# Wolfgang Amadeus Mozart

# Wolfgang Amadeus Mozart

## A BIOGRAPHY *Piero Melograni*

Translated by Lydia G. Cochrane

The University of Chicago Press   *Chicago & London*

PIERO MELOGRANI was born and educated in Rome, Italy. Among his many publications are, most recently, *La guerra degli italiani, 1940–1945*. His English-language publications include, most recently, *Lenin and the Myth of World Revolution: Ideology and Reasons of State, 1817–1920*.

LYDIA G. COCHRANE's many translations include Luc Ferry's *What Is the Good Life?* and Renzo Dubbini's *Geography of the Gaze*, both recently published by the University of Chicago Press.

The University of Chicago Press, Chicago 60637
The University of Chicago Press, Ltd., London
© 2007 by The University of Chicago
All rights reserved. Published 2007
Printed in the United States of America

16 15 14 13 12 11 10 09 08 07     1 2 3 4 5

ISBN-13: 978-0-226-51956-2 (cloth)
ISBN-10: 0-226-51956-2 (cloth)

Originally published as *WAM: La vita e il tempo di Wolfgang Amadeus Mozart.* © 2003 Gius. Laterza & Figli.

The translation of this work has been funded by SEPS,
Segretariato Europeo per le Pubblicazioni Scientifiche

Via Val d'Aposa 7 - 40123 Bologna, Italy
seps@alma.unibo.it - www.seps.it

Library of Congress Cataloging-in-Publication Data

Melograni, Piero.
    [WAM. English]
    Wolfgang Amadeus Mozart : a biography / Piero Melograni ; translated by Lydia G. Cochrane.
        p.   cm.
    "Originally published as WAM : La vita e il tempo di Wolfgang Amadeus Mozart, 2003, Gius.
Laterza & Figli"—T.p. verso.
    Includes bibliographical references and index.
    ISBN-13: 978-0-226-51956-2 (cloth : alk. paper)
    ISBN-10: 0-226-51956-2 (cloth : alk. paper)
        1. Mozart, Wolfgang Amadeus, 1756–1791.  2. Composers—Austria—Biography.
I. Cochrane, Lydia G.  II. Title.
ML410.M9M4313 2007
780.92—dc22

                                                                2006010705

⊗ The paper used in this publication meets the minimum requirements of the American
National Standard for Information Sciences—Permanence of Paper for Printed Library Materials,
ANSI Z39.48–1992.

# Contents

*A gallery of color plates appears after page 176.*

# Preface

The original edition of this book often refers to Wolfgang Amadé Mozart with the acronym "Wam," a word without meaning. In Italian the sound (pronounced "Vahm") recalls a sudden burst of flame; it transmits an image of power, but also sounds like a joke. Mozart was a burst of flame, of power, of jokes, and much more. In English, however, "Wam" evokes a door shutting or a body blow, images that just won't do. Mozart himself played with his names, reversing the letters as Trazom or Gnagflow. At times he abbreviated his surname as "Mzt" or italianized it as "De Mozartini." Past the age of thirty he gave himself the nickname "Pùnkitititi." He even signed one letter, dated 18 July 1787, with an explosive "WAM" and may have done so on other occasions as well.[1]

Mozart was great (among other reasons) because he knew how to have fun. He carried within him all of the moods that music is capable of expressing: the ironic and the tragic, the merry and the sad, the passionate and the detached, the angelic and the demonic. He always worked with zeal and commitment. Some people believe that music flowed from him almost spontaneously, thanks to his genius. In reality, from earliest childhood he practiced for thousands of hours every year, and if later he could compose page after extraordinary page with incomparable speed, it was thanks to hard-won experience, an ability to think through the music before writing it down, and an exceptional memory.

In spite of the brevity of his life, Mozart produced more than twenty theatrical works, over forty symphonies, at least twenty-seven piano concertos, some twenty masses or parts of masses, over a hundred other keyboard compositions, over two hundred dances, some seventy chamber works: quintets, quartets, trios, and duets. As if that were not enough, he also wrote a large number of arias, divertimenti, canons, serenades, sacred and Masonic compositions, and concertos for violin, flute, clarinet, oboe, and bassoon. Calculating the total number of his compositions is a nearly impossible task. The Köchel catalog (which provides the standard listing of Mozart's compositions as a "K." followed by a number) lists six hundred twenty-six works, but many brief pieces (dances, contredanses, and minuets, for example) are grouped under one number. Moreover, some of Mozart's compositions have been lost, and of course we have no trace of the concert improvisations for which he was famous.

Mozart never saw his thirty-sixth birthday, and even the place of his mortal remains is unknown. But his music and his myth accompany us to this day — more than ever today.

In June 1997 Antonella Laterza asked me if I might like to write a life of Mozart in seventy pages, to be published in a Laterza collection of children's books. Probably Antonella, who has known me for decades and who knows that I am not a musicologist, remembered that I had studied piano and singing as a boy and loved Mozart. Without giving the matter a second thought, I immediately agreed, as if writing a biography for young people were just an easy stroll. Vito Laterza telephoned me the next day to give his stamp of approval to his wife's idea, and he sent me a contract. The deadline for the text was the end of the year.

I set to work immediately, and by autumn 1997 I had already written some fifty pages. I gave them to Margherita Guzzinati (who has since died) to read, and she gave me her criticisms. I agreed with her, and I realized that my approach was completely wrong. The fact is that for many reasons I felt ill at ease recounting Mozart's life to young people. For one thing, I had no experience with literature for adolescents. Writing for the young is easy only in appearance: in reality it is much more difficult than writing for adults. The biography of Mozart obliged me to deal with complex themes such as the composer's relationship to the marketplace, with women, and with his father, Leopold, all of which demanded a wider scope than the seventy pages contracted for. But also, as I was writing about Wolfgang, his troubled relations with Leopold began to take on deeper meaning, and his father, in my opinion, bore a great deal of the responsibility for the tension between them. It did not seem to me an encouraging topic for young readers, even though my friends laughed at me and assured me of the contrary. Still, we live in an era when parental authority is already weak, and I preferred not to weaken it further. The events of 1791, which include the suicide of Franz Hofdemel after his attempt to murder his wife, and the suspicion that Franz Xaver Süssmayr may have been the actual father of Constanze's second living son, eliminated my last doubts: the biography would be better aimed at an adult readership.

This is how I came to spend more than five years completing this book. I have sought to be faithful to the method that has served me in writing my other books, relying above all on the sources, which in this case means the letters that the Mozart family sent to one another between 1756 and 1791, and other reliable documents. I have sought to conceal nothing of what I learned in my investigation of Mozart. I have also attempted to identify, to my own satisfaction, all the persons described, although I fear I have not always been impartial. In any event, I am enormously grateful to Antonella Laterza for having given me a completely unexpected opportunity to rediscover Wolfgang, his music, and his times.

When I was young I dearly loved Mozart, and I remember as if it were yesterday how moved I was when I heard my first performance of *The Abduction from the Seraglio* in January 1949, a splendid production at the Rome Opera House conducted by Josef Krips. My intense love of Mozart continued in the following years, but as decades went by, I must confess, I drifted away from him. Perhaps it seemed to me that I had heard too much of his music; perhaps I felt that it had become too much of a consumer product, with too many performances, too much exploitation, and so commercialized that one hears Mozart at every turn. Thanks to this book, however, I have, once and for all, become aware of the greatness of Mozart and of the extraordinary newness of his music.

# In a London Tavern

In July 1765, in a London tavern with the inviting name the Swan and Harp, in Cornhill, a district not far from St. Paul's Cathedral, Leopold Mozart presented his two children, Maria Anna, called Marianne or Nannerl (who was fourteen) and Wolfgang (who was nine) to the public. In a flier written by their father the two children were presented as "Prodigies of Nature."[1] Both children played the harpsichord well, but little Wolfgang was exceptional. He could read any piece of music at sight, improvise on a theme suggested to him, and name any note produced by any instrument or even a bell, a drinking glass, or a mechanical clock. What is more, he was an elegant child, self-assured and charming. The father glowed with legitimate pride at the prowess of his son. Leopold had not only fathered the child, but had provided him with his musical training and taught him to read, write, and figure sums. In short, Wolfgang Amadé Mozart was his father Leopold's biological and pedagogical masterpiece.

London was one halt in a trip throughout Europe that Nannerl, Wolfgang, and their parents had begun two years earlier. They had already played before bankers, dukes, princes, and sovereigns, among them Maria Theresa of Austria and Louis XV, the king of France. They had been in London for over a year and had been received at Buckingham Palace by King George III and his consort, Queen Charlotte Sophia. They had been received with honor in many aristocratic houses in London and had already given a concert with a paid admission set at half a guinea (10s. 6d.) in the Great Room of Spring Garden, near St. James Park.

Before the two siblings left England (never to return), however, they gave a concert in the Cornhill tavern for the bargain price of 2s. 6d., as stated in the announcement written by Leopold and published in the *Public Advertiser* of 8 July 1765. Wishing to earn money, Leopold Mozart had decided to turn to the middle class of shopkeepers, professional people, and craftsmen, declaring that the two child prodigies would play for several days from noon to three in the afternoon in that smoky London tavern. The announcement invited anyone who wanted to hear and admire them to hurry, and in fact by the end of July the entire Mozart family would leave England to return to the continent.

In the summer of 1765 Leopold was forty-five years old. He was a musician of solid training and a certain talent, employed by the small archiepiscopal court of Salzburg. He had published a useful manual for violinists,[2] but his talents were not sufficient for a glorious career. We can presume that without the extraordinary resource of his children, he would have never have known success or traveled throughout Europe. He was an anxious man, often discontent and even depressed, but he was intelligent, and for years he had concentrated on refining Wolfgang's and Nannerl's talents. He realized that if he wanted to guarantee his own success and financial security, he needed to move swiftly to exploit his children's gifts, since the magical appeal of the child prodigy soon dissipates.

This is why, after organizing the usual concerts before sovereigns, dukes, baronets, and London bankers, Leopold arranged to have his children perform in a much humbler locale, before the avant-garde of the new middle class and the emerging would-be middle class, who were beginning to have real money jingling in their pockets. London was the capital of England, the nation at the forefront of the emergence of a new industrial civilization. After ten thousand years of an agricultural economy, England—just at the time of the Mozarts' visit—was in the lead in an economic and social revolution that later transformed the entire structure of society—including relations between musicians and their public. Few were aware of it, but the paid concert in the Cornhill tavern was already a sign of new times.

Nannerl, Wolfgang's sister, was a graceful and obedient girl who played the harpsichord well. She had begun to play much earlier than her brother, which would rightly have led her to think that Wolfgang was so skilled because he had her example before him in the family home. Siblings can be highly competitive, even in their tender years, and this was very probably the case with the two little Mozarts. Nannerl had always provided a model and a point of comparison for Wolfgang. Almost as soon as he opened his eyes to the world, the younger brother could have observed that his sister was rewarded, praised, and indulged because she played so well, and he was probably motivated to do as well as she or even better. Both Nannerl and Leopold were Wolfgang's teachers. By the time the family reached London, however, she had to watch her little brother triumph, stifling mixed emotions of admiration and jealousy, protection and envy, rivalry and self-confidence. The London public also applauded her, but it preferred him. Because he was younger? Or perhaps because he was the better musician?

Some time before, in Vienna, Count Karl von Zinzendorf had occasion to hear the two children, and the judgment that he noted in his diary was unequivocal: Nannerl played with expertise, but Wolfgang was absolutely astonishing.[3] Probably Zinzendorf and many others who heard her play were careful not to humiliate Nannerl by explicitly proclaiming her inferior to her brother, but not everyone was so well-mannered and, in any event, the public's applause was always louder and more spontaneous after Wolfgang played. Nannerl must have realized that she was less talented than her brother. As if that were not enough, after she turned fourteen she no longer belonged (even in theory) to the category of the child prodigy, even if Leopold attempted to keep her there by giving out her age as younger.

Wolfgang was small in stature, of slight build and a somewhat pale complexion, and he almost always looked serious, even austere. The public was struck, at times intimidated, by his appearance. Two years earlier, at Frankfurt am Main, Johann Wolfgang von Goethe, who was fourteen at the time, had attended a concert given by the Mozart children. He stated later that he could "still quite clearly remember the little fellow with his wig and his sword," already famous in many parts of Europe, who performed before an audience sitting perfectly erect.[4] Little Wolfgang was aware of his celebrity and of the power that his musical talent gave him over the public. He already was familiar with the art of seducing and dominating an audience. He managed to do so without effort, with grace and a light touch, either in a great court before princes and sovereigns or in a London tavern playing for commoners. He was sure of himself: as Leopold wrote in a letter from London dated 8 June 1764, "My boy knows in this his eighth year what one would expect only from a man of forty."[5] This composure induced his father to display him like some sort of carnival attraction, playing flawlessly while blindfolded.

The fourth and final member of the family, the mother, Anna Maria née Pertl, was at the time forty-four years old, one year younger than her husband. She never left the family's side, since her task was to take care of Leopold and the children. She attended the popular concert in London seated on a bench. We do not know much about her. She was not beautiful, her ways were simple and her culture limited. She made spelling errors when she wrote and played no instrument. She was gifted with common sense, however, and was good-natured, well-mannered, and discreet, thus providing exactly what was needed to soothe her agitated husband's anxieties and attacks of nerves. For Wolfgang, his mother was a solid base; she provided an equilibrium without which he would have found it much more difficult, and perhaps impossible, to express his talent.

With hindsight, the 1765 concert in the Cornhill tavern seems significant not only for the reasons we have seen, but for two others as well.

First, it signaled the end, even for Wolfgang, of the magical stage of the child prodigy. As he approached the age of ten he was less stupefying than he had been four years earlier, when he played in Vienna before Empress Maria Theresa. This was precisely why his father, after exploiting wealthier circuits, decided to peddle him at a discount price in a tavern. After London, the Mozart family continued their vagabond life across Europe for several more years. They had other successes, but on the whole these were less prestigious and less memorable than in earlier years. When they returned to Salzburg at the end of 1766, Wolfgang was nearly eleven. In September 1767, when he left for Vienna, the stamp of the former child prodigy was not only of little help to him, but hindered him: many listeners still saw him as a child, failing to recognize in the twelve-year-old the qualities of greatness of the budding composer.

Second, the Cornhill concert is significant because it attests to the importance of the consumer market for Mozart, even as a child, and it was at the same time an early sign that the market value of a product can decline, a hard fact from which he was to suffer during the course of his life. We cannot exclude the notion that even the Cornhill tavern concert harmed him in the long run. The London aristocracy in fact reacted with indignation. Without realizing it, Leopold had perhaps committed an error of judgment and a discourtesy: with the aim of earning a little more money, he succeeded in irritating those who had already been generous to him. How is it possible, some aristocrats grumbled, that Mr. Mozart, after having obtained so much from us in the form of sumptuous receptions, pounds sterling, gold snuffboxes, jewels, other gifts, and exquisite attentions, should then offer his children to the petty bourgeois for pennies. And in a tavern! Showing them off like sideshow freaks! Leopold's greed was judged disgraceful and an obvious discredit, and rumors began to spread to the courts of Europe. Several years later, in a letter dated 12 December 1771, Empress Maria Theresa advised her son, Archduke Ferdinand, not to take the Mozarts into his service, because "these people go about the world like beggars" ("ces gens courent le monde comme des gueux").[6]

Throughout his life, Wolfgang was unable to rid himself of the stigma of being an unreliable wanderer, and if he never found the well-paid permanent court post that he yearned for and that almost all the better musicians of the age obtained, it was because the empress, her children, and other powerful lords of Europe denied it to him. He was to live primarily on the resources offered him by the consumer market, to which he in turn offered the treasury of experiences that he had stored up since infancy. If we think about it, this was not a misfortune. Perhaps it was precisely thanks to the market that Mozart became the sublime composer we know. In order to remain a viable market commodity, organize paid concerts, and obtain contracts, Wolfgang Amadé Mozart, throughout his life, had to strike a balance between tradition and innovation; between his genius, which pointed him toward an avant-garde inventiveness, and a need to earn money, which urged him not to disturb the public with too many novelties. By not putting himself in the service of an old-style prince, he encountered a new and more modern prince, the public of consumers. A new prince and a new principle that were to furnish him with new stimuli, assure him greater liberty, and open the way to modernity in ways that enabled him to continue to occupy center stage on the musical scene even two and a half centuries after his death.

# The Rise and Decline of
# the Child Prodigy

## Beginnings (1756–1761)

One day in December 1761, Wolfgang sat down at the harpsichord in the family home in Salzburg in the company of his parents, his sister Nannerl, and some family friends and played two or three very short, very simple pieces of his own composition. He was five years old, a slight, blond boy passionately fond of music, if not downright engulfed by it. All those present applauded and complimented the young composer and his proud father and teacher. No one could have imagined it at the time, but on that day one of the most portentous musical careers in history was launched.

In the Köchel catalog of Mozart's works, as item number 1 we find a piece long considered his first composition: the Minuet for Harpsichord in G Major with a playing time of a bit over one minute. Years later scholars concluded that the Minuet (K. 1/1e) was preceded by an andante, two allegros, and another minuet, all very brief pieces (K. 1a, 1b, 1c, and 1d). As we listen to these childish works, it is hard to tell whether they contain a hint of Mozart's genius or are mere school exercises written in collaboration with his father. To be truthful, these little works elicit emotion only because we know what is to come.

Wolfgang began playing at the age of three. He lived in a family of musicians and heard them making music every day. He began by sitting on the bench next to his sister and putting his hands on the keyboard, almost in play—which reminds us that in many languages "playing" and "playing an instrument" use the same word. This is true in English, but also in German and French (*spielen, jouer*). The child Mozart took to the game of music with a passion, and soon showed extraordinary talent. Given his very young age he could not have been aware of the fact, but his play with musical instruments was teaching him one of life's greatest secrets: success comes only from working with passion, ease, and pleasure, as if in play. Only when we enjoy ourselves can we find the energy for the hours and hours of study, the practice, and the inevitably monotonous training that accompanies all worthwhile human activities, the arts in particular. Before a great pianist or violinist can win over the public, he or she has to have the motivation and patience to devote thousands of hours to what are called "exercises."

As soon as Leopold became aware of the extent of Wolfgang's gifts, he gave the child regular lessons on the harpsichord, using a manual that he had compiled for Nannerl, the manuscript of which still exists. The book contains 135 pieces, minuets in particular, organized didactically by increasing difficulty. The father imposed a rigorous discipline on his son, which the boy accepted, intuiting that it was necessary if he were to "play" well. Little Wolfgang became a great musician because of his intense love of the world of musical notes. He entered into that world by beginning at an early age to cultivate his mind and construct an extraordinary musical memory. Learning was facilitated by his unusual talent for imitation, which he maintained even as an adult. Leopold threw himself into his task, sensing that his two talented children could provide an indirect road to an artistic, social, and economic success that he never could achieve alone.

Johann Georg Leopold Mozart was born in Augsburg, in Swabia, on 14 November 1719; hence he was not Austrian-born but a Swabian transplanted to Salzburg. He was thirty-six years old when Wolfgang was born. A short man with a large nose, he had been born into a Catholic family, had been educated by the Jesuits, and as a young man seems to have considered becoming a priest. In spite of this early exposure, he was no religious conformist, however. A man of modest means, he was the son of a bookbinder and a member of the lower middle class, and he harbored a lively hostility toward aristocrats that he passed on to his son. In 1756, the year in which Wolfgang was born, Leopold had achieved modest fame thanks to the publication of his treatise on mastering the violin, but he remained vice-Kapellmeister at a small court, that of the prince-bishop of Salzburg. Those who knew him described him as intelligent and prudent but pedantic, anxious, tormented by pangs of guilt, and prone to discouragement. He had been disinherited by his widowed mother and was no longer in contact with her.

His wife, Anna Maria Walburga Pertl, was born on 15 December 1720 in the small village of St. Gilgen, near Salzburg, where her father served as deputy prefect. Leopold and Anna Maria, who were almost the same age, were married in Salzburg in 1747; they had six children before the birth of Wolfgang, all of whom died in infancy except Nannerl, christened Maria Anna Walburga Ignatia, who was born 30 July 1751. Joachim, born in 1748, died at five months; then came Anna Cordula, born in 1749, who lived only one week; Nepomucena, born in 1750, dead at two months; Karl Amadeus, born in 1752, dead at three months; and Francisca, born in 1754, dead at seven weeks. Women of the time gave birth at home attended by untrained midwives. There were no pediatricians or gynecologists. Babies born in the winter were often stricken with respiratory illnesses and in the summer with gastric troubles; the pharmaceutical arts of the time could do nothing to save them. Statistics show that in Austria in that period, 20 percent of newborns died before reaching one year of life. In the Mozart family, the figure was 71 percent.

Anna Maria was delivered of her last child, Wolfgang, at 8:00 in the evening on 27 January—one of the coldest months of the year—1756 in the family house at Getreidegasse 9, now the Mozart Museum. Anna Maria must certainly have thought that the baby would suffer the same fate as Joachim, Anna, Nepomucena, Karl, and Francisca. Mothers usually faced sad thoughts of the sort with more Christian resignation than anguish, comforted by the belief that their innocent babes would have an enviable life in the other world. It is even probable that the newborn Wolfgang faced particular dangers, since we know that his mother's milk was insufficient and he was nourished with barley water and oat gruel. Powdered or artificial milk and homogenized baby food were inventions of the future, and a wet nurse would have been beyond Leopold's financial means. Leopold stated later, in a letter dated 3 August 1778, that childbirth had brought his wife to death's door.[1]

The new baby was baptized in a Salzburg church with the name Johann Chrysostom Wolfgang Theophilus. The family soon changed Theophilus (beloved of God) to Amadé; they never used the more solemn "Amadeus," unless in jest. "Wolfgang Amadeus Mozart" used to be the preferred form, but scholarship today prefers "Amadé," as did Wolfgang himself. The name Wolfgang ("walks like a wolf") predicted hardiness, alertness, and rapidity, while Amadé suggested faith in God, an anchor of salvation that Mozart, given the precariousness of life in those days, relied on, repeatedly proclaiming his devotion and piety. He lived only thirty-five years, but he lived them at a wolf's pace and went far in that short time.

Some maintain that, given Mozart's innate gifts, he would have become a great musician even without his father's help and his sister's example. They may be wrong, because it is unlikely that any individual would possess such inborn, absolute musical talent. I prefer to think that certain predispositions can be developed from childhood by familiarity with music and early training. This is exactly what happened to Mozart. As Norbert Elias has said, "He must have been exposed continually to musical stimuli, the changing sequences on the violin and the piano from the first day of his life; he heard his father, his sister and other musicians practicing and correcting their mistakes."[2] An exceptional natural predisposition enabled Mozart to develop very early a keen sensitivity to differences in sound and to musical construction. We can only guess what his fate might have been away from the environment that surrounded him from his birth.

The atmosphere in the Mozart house was highly protective. The children played with a cat and a fox terrier named Pimperl. Until December 1769, when Wolfgang was thirteen and Nannerl seventeen and a half, the entire Mozart family slept together in one big room. This intimacy and the absence of a lavatory explain the somewhat crude language that we often find shocking in Mozart's letters and those of his mother and other family members. One example is a letter in verse from Wolfgang to his mother dated 31 January 1778, which is largely dedicated to the topic of defecation.[3] Such frank language might be read as a reassuring sign of reciprocal trust.

We should remember too that Salzburg was a small city with fewer than twenty thousand inhabitants, and it was provincial and conformist. It enjoyed a measure of independence, and it looked to nearby Bavaria for stimulation. In the years of Mozart's adolescence Salzburg was governed by a prince-bishop, Sigismund von Schrattenbach. Although the court's financial resources were modest, the prince-bishop sought to imitate the pomp of wealthier courts. Social life in the city was all too tranquil. Families gathered for conversation and parlor games in which children took part. We have the impression that although Salzburg may have been gray and unassuming, its very limitations offered a child like Wolfgang protection and serenity.

When Mozart was still quite small, he was also smitten by mathematics. "When he was doing sums," Friedrich von Schlichtegroll, Mozart's first biographer, recounted in 1793, "the table, chairs, walls, even the floor were covered with chalked figures."[4] The Mozart family appears to have taken a keen interest in puzzles and numerology. It is a common notion that small children who are given piano or singing lessons usually demonstrate a greater aptitude for mathematics. If so, it is hardly surprising that Mozart, with his musical gifts, should have found numbers stimulating. Like all aspiring musicians, he did solfeggio exercises, which helped him learn to read music and to follow rhythmic patterns that correspond to fairly complex mathematical rules. Studying music involves mathematical training: Pythagoras himself used musical rules to explain the geometrical complexity of the universe.

At the age of six Wolfgang played the harpsichord astonishingly well, better than his sister. Placidus Scharl, a Benedictine who had heard him in Salzburg, wrote in his memoirs that the six-year-old Mozart played very difficult pieces with speed and accuracy. "He skimmed the octave which his short little fingers could not span."[5] By then Wolfgang also played the violin with some confidence, and legend has it that he had learned to play the instrument without help by listening to others and imitating them.[6]

All of Wolfgang's extraordinary achievements were made at the cost of an intense application that his family and their friends found worrisome. In a letter dated 16 February 1778, when Wolfgang was twenty-two, Leopold Mozart reminds him of the disconcerting gravity he had displayed as a child. Leopold states, "As a child and a boy you were serious rather than childish and when you sat at the clavier or were otherwise intent on music, no one dared to have the slightest jest with you. Why, even your expression was so solemn that . . . many discerning people of different countries doubted whether your life would be a long one."[7] Wolfgang was so thin that he seemed too fragile to bear up under his study regimen.

Leopold regarded his fragile but powerful child as if he himself were God and Wolfgang the baby Jesus, and his little son probably thought his father Leopold next to God in importance. He said as much in a letter dated 7 March 1778: "*Next to God comes Papa* was my motto and my axiom as a child."[8] It is understandable that Leopold-Father-God should decide in 1762 to take his extraordinary boy on a European tour, away from a Salzburg that he considered totally inadequate to appreciate this miracle child.

## The Trip to Munich and Vienna (1762)

Leopold was excited by the idea of traveling about the vast world with his children and his wife, but he was also anguished at the thought of the enormous risks involved. The unpaved roads of the time were often in terrible condition and so full of potholes that a day's travel in a horse-drawn coach covered little ground. Travelers were continually jostled and the coach made frequent halts. On 24 December 1762, to cite one example, it took the Mozart family twelve hours to go from Pressburg (Bratislava) to Vienna, a distance of some thirty miles, at an average speed of about 2.5 miles per hour. All cities closed their gates at sunset, highway robbers were a threat to travelers, and inns were primitive, poorly lit by torches and candles, without running water, and often quite dirty. Travelers supplied their own pillows and sheets. The danger of illness and accident was so great than many prudently drew up a will before setting off on a journey. To top it off, Leopold, as we know, was anxious by nature. Some years later, in letters dated 25 February, 3 August, and 3 September 1778, he explicitly admits to "nervous palpitations," "fits of melancholy," and a depressed, anxious heart.[9]

It is highly probable that Leopold relied on Freemasonry to quell his fears and reduce the risks of travel. There were several Masonic lodges in Salzburg, and we can suppose that Leopold established relations with one of them on the eve of his first journey, perhaps even becoming a member. Freemasonry was a powerful mutual-aid association with branches throughout Europe: why not make use of its protection? At the time there were two other networks that offered protection, the aristocracy and the church, but Leopold had only limited ties to either of them. He belonged to the lower echelons of the middle class, and he was chary of aristocrats. Although he had been educated by the Jesuits, he subsequently rejected a priestly career, and in 1753 he had written a tract denouncing nobles and priests. He was an Enlightenment man, rational and concrete.

Turning to the protection of Freemasonry was the most congenial and perhaps Leopold's only recourse. It is worth anticipating later developments to recall that Wolfgang became a member of a Masonic lodge in Vienna in December 1784, and that when his father joined him there the following year, Leopold was welcomed into his son's lodge as a longstanding "brother," not a postulant. In any event, Wolfgang's career, which began in childhood with probable Masonic support, concluded with *The Magic Flute*, a great Masonic work, and with the Masonic Cantata, *Laut verkünde unsre Freude* (K. 623). He also composed a number of other works of Masonic inspiration, including *Thamos, König in Ägypten* (K. 345/336a), a heroic drama filled with esoteric echoes on a libretto by Tobias Philipp von Gebler. Many of Mozart's minor Masonic works convey a striking intensity.

In January 1762 Leopold Mozart decided to risk a trip to nearby Munich with the entire family. The two children are reported to have played before Maximilian III, the prince-elector of Bavaria, and to have received high praise. The family apparently returned to Salzburg excited by their trip, by the splendor of the Bavarian court, and by the children's success there, which encouraged them to work to improve their art. They began to play a radically new percussion instrument, the pianoforte, which was just beginning to be more widely available and which, unlike the harpsichord, could produce soft and loud notes and even play pianissimo and fortissimo.

We know little about the trip to Munich, but much fuller documentation exists about the succeeding and more challenging sojourn in Vienna. On 18 September 1762 the Mozart family left Salzburg for the capital of the Hapsburg empire, beginning a journey that was to last almost four months. On 20 September the Mozarts arrived in Passau, where Wolfgang was awarded the honor of giving a solo concert attended by the prince-bishop, Joseph Maria Thun-Hohenstein. On 26 September they arrived in Linz, where both children gave a concert. On 4 October they stopped at Mauthausen and, on 5 October, in the town of Ybbs, where Wolfgang played the organ in the Franciscan church so energetically and so skillfully that the friars, gathered in the refectory with their guests, interrupted their meal to rush to the church, where they were amazed to see a six-year-old at the keyboard.

On 6 October the Mozart family arrived in Vienna at long last. Wolfgang played the violin in the customs office, so charming the customs officials that they passed through the family's baggage without inspection. The two children gave their first Viennese concert on 9 October in the house of Count Tommaso Vinciguerra di Collalto. This was followed on 10 October by a concert in the house of Count Wilczek, and one in that of the vice-chancellor, Rudolph Joseph Colloredo-Mels und Waldsee, on 11 October.

Rumors of the talented pair (and of Wolfgang in particular) spread so rapidly throughout the city that as early as the evening of 10 October Leopold Mozart, who had gone alone to the Burgtheater, the court theater, overheard the fifteen-year-old Archduke Leopold (the future grand duke of Tuscany, later emperor as Leopold II) announce to the people in the adjoining box that he had heard that an extraordinarily talented little boy had come to Vienna. That very evening the Mozarts were summoned to give a command performance at Schönbrunn Palace.

On the afternoon of 13 October the imperial couple, Maria Theresa and Francis I, conceded a three-hour audience to the Mozarts at Schönbrunn. Leopold describes these events in a letter written three days later. The empress and the emperor were affable beyond all imagination. Francis I sat down next to the boy, and after the concert, little Wolfgang jumped up into the empress's lap, threw his arms around her, and kissed her. His prestige and charm had immediately broken all ceremonial conventions.[10]

On 15 October empress Maria Theresa gave orders to her treasurer to prepare a gift to Wolfgang of a lilac-colored suit with gold braid that had been made for her son Maximilian Franz, who was the same age as Wolfgang, while Nannerl received a pink silk ball dress that had been part of the wardrobe of her seven-year-old daughter Maria Antonietta (better known to history as Marie Antoinette, who a few years later married Louis XVI of France and was subsequently guillotined by Paris revolutionaries in 1793). There is a famous portrait of Mozart wearing the suit given him by Maria Theresa, a small sword at his side, his left hand slipped into his vest and gazing proudly into the distance with a somewhat ironic smile.[11] We can only wonder what adjustments were needed to make seven-year-old Marie Antoinette's ball gown fit the eleven-year-old Nannerl.

The empress gave Leopold the round sum of a hundred ducats (equivalent to the going rate for composing an opera), and he received other sums from the noble families of Vienna in whose houses the two children played. As early as 19 October Leopold was able to deposit 540 florins in the bank—twice his annual stipend in Salzburg.

Wolfgang charmed the court and the nobility of Vienna by his skill and by such feats as playing blindfolded or with the keyboard masked. His command of music theory was by then strong enough to enable him to "fake" musically—that is, to improvise and correct errors in such a way that his listeners were unaware of them, and thus resorting to tricks expected of a mature artist. From the beginning, little Wolfgang was not only well aware that his talent gave him enormous powers over his listeners (and over his family), but also well pleased by the thought. From the viewpoint of his listeners, life in the courts of Europe was often monotonous and boring, and the arrival of a child prodigy who could conquer and dominate his audience constituted a rare event. He offered an opportunity to escape from routine.

Nannerl was talented, and although she too was praised and rewarded, she was jealous of her brother. During that first trip to Vienna she undoubtedly harbored a growing hostility toward him, repressed only by her good manners and the influence of her parents. Like many older siblings, Nannerl could hardly have been pleased that her little brother had taken her place in her parents' affections, and now the same little brother was robbing her of public attention. In a letter dated 20 August 1763, Leopold declares that Nannerl "no longer suffers" from the comparisons being made between the two children.[12] If her father mentions her suffering, it must have been apparent. People were more generous in their praise for Wolfgang not only because he was younger and more gifted musically, but also because he was more appealing, free in his ways, and spontaneous. After all, he was the one who had jumped into the empress's lap and hugged and kissed her.

On 21 October 1762 their imperial highnesses ordered the extraordinary boy to give a second command performance before the court at Schönbrunn. In the evening, after the concert, however, Wolfgang fell ill, either of scarlet fever or some similar illness.[13] In those times doctors were not only unable to cure diseases, but they even had difficulty identifying them. Leopold Mozart was beside himself with worry, both because he adored his son and because Wolfgang's illness cut down the incoming flow of ducats. We can see from his letters that Leopold was obsessed with money. He was aware of the fact and excuses his cupidity by the high cost of travel and the large sums his family was obliged to spend for servants, hairdressers, and other luxury items in order to keep up their "image" and present themselves properly before nobles and sovereigns.

Whatever his illness may have been, Wolfgang was treated with black powder and magnesium powder and given boiled bread and barley broth. On 5 November, when he had finally recovered, he gave a concert in the house of Dr. Johann von Bernhard, who had attended him in his illness. Two weeks later the Mozarts attended a grand banquet given by the imperial family. On 23 November they visited the Burgtheater, which up to then only Leopold had seen and which would later be the site of the premieres of *The Abduction from the Seraglio* and many other Mozart operas. On 11 December the family left for Pressburg (Bratislava), returning to Vienna on Christmas Eve. In the weeks following Wolfgang's recovery, the two children performed in other concerts and Leopold raked in money and gifts, to the point that toward the end of December, after four months of triumphs and excitement, he permitted himself the great luxury of acquiring a carriage for the return trip to the remote corner of the world called Salzburg.

## From Salzburg to Paris (1763–1764)

When he returned home to Salzburg from Vienna in 1763, Leopold was dazed and giddy with excitement. Thanks to Wolfgang and Nannerl, he had known a fairy-tale environment that had an irresistible appeal. In Vienna he had promised the French ambassador that he would take the children to Paris. This determined him to plan a new, long voyage through Europe during which the two children could be exhibited as rare marvels. Their gifts had to be exploited quickly, not only because child prodigies grow up fast, but also because he feared that, with age, he himself would find travel too demanding. At the time a forty-year-old man was considered to be getting along in years, if not downright old, and Leopold was already forty-three in 1762.

The Mozart family remained in Salzburg for the first five months of the year, but on 9 June 1763 they left for the longest trip of their lives, a voyage that was to last more than three years, ending only on 30 November 1766. Lorenz Hagenauer, a wealthy Salzburg merchant, lent Leopold money to launch his great adventure. Hagenauer was not only a friend, but the owner of the house in which the family lived and in which Wolfgang was born. During the long voyage Leopold sent his friend and creditor some seventy letters crammed with information, which provide a highly important source for a reconstruction of all the events of that long pilgrimage. Leopold wrote them both to reassure Hagenauer that he was putting the money he had borrowed to good use and to create a documentation that might prove to be precious in the future. Leopold was in fact thinking of one day writing a biography of his son.

Between June 1763 and November 1766, the Mozarts covered thousands of miles. They stopped in eighty-eight cities, among them Augsburg, Mannheim, Mainz, Frankfurt, Koblenz, Bonn, Cologne, Brussels, and Paris. They crossed the Channel and went to London. They returned to the Continent, stopping at Lille, Ghent, The Hague, Amsterdam, and Paris once more. They then headed south, passing through Lyon, Geneva, Lausanne, Berne, and Zurich. Few people of the time would have had the courage to face so long a journey. Schrattenbach, the prince-bishop of Salzburg, authorized the trip, temporarily liberating his vice-Kapellmeister from his duties, with the idea in mind that the Mozarts' successes in the cities of Europe would eventually rebound favorably on the city of Salzburg and on his court.

The personality of young Mozart, who was seven at the start of the trip and ten and a half at its end, was strongly marked by the experience. In the first place, it gave him an extremely useful and precocious knowledge of the world; second, it assured his fame throughout Europe; and third, it enabled him to meet excellent musicians, much more talented than the father who had helped him to mature musically.

The first stage of their long journey took the Mozarts north to the Bavarian town of Wasserburg, some thirty miles from Salzburg. A carriage wheel broke on the first day of their trip and was replaced with a borrowed but smaller wheel. So as to avoid overloading the carriage, Leopold and his faithful servant Sebastian Winter, who also functioned as his valet and hairdresser, reached Wasserburg on foot, while Wolfgang, Nannerl, their mother, and the baggage went on in the carriage. The Mozarts stayed two days in Wasserburg, and Leopold took Wolfgang to a church there to teach him to use organ pedals. The boy astonished all present by learning to use them in record time, to some extent repeating the experience of a few months earlier with the organ (without pedals) in the Franciscan church in Ybbs.

The second stop was Munich, where Wolfgang and Nannerl performed before both the prince-elector of Bavaria, Maximilian III (who had heard them the previous year) and in the house of Duke Franz Clemens, Maximilian's cousin. Leopold was made to wait several days for the expected gratuities: a hundred florins from the prince and seventy-five from the duke. These sums were duly noted, along with many other details, in the long letters that Leopold sent to his friend Hagenauer. We also learn, among other things, that Wolfgang played the violin before the prince-elector, an instrument on which he had acquired notable skill.

On 22 June 1763 the Mozarts left Munich, arriving that evening in Augsburg, Leopold's native city. There they encountered difficulties. Catholic circles in the city held Leopold's nonconformist religious attitudes against him, not to mention his ties with Protestant circles and even his affiliation with Masonry. Nearly all of his relatives had broken with him: Leopold's mother refused to meet her talented grandchildren or her son. As Leopold reported in a letter dated 11 July 1763, the audience for the three concerts the children gave there consisted almost entirely of Lutherans.[14]

In Augsburg Leopold and Wolfgang met Pietro Nardini, a violinist from Livorno who was considered to be the best in Italy, a pupil of Giuseppe Tartini and a composer in his own right. After hearing Nardini, Leopold wrote that it would be "impossible to hear a finer player for beauty, purity of tone, and evenness of tone and singing quality."[15] It might even be said that the meeting with Nardini signaled the true beginning of Wolfgang's "italianization," a process that would have a long history.

After Augsburg the Mozarts went to Ulm, then to Ludwigsburg, where they attempted to arrange a reception by the duke, Karl Eugen of Württemberg. While they were there they met Niccolò Jommelli, an Italian composer of some fifty years of age (born in Aversa, near Naples) who was the duke's Kapellmeister. Jommelli was well paid, and he held a good deal of power, which he used to keep all musicians who were not Italian (such as the Mozarts) away from the ducal court. At the time, the "Italian party" was strong not only in Ludwigsburg but in many European courts, which meant that Wolfgang, a little Austrian, had to wait almost ten days before receiving permission to perform before the court. The overwhelming presence of the "Italian party" in musical life was a problem that young Wolfgang was to encounter again and again in his life.

In August of that year Wolfgang and Nannerl gave four concerts in Frankfurt am Main, and it was at one of these that the fourteen-year-old Goethe saw Mozart sitting proudly erect on his piano bench, well on his way to becoming famous throughout Europe. Behind the facade of a self-contained, impeccable child prodigy there remained the reality of a seven-year-old subjected to trials inappropriate for his young age. Traveling without cease, giving concerts in unlikely venues, having to dominate audiences, meeting important personages, may all have been exhilarating experiences, but they were also exhausting. One result was that, one fine morning during the summer of 1763 (Leopold did not remember whether this was in Augsburg or somewhere else), little Wolfgang woke up with a start, weeping, and explained that he missed his friends in the small, familiar city of Salzburg. Clearly he lacked the protective tranquility that only Salzburg, his city of birth, could offer, and which he was unable to find in a life of continual movement. Nannerl, too, showed signed of stress (although less than before): this was the period of Leopold's letter to Hagenauer of 20 August stating that his daughter suffered less than previously from being compared to her brother.[16]

Leopold, meanwhile, worried about everything, even about the remote possibility that the houses in which they lodged might catch fire, either during one of Germany's summer thunderstorms or for some other reason, and force the family to jump out of the windows. Benjamin Franklin had invented the lightning rod only a few years earlier, and his invention had not yet spread around the world. This means that while all the other members of the Mozart family were worrying about one thing or another, only Anna Maria, the exemplary wife and mother, managed to stay calm.

Mainz, Koblenz, Cologne, Aachen: the list of German cities they visited grew inexorably longer. In Aachen the two small Mozarts performed in the presence of Princess Amalia of Prussia, the sister of Frederick II, and money-conscious Leopold complained in a letter that the princess, who was not wealthy, limited her thanks to compliments and a kiss. "If the kisses she gave to my children, and to Wolfgang especially, had been all new louis d'or, we should be quite happy; but neither the innkeeper nor the postmaster are paid in kisses."[17]

On 2 October 1763 the Mozarts finally got to Belgium, arriving in Liège, then moving on to Tirlemont, Louvain, and Brussels, where the two children gave further concerts. Between gifts and monetary rewards, Leopold had by now succeeded in accumulating a sizable sum. He wrote in a letter sent from Brussels on 4 November 1763 that he could "rig out a stall" with all the "snuff-boxes and étuis and such stuff" that they had received as gifts, but that he was looking forward to being able to "haul in fat thalers and louis d'or."[18] On 15 November 1763 the Mozart family left Brussels and set off for Paris. They covered the 135 miles in three and a half days, arriving on 18 November 1763. The Mozarts remained in Paris for nearly five months.

From Liège to Paris the route was no longer a dirt road, but paved, hence "modern." Coach travel involved discomfort, continual jostling, and the threat of broken carriage wheels. The inns lacked all conveniences and even the most elementary necessities were difficult to obtain. Nostalgics who sigh for the good old days may well imagine that in the late eighteenth century fresh water flowed everywhere from uncontaminated fountains, but nothing could be farther from the truth. In a letter dated 20 August 1763, Leopold Mozart relates that in many places in Germany the well water was so bad, smelly, and muddy that it was habitually mixed with wine.[19] It was worse in Paris. Parisians drank the repugnant water of the Seine, into which the city's garbage was thrown. The Mozarts, like many others, let it settle in a pitcher for a few hours, where it formed a worrisome solid layer.[20] Leopold also reported that nearly all foreigners had a touch of diarrhea at first. The consequences could be much worse, however, and it is probable that when Wolfgang and his mother returned to Paris in 1778, it was the Seine water she drank that proved fatal to her.

In his letters Leopold often uses somber tones to describe the prerevolutionary Paris that they visited. This was twenty-five years before the fall of the Bastille, but Leopold already sensed that France was about to fall apart, exactly as the Persian Empire had done under Alexander the Great, as he wrote in a letter dated 1 February 1764. In his opinion, Parisian families lived in moral disorder. The women were disfigured by wearing too much makeup. Parents got rid of their newborn children by sending them off to pitiless wet nurses in the country. Moreover, this reprehensible behavior had spread from top to bottom in French society, even to some worker circles, given that the wet nurses were paid little. The consequences were terrifying, and Paris seemed to be full of cripples, blind people, and paralytics, many of whom had been damaged physically during the time they spent with such monsters. On the streets of Paris one could encounter beggars whose hands had been eaten by pigs as children, and others whose arms had been totally or partially burned off.[21] Leopold Mozart was hardly exaggerating. Even Prince Charles-Maurice de Talleyrand-Périgord, later Napoleon Bonaparte's foreign minister, who was born in 1754 (two years before Wolfgang), limped through life because the miserable country nurse with whom his wealthy and noble parents had deposited him—on the day of his baptism—had been negligent in her care.

In a letter dated 9 March 1764 Leopold reported to Hagenauer that the Parisian authorities were in the habit of hanging prisoners in the center of Paris, in the Place de Grève, on a nearly daily basis. "Recently they have hanged together, one next to the other, a chambermaid, a cook, and a coachman. They were in the service of a wealthy widow who was blind, and they had robbed her of about 30,000 louis d'or." Domestic servants might also be hanged for the theft of small sums: "All that is necessary here, otherwise no one would feel safe." On the other hand, domestics were freely permitted to pad their expenses: "It is called a *bénéfice*, and is not considered theft."[22] Although living in the midst of the age of rationalism and enlightenment, many Parisians believed in the most archaic superstitions. In a letter dated 1 April 1764 Leopold reported that when an eclipse of the sun had occurred, Parisians rushed into the churches to protect themselves from being poisoned by the air during the temporary disappearance of the sun's light.[23] Many were persuaded that eclipses spread the plague.

At the same time, however, the French capital was a great, modern city full of new things. Leopold was astonished to learn that, unlike in other cities, the city gates remained open day and night, and he was struck by the fact that many stores left their doors open, summer and winter, in order to entice people to come in.[24] Many Parisians owned an umbrella, an object that had been invented in England only a few years earlier and that Leopold had probably never seen before. Then there was the other bewildering novelty imported from England, the "water closet," a sanitary apparatus whose hydraulic complications Leopold sought to explain to his friends.[25] Up to then the Mozarts, like almost all other European families, had used chamber pots, pails, and urinals, when they did not simply take care of their bodily functions outdoors.

Paris had other positive aspects. The city postal system, for example, was efficient and speedy, much facilitating exchanges and the dissemination of news. Although doctors still sent many of their patients to their maker by copious bloodletting, they were beginning to practice wide-scale "variolation"—inoculation with material extracted from human smallpox pustules. This was not yet the vaccination with which Edward Jenner experimented in 1796, but a rougher method that led to death now and then. Fearful of this innovation, Leopold refused to have his children be vaccinated.[26] He was favorably impressed by the night lighting in Paris, observing that some Paris shops were lit by "as many as ten candles" and concert halls by as many as sixty candles.[27] We imagine the salons in which the two child musicians from Salzburg performed to have been brilliantly lit, but nothing could be farther from the case. The minute the sun went down interiors were dark, or at best gloomy, and the sixty candles in a concert hall extolled by Leopold were nothing in comparison to the lighting available to us today (or to the lighting we see in the fantasy world of cinematic or theatrical reconstructions of the life of Amadeus and his family).

In Paris the Mozarts were the guests of the Bavarian minister in Paris, Count van Eyck, at the Hôtel Beauvais, rue St. Antoine (now rue de François-Miron), not far from the Hôtel de Ville. Baron Friedrich Melchior von Grimm, a German who had lived in Paris for nearly fifteen years and was the editor of the *Correspondance littéraire*, an artistic and literary gazette, published an article about the Mozart children in the journal's issue of 1 December 1763. Baron Grimm had ties with the *Encyclopédie* philosophers Diderot and d'Alembert, and he figured prominently in fashionable circles in Paris because he was also the lover of the famous Madame Louise d'Épinay. Grimm's article on the Mozart children gave Leopold an excellent entree into Parisian high society. We do not know the names of all the people from whom the Mozarts received invitations in the days that followed, but we do know that on 24 December 1763 they were invited to the royal palace of Louis XV at Versailles.

The Mozarts attended the king for about fifteen days. The two children performed before the sovereign, and on 1 January 1764 the entire family took part in the grand festivities at Versailles to celebrate the New Year. In a letter dated 1 February 1764 Leopold Mozart describes the event with evident satisfaction.[28] During the *grand couvert* banquet held on the evening of New Year's Day the Mozart family had the great privilege of being brought to the side of the king and the queen. Wolfgang of course remained standing, as court protocol required, but he spoke with the queen, Maria Leszczyńska, who was Polish of origin and spoke German, and who translated the child's words to the king. The queen even deigned to give the boy something to eat with her own hands, and in return, grateful and deeply touched, Wolfgang thought it proper to kiss her royal hand repeatedly. Later Louis XV gave the Mozarts a costly snuffbox with an inscription inside stating that in case of need it could be returned to the king of France, who promised to pay a thousand florins for it—a sum four times Leopold Mozart's annual stipend. Louis XV was known (and criticized) for being frivolous and spendthrift.

Little Wolfgang had won over the Paris public by his mastery of the keyboard: aside from his usual feats of playing blind and displaying his perfect pitch, he composed on-the-spot accompaniments to any melody suggested and demonstrated his ability to improvise for hours at the pianoforte. At just eight years of age, he was beginning to reveal musical abilities beyond virtuosity and was fast becoming a composer. By February 1764 he had already composed four sonatas for keyboard and violin, two of which he dedicated to Madame Victoire, the daughter of Louis XV, and two to a lady of the court, Madame de Tessé (K. 6, 7, 8, 9). It is probable that Leopold collaborated in the writing of these somewhat academic pieces, but already they contain vague hints of Mozart's later style. Leopold had them published immediately, as a promotional venture, by Vendôme in Paris. The four sonatas also reflect the profound and positive influence of two German musicians who were living in Paris at the time, Johann Schobert (who was twenty-four years of age) and Gottfried Eckard (who was thirty). Both men had given young Mozart some of their compositions as a sign of their admiration for their very young colleague. Eckard, like Leopold, was born in Augsburg. Schobert is remembered even today for his new synthesis of the German style and the Venetian tradition of Domenico Alberti and Baldassare Galuppi, which thus furthered the italianization of young Wolfgang.

On 10 March 1764 Wolfgang and Nannerl gave a public concert in the theater in the house of Monsieur Félix, rue Saint Honoré, which rendered a profit of 112 louis d'or. In a letter dated 1 April Leopold explained in detail to his friend in Salzburg how such concerts—a novelty at the time—were organized:

> Not a farthing is paid at the door. But whoever is without a ticket is not admitted, no matter who he is. My friends sell the tickets a week beforehand, each for a laubthaler or a federthaler, four of which make a louis d'or; and they collect the money. But most of the tickets, in blocks of twelve and twenty-four, are given to ladies, who sell them the more

easily, as out of politeness one cannot refuse to buy them. *Est modus in rebus,* or, in our language, *Frenchmen like to be fooled.* On the billet (which is written on a card and bears my seal) there are only these words: "Au Théâtre de M. Félix, rue et Porte St. Honoré, ce lundi 9 avril à six heures du soir." That is a hall in the house of a distinguished gentleman, in which there is a small theater where the nobles often act and produce plays among themselves; and I got this room through Madame de Clermont, who lives in the house.[29]

After a second concert on 9 April the Mozarts left for London still richer.

## London (April 1764–July 1765)

In 1764 London was the capital of an England much wealthier and more powerful than Austria or France. England had just defeated France in the Seven Years' War, a conflict that had begun in 1756, the year of Wolfgang's birth, and ended in 1763, the year he arrived in Paris. France had been obliged to cede Canada and almost all its other colonies to the English.

But if England was strong, wealthy, and vital in 1764, it was above all because it was launching a great industrial revolution. The productivity of the textile industry had already grown enormously, thanks to the flying shuttle, invented by John Kay and patented in 1733; to cylindrical sliver cans for twisting thread, patented in 1738; and to water-powered spinning machines developed around 1743. Between 1756 and 1763—during the war—a number of coke-fueled blast furnaces had been built. Thus precisely when the Mozarts arrived in London, English society was going through a phase of exceptional and optimistic ferment. This was in part why the family remained in England for over a year, from April 1764 to July 1765, much longer than the five months they had spent in Paris. Another reason for the longer stay, however, was that Leopold fell ill in London and needed a long convalescence. He gives rather inconclusive information on his illness, in part due to the inability of the physicians of the time to make accurate diagnoses. In a letter dated 13 September 1764, he tells his friend Hagenauer that in England he caught "a kind of native complaint, which is called a 'cold' (*Verkältung*)," which the English tried to ward off by wearing heavy clothing in all seasons.[30] The symptoms were a sore throat, inflamed tonsils, loss of appetite, and, in "people who are not constitutionally sound," what the English called "consumption" but Leopold calls *febrem lentam,* a persistent fever. The typical English remedy for this complaint was to leave immediately for the Continent for a change of climate. Leopold used his usual remedies, which included clysters, purgations, and bloodletting; gargling with various substances; taking antispasmodic powders, barley tea, and a tincture of opium, vinegar, and ammonium; or applying Peruvian balsam, nutmeg, and other products. Leopold's condition finally improved when a competent physician of Portuguese origin arrived on the scene and had him back on his feet in only a few days, thanks to a rhubarb infusion.

Wolfgang left no letters that might help us understand his emotions during his London sojourn. His first letter—or at least the first that has come down to us—was sent from Salzburg and is of uncertain date but certainly not before 1769. Leopold continued to write regularly to his friend Hagenauer, however, to report on the family's extraordinary adventures, reassure him that his money had been well-lent, and justify his own long absence from his post at the court in Salzburg.

Leopold was much impressed by the vastness, the wealth, and the efficiency of London. If someone were to look at the Thames from the bridge, he wrote, he would feel himself in the midst of a forest, so many were the ships' masts. New houses were constantly being built. Public lighting was the most efficient that he had seen. In London as in Paris, the city gates were never closed. Of course, there were poor people even in London, but few of them dared to beg, because begging was against the law. Beggars got around that prohibition by offering little bunches of flowers, toothpicks, popular prints, spools of thread, or ribbons of many colors. In his descriptions of London, Leopold often displays his pedantry by providing exact numbers of ships, sailors, houses, churches, hospitals, policemen, and more, thus giving the impression that he is painstakingly copying his information from a book or guidebook to the city.[31]

Leopold had severely criticized Parisians for their immorality, and he had much the same to say about Londoners. "I will not bring up my children," he writes in a letter to Hagenauer dated 19 March 1765, "in such a dangerous place (where the majority of the inhabitants have no religion and where one only has evil examples before one)."[32] He was perturbed by the fact that London Jews did not wear beards or dress in the Hebrew fashion. He was anguished by the idea that no one had much faith in God any more—not Jews, nor society people, nor Christians of French, Italian, Portuguese, or English origin. Instead of respecting the Lord's day, all well-off Londoners preferred to spend the weekend in their country houses. Society—"good" society in particular—was becoming a secular one, corrupted by wealth. Still, Leopold considered it very important to make a good personal impression in this frivolous world. When they left Paris, Leopold had been wrongly assured that no one wore a sword in London, so he left both his own sword and Wolfgang's little one in Paris, and when they arrived in London, he was obliged to pay a pretty price to rent swords for them both.

On 27 April 1764, four days after their arrival, the Mozarts were received at court by George III and the queen, Charlotte Sophia. Leopold reports in a letter:

> The present was only twenty-four guineas, which we received immediately on leaving the King's apartment, but the graciousness with which both His Majesty the King and Her Majesty the Queen received us cannot be described. In short, their easy manner and friendly ways made us forget that they were the King and Queen of England. At all courts up to the present we have been received with extraordinary courtesy. But the welcome which we have been given here exceeds all others. A week later we were walking in St. James's Park. The King came along driving with the Queen and, although we all had on different clothes, they recognized us nevertheless and not only greeted us, but the King opened the window, leaned out and saluted us and especially our Master Wolfgang, nodding to us and waving his hand.[33]

In England the Mozarts were received at court on at least two other occasions, on 19 May and 25 October 1764. Wolfgang's talent and that of his sister were clearly appreciated. Moreover, Wolfgang dedicated to the queen, Charlotte Sophia, the six sonatas for keyboard and violin (K. 10–15), published in London at the expense of the Mozart family. To signal her gratitude for this dedication the queen gave Wolfgang fifty guineas.

In London Leopold organized a number of private concerts for his children in the houses of nobles or wealthy burghers, but he also organized public concerts with paid admission such as the one in the Cornhill tavern. From a commercial viewpoint Leopold showed a certain acumen, even though his procedures may appear unpolished to us. It is certain, however, that during the fifteen months that the family spent in England, he managed to accumulate another fortune, despite his continual complaints that earnings had fallen short of his expectation.

The London sojourn contributed to another and much more important form of enrichment: the musical maturity of young Wolfgang. In London during those same years Johann Christian Bach (who was thirty at the time), son of the great Johann Sebastian Bach, was pursuing a highly successful career, and that very year, 1765, he had been named chamber musician to Queen Charlotte Sophia. He was the first composer to introduce clarinets into the orchestra and among the first to play the pianoforte as a soloist. Together with his fellow German, Carl Friedrich Abel (also named chamber musician to the queen in 1765), Bach founded the Bach-Abel Concerts, which became a London institution. Both men exerted a notable influence on Wolfgang, and like Schobert and Eckard in France, they were enchanted by the boy's grace, skill, and musical talent. One might go so far as to say that Bach was young Wolfgang's second teacher after Leopold, but he had much more modern ideas than the boy's father. He introduced Wolfgang to the world of the opera and the symphony, treating the boy as a colleague to the point that during a concert before the king, the queen, and the English court, the two took turns at the keyboard for more than two hours.[34]

Leopold recounts in a letter what happened at one of those memorable royal audiences. George III had given Wolfgang some works by J. C. Bach, Abel, Handel, and Georg Christoph Wagenseil, which the boy read at sight. The boy then accompanied the queen, who sang an aria, and, to general astonishment, improvised a lovely melody on the bass part of a Handel air. "In short," his proud father wrote, "what he knew when we left Salzburg is a mere shadow compared with what he knows now. It exceeds all that one can imagine."[35] It was in London, between late 1764 and early 1765, that Wolfgang composed his first and truly notable symphony, in E-flat (K. 16).

In London there were several reasons that Wolfgang continued his musical italianization. First, his new friend and teacher Johann Christian Bach had spent considerable time in Italy before he transferred to London, to the point that he was known as both "the Milanese Bach" and "the English Bach." Bach had studied in Bologna with Padre Giovanni Battista Martini; he had converted to Catholicism; and he had been appointed organist of the cathedral of Milan. He had also composed a number of operas in the Italian style, some of which were given in London that same year in the Haymarket Theater. Second, Italian operas by Baldassare Galuppi, Giovanni Ferrandini, Mattia Vento, Johann Adolph Hasse (as well as Bach) were also produced at the Haymarket during the Mozarts' London stay. Wolfgang's third Italian influence came through singing lessons from the famous Florentine castrato Giovanni Manzuoli, who lived in London at the time, had a magnificent voice, and was Bach's favorite singer. Thanks to these London experiences, Wolfgang was soon able to penetrate many of the secrets of Italian opera and to write some fifteen arias in the Italian style, all lost except for "Va dal furor portata" on a text by Pietro Metastasio (K. 21/19c), the earliest example of Mozart's vocal compositions. The somewhat conventional aria already displays a firm control of the medium.

In those same days an English judge, Daines Barrington, examined Wolfgang carefully, set him to a number of difficult musical tasks, and wrote a report, published several years later in *Philosophical Transactions*. Barrington concluded that the child possessed "most extraordinary musical talents," which he compared to those of an actor interpreting Shakespeare with extraordinary dramatic intensity or an exceptionally gifted scholar capable of reading Shakespeare commentaries in Greek, Hebrew, and Etruscan.[36]

Wolfgang was a child in chronological terms, and in part he continued to be a child. But another part of him had undergone a profound change that enabled him to acquire a technical prowess and a stylistic equilibrium worthy of an adult. We have already seen Leopold's statement in a letter dated 8 June 1764: "My boy knows in this his eighth year what one would expect only from a man of forty."[37] Leopold himself was forty-five at the time, hence when he gives his son a slightly less mature age than his own, he is indicating his intention to claim musical superiority, however limited, over him. It is also possible that deep within him, along with the pleasure that he felt at having created a spectacular talent, Leopold was already beginning to find it difficult to admit that his eight- or nine-year-old son was in all senses a more powerful musician and was even endowed with a more solid character. Rivalry insinuated itself not only into Nannerl's breast, but into the father's. The only member of the family not in competition with little Wolfgang was his mother.

## The Return Trip to Salzburg
### (August 1765–November 1766)

The morning of 1 August 1765 the Mozarts once again crossed the Channel, leaving the cliffs of Dover behind them and reaching Calais after three and a half hours. They did not return home immediately, however, but continued to travel through Europe for another sixteen months. They spent more than a month in northern France and Belgium, about eight months in Holland, another month in Belgium, then another three months in France, a month in Switzerland, and a month in Germany.

The return trip took so long in part because the two young performers fell seriously ill with typhoid fever in Holland. Nannerl became sick on 12 September 1765, and a month later her condition was so dire that she was given last rites. While his sister lay in bed, Wolfgang continued to play and practice in the next room. When she finally recovered, he fell sick. Their illness and convalescence took several months. At the peak of his illness Wolfgang could not speak for eight days, after which he began to babble incoherently night and day. In four weeks his already slight body had shrunk to skin and bones. He too was judged to be at death's door. "Yesterday and today, however," Leopold wrote Hagenauer on 12 December, "we led him a few times across the room so that gradually he may learn to use his feet and stand upright by himself."[38] As he often did in his letters, Leopold furnishes detailed information on the treatment the doctors prescribed. There were the usual remedies of the time: infusions, bloodletting, enemas, "black powder" (*pulvis epilepticus niger*), and margrave powder. Existence was precarious, and the wisest course was to trust in God rather than in pharmacists and physicians.

Despite his illness, Wolfgang managed to perform in some concerts in Holland. In September 1765, before he fell sick, he played in The Hague before Prince William of Orange and his sister, Princess Caroline of Nassau-Weilburg. In 1766, when he had recovered, he gave three public concerts with paid attendance in Amsterdam. In April he played in Utrecht. He composed another symphony (K. 22), which received its premiere performance in The Hague on 27 February 1766. The concert was held in the middle of Lent, when, in theory, only sacred music was to be played, so that the organizers had to obtain special permission to play the new piece. The symphony was a musical genre that was just beginning to gain acceptance as concert halls became more common and instrumental music began to be conceived as an autonomous art; until the eighteenth century the symphony (or sinfonia) tended to be considered almost simple background "noise," a form inferior to the music that accompanied singing. It is truly stupefying that at the age of ten Wolfgang should succeed in producing compositions of high quality in a new genre. He was no longer the child prodigy improvising at the keyboard: he was beginning to be a composer in the true sense of the word.

The Mozarts returned to Paris, where they had left some of their baggage and perhaps some of the precious objects they had collected during their long but breakneck tour of the courts of Europe. This time Wolfgang had a much cooler reception than three years earlier, perhaps because in the aristocratic and worldly circles of Paris a ten-year-old composer aroused much less enthusiasm than a seven-year-old keyboard prodigy. Appreciating the musical gifts of a ten-year-old composer required a musical training and an effort far beyond what it took to be astonished by infantile virtuoso performance. Moreover, as is true of wealthy and consumption-oriented circles in any epoch, even a "phenomenon" like the little Mozart soon lost his charm. On 9 July 1766 the Mozarts left Paris without regret. Before their departure, Leopold sent off to Salzburg two large cases of costly trinkets, the booty won in a long and exhausting trip that was not yet over.

In Dijon, Nannerl and Wolfgang played before the Prince de Condé, and after their concert in October in Schaffhausen, the prince of the city rewarded their father with twenty-four louis d'or and gave each of the two children a diamond ring. They also performed in Geneva, Lausanne, Zurich, and Munich.

By the time they at last reached Salzburg in November 1766, after three years of exhausting adventures and hard work, Wolfgang had become famous and his father had managed to put aside a tidy fortune. The trip had cost enormous sums, but the earnings were sufficient for Leopold to accumulate thousands of florins, a sum perhaps fifty times his annual stipend. The cases sent from Paris contained the gifts of kings, queens, princes, dukes, counts, and countesses: watches, inlaid snuffboxes, rings and necklaces set with precious stones, earrings, and gold tableware in such numbers as would be hard to count. One commentator has remarked that only the cathedral of a great city could accumulate a more dazzling treasury.[39]

## Salzburg (December 1766–September 1767)

After three emotionally charged years Salzburg offered a more modest reality, which was why Leopold arranged it so that the family would remain home only nine months. During that time Wolfgang had a chance to meditate on his experiences, compose new works, and study.

Only a few days before their return to Salzburg, Leopold had shared with Lorenz Hagenauer his program for the coming months: "God, who has been far too good to me, a miserable sinner, has bestowed such talents on my children that, apart from my duty as a father, they alone would spur me on to sacrifice everything to their successful development. Every moment I lose is lost forever. . . . If with the excuse that one thing prevents another they were to accustom themselves to hours of idleness, my whole plan would crumble to pieces."[40] Luckily, his children were obedient, hardworking, and accustomed to knuckling down. As Leopold said, "Habit is an iron shirt." Wolfgang in particular not only practiced his instrument but also disciplined himself to study counterpoint and three foreign languages, Italian, English, and French. As a cosmopolitan artist he would need to communicate with the world, and a good command of Italian was imperative if he wanted to compose arias and operas. He was eleven, but he worked like an adult. As if study and practice were not enough, during the nine months that the family spent in Salzburg he managed to write the first act of a sacred oratorio, an intermezzo in Latin for voices and orchestra, four concertos for keyboard and orchestra, a tenor aria, a cantata for soloists, chorus, and orchestra, and other compositions now lost.

It is often noted that the four keyboard concertos (K. 37, 39, 40, 41) are reelaborations of other composers' works. This was by Wolfgang's choice, however, both because imitation was common practice among musicians of the time and because, by developing other composers' themes, he intended to demonstrate his superiority to them. This consideration seems particularly true for the Concerto in B-flat (K. 39), which uses themes by Hermann Friedrich Raupach and Johann Schobert. Even the sacred drama, *Die Schuldigkeit des erstern Gebots* (The Obligation of the First Commandment; K. 35), and the intermezzo *Apollo et Hyacinthus* (K. 38) were serious works of notable quality. The sacred drama, performed in Salzburg on 12 March 1767, had been commissioned by Sigismund von Schrattenbach, the prince-bishop of Salzburg.[41] This was his native city's first official recognition of Mozart's gifts as a composer. According to legend, Wolfgang composed this oratorio in total isolation, under the strict personal supervision of the archbishop, in order to counter any suspicion that others might have aided him.[42] Mozart's reward was a gold medal and twelve ducats. The Latin intermezzo, *Apollo et Hyacinthus*, had been commissioned by the Jesuit University of Salzburg to celebrate the end of the academic year. Its performance took place in the great hall of that university on 13 May 1767.

By this time eleven-year-old Wolfgang had to his credit something like a hundred compositions, including sonatas, dances, symphonies, preludes, arias, and oratorios. No other composer had ever succeeded in producing this much material and of like quality at that age. Leopold must have been happy indeed over his son's successes, which was precisely what induced him to press on. The European trip had already demonstrated the provinciality of Salzburg, and Wolfgang's growing musical powers seemed to Leopold to merit a permanent post in a city such as Vienna or Munich. In Leopold's imagination, by offering their joint services, he and his son could find a comfortable berth in a wealthier and more powerful court than that of a modest prince-bishop. The mirage of Vienna, which had already enchanted him five years earlier, endured. As he wrote to Hagenauer on 10 December 1762, "You will say that Vienna makes a fool of everyone. And indeed, when I compare Salzburg with Vienna, in certain respects I soon become confused."[43] The dream of a joint position in a great European court was to last another fifteen years.

In September 1767 the entire Mozart family left once more for the Austrian capital, where festivities to celebrate the marriage of Maria Josepha, the daughter of Empress Maria Theresa, were about to begin. Archbishop Schrattenbach, thinking that the Mozarts' absence would be brief, gave Leopold permission to leave his post once more.

# Searching for a Post
# with His Father

## Disappointments in Vienna
## (September 1767–January 1769)

Archbishop Schrattenbach never imagined that the Mozart family would stay in Vienna nearly a year and a half. Nor could Leopold have predicted that Vienna's fascination with Wolfgang would dissipate so alarmingly. The father and the son faced bitter days between September 1767 and January 1769.

The family's stay in Vienna opened inauspiciously, due to an epidemic of smallpox, a highly contagious disease not easily cured in those days and one which often led to death. On 15 October 1767 the young archduchess Maria Josepha, the empress's daughter, who was to marry King Ferdinand IV of Naples, died of smallpox. Leopold, who had organized the Mozarts' expedition to Vienna in the hope of performing during the festivities to celebrate the marriage, was upset. But he was downright panicky at the notion that Wolfgang and Nannerl might also catch the disease. He decided to leave Vienna and take them to Bohemia, but the precaution proved useless, as Wolfgang fell seriously ill with smallpox. He was blind for nine days and hovered between life and death, for the second time, after his bout with typhus in 1765. Around 10 November 1767 Wolfgang began to recover but then Nannerl fell ill. She recovered after three weeks, but both siblings were left pock-marked for life. Leopold wrote Lorenz Hagenauer twice that November, asking him to have six masses said in thanks for Wolfgang's recovery and just one for Nannerl's. If there is any meaning in this discrepancy, it tells us something about how Leopold valued his son, as compared to his daughter.

The only known remedies for smallpox were the usual useless powders. Some form of inoculation was beginning to be practiced, but as we have seen, three years earlier in Paris Leopold had refused to have his children subjected to it. We know from a letter of Leopold's written on 6 August 1768 that the Viennese physicians of the time were also fiercely hostile to inoculation, but when the empress finally determined to have her children inoculated, the majority of the medical profession changed its opinion and pronounced in favor of the new practice.[1] This change of mind did not affect Wolfgang and Nannerl, whose illness had provided them with immunity to further infection.

As the family might have learned from its recent experience in Paris, when the two child prodigies were no longer children, the enchantment of the earlier trips was shattered. Nannerl was sixteen when they arrived in Vienna and eighteen at the end of their stay; Wolfgang was eleven at the start and thirteen at the end. He was past the age for jumping up into Empress Maria Theresa's lap and kissing her, as he had done in 1762.

Moreover, the Viennese began to accuse Wolfgang of deception: of pretending to sight-read scores that he had studied previously, of claiming to have composed sonatas and symphonies that had really been written by others, and even of lying about his age by saying he was younger than he was. Many adult keyboard players resented Wolfgang and felt humiliated by the youngster's superior talent.[2] Moreover, the court's attitude toward the Mozarts had changed in the intervening five years. Emperor Francis I, who had been so amiable with Wolfgang in 1762, had died two years before, and Maria Theresa, now a widow, was sharing the imperial throne with her son, Joseph II, who proved to be somewhat indecisive and inclined to avarice. Joseph II's thanks to Mozart came in the form of a single medal of little intrinsic value. Moreover, the court was in mourning for the death of Maria Josepha.

Leopold was on the verge of packing up and returning to Salzburg when a casual remark of Joseph II's, asking Wolfgang if he would like to compose an opera, persuaded him that they should remain in Vienna. Viennese musical society demanded that Wolfgang, no longer a child prodigy at the keyboard, find new ways to charm an audience, and Leopold understood that his son needed to accept the challenge. Any genuine composer was expected to write operas.

The experiment failed. There was nothing wrong with the opera that Wolfgang composed in Vienna between April and July 1768, *La finta semplice* (The Pretended Simpleton; K. 51/46a), but it was never even produced. The libretto, written by the Livornese Marco Coltellini, was a capable adaptation of a text by Carlo Goldoni. Some parts of the opera were delightful, and as a whole it was more than pleasing, but—according to

Leopold—many in Viennese musical circles conspired to prevent its success. Still according to Leopold, Coltellini, the librettist, was also to blame for providing the texts of the arias very late, and all the composers in Vienna, the great Christoph Willibald Gluck first among them, moved by jealousy or their own interests, worked to block the work's performance. The singers could not read music. The members of the orchestra felt humiliated at the thought of a twelve-year-old conductor. "Some people," Leopold complained, "spread the report that the music was not worth a fig; others said that it did not fit the words, or was against the meter, thus proving that the boy had not sufficient command of the Italian language."[3] The impresario of the court theater, a Neapolitan named Giuseppe Affligio, canceled the performance and refused to pay Mozart the hundred ducats he had been promised. Leopold had made the mistake of setting Wolfgang to the task without a properly drawn-up and signed contract and an appropriate down payment. Affligio was an adventurer and a swindler who had become wealthy by running the court theater on his own, thus relieving the court itself of risks and responsibilities. Some years and many illicit maneuvers later, he was tried in Tuscany and sentenced to life imprisonment, a sentence that was commuted to a number of years in prison in Portoferraio. In 1767 Affligio had already experienced financial difficulties in Vienna, and he probably thought that an opera written by a twelve-year-old was a poor business move.

We can well imagine Leopold's irritation at this affront. He knew *La finta semplice* to be of perfectly acceptable musical quality and felt that its cancellation could only be explained by intrigues and ill will. Yet his irritation only isolated him even more from influential circles in Vienna. He went so far as to present Joseph II with a petition in which he listed the wrongs done to him, accusing Affligio, and asking that Wolfgang's musical capacities be tested.[4] Joseph II had turned over all responsibility for managing the court theater to Affligio, but to forestall talk he ordered an investigation, the outcome of which was to declare Leopold's accusations unfounded. From then on, the idea took hold in the Viennese court that Leopold was a meddlesome bore and Wolfgang an ambitious youngster unable to get over having been a child prodigy. Opinion had changed to the point that the Mozart family's earlier successes began to be seen in a negative light. It was said that Leopold had carted his children around Europe only to exploit them and exhibit them like a circus act. Three years later Maria Theresa sent one of her sons, Archduke Ferdinand, the famous letter in which she speaks so severely of the entire Mozart family: "You ask me," she wrote to her son, "to take the young Salzburger into your service. I do not know why, not believing that you have need of a composer or of useless people."[5]

The empress's hostility proved a notable obstacle to Mozart's career, particularly since it is very probable that she expressed her aversion to the Mozarts to members and representatives of other European courts, not only to her son Ferdinand. Mozart never knew of Maria Theresa's letter, but he must have received other evidence of her dislike. When the empress died in November 1780, Wolfgang took care to wear black to show formal respect, but in a letter to his father he clearly hinted that her death meant nothing to him.[6]

Luckily for Wolfgang, the trip to Vienna was not exclusively one of disappointments and bitterness. He had several successes as a concert artist, playing portions of *La finta semplice* on the pianoforte and thus enabling his father to put away some money. He also composed a short opera in German, *Bastien und Bastienne* (K. 50/46b), a charming work still popular in Germany today. Tradition has it that this one-act operetta was commissioned by the famous physician and theorist of magnetism Franz Anton Mesmer, but there is no real proof of this. Mesmer is mentioned more than once in the letters that Leopold wrote in 1773, but not in 1768.[7] In any event, *Bastien und Bastienne* was Wolfgang's first singspiel—a partially sung, partially spoken theatrical work. Its libretto was based on *Le devin du village,* a theatrical intermezzo published by Jean-Jacques Rousseau some years earlier. We should point out that the negative reaction to *La finta semplice* helped Mozart to understand the jealousies, animosities, and risks involved in opera production. A good product was not enough to persuade patrons and impresarios to invest large amounts of money in singers, scenery, and musicians: the work had to be excellent, and every step of the process required diplomacy, a lesson that Wolfgang remembered nearly all his life. Given that we learn more from failures and errors than from easy victories, the whole affair of *La finta semplice* helped Wolfgang to grow and to learn.

On 7 December 1768, toward the end of his stay in Vienna, Wolfgang experienced genuine triumph when he conducted a mass of his own composition in the presence of the entire court during the ceremonies connected with the consecration of the church of the Landstrasse orphan asylum. We can surmise that Joseph II commissioned the work to compensate Mozart for the humiliation he had received with *La finta semplice*. The mass in question may have been the Missa brevis (K. 49/47d), or perhaps the Missa solemnis (K. 139/47a), a work so extraordinarily innovative that scholars long hesitated to attribute it to a twelve-year-old and dated it to 1772 or even later. Today the 1768 date is no longer disputed. As he convalesced from smallpox, Wolfgang probably composed a new symphony as well, the Symphony in F (K. 43). The year he spent in Vienna had been of fundamental importance for his musical education, perhaps even more so than the fifteen months he spent in London.

Johann Adolph Hasse, a famous German musician who had lived for long periods in Italy, had become the official composer of the court in Vienna in 1764. After examining Wolfgang, he wrote of him, "I took him through various tests on the harpsichord, on which he let me hear things that are prodigious for his age and would be admirable even for a mature man." Hasse adds, "The boy is moreover handsome, vivacious, graceful, and full of good manners; and knowing him, it is difficult to avoid loving him. I am sure that if his development keeps due pace with his years, he will be a prodigy."[8]

Hasse emitted this rosy prediction because, given his own professional competence, he had insisted on listening to Wolfgang and examining him personally. Leopold in fact stated that his son's detractors had never met the child or heard his compositions. In a letter dated 30 January 1768 Leopold writes that "the chief maxim of these people" was to avoid any possible occasion for direct acquaintance with the young composer, so that if questioned about the lad's qualities they could answer that they had never heard him play, thus reinforcing the notion that his compositions were forged, "all humbug and foolishness," since a twelve-year-old boy could never achieve the qualities of an experienced composer.[9] In other words, Wolfgang's rivals had deliberately woven a curtain of indifference and silence around him. It may be odd to say so, but we have the impression that an involuntary curtain of silence continued to surround the works of the very young Mozart for centuries. Until recently many of his early works remained buried in the archives, were rarely if ever performed, and were seldom recorded, and thus have remained totally or relatively unknown. The authors of some of the best-known biographies of Wolfgang (perhaps even the excellent Massimo Mila) may have written about such early works as La finta semplice without having had an opportunity to hear them or read them over, hence they write of those works without fully appreciating their qualities. They may not have realized it, but in some respects they were acting like Mozart's Viennese detractors in 1768.

## Back to Salzburg in 1769

On 5 January 1769 the Mozart family returned to Salzburg. For almost a year the prince-bishop, Schrattenbach, had shown signs of irritation over Leopold's long absences, and he had suspended his pay. Schrattenbach may have learned that Leopold was hoping to find an appointment in Vienna or elsewhere and considered it an act of betrayal of the diocesan court which had done so much to help him and encourage Wolfgang. Nor can we exclude the notion that word might have reached Salzburg of Empress Maria Theresa's hostility toward the Mozarts. Archbishop Schrattenbach had not only encouraged but financed the Mozarts' voyages in the hope of enhancing Salzburg's prestige throughout Europe, and if that aim was not to be fulfilled, there was no longer any reason to guarantee the stipend of the ever-absent Leopold. Nevertheless, soon after his return, Leopold presented the prince-bishop with a petition to be reinstated, with back pay, a request that the prince-bishop deigned to grant.

In spite of his misadventures in Vienna, Wolfgang possessed an enormous talent, and the diocesan court was well aware of the fact. His achievements numbered more than one hundred compositions listed by Leopold,[10] including two brief operas, *La finta semplice* and *Bastien und Bastienne*. In May 1769 *La finta semplice* was put on in the court theater in Salzburg. During the same year, which the thirteen-year-old Wolfgang spent almost entirely at home, he wrote a Missa brevis (K. 65/61a) and the longer *Dominicus* Mass (K. 66), composed on the occasion of the first mass celebrated by his childhood friend, Cajetan Hagenauer (the son of Lorenz Hagenauer, the Mozarts' landlord, who had financed their voyage around Europe), who had become a priest and taken the name Father Dominicus. The *Dominicus* Mass diverged from traditional schemes, even containing a waltz-like section in the Kyrie. During the same period Wolfgang composed a *licenza*, or farewell aria, to be sung at the end of an evening at the opera, which he dedicated to the most powerful person present, Prince-Bishop Schrattenbach. This concert aria for soprano and orchestra, "A Berenice"/"Sol nascente" (K. 70/61c), is a truly magnificent work, much superior to the tenor aria (K. 21/19c) that Wolfgang had composed in London four years before. Wolfgang was making continual and astonishing progress. On 27 October 1769 the prince-bishop named the thirteen-year-old as court concertmaster, though without stipend.

Leopold was still dissatisfied. His son's talent was an irresistible inducement to move on and seek a larger stage than Salzburg. What had happened in Vienna in 1768 had persuaded him that a change of direction was called for. Wolfgang, once a child prodigy, had the capacity to become a great composer, but he needed help to make the transition. Italy was relatively close to Salzburg, and Italy might encourage just such an evolution, given that it was a great musical nation, perhaps the greatest in Europe. In no other country in the world was there such a large number of opera houses and musical academies. Italian composers held a dominant position in almost all European courts. Indeed, Wolfgang himself had already begun the process of his musical italianization as early as 1763, when he had written an entire opera on an Italian libretto, and he could not afford to ignore the latest fashions of the Italian peninsula. A trip to Italy was just about obligatory for anyone who sought entry into the world of opera.

Leopold Mozart was counting on a trip to Italy to provide an opportunity for Wolfgang to complete his musical training, consolidate his fame, and even—thanks to Leopold's connections—to obtain a permanent and well-paid post at one of the many Italian courts. Italy of that time was in fact subdivided into many states, and the influence of the Hapsburg Empire, which administered Lombardy directly, was strong throughout the peninsula. Leopold had a letter of introduction to one of the most prominent representatives of the empire, the governor-general of Lombardy, Count Karl Joseph Firmian, a nephew of Leopold von Firmian, who had served as prince-bishop of Salzburg until 1744. Empress Maria Theresa's son Leopold, who had reacted with enthusiasm on hearing Wolfgang play some years earlier in Vienna, was now, at twenty-two, grand duke of Tuscany as Leopold I (but better known in Italy as Pietro Leopoldo). The king of Naples, Ferdinand IV, had married Maria Carolina, another of Maria Theresa's children. In other words, Leopold, who was unaware of any hostile sentiments of the court in Vienna, might have deluded himself that someone—in Milan, Florence, Naples, or another Italian capital—might step up and offer Wolfgang a permanent position. Prince-Bishop Schrattenbach not only agreed to a voyage that might cause him to lose two composer-musicians, but magnanimously granted them 120 ducats to finance their trip. In the letters that Leopold sent back from Italy, which might well have been intercepted by the Salzburg censors, he used a pre-established code whenever he wrote about the money they earned or anything else that might irritate the prince-bishop.

Thus Leopold left for Italy with his son on 14 December 1769, just under a year after the family's return to Salzburg. They went alone, without Anna Maria and Nannerl. Nannerl, now nearly eighteen, did not have her

brother's talents; her career as a child prodigy had ended some time earlier, so there was little sense in paying her way. She remained in Salzburg,
with her mother taking care of her, and gave piano lessons. She had become quite the little lady and was demanding and spoiled. Since she could
not do her daily *toilette* unaided or dress her own hair, she needed someone to serve her. Left alone in Salzburg, the mother and the daughter were
jealous of the two men of the family, who were privileged to wander freely
in the land of flowers, lemon trees, sunshine, and love.

## The First Italian Trip: From the Brenner Pass to Florence (December 1769–April 1770)

Between December 1769 and March 1773, Leopold and Wolfgang took
three trips to Italy, spending some twenty-four months there in all. The
first and longest of these lasted fifteen and a half months. Each time they
traversed the Alps over the Brenner Pass. *Mozart in Italy,* by Iwo and
Pamela Zaluski, gives detailed information on the places they saw, the
persons they met, the roads they took, and the sums they earned.[11]

On their first trip, after making their way over the Brenner Pass, they
reached Bressanone (Brixen) toward the end of December 1769, where
they lodged at the Aquila Nera, an inn that exists to this day, then moved
on to Bolzano and Rovereto, where Wolfgang and his father played their
first concert before an Italian audience. The concert took place in the
house of Baron Giovanni Battista Todeschi on via Nuova (now via Mer-
cerie 14), where a wall plaque recalls the event. The evening of 27 December the pair arrived in Verona, where they slept at the Albergo Due
Torri. On 5 January 1770 Wolfgang gave a concert at the Accademia Filarmonica of Verona, and Saverio Della Rosa painted a portrait of him, ele-
gantly dressed, his hands poised over the keyboard, one of his own compositions laid out on the music stand, and his serious gaze turned to the
painter.

On 10 January father and son reached Mantua. The program that was
printed for the concert held on 16 January in the small but elegant Teatro
Scientifico, recently constructed by Antonio Bibiena (and still standing),
is further confirmation that Leopold continued to exhibit his son as if
he were a circus spectacle. The program states: "The most highly skilled
youth, Signor Amadeo Mozart" would play a concerto for harpsichord at
sight; would then compose and sing "extempore" an aria "to words made
for the purpose, but not previously seen by him." After this he would play
another sonata "on a musical theme proposed to him extempore by the

first violin."[12] Toward the end of what must have been a long program, Mozart would leave the keyboard to improvise the violin part of a trio. Aside from being an extraordinary pianist, Wolfgang played both the viola and the violin acceptably. It is too much to ask that he excel in everything; it is surprising enough that at fourteen he could play three instruments in public, one of them splendidly. All of this concertizing took place in extremely cold weather, playing in halls that were unevenly or scantily heated, if at all. As Leopold wrote his wife from their Mantua lodgings, "No warm room, so that one freezes like a dog. Everything I touch is as cold as ice."[13] Wolfgang's face and hands were so red from the cold and from the fires they huddled over that a local lady took pity on him and gave him a pomade to use on them.

On 23 January the two Mozarts reached Milan, where they remained for almost two months, staying at the Monastery of San Marco on via Fatebenefratelli. Wolfgang had free access to Palazzo Melzi, the residence of Governor-General Firmian, where a spinet was put at his disposal (it is now displayed in the Museum of Musical Instruments in Milan's Castello Sforzesco). On 2 February Leopold and Wolfgang went to the Regio Ducal Teatro, the theater located in the right wing of the royal palace, near the Duomo, to attend the dress rehearsal of *Cesare in Egitto*, an opera by Niccolò Piccinni, the famous composer born in Bari, forty-two at the time, who composed 120 operas during his lifetime. Leopold and his son liked the opera very much, and Piccinni and Wolfgang, who was intrigued by some technical aspects of Piccinni's music, became friends, meeting on other occasions in the years to come.

While in Milan, Mozart gave a number of concerts in Palazzo Melzi, and he received a beautifully bound nine-volume edition of the works of Pietro Metastasio as a gift from Governor Firmian. Wolfgang had already set to music two arias by Metastasio, and he wrote six others in the months that followed. Most important, it was in Milan that Wolfgang was commissioned to write an opera, *Mitridate, Re di Ponto,* on a libretto by Vittorio Amedeo Cigna-Santi (after a play by Jean Racine, translated by Giuseppe Parini), a work that was to be produced during Carnival the following year. We learn from Leopold Mozart's letters that they both enjoyed the cordial and friendly atmosphere that surrounded them everywhere in Italy. Leopold wrote his wife on 17 February 1770 that "on the whole we shall not earn much in Italy," but in compensation "everywhere we have been received with the greatest courtesy imaginable, and . . . on all occasions we have been asked to meet the leading nobles."[14] Wolfgang amused himself italianizing and ennobling his surname, suggesting that he should be addressed as "Amadeo De Mozartini."[15] For many Italians, "Wolfgang" was in fact a mouthful, and in some of his letters from Italy he signed himself "Wolgango." We should not be surprised by Leopold's complaints about their modest earnings: he habitually cried poverty and, as we have seen, he feared that the Salzburg censors would read his correspondence and inform the prince-bishop of any sums earned in Italy. It is also true, however, that Italy was less wealthy and powerful than France or England.

After nearly two months in Milan the two Mozarts went to Lodi, where Wolfgang composed his first string quartet (K. 80/73f), a work inspired by similar compositions by the Milanese composer Giovanni Battista Sammartini, whom he had met in Milan. From Lodi they moved on to Piacenza, then to Parma, where they were received by the famous and well-paid singer Lucrezia Agujari, known as "La Bastardella" because she was the illegitimate daughter of a Ferrarese nobleman. Wolfgang was much impressed by the quality and the range of Lucrezia's voice, and in a letter to Nannerl he transcribed her runs and trills, in particular a "C sopra acuto" (an octave above high C) that has remained famous in musical history thanks to his transcription.[16]

On 24 March 1770 Wolfgang and Leopold arrived in Bologna, where they lodged at Il Pellegrino di San Marco in via Bettorini (now via Ugo Bassi), the best inn in the city, which they thought extremely expensive, as it cost a ducat a day. They remained there only five days, but during that time Wolfgang met twice with Padre Giovanni Battista Martini, a noted music theorist and composer whom he would meet again between July and October of the same year. On 25 March Wolfgang and Leopold paid a call on Count Gian Luca Pallavicini, a former field-marshal and representative of the court of Austria, in whose palace they and other artists gave a concert the following day. Wolfgang received an honorarium of about two hundred lire, and Leopold received twenty zecchini (sequins). The audience for the concert, which was given in honor of Count Joseph Clemens Kaunitz, the son of Wenzel Kaunitz, the powerful Austrian state chancellor, included many Bolognese nobles, two German princes, and two cardinals, Antonio Branciforte and Vincenzo Malvezzi. A genuine friendship sprang up between the two Mozarts and the Pallavicini family, in part because the count had a highly accomplished son, Giuseppe, just Wolfgang's age (the two boys were born three days apart). When Leopold and Wolfgang returned to Bologna in August of the same year, they were the guests of the Pallavicini in their country residence at La Croce del Biacco, not far from the city, where they remained for two months. In all the cities they visited, in fact, Leopold and Wolfgang managed to meet the right people in both the better social classes and musical circles. This guaranteed Leopold economic success and permitted Wolfgang to continue to expand his musical horizons.

The two Mozarts left Bologna for Florence on 29 March 1770, arriving the following day. They stayed for a week, lodging not far from the Arno in the Albergo Aquila Nera in Borgo Ognissanti. Leopold and Wolfgang were immediately received by the many English people who lived in Florence, and Wolfgang played in the salon of Sir Horace Mann and that of Lord and Lady Cowper. On 1 April the grand duke received them in Palazzo Pitti, and the following day they were taken in a grand-ducal carriage to Poggio Imperiale, Pietro Leopoldo's summer residence, where Wolfgang showed off his technical prowess, playing with the violinist Pietro Nardini, whom he had met in Augsburg seven years earlier. He was rewarded with over three hundred lire.

Leopold found Florence enchanting. He wrote his wife: "I should like you to see Florence itself and the surrounding country and the situation of the town, for you would say that one should live and die here."[17] While in Florence, Wolfgang paid a visit to Giovanni Manzuoli, the famous Florentine castrato who had given him singing lessons in London. He also got to know a young English violinist just his own age, Thomas Linley, with whom he established a strong though brief friendship. Linley, a pupil of Pietro Nardini's, was extraordinarily gifted, and the two fourteen-year-olds gave several concerts, one of them in the house of Giuseppe Maria Gavard des Pivets, administrator-general of the grand-ducal finances. Linley wept when he learned that his friend Wolfgang was about to leave for Rome, and on the day of the Mozarts' departure he accompanied them as far as the city gates. Linley soon returned to England, where he became well known as a violinist, a conductor, and a composer, but he drowned in a boating accident at the age of twenty-two.

## The First Roman Sojourn (April 1770)

Leopold and Wolfgang left Florence for Rome on 7 April 1770. The trip took five days; it rained constantly, with a freezing wind, and they judged the territory between the two cities to be barbarous. As Leopold wrote to his wife, "I will not give you a long description of that dreadful journey. Picture to yourself a more or less uncultivated country and the most horrible filthy inns, where we got nothing to eat save here and there eggs and broccoli; while on fast-days they sometimes made a fuss about giving us the former. Fortunately we had a good supper at Viterbo and slept well."[18] On Tuesday 11 April they entered Rome through the Porta del Popolo in a severe thunderstorm, stopping at the coach station in Piazza di Spagna at noon.

That very afternoon, they went to the basilica of St. Peter's in the Vatican. Leopold and Wolfgang were both profoundly religious, and entering that impressive edifice for the first time must have been an emotional experience, in particular because it was Holy Week. Thanks to the elegance of their dress and Leopold's nonchalance as he told their servant in German to ask the Swiss Guards to let them pass, they went right through a number of checkpoints. The Swiss Guards took Wolfgang for a young German prince and Leopold for his tutor. The two Mozarts managed to speak briefly with Cardinal Lazzaro Pallavicini, the secretary of state to the Vatican and a distant cousin of the Count Pallavicini they had met in Bologna. They even found themselves standing quite close to Pope Clement XIV as he was serving the poor at mass, as was customary during Holy Week. They then entered the Sistine Chapel.

In the Sistine Chapel Wolfgang had an opportunity to hear the famous Miserere in Nine Parts for Two Choirs composed a century earlier by Gregorio Allegri. The Roman popes had reserved to themselves the exclusive use of this Miserere, forbidding its publication. Leopold boasts, however, that Wolfgang worked around the prohibition. He explains to his wife:

> You have often heard of the famous *Miserere* in Rome, which is so greatly prized that the performers in the chapel are forbidden on pain of excommunication to take away a single part of it, to copy it or to give it to anyone. *But we have it already.* Wolfgang has written it down and we would have sent it to Salzburg in this letter, if it were not necessary for us to be there to perform it. But the manner of performance contributes more to its effect than the composition itself. Moreover, as it is one of the secrets of Rome, we do not wish to let it fall into other hands, *ut non incurramus mediate vel immediate in censuram Ecclesiae.*[19]

Leopold was probably exaggerating, and doubly so. First, it seems a bit much that Mozart, for all his genius, could really memorize a rather complex work for two choirs of nine voices each, with a performance time of thirteen minutes, after hearing it only once. Despite the legend, I suspect that rather than transcribing the entire work, Wolfgang managed to remember and note down some parts of it, which is already quite an enterprise. Second, Pope Clement XIV could not have guarded the Miserere quite that jealously, given that he showed no anger on learning that an Austrian lad had arrived in the city who was purported to have reproduced that inaccessible score. To the contrary, the pope conferred the cross of the Order of the Golden Spur on Wolfgang. Moreover, various copies of Allegri's work were circulating in Europe, and the Vatican did not protest, perhaps because, as Leopold says, "the manner of performance contributes more to its effect than the composition itself."

On this first visit to Rome the two Mozarts remained for almost a month, lodging first in a rented room and then in Palazzo Scatizzi (now demolished) in Piazza Nicosia, a palace not far from the Tiber that provided a good view of the famous fireworks shot off from Castel Sant'Angelo on Easter. Leopold, who clearly intended to put their Roman sojourn to good use and show off his son's extraordinary talents before the high society of the city, had brought with him some twenty letters of introduction to nobles and ecclesiastics. On 20 April, at the invitation of Cardinal Pallavicini, Wolfgang gave a concert in the Golden Hall of Palazzo Chigi, receiving much applause. On 26 April he had a similar success in Palazzo Barberini, and on 29 April another in the palace of Giuseppe Maria Altemps, duke of Gallese. Wolfgang did not neglect more frivolous pursuits, however, and the literature tells us that during this stay in Rome he learned how to play bocce.

## Naples (May–June 1770)

After their month in Rome, Wolfgang and his father went to Naples, where they stayed for more than a month. On 8 May, just before leaving Rome, they were disconcerted to learn that the roads to Naples were infested with dangerous bandits. They heard that recently an armed skirmish had taken place during which three highway robbers and five *sbirri* (policemen) had been killed. They left only when they felt sure that the way was clear on the Via Appia, and for safety's sake they traveled in a convoy with other coaches. At Terracina they sighted the Mediterranean for the first time. They arrived in Naples on the evening of 14 May, remaining in that city until 25 June.

Wolfgang's reception in Naples left both Mozarts somewhat perplexed. The Neapolitan audiences welcomed them warmly enough, but the Bourbon court was very chilly toward them. Ferdinand IV, the king of Naples, although married to Maria Theresa's daughter Maria Carolina, may have been prejudiced against the Mozarts because he had very likely learned about what had occurred in Vienna two years earlier regarding the canceled performance of *La finta semplice*. Wolfgang was not even invited to court, and his reaction to this discourtesy was to take a dislike to the king. He writes in a letter to his sister dated 5 June: "The King has had a rough Neapolitan upbringing and in the opera he always stands on a stool so as to look a little taller than the Queen."[20]

The king's subjects, by contrast, showered Mozart with applause and even with gifts. One public concert brought in 150 zecchini, perhaps more. Mozart performed several times on the harpsichord, astonishing his listeners with the agility of his hands, his left hand in particular. Some Neapolitans, perhaps influenced by a culture that tended to superstition and liked mysteries, asserted that the boy played as well as he did thanks to a magic ring that he wore. When they demanded that he take off the ring and play without it, they saw that his playing depended on talent rather than spells, and they applauded all the more.[21] We can imagine the scene: Neapolitans first crying out in dialect that they had no intention of being *fatti fessi da o' guaglione* (made fools of by an imposter) and then breaking out in enthusiastic cheers.

Wolfgang and Leopold met many members of Neapolitan high society. They paid a call on the prime minister of the Kingdom of Naples, Bernardo Tanucci, a powerful member of the government and an enlightened reformer. They were received by William Hamilton, the English ambassador, whom they had met six years earlier in London. Wolfgang gave a concert on 18 May at the ambassador's residence, playing a valuable harpsichord made in England that had two manuals that were activated or disconnected by foot pedals. Hamilton was still living with his first wife, Catherine Barlow, and not yet with the famous Emma, who in turn later left him for Admiral Horatio Nelson. On 28 May, Countess Kaunitz, the wife of the Austrian ambassador, organized a reception in Wolfgang's honor, at which he played a harpsichord or a spinet. On 7 July, Abbé Ferdinando Galiani wrote to Madame d'Épinay, Baron Grimm's companion, "I think I wrote you that little Mosar is here, and that he is less of a miracle, although he is always the same miracle; but he will never be anything else than a miracle, and that is all."[22] It is not entirely clear just what kind of keyboard instruments Wolfgang used in Naples, in part because a 1771 portrait by Pietro Fabris shows him in a Naples salon playing an instrument so small that it is placed on a chair.

In May the two Mozarts were also invited to call on Princess Francavilla. On 30 May they met the composer Niccolò Jommelli and attended rehearsals of his *Armida abbandonata*, the work that was slated to begin the opera season at the Teatro San Carlo. Jommelli was fifty-six years old, and Wolfgang pronounced the work "beautiful, but too serious and old-fashioned for the theater."[23]

Leopold and Wolfgang went on excursions to Pompeii and Herculaneum and visited Mount Vesuvius. They were impressed by the volcano, which at the time was "smoking furiously. . . . Thunder and lightning and all the rest."[24] Wolfgang wrote his sister that Naples was beautiful, but even more crowded than Vienna and Paris, adding, "And of the two, London and Naples, I do not know whether Naples does not surpass London for the insolence of the people; for here the lazzaroni have their own general or chief, who received twenty-five ducati d'argento from the King every month, solely for the purpose of keeping them in order."[25] Mozart, who himself was always hyperactive, developed a real disdain for the laziness of the Italians. "Naples and Rome are two sleepy towns," he writes his sister on 5 June, a sentiment he repeated in a letter of 4 August: "Italy is a sleepy country! I am always drowsy!"[26] It is unclear whether it was the filth that he encountered in the city's streets or his own mocking turn of mind that inspired him, but in a letter dated 16 June, Wolfgang defined the sea lapping at the feet of Naples with the scatological humor common in Mozart family letters as the "Merditerranean."

Leopold, too, although recognizing the extraordinary beauty of Naples, listed its defects. The city was dirty and its people unbelievers. Superstition, he stated, was so deeply rooted in its population that "heresy now rules supreme and that everyone treats this state of affairs with indifference."[27] Later he wrote to his wife, "The situation of the town, the fruitfulness of the country, the liveliness of the people, the rare sights and a hundred beautiful things make me sorry to leave. But the filth, the crowds of beggars, the hateful and godless populace, the disgraceful way in which children are brought up, the incredible frivolity even in the churches, make it possible quite calmly to leave behind what is good."[28] He also felt himself far from home: a letter took fifteen days to get to Naples from Salzburg.

Their stay in Naples left Leopold with a bitter taste in his mouth. One of his dearest objectives had failed: that of finding a stable, well-paid position in the service of the great court at Naples for Wolfgang (and for himself).

## Back to Rome, then on to Bologna (June–October 1770)

Leopold and Wolfgang left Naples at six in the afternoon on 25 June, but it took them twenty-seven hours to reach Rome, sleeping only two hours during the entire trip. They were hungry as well as sleep-deprived, as all they had eaten was "four cold roast chickens and a piece of bread in the carriage." Leopold reports: "As soon as we got to our bedroom, Wolfgang sat down on a chair and at once began to snore and to sleep so soundly that I completely undressed him and put him to bed without his showing the least sign of waking up. Indeed he went on snoring, although now and then I had to raise him and put him down again and finally drag him to bed sound asleep. When he awoke after nine o'clock in the morning, he did not know where he was nor how he had got to bed. Almost the whole night through he had lain in the same place."[29]

Leopold then told his wife a white lie: "God be praised, we are well." This wasn't exactly true. At the last coach halt before Rome, Leopold had received a rather serious wound on his right leg when one of the coach horses fell down, pulling the front part of the coach down with him. Leopold, thoughtless of his own danger, reached out to keep Wolfgang from falling forward, thus hitting his leg on an iron bar on the dashboard, which gave him a nasty gash in his shin. A month later, to lessen the pain and hasten his recovery, he was still resting in bed or sitting with his leg up on a footrest as much as possible. He recovered fully only at the end of the summer. This adventurous trip from Naples to Rome gives us an emblematic representation of the character of the two Mozarts: Leopold, dedicated to the protection of his beloved son, even at the risk of his own life, but also determined to force him to terrible exertions; Wolfgang docilely taking on the challenge and willing to place himself into the hands of his father-protector.

On 5 July Cardinal Lazzaro Pallavicini received Wolfgang in the Palazzo del Quirinale in his role as papal secretary of state and presented him with the pontifical decree naming him a Cavalier of the Order of the Golden Spur. The great German composer, Christoph Willibald Gluck, who was forty-two years older than Mozart, had already received this honor, but the title conferred on Mozart was of a higher rank. "Divine Providence" had obviously shown the pontifical court that future generations would judge the qualities of the young man from Salzburg to be clearly superior to Gluck's. On 8 July Pope Clement XIV himself received Wolfgang in the Palazzo di Santa Maria Maggiore.

Two days later the pair left Rome, trailing glory. They departed at six in the evening and arrived in Civita Castellana (some twenty-five miles north of Rome) at five o'clock the next morning, leaving that same afternoon for Terni, Spoleto, and Foligno on their way to Bologna, where the two Mozarts intended to rejoin their friends Gian Luca Pallavicini and

Padre Martini. They chose this route in order to go to Loreto, probably for religious reasons, either because there was a chapel of Our Lady of Loreto in Salzburg in which it was Leopold's habit to have masses said for himself and his family, or because he wanted to pray for Our Lady's intercession to heal his leg. In Rome, Leopold had acquired a number of relics, among them a piece of wood that, he was assured, had been part of the cross on which Christ was crucified. There was a thriving market for false relics at the time.

On 20 July, after passing through Senigallia, Pesaro, Rimini, and Imola, father and son finally reached Bologna. Leopold wrote home that the entire coastal area around Rimini was crawling with soldiers and police, placed as sentinels on the hillsides and along the road from one hundred and fifty to three hundred paces apart, so as to prevent "sea pirates" from going ashore and robbing travelers.[30] The trip was fairly uncomfortable, not only because of the fleas and bedbugs that tormented them, but because Leopold's leg was hurting him. In Bologna they stayed in an inn, where Leopold remained in bed for nine days in acute pain, then moved to Count Pallavicini's summer residence outside the city, where Leopold finally recovered.

Leopold was much impressed by the luxury of Pallavicini's residence. He told his wife:

> Our sheets are of finer linen than many a nobleman's shirt, everything is of silver, even the bedroom sets, and the nightlights and so forth. Yesterday we went for a drive in two sedias, that is, Wolfgang, the Countess and the young Count in one, and I and His Excellency the Field-Marshal in the other. We have two servants to wait on us, a footman and a valet. The former sleeps in our anteroom in order to be at hand in case of necessity. The latter has to dress Wolfgang's hair. His Excellency has put us into the first rooms, which in Salzburg we should call the ground floor. Since in summer the upper rooms get all the heat, these are the best rooms, as we do not feel the slightest heat the whole day long nor particularly during the night. In addition to our rooms we have the *sala terrena* where we take our meals and where everything is fresh, cool and pleasant. The young Count, who is about Wolfgang's age and is sole heir to the property, is very talented, plays the clavier, speaks German, Italian and French and has five or six masters every day for lessons in various sciences and accomplishments.[31]

Wolfgang set to work with a will, taking counterpoint lessons from Padre Martini, a master in the art. Given that one purpose of their Italian voyage was to pursue Wolfgang's musical education, no one could have helped him attain that goal better than Padre Martini. A strong sympathy grew up between the fourteen-year-old composer and his much older teacher (Martini was sixty-four in 1770). Wolfgang was already familiar with the rules of counterpoint, but where Leopold Mozart had brought pedantry to his exercises, Martini was able to bring to life the extraordinary expressive possibilities inherent in certain compositional techniques.

On 9 October 1770 Wolfgang underwent the examination required for entry into the ancient (over one hundred years old) and highly prestigious Accademia Filarmonica of Bologna. At four in the afternoon the academicians gathered in one of the halls of the academy and their *princeps* gave Mozart a bit of Gregorian chant (in Wolfgang's case, an antiphon) and set him the task of composing a four-part composition on it, respecting the many rules of the polyphonic style laid out by Giovanni Pierluigi da Palestrina. They closeted him in a room set aside for the purpose and they waited.

At this point I have to say that we have more than two versions of what happened. The first is the one that Leopold gave his wife in a letter dated 20 October, according to which the young Mozart emerged from the room, his task well done after "less than half an hour."[32] (Wolfgang himself stated later, in a conversation in 1777 with Maximilian III of Bavaria, that it took him "an hour.")[33] Another version is that of Alfred Einstein, one of the most serious of Mozart's biographers: "Mozart failed completely" in this task, hence Leopold's account was totally fallacious.[34] Einstein's version of the affair is confirmed by three documents in the archives of the Accademia Filarmonica and the Liceo Musicale of Bologna: the draft that Mozart wrote in the closed room, the corrections that Padre Martini secretly made to it, and the fair copy that Wolfgang presented to the jury. The academicians, notes Einstein, were not enthusiastic. The minutes of the academy state, "At the end of less than an hour, Signor Mozart completed his trial which, considering the circumstances, was judged to be sufficient."[35] Each member of the jury had a white ball and a black ball. Wolfgang obtained only white balls, thus, as is the custom in such cases, the academicians rose to their feet and proclaimed him enrolled in the academy as a master.

Without any doubt, this diploma, however it was obtained, signaled a meaningful and symbolic moment in Mozart's maturing process. After 1770 Mozart could no longer be accused of inexperience in technical matters. Thanks to Padre Martini's lessons he had complete command of the composer's craft, and the difficulties he encountered in the Accademia's examination were irrelevant. As Einstein says, Mozart "quickly forgot this experience in Bologna. Nothing connected with sixteenth-century style, whether authentic or anachronistic, had any interest for him: he, who was able to imitate all styles and composers, never felt the need of imitating Palestrina, at least not directly."[36]

According to Vernon Lee, Padre Martini was even capable of scolding Pergolesi because he had not written his *Stabat Mater* in the "more scientific fugued style of the sixteenth century."[37] It is hardly any wonder that he corrected Mozart's test composition, judging it too modern.

It was also in Bologna that Leopold began to mention to his wife that their son was undergoing physical changes normal for his age, fussing that "I shall have nearly all Wolfgang's cravats and shirts altered." He quickly adds: "You must not think that he has grown very tall. It is only that his limbs are becoming bigger and stronger. He has no longer any singing voice. It has gone completely. He has neither a deep nor a high voice, not even five pure notes. He is most annoyed, for he can no longer sing his own compositions, which he would sometimes like to do."[38]

Four months later, in Milan, Leopold was obliged to overcome his usual stinginess and order a new scarlet suit for the fourteen-year-old Mozart. His shirts were by then much too small, but in order to save money Leopold decided to keep to his plan to have them altered and wait until they returned to Salzburg to replace them.[39] The former child prodigy was clearly becoming a young man. For this reason and others, as Leopold wrote his wife from Venice early in 1771, when they returned in Salzburg, it would no longer be convenient for all four of them to sleep in the same room.[40] Back in the Pallavicini's house in Bologna, Wolfgang discovered a copy of *A Thousand and One Nights* in Italian, a story of love, jealousy, and beautiful girls that he immediately set to reading.[41]

Anna Maria Mozart and Nannerl, who had remained cooped up in their house in Salzburg, felt themselves excluded from all the novelties, joys, and luxuries in which the men of the family were wallowing. Leopold was hardly tactful in his letters, which did not help. At times he exaggerated the dangers of travel, almost as if to suggest to his wife that Salzburg was admirably comfortable in comparison, but at other times he imprudently praised the marvels of Italy. "We invite you to partake of the finest figs, melons and peaches!"[42] he wrote from Count Pallavicini's residence near Bologna, where even the chamber pots were made of silver. And then there were the watermelons: "In the evening, two hours before supping, we eat a fruit which I have never seen except in paintings, which tastes something like a cucumber. It is a big, round fruit with a green skin. When it is opened and cut into several pieces, it is lovely to behold, because the fruit is pale red inside. It is called *angurie* or cucumber or squash, but it is a sweet squash and not a wild one. It is eaten with sugar and cinnamon."[43]

The two women back in Salzburg were devoured by envy. Nannerl took revenge on her brother by not responding to his letters. Her mother was resigned, up to a point. Leopold wrote her on 18 September, "If you are so keen to travel to Italy, we invite you to the opera at Milan."[44] This was a nice thought, but hastily written in a brief postscript without real conviction. The two women remained in Salzburg.

## To Milan for *Mitridate* (October–December 1770)

On 18 October 1770 Wolfgang and Leopold, who had lived in Milan for nearly two months the previous winter, returned there. Milan was already an extremely active and vital urban center. Its network of canals, called *navigli*, was crowded with commercial traffic. At the Piazza del Duomo, as was true of many other open squares throughout Europe, malefactors were hanged, and Wolfgang witnessed four such events. In autumn and winter the Milanese climate was far from comfortable because, as Leopold wrote to his wife, "it still rains here most of the time and we have thick mists, which, after one fine day, then settle down upon us."[45] It snowed in December, after which the weather turned dry but the roads were icy. The Mozarts, who had no heating stove in their quarters, suffered much from the cold, especially their unprotected hands (their feet were protected by felt boots and their bodies by furs). Wolfgang was also in pain because of a toothache that left him with one side of his face swollen.

In spite of these contretemps, on 26 December Mozart inaugurated the Milanese opera season, personally directing from the harpsichord his first *opera seria*, *Mitridate, Re di Ponto* at the Regio Ducal Teatro (La Scala had not yet been built). The libretto for this opera (which had been commissioned the preceding March by Count Karl Joseph Firmian, the governor-general of Lombardy) was turned over to Mozart only in July in Bologna, and it was not until much later that he met most of the singers. In those days, a composer would not dream of writing the arias for an opera without consulting the singers who were to interpret them. He might write the recitatives beforehand, but never the arias. As Iwo and Pamela Zaluski tell us, composers were craftsmen, paid by the piece, and were completely subservient to the true superstars of the age, who were the singers. Every composer wrote arias with particular singers in mind, shaping the music to their specific aptitudes and technical vocal abilities and respecting their caprices.[46] This is a more important point than it may seem, because it demonstrates how a composer and his musical scores did not enjoy the same respect they do today. Now it is generally the singers who have to adapt to the composer's will, not the other way around.

Composers then occupied a low rank on the social scale. Those who obtained the post in a princely household that they so ardently desired were considered servants, wore livery, ate in the kitchen with the rest of the staff, and could be arrested if they tried to quit their post without their patron's permission. Even the great Johann Sebastian Bach was held in prison for nearly a month in 1717 when he announced his intention to leave his post at the court of Weimar,[47] and Franz Joseph Haydn was already sixty years of age before he could leave his patrons, the Esterházy family. Copyright had not yet been introduced in Mozart's day, which meant that a musician was happy to find a stable post, with all its servile overtones, under a prince who assured his survival by paying a regular stipend.

It is also important for an understanding of the musicians of the time, however, to add that the public did not listen to music in the religious silence that is the rule today. People went to the opera house to converse, eat, drink, play cards, and even flirt. The curtains could be drawn around a box, thus transforming it into a very private miniature drawing room. Every opera theater was in reality one big drawing room financed by the sovereign and the proprietors of the boxes (*palchi*), known in Italy as *palchettisti*, who might go to the theater every evening. This means that the audience listened to the opera with the same attention (or inattention) of people of today who leave the radio on as they go about their business. What is more, servants of the *palchettisti* who attended the theater with their masters paid no admission fee. Their habits were free indeed. What would be the main floor in a modern theater was only partially furnished with benches, with the front rows usually reserved for army officers in uniform. Everyone talked continually, and the opera was performed to the accompaniment of all this noisy social life. Only once in a while did what was taking place on the stage attract enough interest to make the public listen in silence.

In practical terms, then, Mozart could work seriously on the composition of *Mitridate* only from late September. During the next few weeks Wolfgang seemed very serious, very busy, and very preoccupied, to the point that his father declared himself happy if he could distract his son with some amusement now and then. But after the failure of *La finta semplice*, Mozart was anguished at the idea that *Mitridate* might fail as well: "Mamma, I beg you to pray for me, that my opera may go well," he wrote to his mother on 20 October.[48]

The new opera portrayed events in the tragic story of Mithridates VI, Rome's bitter enemy, who reigned over the region of Pontus, on the Black Sea, from 120 to 63 BC and conquered all of Asia Minor and Greece. At the end of his life, however, misfortune descended on him: defeated by the Romans, ignominiously betrayed by his sons and by his mistress, Aspasia, Mithridates committed suicide. In Mozart's opera, before dying, Mithridates becomes reconciled with his sons and with Aspasia.

Rehearsals for the opera took place in a fairly agitated climate of rumors spread by jealous fellow-composers and rivalries among the singers. The two Mozarts had learned a thing or two since the Vienna episode of *La finta semplice*, and they moved with diplomacy and tact to overcome all difficulties. On 17 November Leopold was still worried, however, and he wrote his wife that if an opera was a complete success it was "a stroke of luck which in Italy is very rare." He explains why: "There are so many factions [and] an indifferent, indeed even a bad solo dancer has her supporters who combine to shout 'Bravo' and to make a great noise."[49] On opening night, *Mitridate* lasted six hours, given that it was performed with entr'actes in the form of two hours of ballet, as was the custom of the time. Luckily, the opera was a great success and was greeted with general applause, with the Milanese audience rising to its feet and crying, "Viva il maestro" and "Viva il maestrino." Thus Father Martini's lessons had borne fruit. Such impetuous music had probably never before been heard in an *opera seria*. Even in rehearsal the singers had expressed their enthusiasm for the musical style of the young composer. One particularly auspicious sign was the warm approval of the copyist, given that (as Leopold observed) he was "absolutely delighted, which is a good omen in Italy, where, if the music is a success, the copyist by selling the arias sometimes makes more money than the Kapellmeister does by his composition."[50] By the time the two Mozarts left Milan, the copyist had already received orders for five complete copies of the opera, one for the impresario of the theater in Milan, two for Empress Maria Theresa, one for the duchess of Parma, and one for the court of Lisbon, not to mention the many orders for copies of individual arias.[51]

Mozart was now considered a technically expert composer and also an innovative one. At the premiere and during the next two performances, seated at the harpsichord in the middle of the orchestra and wearing his new scarlet suit with a light blue lining, he directed the music himself.[52] There were some twenty performances in all, and Leopold declared himself very satisfied, also because Wolfgang was given the sum of four hundred ducats for *Mitridate* and they were reimbursed for their living expenses for three months. In a further demonstration of faith in his qualities as a composer, Wolfgang was commissioned to write a so-called *festa teatrale, Ascanio in Alba*, on a text by Giuseppe Parini, to be performed in Milan in October 1771 on the occasion of the marriage of Archduke Ferdinand, one of the sons of Empress Maria Theresa.

In recent times, commentary on *Mitridate, Re di Ponto* has often stressed the work's limitations and the immaturity of its young composer. It is true that the opera is somewhat conventional in some of its parts and overly dependent on the styles of the times, but we should keep in mind that it was an extraordinary accomplishment for a boy of fourteen to write an opera (in record time) judged good enough to be welcomed with applause and shouts in one of the major theaters of Italy. I might add that when we listen to *Mitridate* today, we are struck by the quality of many of the arias, by the pathos of many of the recitatives, and by Mozart's mastery in putting together a complex three-act opera with twenty-one arias, a duet, and a final chorus. In short, *Mitridate* promised even more amazing achievements to come.

## Turin and Venice (January–March 1771)

After the great success of *Mitridate,* Wolfgang and his father went to Turin in mid-January 1771, where they met the composer Giovanni Paisiello, who was supervising the staging of his new opera, *Annibale in Torino*. Paisiello, who was born in Taranto in 1740, was already renowned in Italy and would be more widely known in the future, thanks to his active presence in the courts of St. Petersburg and Paris. As a recognized master opera composer, he received commissions continually, which means that he produced a great many stage works, and with an intense creativity that permitted him to dominate the theaters of Europe in a way that Mozart would never achieve in his lifetime.

In Turin the two Mozarts also met Gaetano Pugnani, whose new opera, *Issea,* was also being produced at the time. Pugnani, who was born in Turin in 1731, was not only a composer but a highly successful violinist. When he met the Mozarts he was the first violinist and the director of the orchestra of the Teatro Regio of Turin. Leopold Mozart wrote to his wife that he had seen a "magnificent opera" in the Piedmontese capital, but without specifying whether it was Paisiello's or Pugnani's.[53] In any event, the work greatly impressed the young Wolfgang as well.

After Turin, the two Mozarts returned to Milan in February, with the intention of leaving from there for Salzburg. They decided to go through Venice, Padua, Verona, Rovereto, and Bressanone on the way, however. They stayed for a month in Venice, from 11 February to 12 March 1771. During this stay father and son made frequent use of gondolas, a means of transportation that impressed Leopold by its strangeness, as did the canals and the lagoon. He stated in a letter home that "during the first days the whole bed rocked in our sleep."[54] The day they arrived, 11 February, was Carnival Monday, the day before Mardi Gras, and we can imagine that the elaborate celebrations for Carnival in Venice made the Mozarts' first encounter with the city on the lagoon even more magical. They took lodgings in the *contrada* of San Fantin, near the Ponte dei Barcaroli, probably in Ca' Falletti. In any event, their lodgings were in the center of the city, not too far from Piazza San Marco.

The afternoon of their arrival they hastened to pay a call on Johann Wider, a wealthy Salzburg merchant who had lived for some time in Venice, where he was known as "Signor Giovanni." Wider had married a Venetian, Venturina Rossetti, who had presented him with nineteen children, thirteen of whom died before the age of six. Six children—all girls—had survived, and Wolfgang took an immediate liking to them. That very evening they all went to the theater, since the Carnival opera season was about to draw to a close. The next afternoon they all went to the theater again, dining and supping together, with Wolfgang dancing with the six Wider "pearls," and around midnight the whole group attended the great masked ball in Piazza San Marco celebrating the end of Carnival.

Wolfgang's excitement is clearly reflected in a letter sent to his young friend Nepomuk Hagenauer, the son of their landlord: "The particularly splendid pearl [probably the eldest of the Wider sisters] and all the other pearls too admire you very greatly. I assure you that they are in love with you and that they hope that like a Turk you will marry them all, and make all six of them happy."[55] Catarina, the eldest, was twenty-eight; Rosa, twenty-three; Maria Teresa, nineteen; Marianna, fourteen; Maria Girolama, seven; and Maria Leopolda, five. Their mother, Venturina, was forty-eight. "I am charmed with Venice," Wolfgang told his friend Nepomuk. On 20 February Wolfgang gave his sister Nannerl a message for his friend: "Tell Johannes that Wider's pearls, especially Mademoiselle Catarina, are always talking about him, and that he must soon come back to

Venice and submit to the *attacca,* that is, have his bottom spanked when he is lying on the ground, so that he may become a true Venetian. They tried to do it to me—the seven women all together—and yet they could not pull me down."[56]

Leopold was disturbed: he understood that his son was growing fast and becoming interested—perhaps overly interested—in persons of the opposite sex. In his book about Mozart's month in Venice, Paolo Cattelan quite rightly observes that Leopold may have been visited, perhaps for the first time, by "the feared phantasm of his detachment from his son."[57] Leopold wrote his wife in a letter dated 14 March that Venice was "the most dangerous place in all Italy" for young people.[58]

It is worth mentioning that at precisely that same time Gian Maria Ortes, an abbé and a philosopher who lived in Venice, and Johann Adolph Hasse, the composer, whom the Mozarts had met in Vienna in 1768, exchanged letters in which both men drew a clear distinction between Leopold and Wolfgang. "Il sig. Maestro Mozard is here in Venice from the last days of Carnival with his son, having left the daughter in Salzburg," Ortes wrote to Hasse. "I see them now and then, with greatest satisfaction for the son, who is truly likable and pleases me much." Thus his pleasure lay more in meeting Wolfgang than his father. Ortes adds, "I do not think, however that they are very much pleased with this city, where they probably expected that others would seek after them, rather than they after others, as will have happened to them elsewhere." He closes with the comment, "What a curious thing it is, this unconcern with which the boy notes this difference, whereas the father appears to be somewhat piqued by it."[59]

Hasse responded to Ortes on 23 March, and his judgment of Leopold was even more severe: "Young Mozard is certainly marvelous for his age, and I do love him infinitely. The father, as far as I can see, is equally discontented everywhere, since here too he uttered the same lamentations. He idolizes his son a little too much, and thus does all he can to spoil him; but I have such a high opinion of the boy's natural good sense that I hope he will not be spoilt in spite of the father's adulation, but will grow into an honest fellow."[60]

Hasse thus confirms the notion that at fifteen years of age Wolfgang had already shown more character than his father and more common sense, which tells us something about a growing ambivalence in the relationship between the father and the son. Leopold had created Wolfgang, but he ran the risk of destroying him as well. We might presume that the elderly Hasse, seventy-two at the time and a highly successful composer, had no reason to harbor any hard feelings toward Leopold, but might have seen Wolfgang as a rival; yet here we see him speaking highly of Wolfgang and judging Leopold with some severity. He did not say so, but he may have thought that if the Mozarts felt isolated in Venice, it was Leopold's fault.

They were not to be isolated for long. On 6 March, a few days before their departure, Leopold wrote his wife that he was sorry not to be able to remain longer in Venice because they had gotten to know "the whole nobility very well." He adds, "On all occasions we are so overwhelmed with honors that our hosts not only send their secretaries to fetch us and convey us home in their gondolas, but often the noble himself accompanies us on our return; and this is true of the greatest of them, for instance, the Cornaro, Grimani, Mocenigo, Dolfino, Falieri and so forth."[61] While they were in Venice Wolfgang received a commission to write a new opera for the Regio Ducal Teatro in Milan, which would become *Lucio Silla*, on a libretto by Giovanni De Gamerra (the libretto and title were unknown at that point). It is hardly surprising that some years later Wolfgang confided to his father, "When I think about it, in no other country have I received so many honors, in no other place have I enjoyed more consideration, as in Italy."[62]

On 13 March 1771 the two Mozarts hired a boat and went up the Brenta Canal to Padua in the company of Abbé Ortes, the Wider parents, and the two elder Wider daughters, all of whom stayed the night at Padua. They returned to Venice the next day, but the Mozarts stayed over in Padua for a day, which proved to be time enough for Wolfgang to receive a commission for a sacred oratorio in two parts, *La Betulia liberata*, on a text by Metastasio, to be performed in Padua during Lent 1772. Giuseppe Ximenes, Giovanni Domenico Ferrandini, and other Paduan patrons of the arts who gave concerts in their palaces invited Mozart, Giuseppe Calegari (a Paduan composer), and the Bohemian Josef Mysliveček to set to music *La Betulia liberata*, a text that had already been used by at least a dozen composers. Leopold, who had learned his lesson from the Vienna affair of *La finta semplice*, probably obtained a contract and an appropriate advance before he permitted Wolfgang to contribute to the score.

Leopold and Wolfgang soon left Padua and their friends, and after halts in Verona, Rovereto, Bressanone, and Innsbruck, they returned to Salzburg on 28 March. Their first trip to Italy had lasted more than fifteen months.

## A Brief Stay in Salzburg (March–August 1771)

Their first long Italian journey finally concluded, Leopold and Wolfgang embraced Anna Maria and Nannerl tenderly, but the family was to remain together for only four months, from 28 March to 13 August 1771. At least for some time the two women and the two men had to live separately, because the family apartment was being redone, a change perhaps motivated by a desire to move Wolfgang and Nannerl out of the bedroom in which the entire family had slept until then. Anna Maria and Nannerl were taken in by the Hagenauer family, while Leopold and Wolfgang found a room on Lochlplatz, today Hagenauerplatz 2.

Wolfgang set right to work to catch up with the commissions he had received. He soon completed *La Betulia liberata* and wrote the recitatives for *Lucio Silla,* for the moment leaving aside the *festa teatrale, Ascanio in Alba,* because Parini's text had not yet been delivered. He also wrote two symphonies (K. 73/75a and K. 110/75b) and a sacred work, Regina coeli (K. 108/74d) for soprano and chorus, orchestra, and organ. He began and perhaps even completed the Litaniae Lauretanae (K. 109/74e), dedicated to Our Lady of Loreto, an object of particular devotion for the Mozarts.

The most important work that Wolfgang completed during his four months at home in Salzburg was clearly *La Betulia liberata* (K. 118/74c), a two-act sacred oratorio commissioned in Padua. Metastasio's text was based on the biblical story of Judith and Holofernes. At some unspecified time the Assyrian army commanded by Holofernes was laying siege to Bethulia (a city historians have never succeeded in identifying). Judith left the city and went alone to the enemy camp, where she decapitated the drunken Holofernes after a banquet, thus liberating her city. It does not appear that Mozart's *Betulia* was ever performed during his lifetime, either in Padua or elsewhere, but we know that the composer did not forget it. Writing to his father from Vienna in 1784, he asked Leopold to send him the score in the hope of being able to utilize the music in some manner. This oratorio in the style of Hasse may be little known and long buried in the archives, but is a notable achievement that contains some excellent pages. In short, Wolfgang was still making progress.

During the spring that he spent in Salzburg, before producing symphonies and sacred music, Wolfgang also cultivated some more profane interests, developing a crush on a friend of Nannerl's. Even before, on 20 October 1770, he had declared in a letter to his mother, "I have many things to say to my sister, but what? God and I alone know. If it is God's will, I shall soon, I hope, be able to tell them to her myself."[63] Writing from

Milan on 24 August 1771, several days after he and his father left for Salzburg, Wolfgang refers to his ardors again. He tells his sister, "What you
promised me (you know what, you dear one!) you will surely do and I shall
certainly be most grateful to you."[64] In his next letter, dated 31 August, still
from Milan, he adds, somewhat pessimistically, "I beg you to remember
the other matter, if there is nothing else to be done. You know what I
mean."[65] The object of this unrequited passion may have been Teresa
Barisani, the daughter of the Salzburg court physician, or perhaps Waberl
von Mölk, the daughter of the court chancellor, whose brother was court-
ing Nannerl.

## The Second Journey to Italy: To Milan for *Ascanio in Alba* (August–December 1771)

On 13 August 1771 Leopold and Wolfgang left once more for Italy, following the usual route over the Brenner Pass. By 17 August they were in
Ala, where they thought it prudent to spend the night rather than arrive
in Verona after sundown and risk finding the gates of the city closed.
Leopold's stipend had been suspended upon his departure, so his wife and
daughter, left behind in Salzburg, were all the more irritated and envious.
Leopold's friend Paul Anton Troger reprimanded him for not taking them
along, and Leopold himself made awkward attempts in his letters to placate the women's jealousies. He wrote that it was unspeakably hot in Italy
and too crowded, and he promised them "perhaps some day you will have
an opportunity of hearing operas in Italy," without the "great inconvenience" of facing "the crowd"—an inconvenience occasioned by Wolfgang's successes, which both the mother and the sister would have loved
to witness. "Troger has made your mouth water for Italy far too much," he
concludes. He hints that his wife and daughter had no reason to complain,
since they had traveled a good deal in the past, and he states that "for
people who have not seen as much of the world as you have, there are
many strange things to be seen here. But for you they would not be very
wonderful, and Italy can always be visited."[66] In another letter he reports
that during some popular outdoor festivities in Milan arranged in honor
of the forthcoming imperial wedding, a viewing stand had collapsed, in-
juring many and killing several people. He and Wolfgang escaped injury
only because they had arrived late.[67] The message was that it was just as
well that Nannerl and Anna Maria were not there, or they would have
risked their lives as well. In short, Leopold was doing his best to continue
to present Italy as a place full of dangers, thus to be avoided if possible.

On 30 August the libretto of *Ascanio in Alba* (K. 111) finally arrived from Parini, and Wolfgang went to work immediately to set it to music. The text was late because it had to be sent first to Vienna so that it could pass inspection by the censors. Labeled a *festa teatrale* or *serenata*, the work was really a shorter opera combining singing and ballets in a manner more harmonious than dramatic, as was appropriate for its intended task of entertaining the guests assembled for the marriage celebrations of the Archduke Ferdinand, the seventeen-year-old third son of Maria Theresa of Austria, and the twenty-one-year-old princess Maria Beatrice Ricciarda d'Este. The allegorical work based on mythology presents Ascanius (son of Aeneas and founder of Alba Longa) and attendant nymphs, fauns, shepherds, and shepherdesses, all guided by Venus, the goddess of love. Ascanius weds the nymph Sylvia on stage just as in real life Ferdinand was to wed Maria Beatrice. Leopold boasted that his son managed to finish *Ascanio* in less than two weeks, although this was probably a slight exaggeration. The "theatrical serenata" was performed in the Regio Ducal Teatro of Milan in alternation with Hasse's heroic opera *Ruggiero*, also composed in honor of the archducal nuptials.

When we listen to *Ascanio in Alba* today, we are struck by its fine musical qualities, especially when we remember that it was written by a fifteen-year-old. Like *Mitridate*, it hints at masterpieces to come. Some scholars, the musicologist Alfred Einstein among them, have remarked that *Ascanio* was much more appropriate to the age and talents of the very young Mozart than *Mitridate*.[68] The work is in fact largely a "decorative" piece in which the composer was required only to write elegant connections between choruses, dances, recitatives, and virtuoso arias. Among the singers brought to Milan for *Ascanio* there was the able castrato soprano, Giovanni Manzuoli, whom Wolfgang had known in London and had met again in Florence. But at the age of forty-seven the singer's voice was not what it had once been. Manzuoli was also somewhat irascible, prone to fits of temper, and jealous of younger singers. Mozart was apparently constrained to modify an aria assigned to Adamo Solzi, a younger castrato soprano in the cast, simply because Manzuoli thought it too beautiful for his rival.[69] As we have already seen, the singers were the real dictators in the opera world, and Manzuoli was a man given to bizarre caprices. Wolfgang rendered a rather severe judgment of him in a letter to Nannerl of 24 November 1771:

> Manzuoli, who up to the present has been generally looked upon as the most sensible of the castrati, has in his old age given the world a sample

of his stupidity and conceit. He was engaged for the opera [Hasse's *Ruggiero*] at a salary of five hundred cigliati [more than two thousand florins], but, as the contract did not mention the serenata [*Ascanio in Alba*], he demanded another five hundred for that, that is, one thousand cigliati in all. The court only gave him seven hundred and a fine gold snuff box (quite enough, I think). But he, like a true castrato, returned both the seven hundred cigliati and the snuff box and went off without anything. I do not know how it will all end—badly, I expect.[70]

In any event, *Ascanio* was an enormous success, and even Manzuoli declared himself satisfied by the part that Mozart had written for him. The serenata was greeted with ovations and repeated in four more performances, alternating, as we have seen, with the *Ruggiero* of Johann Adolph Hasse, a composer who had declared his esteem for Wolfgang. Leopold was delighted to communicate that his fifteen-year-old son had completely eclipsed the seventy-two-year old Hasse. "We are constantly addressed in the street by courtiers and other persons who wish to congratulate the young composer. It really distresses me very greatly, but Wolfgang's serenata has killed [*niedergeschlagen*] Hasse's opera more than I can say in detail."[71] Mozart and Hasse both celebrated their musical contribution to the imperial marriage by participating in a banquet given by Count Firmian. During one of several evenings in the Firmian residence, probably on 22 November 1771, Wolfgang presented a new and notable symphony that he had composed in Milan (K. 112), which might well deserve the title of "Firmian," given all the aid that the count gave Mozart during his Italian journeys. Some weeks earlier, also in Milan, Wolfgang had composed another symphony with a very festive, Italian, and impetuous initial and final allegro (K. 96/111b) as well as yet another symphony (K. 120/111a) and a divertimento in E-flat (K. 113), the last of them evidently performed in November.[72]

The young Archduke Ferdinand was enthusiastic in his approval of Mozart, and he wrote to the empress, his mother, that he wished to take him into his service. Were Leopold's aspirations about to be realized, and was Wolfgang was actually about to win the well-rewarded permanent post that he had yearned for so long and that would have enabled the whole family to live decently in a city less provincial than Salzburg? This was not to be. The empress wrote back to Ferdinand, practically ordering him not to take Mozart into his service. Maria Theresa, annoyed by the controversy that had arisen three years before surrounding *La finta semplice*, sent her son the atrocious letter that we have already seen. It merits more extensive citation here because it gives clear, blatant testimony to a hostile atmosphere that plagued Wolfgang to his dying day. In the postscript to her letter dated 12 December 1771 Maria Theresa wrote her son:

> You ask me to take the young Salzburger into your service. I do not know why, not believing that you have need of a composer or of useless people. If however it would give you pleasure, I have no wish to hinder you. What I say is intended only to prevent your burdening yourself with useless people and giving titles to people of that sort. If they are in your service it degrades that service when these people go about the world like beggars. Besides, he has a large family.[73]

The archduke, obedient to his mother's admonition, did not hire Mozart. In early December, while Maria Theresa's harsh letter was making its way from Vienna to Milan, the two Mozarts set off from Milan to return to Salzburg, where they arrived on 15 December. The very next day the prince-bishop of the city and their protector, Sigismund von Schrattenbach, died. December 1771 was thus a moment in the young Wolfgang's life when fortune refused to smile on him: he had lost both his princely protector in Salzburg and his hopes of finding another princely protector in Italy. In reality, however, it may have been thanks to these adverse blows of fortune that Wolfgang succeeded, little by little, in achieving the equilibrium, the strength, and the power that permitted him to compose the extraordinary music that we know.

## The Arrival of the New Prince-Bishop, Colloredo (December 1771–October 1772)

Leopold and Wolfgang remained in Salzburg for about ten months, from December 1771 to 24 October 1772, at which time they left for the third and last time for Italy. Early in 1772 Wolfgang fell sick. Details are slim, but we know that his illness was serious. He looked sickly, with a yellowish complexion: it may have been viral hepatitis.[74] Mozart's frequent childhood illnesses give us a picture of delicate health that may go far to explain his early death.

On 14 March 1772 the forty-year-old Count Hieronymus Joseph Franz von Colloredo, a reform-minded man of the Enlightenment, was elected prince-bishop of Salzburg, taking the place of Schrattenbach, who had died three months before. It was an absolute necessity, if Wolfgang were to be looked on favorably by the new prince-bishop, that he dedicate a

composition to him. Wolfgang already had, tucked away in his compositions box, a new and ambitious dramatic serenata on a text by Metastasio, *Il sogno di Scipione* (Scipio's Dream). The work, which had a playing
time of almost two hours, had originally been written to be offered to
Schrattenbach, but Leopold and Wolfgang decided to recycle it for the
new prince-bishop. The dedication of the final recitative as well as the
vocal text, which formerly had contained the name "Sigismondo," was
promptly changed to "Girolamo."[75]

The subject for Metastasio's text for *Il sogno di Scipione* came from a
well-known passage in Cicero's *De republica*. It told the story of Scipio Ae-
milianus, the destroyer of Carthage (second century BC), who in a dream
talked with his father about the immortality of the soul. In the dream the
goddesses Constancy (Costanza) and Fortuna force Scipio to choose between them, and he opts for Constancy. This imaginary voyage to the beyond had been highly influential in the culture of medieval philosophy,
in particular for its religious implications. Scipio's dream-voyage, as nar-
rated by Cicero, had been compared to Dante's journey in the *Divine Comedy*. Among other points of comparison, both authors cast the Earth in a
new light, with Scipio describing it as a planet in which everything (save
human souls) appears as transitory, mortal, and fleeting.

Some of Mozart's biographers have spoken of his *Sogno* as a mediocre
composition lacking structure and vitality. Even Massimo Mila joined the
chorus of critics to define the work as an "insignificant work of circum-
stance."[76] In my opinion these critics are wrong, and I even suspect that
some of them have passed judgment on *Il sogno di Scipione* (and on *Ascanio
in Alba* and *Mitridate*) without ever having actually heard these works. The
events surrounding *Il sogno* are instructive in this connection. The opera
was not performed in public for two centuries—that is, until 20 January
1979, when it was exhumed for Mozart Week in Salzburg. For over two
hundred years the work remained buried in the archives, and we can conclude that even Mozart himself never had occasion to hear it in its entirety, either in a theater or in a salon setting. Indeed, it appears that in
May 1772, when *Il sogno di Scipione* was performed in Salzburg in homage
to the prince-bishop, only one aria, the final chorus, and the recitative
containing the dedication itself were actually sung. Nothing more. Perhaps Prince-Bishop Colloredo wanted to save money; perhaps there were
other reasons unknown to us.

Leopold was not named first Kapellmeister to the new prince-bishop,
a post that he had ardently desired for some time. Colloredo, who liked
Italian music, preferred to give the title to Domenico Fischietti, a Nea-

politan composer who was well known at the time and who had worked previously in Dresden. Leopold was crushed, but the stipend that had been suspended during his recent Italian journey was reinstated.[77] Colloredo was also the first ruler to give Wolfgang a regular stipend. Before then, Schrattenbach had appointed Wolfgang to a position as "third Kapellmeister," but without retribution. In a decree dated 9 August 1772, however, the new prince-bishop granted Wolfgang the title of *Konzertmeister* at an annual pay of 150 florins. As Wolfgang himself explained in a letter dated 1 August 1777, this made him "only a half-time servant."[78] His pay was indeed small in comparison with the Mozarts' expectations and the sums that Wolfgang had already earned in his voyages, as well as with his extraordinary capacities. But it was nonetheless a fixed stipend and not to be scorned, especially if we consider that the beneficiary was only sixteen years old and that his father, even after many years of service at full pay, did not earn much more (probably some 354 florins a year).

One might well wonder why Leopold should want his son to become a paid servant of the Salzburg court, even at half pay, given all the difficulties that such service entailed when it came to obtaining a better appointment at another court. From this moment on, in fact, any other European ruler who wanted to assume Wolfgang into his service would first have to obtain the assent of Archbishop Colloredo. Leopold was probably well aware of this risk and willing to take it for a number of reasons. First of all, 150 florins were useful; second, the title of *Konzertmeister* constituted something like an official recognition of Wolfgang's qualities; third, Leopold might have thought that if Wolfgang were a servant of the Salzburg court, as he himself was, it would link their fortunes together forever. They would have to face the same difficulties if they wanted to emigrate. Above all, Wolfgang, who was now sixteen, would have been less free to separate from his father and decide his future on his own.

During the months he spent in Salzburg in 1771 and 1772 Wolfgang produced many works, perhaps because he was stimulated by the appointment he had just received; or perhaps because he was seized by an impetuous need to compose. He wrote nine symphonies, some of them exceptionally beautiful (K. 114, 124, 128, 129, 130, 132, 133, and 134, in addition to the symphony [K. 161/141a] from the overture to *Il sogno di Scipione*). Many commentators consider the Symphony in F (K. 130) the first truly great Mozartian symphony. But it had been preceded by the Symphony in A (K. 114), written in December 1771, not long before Wolfgang fell ill and before Colloredo's election. The latter work contains an engaging allegro that stands as witness to the fact that the young Mozart had already arrived in the promised land of musical maturity.

In those few months Wolfgang also composed four divertimentos (K. 131, 136/125a, 137/125b, and 138/125c), complex, passionate, and technically advanced chamber works. His service in Colloredo's court involved providing a number of sacred pieces, including a new and ambitious *Regina coeli* (K. 127) for soprano solo, four-part chorus, and orchestra; and the *Litaniae* (K. 125). He also wrote six minuets for orchestra and two songs for voice and keyboard. One of these *lieder* (K. 148/125h), entitled "O heiliges Band," was explicitly Masonic, which is why until recently it was thought to have been composed in 1784, the year in which Wolfgang became a Freemason. Today the date 1772 is accepted, providing further evidence of the Masonic protection that I have supposed Wolfgang and his father received during their first voyages in Europe.[79] If this is the case, the song was composed in recognition of the aid that Wolfgang received even before his official affiliation with a lodge. The text of this work asserts:

> Up, Masons, and sing; today, let the entire globe hear,
> This is the day which this song consecrates,
> A glorious, great day of honor,
> A high feast of devotion and unity.[80]

Wolfgang also composed some choral scenes and some of the recitatives for *Lucio Silla*, a *dramma per musica* with a libretto by Giovanni De Gamerra that had been commissioned in March 1771 by the Regio Ducal Teatro of Milan.[81] In order to fulfill Wolfgang's obligations for this engagement, Leopold and he left for Italy once more, on 24 October 1772, with the authorization of their prince-bishop and patron, but again without Anna Maria and Nannerl, perhaps because Leopold's stipend (possibly Wolfgang's as well) had been suspended for the duration of their absence from Salzburg. Milan had already been the setting for performances of both *Mitridate* (which had opened the opera season in December 1770) and *Ascanio in Alba* (October 1771). Now, with *Lucio Silla* (K. 135), the opera season would be inaugurated for the second time by a work of Wolfgang's. Colloredo could not refuse to authorize the trip, both because the Milanese theater operated under the aegis of the Hapsburgs and because the honor of opening the opera season in Milan with a composition by Mozart conferred prestige on the Salzburg court.

## The Third Italian Voyage: To Milan for *Lucio Silla*
## (October 1772–March 1773)

Wolfgang and Leopold left Salzburg on 24 October 1772, traversing the Brenner Pass for the third time and arriving in Bressanone on 27 October. The next day they stopped by Bolzano, even though Wolfgang was not fond of that city. He said in fact that it seemed to him a genuine "pigsty" and quoted two lines of mocking verse about it:

> If to Bozen I must come,
> Faith, I'd rather cut my thumb.
> (*Soll ich noch komen Botzen*
> *so schlag ich mich lieber in d'fozen.*)[82]

In the same letter to his sister he refers indirectly to a girl in Salzburg who had interested him, whom he does not name but who probably was Maria Daubrawa von Daubrawaik, who was thirteen at the time.[83]

In the autumn of 1772 even Leopold was in good spirits. The opportunities offered by their new journey and the upcoming performance of *Lucio Silla* energized him. He wrote to his wife that his health was good, so good, in fact, "that I am really surprised, for we have been living very irregularly."[84] The two traveled through Trento, Rovereto, Ala, Verona, and Brescia, arriving in Milan on 4 November. Leopold gave his wife a discouraging account of Milanese life, perhaps in the interest of diminishing the envy of the two women left at home, once again excluded from the journey. At the end of November he wrote that most members of the better society of Milan were still out of the city in their country homes, and he claimed that he and Wolfgang were eating only one meal a day at two in the afternoon. "In the evening," he adds, "we have an apple and a slice of bread and we drink a small glass of wine."[85] Wolfgang announced to his sister, "I have learnt a new game here in Milan, called *Mercante in fiera,* and as soon as I come home, we shall play it."[86]

On 18 December, the evening of the first orchestral rehearsal of *Lucio Silla*, Wolfgang sent his sister a message full of nonsense phrases written around a drawing of a heart, with every other line written upside down, so that the reader has to turn it around and around in order to read it. In the future, these somewhat infantile jests contributed to the legend of a totally frivolous, immature, and eccentric Mozart, as he is portrayed in *Amadeus,* the film by Miloš Forman. The real Mozart loved games and jokes, but he did not have the split personality, totally serious in music and totally superficial in life, that many imagine.[87] In any event, when he wrote the curious letter dated 18 December 1772, he was not yet seventeen.

In Milan Wolfgang gave further proof of his seriousness and mastery of his art in the production stages of *Lucio Silla*. He composed all of the arias with the vocal capabilities of each singer in mind, which meant that he had to wait for each one's arrival in Milan. Venanzio Rauzzini, the castrato soprano who was to play the leading male role of Cecilio, reached Milan only about 20 November. Anna Lucia De Amicis, the famous soprano who was to play Giunia, the prima donna, arrived two weeks later, after a dreadful trip from Venice to Milan in bad weather that had taken eight days. What is worse, De Amicis initially mistrusted the young Wolfgang. As if this were not enough, the tenor who was to sing the part of Lucio Silla fell ill and was replaced, at the late date of 17 December, by another and rather inexperienced church singer, Bassano Morgnoni. Given that the premiere was set for 26 December, Wolfgang worked like a madman. He was forced to cut down the role of Lucio Silla because of Morgnoni's limitations and to make up for it by composing more striking arias for De Amicis and Rauzzini.

Opening night did not go as smoothly as desired. The theater was packed, but the opera began three hours late, which made for a high degree of nervousness on the part of both the audience and the singers. Morgnoni's performance inspired general hilarity, and when De Amicis sang her duet with him, she became extremely upset because she thought the audience was laughing at her. She sang poorly for the rest of the evening and became increasingly jealous of Rauzzini's success. In the following days, however, De Amicis received many honors, tension died down, and *Lucio Silla* went on to have a total of twenty-six performances.[88] Some commentators claim that in spite of those twenty-six performances, the opera was not a genuine success because it was not revived in Mozart's lifetime, either in Milan or elsewhere.

Once again, however, I am compelled to note that this youthful work of Mozart's is of a quality that has escaped many of his critics and biographers. Obviously, when compared with the masterpieces of Mozart's mature years, a youthful work like *Lucio Silla* might be judged "minor" and unbalanced. Still, it expresses the composer's genius, and it seems hardly "minor" in comparison with the musical production of other popular composers of the time. As Roberto Parenti has written, *Lucio Silla* attests to Mozart's surprising musical maturity. If anything, it was the court theater audiences, with their exclusive focus on virtuoso singing, that were unprepared to appreciate Mozart's novelty and style.

Mozart gave at least two concerts in Milan during the month of December 1772, one of them in the presence of Archduke Ferdinand and his bride, Maria Beatrice d'Este. On 17 January 1773 the first performance of his "Exsultate, jubilate" (K. 165/158a), which contains the famous "Alleluia" section, took place in the Theatine church in Milan. Mozart had composed the work for the castrato Rauzzini, who had sung in *Silla* and who, aside from possessing an extraordinary voice, was also notably cultivated, musically speaking. While in Italy, and in Milan in particular, Mozart also composed six string quartets (K. 155/134a, 156/134b, 157, 158, 159, 160/159a) in the months between the end of 1772 and the beginning of 1773.

Although Wolfgang now had a permanent post in Salzburg, Leopold continued to be interested in finding him a stable and better position in Italy. He still had hopes for Milan, governed by Archduke Ferdinand of Hapsburg, but he also made inquiries regarding the court of Florence, now ruled by Grand Duke Pietro Leopoldo (Ferdinand's brother Leopold, whom we met earlier). In a letter to his wife dated 9 January 1773, partially written in code to circumvent the censors in Salzburg, Leopold notes, "I hear from Florence that the Grand Duke has received my letter, is giving it sympathetic consideration and will let me know the result. We still live in hopes."[89]

But the grand duke was not persuaded. He may have been held back by the anathema that Maria Theresa had pronounced in December 1771, or perhaps he considered Wolfgang to be too young. Early in March 1773 Wolfgang and Leopold left for Salzburg, abandoning Italy once and for all.

## Four and a Half Years in Salzburg; Two Trips to Vienna and Munich (March 1773– September 1777)

After his three trips to Italy, Wolfgang remained in Salzburg for more than four years, until September 1777. Still, even during this pause in his career, he left Salzburg twice, first during the summer of 1773, when he went to Vienna with his father in the hope, once again, of obtaining a post at court. The second time was in the winter of 1774–1775, when he went to Munich.

During the summer of 1773 Leopold learned that the post of Kapellmeister at the imperial court might soon be open. The position was then held by Florian Leopold Gassmann, a famous Bohemian composer forty-four years of age with many operas to his credit, who had studied in Bologna with Padre Martini. Gassmann had suddenly fallen seriously ill.

Thinking that he might soon die or be retired, Leopold rushed to Vienna with Wolfgang, hoping to beat other possible contenders. His hopes were in vain, however: not only did Gassmann recover, but more important, Maria Theresa, for reasons that we know, granted the Mozarts only one audience, during which her attitude was extremely cold. Leopold himself was aware of the chill. In a letter to his wife of 12 August he stated, "Her Majesty the Empress was very gracious to us, but that was all. I am saving up a full account until our return, for it is impossible for me to give it in writing."[90] Archbishop Colloredo happened to be in Vienna during the summer of 1773, and it cannot be excluded that while conversing with Maria Theresa he may have expressed opinions regarding the Mozarts that exacerbated her negative opinion. In any event, the court of Vienna did not seem to be about to offer the post the Mozarts longed for. After two and a half months in Vienna, Leopold and Wolfgang returned, crestfallen, to Salzburg.

During the course of the year 1774 (we do not know in what month) Wolfgang asked Archbishop Colloredo for permission to go again to Vienna, but permission was refused and he was advised that there was nothing for him to hope for in Vienna; hence he would do better to try his fortunes elsewhere. This advice can be deduced from a letter that Wolfgang sent to Colloredo three years later, dated 1 August 1777, which gives an indication of the extent to which the prince-bishop was perfectly aware that his young subject and servant was harboring projects for flight.[91] This may have worried the prince-bishop, but only up to a point. He knew that other European courts would not risk offending him by taking Wolfgang into their service without asking his permission. He also knew that he had an ally in Leopold, who had no desire to be separated from his son. Perhaps Colloredo was aware as well of the fact that Leopold was willing to leave Salzburg if he too were taken on by another court, along with Wolfgang, but this prospect was unlikely, and in any event the other court would have to ask his permission—or rather two permissions. Wolfgang was thus Colloredo's prisoner. He was also the prisoner of his father, who cried poverty, stated that he had been obliged to go into debt because of the voyages he had organized for Wolfgang, and claimed that he could not fulfill his financial obligations without Wolfgang's earnings, which he in fact sequestered. The fact that the father took over almost all of his son's pay is confirmed by Wolfgang's letter to Leopold of 26 May 1781: "Why, where could I have learnt the value of money, when up to the present I have had so little to handle? All I know is that once when I had twenty ducats, I considered myself wealthy."[92]

Leopold obviously intended to prove to his son that Salzburg was not such a prison after all, because Colloredo gave them permission to leave now and then. They indeed managed to do so for three months, from 6 December 1774 to 7 March 1775. Wolfgang had to go to Munich for the premiere of La finta giardiniera (The Make-Believe Garden-Girl; K. 196), an opera buffa commissioned by the prince-elector of Bavaria, Maximilian III. Wolfgang had begun to compose the work in September 1774, using a text perhaps by Giuseppe Petrosellini, who had written librettos for Domenico Cimarosa, Baldassare Galuppi, and Giovanni Paisiello.[93] In 1768 Mozart had composed the music for another opera about a "make-believe" personage, La finta semplice. During the eighteenth century, in fact, dozens of theatrical texts were written about pretend persons—feigned countesses, baronesses, invalids, Tartars, Poles, and more—a custom that confirms the central importance, in the theater of the period, of the relationship between fiction and reality. In the opera that Mozart was commissioned to write for the Munich theater, a Milanese marchioness, Violante Onesti, pretended to be a humble garden-girl as a way to meet the young Count of Belfiore, of whom she was madly enamored.

On 7 December 1774 Wolfgang and Leopold left for Munich with the permission of Archbishop Colloredo, who could not have refused to deny their request without offending Maximilian of Bavaria, the commissioner of Mozart's new opera. This time the trip from Salzburg to Munich was fairly speedy, given that the two Mozarts left their city at eight in the morning and had already arrived at their destination at three-thirty the next afternoon. It was an extremely cold trip, however, to the point that they were obliged to wear great felt slippers over their shoes and cover both the slippers and the floor of the coach with hay.[94] In Munich they found comfortable quarters and warmed themselves again, in Wolfgang's case, aided by the thought of a new young flame he had temporarily left behind in Salzburg. Once again, she was a friend of Nannerl's, and on 28 December Wolfgang wrote to his sister to beg her to visit her friend and "convey my greetings there—but in the most definite way—in the most tender fashion."[95] Thus relations were still harmonious between the nearly nineteen-year-old Wolfgang and his older sister. In fact, Nannerl arrived in Munich several days later, without her mother, to join her father and brother and attend the premiere of the opera.

After several postponements, La finta giardiniera had its first performance on 13 January 1775, when it was greeted by loud applause, general enthusiasm, and cries of "Viva Maestro," as Wolfgang wrote to his mother the next day.[96] Archbishop Colloredo was also in Munich, but according to what Leopold wrote his wife, he did not show the least enthusiasm when congratulated on the excellent reception of *La finta giardiniera* and indeed seemed "embarrassed."[97] The prince-bishop was obviously not very happy at the thought of Wolfgang's spreading fame.

Although *La finta giardiniera* was declared a great success at its premiere, the follow-up was less brilliant. The musicians in the Munich orchestra were mediocre, as were the singers, one of whom had the bad taste to be taken ill. There were only two performances after the premiere, and in its original Italian version the opera thereafter disappeared from the stage. Some years later it was substituted by a reelaboration in German, with Mozart's authorization, and that version had a certain success with the public in the course of the nineteenth century.[98] In any event, the opera in its original Italian form, as it was performed in Munich, was rediscovered only in 1956, and it returned to the stage only in 1978, after a silence of more than two centuries (as was more or less the case with *Il sogno di Scipione*). Like many of the young Mozart's compositions, *La finta giardiniera*, in the original Munich version, was a work of notable value. The poet, composer, and music critic Christian Friedrich Schubart, who attended the premiere in Munich, was struck by the opera and sensed the enormous potential of its young composer: "I also heard an *opera buffa* by that wonderful genius *Mozart;* it is called *La finta giardiniera.* Flashes of genius appear here and there; but there is not yet that still altar-fire that rises toward Heaven in clouds of incense—a scent beloved of the gods. If *Mozart* is not a plant forced in the hothouse, he is bound to grow into one of the greatest musical composers who ever lived."[99] *La finta giardiniera* was in fact impetuous, brilliant, ironic, and a far cry from any quiet incense of the altar fires. As Schubart sensed, Mozart urgently needed to leave the hothouse. Schubart's prediction of a brilliant future also turned out to be accurate.

If we consider Mozart's musical production during the four and a half years he spent in Salzburg, we are impressed not only by its quantity (over one hundred titles in the Köchel catalog), but also by the quality of many of his compositions. At least some thirty of them still figure on concert programs. I am thinking (among others) of the two violin concertos (K. 219 and 216), the Symphony in A (K. 201/186a), and other symphonies (K. 181/162b, 183/173dB, 184/161a, 202/186b). The last of these is particularly innovative. Among the sacred works written in this period were the Missa brevis (K. 275/272b) and the Gradual "Sancta Maria, mater Dei" (K. 273) for chorus, strings, and organ, a work dedicated to the Blessed Virgin Mary completed 9 September 1777, two weeks before Mozart left for Germany with his mother, as if to ask the Madonna's protection from the risks of the upcoming trip. Mozart was a fine keyboard player, and he enriched his repertory by writing music for pianoforte, including a truly innovative concerto (K. 175), composed in December 1773, and the extraordinary *Jenamy* Concerto (K. 271), completed in January 1777 for Victoire Jenamy, daughter of the celebrated choreographer Jean-Georges Noverre and an excellent pianist, who commissioned the work.[100] Mozart also composed six piano sonatas (K. 279–83/189d-h, and 284/205b), some of which were exceptionally well written. Aside from the two violin concertos, he wrote many other pieces for the violin, an instrument whose resources he understood thoroughly.

Much of this music was so modern that even Leopold thought it prudent to keep the scores closed up in a box for fear of shocking the public. He says so explicitly in a letter to Wolfgang dated 24 September 1778, thus clearly demonstrating just how incapable he was of understanding the extraordinary quality of his son's works. Referring to the excellent symphonies that Mozart wrote between 1773 and 1774, the originals of which had remained in Salzburg, he states, "It is better that whatever does you no honor, remain unknown. That is the reason why I have not given any of your symphonies to be copied, because I knew in advance that when you are older and have more insight, you would be glad that no one has got hold of them, though at the time you composed them you were quite pleased with them."[101]

To do Leopold at least partial justice, I should report that even a Parisian publisher as discerning as Jean Georges Sieber, who had published some of Mozart's sonatas for violin and piano, refused to print the *Jenamy* Concerto (K. 271), judging it insufficiently commercial. The second movement seemed to Mozart's contemporaries too long and too difficult. The last movement was simply too new. Even in later years, Mozart had problems both with publishers and the public because many of his compositions were judged too difficult and too new. In 1785, for example, the Viennese publisher Franz Anton Hoffmeister, who had printed the Piano Quartet in G Minor (K. 478), asked Mozart not to compose the other two quartets stipulated in their contract.[102] Mozart's last symphonies were also judged unpalatable and were only printed several years after his death. Thus when Leopold wrote to his son that certain of his compositions did not do him "honor," he was warning him that they may not have been in the public taste, and thus not remunerative. Today there are many Mozart compositions that seem to us "traditional," but a trained ear can hear the innovations that struck contemporary listeners. In short, by writing works that now define him as a great composer, Mozart stood nearly alone, against his father, a number of publishers, and a large portion of the public.

Mozart was also an innovator in leaning more and more toward instrumental music, at the time considered a minor genre in comparison to vocal music. The majority of the public preferred listening to singers and paid little attention to symphonies and concertos. Public concert halls were almost nonexistent. During Mozart's lifetime, however, musical taste evolved and instrumental music began to grow in prestige. Mozart sought to profit from that change, given that one of his dearest ambitions was to bolster the supremacy and autonomy of the art of music. Instrumental music was one of the best ways to enhance that autonomy. But in time Mozart also sought to assert the supremacy of music over words in opera as well, which explains why singers opposed him when he challenged their traditional primacy.

In the spring of 1775, in Salzburg, Mozart finished a two-act *serenata* on a text by Metastasio, *Il re pastore* (The Shepherd King; K. 208). The work had been commissioned by Archbishop Colloredo to honor Prince Maximilian Franz, the youngest son of Maria Theresa, who was visiting Salzburg. The work was performed on 23 April 1775 in the archbishop's residence. The five characters in the drama were Alexander the Great of Macedon (Alessandro), his counselor Aegenor, Tamyris (Tamiri, a princess disguised as a shepherdess), the shepherd Amyntas (Aminta, discovered to be heir to the kingdom of Sidon), and the nymph Elisa. Metastasio's drama depicts an ideal Arcadia, a notion that writers in the Enlightenment had revitalized so as to exalt the myth of a pure and innocent peasant world similar to the myth of the "good savage" admired by Jean-Jacques Rousseau. In the finale of Metastasio's version of the story, set to music by Mozart, even Alexander the Great declares that if a state is enjoy a *beata sorte* (blessed fate) it must take a "shepherd king" as its leader. Metastasio's text was chosen by Archbishop Colloredo, an enlightened reformer.

The orchestration of this *serenata* displays evident progress over that of *Ascanio in Alba* four years earlier. Even leaving aside its classical content, the libretto is notably conventional and rhetorical in style, especially in the recitatives. The plot is all too respectful of the traditional canons. The first strophe of every aria, for example, is unfailingly repeated several times. Yet Wolfgang managed to give powerful energy to many arias and even many recitatives. We can agree with Stefan Kunze regarding *Il re pastore:* "Even if it is considered by the majority of scholars an 'occasional work' with dramaturgical failings, *Il re pastore* is doubtless the last true *opera seria* that the composer wrote before *Idomeneo*. However, with Mozart we can never speak of occasional works in the sense of merely routine exercises."[103] Mozart himself was fond of his *Shepherd King*, to the point of giving a copy of the score to his friend and fellow-musician Mysliveček in 1777 and including arias from the opera in concerts on a number of occasions.

# In Search of a Permanent Post with His Mother

## Departure with His Mother (September 1777)

Wolfgang's long stay in Salzburg worried him for many reasons. First, his post in the service of the archbishop in no way corresponded to his merits. Second, confined within the city of his birth, he found it difficult to follow developments within the new schools of music, and he lacked opportunities to enrich his formation as an artist. Nor was Salzburg a city that could provide a musical market worthy of the name: it had no public capable of appreciating innovation, and even the court theater had been closed.

Mozart's discontent and solitude is clear in a letter that he wrote to Padre Martini on 4 September 1776. He had sent Martini an offertory, "Misericordias Domini" (K. 222/205a), that he had composed a year and a half earlier following the rules of counterpoint that were Martini's special field of expertise. He opened his heart to Martini in the letter accompanying the score, but he also offered a criticism of life in Salzburg:

> I beg you most earnestly to tell me, frankly and without reserve, what you think of it. We live in this world in order to learn industriously and, by interchanging our ideas, to enlighten one another and thus endeavor to promote the sciences and the fine arts. Oh, how often have I longed to be near you, most Reverend Father, so that I might be able to talk to and have discussion with you. For I live in a country where music leads a struggling existence, though indeed apart from those who have left us, we still have excellent teachers and particularly composers of great wisdom, learning and taste. As for the theater, we are in a bad way for lack of singers. We have no castrati, and we shall never have

them, because they insist on being handsomely paid; and generosity is not one of our faults.[1]

Archbishop Colloredo had in fact done his best to save money. "I am amusing myself by writing chamber music and music for the church," Mozart adds, but he also indicates that two "excellent masters of counterpoint" were working at the court, the forty-seven-year-old Anton Adlgasser and the forty-year-old Michael Haydn, the brother of the more famous Franz Joseph. The Mozarts were not intimate with Michael Haydn, however, and Leopold complained that he drank too much.[2]

In March 1777, anxious to get out of Salzburg, Leopold and Wolfgang once more asked their employer for a leave of absence from their posts. Although both men were still bound in service to Prince-Bishop Colloredo, they persisted in tempting fortune in the obstinate hope of finding a more munificent court willing to hire them both. With this aim in mind, they had decided to travel again, first to Munich. Colloredo did not even deign to respond to the request. In June the two Mozarts presented a second petition. This time Archbishop Colloredo explicitly refused to authorize the voyage for Leopold, but suggested that Wolfgang could leave by himself. He later communicated that Wolfgang's departure would present difficulties as well. In August Wolfgang sent Colloredo a third (undated) petition, signed only by him, but written in his father's unmistakable hand: "Our circumstances are pressing: my father has decided to send me off by myself. But to this too Your Serene Highness made some gracious objections." At this point Wolfgang (that is, Leopold) mentions Wolfgang's musical talent and his filial duties, perhaps attempting to suggest indirectly that the father should be included in the permission to travel:

> Parents take pains to enable their children to earn their own bread, and this they owe both to their own interest and to that of the State. The more talent that children have received from God, the greater is the obligation to make use thereof, in order to ameliorate their own and their parents' circumstances, to assist their parents, and to take care of their own advancement and future. Such usury with our talents is taught us by the Gospel. I therefore owe it before God and in my conscience to my father, who indefatigably employs all his time in my upbringing, to be grateful to him with all my strength, to lighten his burden, and to take care not only of myself, but of my sister also, with whom I should be bound to commiserate for spending so many hours at the *clavier* without being able to make profitable use of it.[3]

Wolfgang was humbly requesting to be relieved of his post, and he expresses his hopes that his request will be granted. In closing he states his hope to serve Colloredo "with greater success in the years of my manhood." We do not know exactly what occurred between the archbishop and Leopold and Wolfgang in the days that followed, but we do know that the archbishop, infuriated, forwarded the petition to the court chamberlain with an annotation that both men had his permission "to seek their fortune elsewhere." In other words, they were both fired. At that point, Leopold took fright and humbly requested to be taken back into the archbishop's service.

Wolfgang, however, decided to leave Salzburg for good, as he declared to Maximilian III of Bavaria in September. Leopold had to accept the notion that his son would go away without him. Since he was well aware of his own worth, Wolfgang was not daunted by the idea of the trip that was about to begin. On the contrary, he thought he could easily find ways to earn money elsewhere, and he looked forward to not having to bow before the prince-bishop of his native city. It is clear that with Leopold's capitulation and Wolfgang's departure, relations between the Mozart family and the court in Salzburg reached a crisis. But so did relations between Leopold and Wolfgang, because they would separate for the first time in their lives, and separation was a first step toward a greater independence for the young composer. By then Wolfgang had gained artistic autonomy; now he was on his way to total autonomy.

To prevent that from happening, Leopold insisted that his wife, Anna Maria, accompany Wolfgang. He claimed that the twenty-one-year-old Wolfgang was incapable of organizing his baggage, changing foreign currency, and confronting all the problems that would arise in a long trip abroad on his own. But although up to this point Wolfgang had lived under his father's guidance, he was no longer a child, and he might quite easily have been able to keep out of trouble on his own. Moreover, his mother, although certainly endowed with common sense, was not likely to be any more experienced than he in changing foreign currencies or resolving unexpected difficulties. She too had always lived under Leopold's watchful eye. But Leopold was evidently firm in his desire that his wife continue to keep control over their son and communicate by letter any information that Wolfgang might prefer not to mention. Leopold was tormented by the idea that Wolfgang might fall in love, marry, settle somewhere else, and live his own life.

So Wolfgang left, accompanied by his mother, separating himself from both his father and his sister. Perhaps Leopold thought that the trip might be a short one, and that in Munich the prince-elector would be moved to take the young genius into his service. The separation turned out to be a long one—nearly sixteen months—and it took mother and son as far as Paris. One consequence that it did have was to give Wolfgang an inebriating sense of independence. Up to that time Leopold had always acted as his impresario, counselor, accompanist, and supervisor. Now Wolfgang, although in the company of his mother, had to make his own way. At the risk of getting ahead of my tale, I will note that Anna Maria died unexpectedly in Paris on 3 July 1778, six months before Wolfgang returned to Salzburg and to his father.

## Munich and Maximilian III (September 1777)

Wolfgang and his mother left for Munich at six in the morning on 23 September 1777. Leopold and Nannerl, having to stay behind at Salzburg, were in despair and depressed. In a letter dated 25 September Leopold related that on the day of their departure Nannerl wept bitterly, developed a nasty headache, vomited, and then took to her bed with the windows and shutters closed tight. Pimperl, their little dog, was melancholy as well and lay down beside her. Leopold had sunk into an armchair as his wife and son left, but realizing that he had not given Wolfgang his fatherly blessing, he ran to the window, hoping to catch sight of the coach going out of the city gates. It was too late. Wolfgang left without the blessing.[4]

Anna Maria and Wolfgang reached Munich the following day. They remained there about three weeks, with Wolfgang spending hours in wearisome conversations with members of the local nobility and court functionaries in a vain attempt to persuade the prince-elector, Maximilian III (who had commissioned *La finta giardiniera*) to take him into his service. But Wolfgang soon became aware that this would be a difficult enterprise. He was told that the prince had responded to the notion with "It is too early yet. He ought to go off, travel to Italy and make a name for himself. I am not refusing him, but it is too soon."[5] Maximilian was unwilling to consider Mozart, perhaps either because he knew that Wolfgang had abandoned his post in Salzburg somewhat brusquely, thus demonstrating a volatile nature, or because he wanted to avoid bad relations with Colloredo, or because he was aware of Maria Theresa's hostility toward the Mozarts. Maximilian III was in fact the brother-in-law of Joseph II, Maria Theresa's son and for some years her coregent as Holy Roman Emperor. On 30 September Wolfgang betook himself to court, having finally

managed to arrange an audience with the elector—a meeting that he describes to his father in a letter. We have no way of knowing whether the
dialog in the interview went exactly as Mozart reports it. But even if Wolfgang sought to embellish his side of the conversation, what he reports reveals a youthful imprudence in the nonchalant way he refers to what he
said regarding his rebellion against Colloredo. According to Mozart, it
even led Maximilian to exclaim: "Good heavens! There's a young man for
you!" The entire conversation, as Mozart reported it, went like this:

"Your Highness will allow me to throw myself most humbly at your feet
and offer you my services."

"So you have left Salzburg for good?"

"Yes, your Highness, for good."

"How is that? Have you had a row with him?"

"Not at all, Your Highness. I only asked him for permission to travel,
which he refused. So I was compelled to take this step, though indeed
I had long been intending to clear out. For Salzburg is no place for me,
I can assure you."

"Good heavens! There's a young man for you! But your father is still
in Salzburg?"

"Yes, your Highness. He too throws himself most humbly at your
feet, and so forth. I have been three times to Italy already, I have written three operas, I am a member of the Bologna Academy, where I had
to pass a test, at which many maestri have labored and sweated for four
or five hours, but which I finished in an hour. Let that be a proof that I
am competent to serve at any Court. My sole wish, however, is to serve
your Highness, who himself is such a great . . ."

"Yes, my dear boy, but I have no vacancy. I am sorry, If only there
were a vacancy . . ."

"I assure your Highness that I should not fail to do credit to Munich."

"I know. But it is no good, for there is no vacancy here."[6]

Having said that, His Serene Highness then moved on, leaving his young
petitioner standing there. In the days that followed Mozart attempted—
in vain—to persuade powerful courtiers to intercede in his favor. In the
same letter Wolfgang complains that "most of these great lords are downright infatuated with Italy,"[7] hence with Italian musicians, thus obstruct-
ing his way.

Franz Joseph Albert, owner of the inn in which the Mozarts were lodging, offered to back Wolfgang by providing 600 florins a year, collected from a group of ten friends. Another 200 florins might come from the court or other sources and, as Wolfgang himself wrote to his father, "if we have had to live in Salzburg on 504 gulden, surely we could manage in Munich on 600 or 800?"[8] Salzburg would offer much less. But Leopold killed this notion of an uncertain private income. He did not find Albert's proposition convincing, and he urged Wolfgang instead to pursue a permanent post. Admittedly, the idea that a composer could trust the market was shockingly new at the time, and it was totally foreign to the mentality of Leopold and many others like him. He states in a letter dated 4 October:

> Herr Albert's scheme is indeed a proof of the greatest friendship imaginable. Yet, however possible it may seem to you to find ten persons, each of whom will give you a ducat a month, to me it is quite inconceivable. For who are these philanthropists or these music-lovers? And what sort of undertaking or what kind of service will they require from you in return? . . . Running about and training singers! That would be a dog's life and quite out of the question! In short, I cannot see where these ten charming friends are to come from. Further, Albert may not be able to see them at once, as some of them are perhaps out of town. . . . *If the arrangement is immediately practicable, well and good, and you ought to accept it.* But if it cannot be made at once, then you simply must not lounge about, use up your money and waste your time.[9]

On 4 October Wolfgang gave a concert in Herr Albert's inn, where with great success he played three piano concertos (K. 242, 246, and 271, the *Jenamy*), and also offered two divertimentos (K. 254, a piano trio, and 287/271h). But a week later, after receiving his father's severe letter, he obediently left Munich for Augsburg, with his mother. The evening before their departure he went to the theater to see a pantomime with a bizarre title—*Das von der Féegirigaricanarimanarischarivariverfertigte Ei*, which stands as proof that extravagance was fashionable at the time. The title is derived from *fée* (French for "fairy"), "girigari" (imitation of a cock's crow), "canary," "manari" (probably rhyming nonsense), the French *charivari* (festive uproar), *verfertigte* (prepared), and *Ei* (egg)—a fine description of celebration and deafening, off-key music. If the Italian Futurists had lived in the eighteenth century they would have applauded enthusiastically. Mozart told his father that he had enjoyed himself immensely.[10]

## The Young Nobles of Augsburg (October 1777)

By leaving Munich at noon on 11 October, Wolfgang and his mother reached Augsburg that evening. Augsburg was the city of Leopold's birth, and one of his brothers still lived there, the fifty-year-old Franz Alois Mozart, owner of a print shop and a book bindery. Wolfgang had visited the city fourteen years earlier, as a child, and had not been very warmly received by his kin. This time, however, Franz Alois's family was much more friendly.

Wolfgang remained in Augsburg for two weeks and gave several concerts there. He paid a call on Johann Andreas Stein, a pianoforte manufacturer whom he had met before, when he was seven. At first he presented himself to Stein with his surname reversed as "il signor Trazom." Stein recognized him immediately, however, and embraced him with joy.[11] Mozart was impressed with the excellent quality of Stein's instruments, which cost some three hundred florins, and Stein was in turn delighted by Wolfgang's skill at the keyboard.

In general, Wolfgang had a cordial reception from the local Augsburg society, but some nobles were openly discourteous to him, laughing at him for exhibiting the medal of the Order of the Golden Spur given to him by the pope, which they declared to be counterfeit. Mozart himself describes the entire unpleasant episode in a letter to his father dated 16 October. He had been invited to supper by a young lord who bore the pompous name of Jakob Alois Karl Langenmantel von Westheim und Ottmarshausen, the son of the chief magistrate, or burgomaster, of the city. During the evening this young man and his brother-in-law began to rag Wolfgang about his decoration, declaring, "We must get our crosses too, so that we may belong to the same body as Mozart." At first Mozart ignored them, but they would not give up: "They asked me, 'About how much does it cost? Three ducats? Must one have permission to wear it? Does this permission cost something too? We really must send for our crosses.'" They laughed, exchanging pinches of snuff, while Mozart grew increasingly uneasy. Mozart's host asked to borrow the cross to show it to a goldsmith the following day, noting, "I am sure that if I ask him what its value is, he will say: 'About a Bavarian thaler. And it is not worth more, for it is not gold at all, only copper. Ha! Ha!'" Wolfgang, angry by this time, responded that it was tin, adding to his father, "I was burning with anger and rage." At that point he decided to react, and he pointed out to Langenmantel, his host, that he shouldn't be jealous of a papal golden spur: "You do not need one, for you have one in your head already. I have one in mine too, but of a very different kind, and indeed I should not care to exchange it for yours." Mozart reports that the young man turned pale, which made Mozart speak his mind even more explicitly: "'That is really very strange,' I began, as though I had not heard what he said, 'but it would be easier for me to obtain all the orders which it is possible for you to win than for you to become what I am, even if you were to die twice and be born again.'" All present were "exceedingly embarrassed" and Wolfgang took his leave.[12]

Probably one reason for the execrable behavior of these young aristocrats was that, as natives of Augsburg, they were well aware of the modest craftsman origins of the Mozart family. The day before, when Wolfgang was received by young Langenmantel's father, the burgomaster, his uncle Franz Alois was obliged to wait outside in the antechamber like a lackey. Wolfgang was furious. When he went to pay his respects to the burgomaster and conversation turned to Leopold, Langenmantel *père* asked, with condescension, "How has he fared all this time?" Wolfgang's swift response was, "Very well, thanks and praise be to God. And I trust that you too have fared very well?"[13] At this proud response the official realized that his interlocutor was a young man of fiery temperament and assumed a more respectful tone of voice.

During the course of his life Mozart showed little love for aristocrats, or perhaps it is fairer to say that his attitude toward them was often ambiguous. He needed them, frequented them, and esteemed them when they were aristocrats in spirit as well. Otherwise he willingly avoided them. In Augsburg he was simply furious at them. He would have loved not to play a concert before them and to tell them exactly what they could do about it. In the long run he did perform for the local nobility, limiting himself to nasty remarks about them in a letter to his father: "A great crowd of the nobility was there: the Duchess Smackbottom [*Arschbömmerl*], the Countess Makewater [*Brunzgern*], to say nothing of the Princess Dunghill [*Riechzumdreck*] and her two daughters, who, however, are already married to the two Princes Potbelly von Pigtail [*Missbauch vom Sauschwanz*]."[14] Tired of provincial nobles, Wolfgang wrote his father, "I shall be honestly glad to go off again to a place where there is a court."[15]

Maynard Solomon, one of the leading modern biographers of Mozart, has observed that Wolfgang showed little deference based on rank or position, social or religious: he was capable of scorning archdukes, archbishops, and emperors.[16] Indeed, as he frequented courts and visited palaces and prestigious salons, Mozart personally experienced the limitations of human nature, even at the very top of the social pyramid. The archduke Maximilian Franz, for example, was a son of Empress Maria

Theresa, yet, as Wolfgang wrote his father in November 1781, "stupidity oozes out of his eyes."[17] He expressed similar sentiments in other letters written in the same year: "It is the heart that ennobles man," not birth or rank, "and even if I am no count, perhaps I have more honor in my body than many a count."[18] Mozart was very much aware of his worth, but he realized that high social circles and the courts of Europe were loath to recognize it in concrete form. This realization may have been responsible for the attitude of disdain and rebellion that he always manifested toward the powerful—which in turn heightened his difficulties with them.

## The "Little Cousin," Maria Anna Thekla (October 1777)

In Augsburg, Wolfgang also met someone of a totally different sort, his cousin, the daughter of his uncle Franz Alois, whose behavior toward her cousin was particularly kind and open. In fact, Wolfgang was strongly attracted to her, and thanks to her he had a complete (or perhaps nearly complete) initiation into sexual experiences. "Our little cousin," he writes his father, "is beautiful, intelligent, charming, clever, and gay." She was also "a bit of a scamp."[19] The girl was nineteen years of age—two years younger than Wolfgang—and her name was Maria Anna Thekla, known to history as the "Bäsle" (little cousin). In the weeks and years to come Wolfgang wrote her a number of letters that are both ingenuous and quite daring, full of sometimes incomprehensible allusions. He considered her a secret confidante, addressing her as "little rabbit" (*häsle*) or "crazy little witch" (*fex hex*), and at one point asking her if she still had the "spuni cuni fait," a term that thus far Mozart specialists have been unable to decode.[20]

One of Leopold Mozart's reasons for fearing what might happen if his son left Salzburg without him was precisely that Wolfgang's beautiful soul might be swept away by a passion for a woman. Up to that time Wolfgang had experienced crushes on a number of girls, but as far as we can tell these were platonic relations. In Salzburg the previous year, for example, he had given music lessons to the daughters of Countess Maria Antonia Lodron, and may perhaps have found them beguiling. Just before his departure from Salzburg in September 1777, a baker's daughter had fallen in love with him at a dance, an event that inspired Leopold to make fun of his son, writing him that the girl was so stricken at his departure that she was becoming a nun, forcing the baker to pay enormous amounts of money for the vestition ceremony, for which Wolfgang, who was responsible for the whole affair, should reimburse him.[21]

Wolfgang's relations with his nineteen-year-old cousin Anna Thekla, on the other hand were soon extremely sensual, although we have no precise information on how far the relationship went. "In Augsburg," Leopold wrote his son several months later, "you had your little romance, you amused yourself with my brother's daughter,"[22] and it is undeniable that Wolfgang's letters to Anna Thekla are so crammed with mysterious erotic allusions and scurrilous matter that when Stefan Zweig decided to print his collection of them in 1931 it was in an expurgated private edition. Customs have changed, and today these letters are published uncensored without causing problems. At the time, Zweig sent a copy to Sigmund Freud, the founder of psychoanalysis, accompanied by a circumspect letter that stated: "I hope that you, as one who understands the heights and depths, will find the enclosed private printing, which I am making available only to a *narrow* circle, not entirely irrelevant: these nine letters of the 21-year-old Mozart, of which I am publishing *one* here in its entirety, throw a psychologically very remarkable light on his erotic nature, which, more so than that of any other important man, has elements of infantilism and coprolalia."[23]

Anna Thekla was a bit free in her ways, and some years later she had an illegitimate child by a canon of the Augsburg cathedral. When Wolfgang wrote Leopold about her charms, Leopold, somewhat maliciously, noted in a letter to his son of 18 October 1777 that Anna Thekla seemed to him to have "too many friends among the priests." In a further indication that he might have been aware of his niece's habits, he adds, "I am quite pleased to hear that she is a bit of a scamp, but these ecclesiastical gentlemen are often far worse."[24]

Given the girl's vivacious nature, we might even suspect that Leopold looked somewhat kindly on their relationship, precisely as a way to give the boy an indispensable supplement to his education. Leopold must certainly have been concerned for some time about the problem of the sexual instruction of his son. His cousin Anna Thekla presented little risk, given that her parents and her aunt could easily counsel the girl to be prudent, but also because it was unlikely (even if a baby were conceived) that a marriage between cousins would be permitted. We would do Leopold too much credit for farsightedness to imagine him as the originator of such a risky scheme, however. Very probably everything happened by chance, without premeditation, as is often the case.

At the time Wolfgang still looked very boyish. From what his parents say in two letters written in December 1777 we gather that at the time he did not need to shave. Scissors sufficed to snip off the first peach fuzz.[25]

## Nearly Five Months in Mannheim
## (October 1777–March 1778)

On 26 October 1777 Wolfgang and his mother left Augsburg and Anna Thekla behind them. After a halt in Hohenaltheim, they arrived in Mannheim on 30 October. They stayed there for the entire winter, and this is where Wolfgang met Aloysia Weber, this time seriously falling in love.

Mannheim, the capital city of the Palatinate, was the residence of a prince-elector, Karl Theodor, who had ruled with notable success for over thirty years. Wolfgang hoped to be hired by him, but once again his hopes were dashed. Mannheim offered him an extremely exciting musical environment, however, and Mozart learned much during his stay there. The city boasted a flourishing music school founded by Johann (Jan) Stamitz, a famous Bohemian violinist and orchestral conductor who had died in 1757, a year after Wolfgang's birth. He and his school had contributed much to developing and imposing what is now the standard model for an orchestral symphony in four movements—an allegro, an adagio, a minuet, and a finale—which was new at the time.

Mannheim also had the fortune to have an excellent court orchestra, perhaps the best in all of Germany—a fact worthy of note, as in those days orchestras were often worse than mediocre, poorly led, and full of amateur musicians. All the players in Mannheim's court orchestra, in contrast, were excellent, as Wolfgang wrote home in a letter. He became a great friend of the director, Johann Christian Cannabich, who was forty-three at the time and had first become a member of that famous orchestra at the age of twelve. In a letter of 9 July 1778 Mozart said that Cannabich was the best orchestral conductor that he had ever known.[26] Wolfgang was often a guest in the family's house and gave keyboard lessons to one of the Cannabich daughters, Rosa, for whom he composed one of his loveliest piano sonatas, the Sonata in C Major (K. 309/284b). In 1781 Johann Cannabich, who had transferred to Munich, conducted the premiere of *Idomeneo*.

Wolfgang was less pleased with the singers he encountered in Mannheim. In a letter dated 4 November he praises the orchestra, but then adds, "You cannot imagine anything worse than the voices here. . . . They have only two castrati, who are already old and will just be allowed to die off. The soprano would actually prefer to sing alto, as he can no longer take the high notes. The few boys they have are miserable. The tenors and basses are like our funeral singers."[27]

Wolfgang was equally severe in his judgment of the deputy-Kapellmeister, the famous Georg Joseph Vogler, who was thirty-eight at the time. He took a great liking, however, to the sixty-six-year-old Ignaz Jacob Holzbauer, the court Kapellmeister and a well-known composer. On the whole, Mozart was fascinated by the artistic and intellectual environment he found in Mannheim.

Leopold became furious when he realized that his wife and son intended to spend the entire winter enjoying the delights of Mannheim, seemingly with no thought of striving to find a lucrative and stable position. It would be better to move on to Mainz, he wrote them, because that city seemed to present greater opportunities for work. In a letter dated 27 November he declares severely, "The object of your journey, the very necessary object was and is and must be, to obtain [an appointment or make money.] So far I see little prospect of the one or the other. . . . A pretty kettle of fish; and yet not a syllable about your plans for your next journey. I keep on racking my brains—and write myself blind. I do want to arrange everything in advance. You, however, make light of everything, you are indifferent, you tie my hands when I want to advise and help, since you do not say a word about where you are going to next."[28] In a letter that he sent off three days earlier Leopold had written even more severely to his son, but also to his wife: "So far you have just had a holiday and have spent the time in enjoyment and amusement. Now the bad weather, short days, and the cold have arrived and these conditions will become worse, while our prospects and purposes become more costly and more distant."[29]

On 13 November Wolfgang reported to his father that his rewards for his musical efforts had been watches—gold watches, to be sure—rather than money. "I now have five watches. I am therefore seriously thinking of having an additional watch pocket on each leg of my trousers," he states.[30] He could then wear two watches, as was then the fashion. What is more, the display might discourage some great lord from giving him yet another watch. Leopold responded with the usual advice: "It would have been much better, I admit, if you had received fifteen louis d'or instead of a watch, which you say has been valued at twenty louis d'or, since for traveling money is very necessary, indeed indispensable."[31] Leopold goes on to list the debts the family had contracted in Salzburg: three hundred florins to family friend Abbé Joseph Bullinger, more than a hundred florins to the merchant Ignaz Weiser, at least forty florins to Johann Kerschbaumer, another merchant, and of course a large sum to Lorenz Hagenauer. Money! Wolfgang had better put his mind to earning some, soon and in abundance, also because the bills for the tailor, for firewood, for candles, would have to be paid. Wolfgang was behaving, Leopold scolded, as if he had strongboxes overflowing with money.

It took several days for a letter to reach Mannheim from Salzburg, which explains the disconnect between the moods of the father and the son. In his letter of 24 November, for example, Leopold was indignant because Wolfgang, writing on 14 November, had dared to send him something like a public confession in which he wrote ironically about himself. A clearly euphoric Wolfgang had written:

> I, Johannes Chrysostomus Amadeus Wolfgangus Sigismundus Mozart, hereby plead guilty and confess that yesterday and the day before (not to mention on several other occasions) I did not get home until midnight; and that from ten o'clock until the said hour at Cannabich's house and in the presence and company of the said Cannabich, his wife and daughter, the Treasurer, Ramm [the oboist] and Lang [the horn player] I did frequently, without any difficulty, but quite easily, perpetrate—rhymes, the same being, moreover, sheer garbage, that is, on such subjects as muck, shitting and arse-licking—and that too in thoughts, words—but not in deeds.

Clearly, scurrilous language was admitted in many social circles at the time, as Mozart indicates:

> I should not have behaved so godlessly, however, if our ringleader, known under the name of Lisel (Elisabetha Cannabich), had not egged me on and incited me; at the same time I must admit that I thoroughly enjoyed it. I confess all these sins and transgressions of mine from the bottom of my heart, and in the hope of having to confess them very often, I firmly resolve to go on with the sinful life which I have begun. Wherefore I beg for the holy dispensation, if it can be easily obtained; if not, it's all one to me, for the game will go on all the same.[32]

Certainly Wolfgang thought he was being funny. He had not yet understood the extent to which his witticisms were capable of infuriating his father even beyond his usual rage.

Leopold was suffering anxieties because his son was wasting precious time, because Wolfgang's letters were too vague, and because the post traveled too slowly. He inundated his wife and his son with practical advice about their imminent voyage to Paris, but the advice he sent them was contradictory. He suggested that they go to Paris, where opportunities would surely not be lacking, but he did not exclude the idea of wintering in Mannheim, where he still hoped that the prince-elector might take Wolfgang into his service. "I repeat," he writes on 13 November 1777, "that I do not doubt but that the Elector will keep you for the winter and perhaps even longer, if Mamma represents to the Electress the discomfort of a journey. If you do spend a winter there, I feel sure that you will be appointed permanently and with a good salary." Leopold could not get over the idea that the world had not yet understood his son's genius: "Your youth and your appearance prevent people from realizing the wealth of the Divine grace which has been bestowed on you in your talents. You have left behind you many places, where people never got to know half of what you can do."[33]

Mozart took offense at his father's severe reproaches. "We spend nothing beyond what is necessary," he responded on 29 November. He adds, "But if you attribute it to my negligence, thoughtlessness, and laziness, I can only thank you for your good opinion of me and sincerely regret that you do not know your son. I am not careless, I am simply prepared for anything and am able, in consequence, to wait patiently for whatever may come, and endure it—provided that my honor and the good name of Mozart are not affected. Well, as it must be so, so let it be. But I must beg you at the outset not to give way prematurely to joy or sadness. For come what may, all is well, so long as a man enjoys good health. For happiness consists—simply in imagination."[34]

Leopold counterattacked. He argued with his son regarding his ideas of happiness, noting that a traveler who hasn't a penny and is mistreated by innkeepers cannot console himself with any abstract idea of happiness. But he agreed to the notion that Wolfgang and Anna Maria should remain for a month or two in Mannheim. It was by then the first week in December and a trip to Paris seemed inadvisable until spring.

Anna Maria Mozart was also somewhat piqued by her husband's reproaches, and on 7 December she had this to report about her less than brilliant routine in Mannheim: "Wolfgang is lunching with Herr Wendling today, December 7th. So I am home alone, as I usually am, and have to put up with the most horrible cold. For even if they light a small fire, they never put any more coal on it, so that when it burns out, the room gets cold again. A little fire of this kind costs twelve kreuzer. So I make them light one in the morning, when we get up, and another in the evening. During the day I have to put up with dreadful cold. As I write I can hardly hold my pen, I am freezing so."[35] Leopold was not moved. He suggested to his wife that she go and visit someone who had a heated room, and afterward she could go back and take to her bed, snuggling under the covers. But Wolfgang and Anna Maria found a more intelligent way to resolve their problem by moving to the house of the privy court councilor, Serrarius, where adequate and less costly heat was available. Mozart knew Serrarius because he was giving keyboard lessons to his daughter-in-law. "Praise and thanks be to God," Anna Maria wrote to Leopold.[36]

In theory, Anna Maria was there to supervise their son, but in her letter of 7 December, as we have seen, she confessed that she was alone most of the time. At the age of twenty-one, Wolfgang was full of energy and went out all over the city, while his mother, by then fifty-one, was tired of traveling, melancholy, prone to chill, and in poor health, and hence could not even think of keeping up with him.

Among other things, Wolfgang was attracted by the intellectual salons of Mannheim, the leading light of which was Christoph Martin Wieland, a well-known poet, writer, and man of the Enlightenment who was forty-four years old at the time. Wolfgang was fully aware of who Wieland was and had read some of his works, but he was by no means intimidated by him. He judged the writer as he would an equal, or even as a lesser man, as he had always judged all aristocrats and all the powerful. He told Leopold of a meeting with the great poet in a letter dated 27 December 1777:

I have now added Herr Wieland to the list of my acquaintances. But he doesn't know as much about me as I know about him, for he has never heard any of my compositions. I had imagined him to be quite different from what I found him. He strikes you as slightly affected in his speech. He has a rather childish voice; he keeps on quizzing you over his glasses; he indulges in a sort of pedantic rudeness, combined occasionally with a stupid condescension. But I am not surprised that he permits himself such behavior here, even though he may be quite different in Weimar and elsewhere, for people stare at him as if he had dropped from Heaven. Everyone seems embarrassed in his presence, no one says a word or moves an inch; all listen intently to every word he utters; and it's a pity they often have to wait so long, for he has a defect of speech that makes him speak very slowly and he can't say half a dozen words without stopping. Apart from that, he is what we all know him to be, a most gifted fellow. He has a frightfully ugly face, covered with pockmarks, and he has a rather long nose. In height he is, I should say, a little taller than Papa.[37]

Leopold replied in his letter of 5 January 1778 that he was not surprised by Wolfgang's portrait of Wieland because others had given him "a most minute description of him."[38]

Wolfgang had found in Mannheim a rich and stimulating musical environment in which he might have been able to survive economically even without a post at court. During the course of his stay there he wrote some twenty compositions, many of which elicited enthusiasm for the new ideas they contained. In particular, there were two piano sonatas (K. 309/284b and K. 311/284c), the first of which, as we have seen, he wrote for Cannabich's daughter. But there were also five sonatas for violin and piano (K. 296, 301/293a, 302/293b, 303/293c, 305/293d), all of them fine works, as well as three quartets for flute and strings (K. 285, 285a, 285b/Anh.171). He also composed two flute concertos (K. 313/285c, 314/285d), both of them commissioned by Ferdinand De Jean, a wealthy Hollander who lived in Mannheim and was passionately fond of the flute.

Wolfgang felt himself to be no longer a keyboard player, but a composer. This change is clear in his letter of 7 February 1778. He explains to his father that he no longer thinks it appropriate to give clavier lessons, even if they paid well. They would be a waste of time, given that his true vocation was to compose music: "I am a composer and was born to be a Kapellmeister. I neither can nor ought to bury the talent for composition with which God in his goodness has so richly endowed me. . . . I would rather, if I may speak plainly, neglect the clavier than composition, for in my case the clavier with me is only a sideline, though, thank God, a very good one."[39] The child prodigy and virtuoso keyboard player was buried, once and for all. If Wolfgang continued to play the piano and give concerts, he did so only to communicate his new ideas.

## Meeting the Weber Family; Love for Aloysia (January 1778)

There was another consequence of Wolfgang's stay in Mannheim: he met the Webers, a family of musicians who were to play a decisive role in his life. There were four Weber sisters: Aloysia, with whom Wolfgang immediately fell in love; Constanze, whom he was to marry in 1782 but to whom he paid little attention in 1778; Josepha, who sang the role of the Queen of the Night in the premiere performance of *The Magic Flute*; and Sophie, who was with Mozart (along with Constanze) during the last days of his life. The girls' mother, Caecilia, was a likeable person but not altogether admirable and somewhat common. Their father, Franz Fridolin Weber, was a musician, a good-humored and honest man, but somehow unfortunate and always poor. He scraped together a living as a copyist, singer, and prompter. Years earlier he had studied law at the University of Freiburg and had worked as a court clerk. His brother Franz Anton, a more successful composer and a Freemason, produced a son in 1786 named Carl Maria (who later himself added the noble "von" to his name), the composer of *Der Freischütz* and *Oberon*. Hence Constanze Weber (Mozart's wife) and Carl Maria von Weber were first cousins.

Wolfgang was immediately enchanted by the personal fascination and the musical talents of the sixteen-year-old Aloysia, an able pianist and an excellent singer. He was also attracted by the gaiety that reigned among her entire family. The first letter to his father in which Wolfgang speaks of the Webers is dated 17 January 1778. In it he writes that Fridolin Weber was a man persecuted because of his honesty and rectitude, and that his daughter Aloysia sang so beautifully that doors were open to her at court. It is possible that even before he received this letter Leopold had been informed of his son's new friends. In a letter of 4 December 1777 he invites Wolfgang to be wary of people: "Mark well, my son, that *to find one man in a thousand, who is your true friend* from unselfish motives, is to find *one of the greatest wonders of this world.*"[40] In a subsequent letter, dated 18 December, he forbade his son to sleep in other people's houses or even in quarters that he did not share with his mother: "You should not and must not leave Mamma alone and at the mercy of other people, as long as she is with you. However small her room may be, space can surely be found for a bed for you."[41] In short, the twenty-one-year-old Wolfgang was not to run the risk of spending even one night with a woman other than his mother. Leopold, who was already furious because Wolfgang was wasting time without either earning money or finding engagements worthy of his talents, must have sensed that there were new dangers afoot. On 29 January, speaking of the perils awaiting his son in Paris (but perhaps also of those besetting him in Mannheim), he warned Wolfgang to be on guard against Parisian women, "who are always on the lookout for strangers to keep them, who run after young people of talent in an astonishing way in order to get at their money, draw them into their net, or even land them as husbands. God and your own good sense will preserve you. Any such calamity would be the death of me!"[42]

Wolfgang sought to reassure his father, but his letter of 7 February probably produced just the opposite effect. He writes that for the moment he excluded marriage because his means were insufficient. He would want to make his wife happy, not use her to make his fortune: "So I shall let things be and enjoy my golden freedom until I am so well off that I can support a wife and children." Nobles marry for interest alone, but

> we poor humble people can not only choose a wife whom we love and who loves us, but we may, can, and do take such a one, because we are neither noble, nor highly born, nor aristocratic, nor rich, but, on the contrary, lowly born, humble, and poor; so we do not need a wealthy wife, for our riches, being in our brains, die with us—and these no man can take from us unless he chops off our heads, in which case—we need nothing more.[43]

We have every right to think that this was the sort of reasoning Wolfgang heard from Fridolin Weber, his wife Caecilia, and their marriageable daughters.

At the end of January, Fridolin, Aloysia, and Wolfgang took a brief trip to the Palatinate, where they gave a few concerts, earned little, and amused themselves thoroughly, especially Wolfgang, who was by then madly in love with the girl. In a letter to his father of 4 February he ingenuously speaks of his passion and describes himself as the possible savior of the entire Weber family, forgetting for the moment that his own family in Salzburg was expecting his salvation for themselves. But by this time Wolfgang was being catapulted toward his own personal and brilliant future. Regarding the Webers he had the imprudence to write: "I have become so fond of this unfortunate family that my dearest wish is to make them happy; and perhaps I may be able to do so. My advice is that they should go to Italy."[44] According to Mozart's plans, Aloysia would become a prima donna in the opera houses of Verona or Venice and he himself, with the Weber family, would go to Italy with her to give her moral support. Leopold, who thought his son incapable of taking care even of himself, was beside himself with anger. Even worse, Wolfgang had the addle-headed idea of writing Leopold that Fridolin had become a new father for him:

> Herr Weber will endeavor to get engagements here and there for concerts with me, and we shall then travel together. When I am with him, it is just as if I were traveling with you. [It is interesting to note that here Wolfgang uses the formal "you" to his father.] The very reason why I am so fond of him is because, apart from his appearance, he is just like you and has exactly your character and way of thinking. If my mother were not, as you know, too *comfortably lazy* to write, she would tell you the very same thing! I must confess that I much enjoyed traveling with

them. We were happy and merry; I was hearing a man talk like you; I had nothing to worry about; I found my torn clothes mended; in short, I was waited on like a prince.[45]

Leopold was immensely put out. He thought that Wolfgang had lost his mind and was about to compromise his career once and for all. He sent his son a sizzling letter, accusing him of allowing himself to be trapped by impostors; of no longer wanting to aid his parents, who had sacrificed everything for him; and, consequently, of being an ungrateful, cruel, and inconsiderate booby. He emphasizes his own physical reactions to Wolfgang's proposals (sleeplessness, exhaustion, depression, near insanity) and declares that his worries over his son "almost kill me." He demolishes the notion that Aloysia could so easily become a prima donna in an Italian opera house. He paints a sorry future for Wolfgang if he were to marry a girl like Aloysia: "Now it depends solely on your good sense and your way of life whether you die as an ordinary musician, utterly forgotten by the world, or as a famous Kapellmeister, of whom posterity will read— whether, captured by some woman, you die bedded on straw in an attic full of starving children, or whether, after a Christian life spent in contentment, honor, and renown, you leave this world with your family well provided for and your name respected by all."[46]

Leopold ordered Wolfgang to leave immediately for Paris, accompanied by his mother. And Wolfgang obeyed. He was still strongly under the sway of paternal authority, but at the same time, he himself wondered whether his dreams had not perhaps taken him too far. In his letter of 19 February he quickly backtracks. He admits that Aloysia, although an excellent singer, is still too young and too little skilled as an actress. Before going to Italy, it would be better if she took lessons to improve her stage presence.

In the previous weeks the family had thought that Anna Maria, who was tired, worried about the hardships of the Paris trip, and anxious to return to Salzburg, might see Wolfgang off to Paris by himself. In a postscript to his letter of 5 February 1787 Leopold indicates that he believed that his son had already left. But then the developments of the Weber affair persuaded Leopold to change his mind. He announces in a letter of 23 February, "Mamma must go with you to Paris and you must confide in her, just as you must confide in me when you write to me."[47] Continual surveillance must be assured by all available means. Wolfgang was being forced into the trip to Paris for several reasons: the notion that Paris was a good place for him to be had circulated within the Mozart family for some time, but also everything possible had to be done to distance him from Aloysia, from the Weber family, from the projected sojourn in Italy, and hence from Mannheim. In the same letter of 23 February Leopold explains to Wolfgang that in order to gain renown in the world as a composer he must go to Paris, to Vienna, and perhaps to Italy, but for the moment Paris was the better choice because it was nearer Mannheim and did not have a large number of composers: "The only other question is: 'Where have I most hope of getting on?' *In Italy*, where in *Naples alone* there are at least three hundred maestri and where, from one end of the country to the other, the maestri have contracts (very often two years in advance) with those theaters that pay well? Or in Paris, where perhaps two or three are writing for the stage, and other composers may be counted on one's fingers?"[48]

Leopold decided, however, that Wolfgang and his mother should wait to set off for Paris until the beginning of the better season for travel, which meant mid-March. On 13 February 1778 Wolfgang gave a concert in the Cannabiches' house in which Aloysia Weber sang two arias from *Lucio Silla*. On 12 March, again at the Cannabich residence, Wolfgang gave a final concert in Mannheim and Aloysia sang the recitative and concert aria "Alcandro lo confesso"/"Non so d'onde viene" (K. 294), which he had composed for her. In a letter describing it to his father, dated 24 March, Wolfgang complained, however, that the Cannabiches were hardly generous to him: not a word, not even a keepsake, no thanks whatsoever, after all the time he had spent giving lessons to their daughter. He stresses the contrast with the behavior of the Weber family, whose means were much more restricted. On 13 March, on the eve of his departure for Paris, Wolfgang paid a farewell call on the Webers, during which Aloysia gave him a pair of lace cuffs and her father presented him with a volume of Molière's plays with an Italian inscription, "Ricevi, amico, le opere del Molière in segno di gratitudine, e qualche volta ricordati di me" (Accept, my friend, the works of Molière in token of gratitude, and think of me sometimes). When the moment came for a final good-bye, the women of the family all wept. We can presume that in saying farewell to Aloysia, Wolfgang did his best to assure her that he would think of her in Paris, not only from a sentimental point of view, but also practically. He would have loved to guarantee her a splendid career as a singer thanks to the many opportunities Paris was reputed to offer. His departure for Paris was thus not a definitive good-bye, but rather an *arrivederci*, with a possible engagement and marriage in view as soon as he had permanent employment. Wolfgang himself alluded to these plans in a letter to his father on 7 March: "Once I am happily settled in Paris and, as I hope, our circumstances with God's help have improved and we are all more cheerful and in better spirits, I shall tell you my thoughts more fully and ask you for a great favor."[49] We can only guess that the favor was Leopold's consent to his son's marriage.

## From Mannheim to Paris (March 1778)

On 14 March 1778 Wolfgang and his mother left Mannheim, on their way to Paris via Metz. Twelve years after their first Parisian experience, the city seemed to them as alluring and grandiose as ever, especially in comparison to Salzburg. The taking of the Bastille was only eleven years in the future, but at this time Paris was effervescent, growing fast, and evolving in positive ways, as nearly all of France seemed to be. The great French historian Alexis de Tocqueville entitled one of the chapters of his book on the French Revolution "How, though the reign of Louis XIV was the most prosperous period of the monarchy, this very prosperity hastened the outbreak of the Revolution."[50] In this prosperous Paris perhaps Wolfgang, too, could make his fortune.

As early as the previous September and throughout the intervening months an anxious Leopold had assailed his wife and his son with his advice about the trip to France. Take with you only louis d'or and always keep them on you. Do not forget to pack black powder, which is an extraordinary medication. When you get to Paris, beware of pickpockets, who often attack foreigners. The journey from Mannheim to Paris took place without incident; it lasted nine and a half days and cost fifteen louis d'or, between paying the coachman, contributing to the cost of the new coach, and buying food and lodging. During the first eight days they had good weather, but on the last few days it rained constantly, with a strong wind. "We both got soaking wet in the carriage and could scarcely breathe," Anna Maria Mozart wrote.[51] At the customs office on the French border Wolfgang had to pay thirty-eight sous, but at the gates of Paris their baggage went through without inspection by the customs officials.

They arrived in Paris on 23 March at four in the afternoon. As Leopold had suggested, they rented a furnished room from Monsieur Mayer, in rue Bourg l'Abbé, not far from Les Halles. Their lodging was truly dreadful, as was often the case in Paris before Napoleon III and Baron Haussmann remodeled the city. In a letter to her husband of 5 April, Anna Maria Mozart gave a disconcerting account of her days:

As for my own life, it is not at all a pleasant one. I sit alone in our room the whole day long as if I were in jail, and as the room is very dark and looks out on a little courtyard, I cannot see the sun all day long and I don't even know what the weather is like. With great difficulty I manage to knit a little by the daylight that struggles in. And for this room we have to pay thirty livres a month. The hall and the stairs are so narrow that it would be impossible to bring up a clavier.[52]

Wolfgang, meanwhile, went off to work wherever someone put a keyboard instrument at his disposal. Anna Maria's description of her life continues:

Thus I never see him all day long and shall forget altogether how to talk. The food which the traiteur sends in is perfectly magnificent. For a lunch which costs 15 sous I get three courses, first of all, soup with some butter which I detest, secondly, a little slice of very poor meat, thirdly, a slab of calf's foot in some dirty sauce, or a piece of liver as hard as a stone. In the evening we don't have any food sent in, but Frau Mayer buys us a couple of pounds of veal and has it roasted at the baker's. So we have it hot for the first time, and afterward cold as long as it lasts, as is the custom in England. We have never had soup in the evenings. I simply cannot describe to you the fast days, which are positively unendurable. Everything here is half as dear again as it was the last time we were here twelve years ago.[53]

On 24 March, the day after their arrival, Wolfgang paid a call on Baron Grimm, who had introduced the Mozarts into society circles in Paris on their earlier visit, but did not find him at home. Leopold was very eager to have his son put himself under the protection of Grimm, and had already sent the baron two letters expressing his concern over his son's libertine inclinations. Grimm must have been more than a bit put out, not only at the thought of having to take on responsibility for Leopold's twenty-two-year-old son, but even more because some months earlier, at a concert that Wolfgang gave in Augsburg, when the baron sat up close precisely so that the young artist would acknowledge his presence, neither he nor Anna Maria recognized him.[54] On 25 March Wolfgang went once more to call on Grimm, and this time found him at home. That same afternoon he also visited Count Karl Heinrich Joseph Sickingen zu Sickingen, the Paris representative of the court at Mannheim, who immediately became a great friend, protector, and admirer of Wolfgang's.

Soon after their arrival Wolfgang also met Jean Joseph Legros, a singer and a Freemason who was prominent in the musical life of Paris at the time. Legros was in fact the director of the Concert Spirituel, a musical institution with a chorus and an orchestra that had been founded in 1725, when Louis XV had given permission to organize "spiritual" concerts in the Tuileries on days on which the theaters remained closed for religious reasons. Legros immediately commissioned Mozart to write some choruses for a miserere, made a clavier available to him, and invited him often to dinner, sparing him the discomfort of the furnished room. The commissioned choruses were to be used in substitution for the original ones in a miserere by Ignaz Holzbauer, a Mannheim musician whom Mozart esteemed.[55] The undertaking was a failure, however. Holzbauer's work did not please the Parisians, who found it too long. As performed, it was accompanied by only two out of the four choral pieces Mozart had written, the ones he himself thought the worst. "But that was of no consequence," Mozart wrote to console himself, "for few people knew that I had composed some of the music and many knew nothing at all about me."[56]

On 9 April, Baron Grimm went to call on Anna Maria Mozart in her gloomy furnished room, and it was probably thanks to him that Anna Maria and Wolfgang moved to a somewhat more pleasant furnished room. Their new lodgings were in rue du Gros-Chenet (now rue du Sentier), still in the neighborhood of Les Halles. In a letter to her husband of 14 May, Anna Maria explained that they hoped to move out of that room as well, because they wanted to rent an apartment, furnish it themselves, and at long last be able to cook their own meals.[57]

## Disappointments in Paris (Spring 1778)

Mozart had known great success in Paris as a child prodigy, but things were different in 1778. One probable reason for the Parisians' diminished enthusiasm is that many saw him as an overgrown child prodigy. "What annoys me most of all here is that these stupid Frenchmen seem to think I am still seven years old, because that was my age when they first saw me," Mozart complained.[58] Except for the professional musicians, everyone treated him as a beginner. They failed to appreciate the young and promising composer, in part because his music was new and they found it unpalatable and often difficult to understand and to play. Mozart's compositions were far from current musical tastes in Paris.

Wolfgang gives a revealing account of Parisian high society's lack of appreciation in a letter to Leopold of 1 May 1778. In it he relates his reception in the palace of the Duchesse de Chabot (to whom Mozart had a letter of introduction and whom he hoped would recommend him to the Duchesse de Bourbon): "I had to wait for half an hour in a large ice-cold unheated room, which hadn't even a fireplace. At last the Duchesse de Chabot appeared. She was very polite and asked me to make the best of the clavier in the room, as none of her own were in good condition. Would I perhaps try it?" Wolfgang explained to the duchess that at least for the moment his fingers were too cold for him to play, at which he was shown into a room where several gentlemen were seated around a table drawing: "I had the honor to wait. The windows and doors were open and not only my hands but my whole body and my feet were frozen and my head began to ache. There was *altum silentium* and I did not know what to do for cold, headache, and boredom." Mozart realized that he was being treated as a servant, and the only reason he did not leave immediately was that he did not want to cause difficulties in his relations with Grimm. After a while he decided to play the terrible pianoforte before the company gathered in the room, who, indifferent to the music, continued their drawing. When he stopped, however, Mozart says, "I received a shower of éloges" and they persuaded him to stay a bit longer. At that point the Duc de Chabot arrived, however, and his comportment was totally different. Mozart re-lates: "He sat down beside me and listened with the greatest attention and—I forgot the cold and my headache and in spite of the wretched clavier, I played—as I play when I am in good spirits. Give me the best clavier in Europe with an audience who understand nothing, or don't want to understand and who do not feel with me in what I am playing, and I shall cease to feel any pleasure."[59] The contrary was true as well: when Mozart found someone who did understand him, he was willing to play with passion even in the worst conditions.

In a letter of 5 February Leopold had admonished his son to call on all of the noble families they had known earlier in Paris and on other influ-ential personages, and to that purpose he added a detailed list of some eighty names. In his 1 May letter Wolfgang explains why he could not possibly visit all of them:

The distances are too great for walking—or the roads too muddy—for really the mud in Paris is beyond all description. To take a carriage means that you have the honor of spending four to five livres a day, and all for nothing. People pay plenty of compliments, it is true, but there it ends. They arrange for me to come on such and such a day. I play and hear them exclaim: "Oh, c'est un prodige, c'est inconcevable, c'est étonnant!" and then it is—Adieu. At first I spent a lot of money driving about—often to no purpose, for the people were not at home. Those who do not live in Paris cannot imagine how annoying this is. Besides, Paris is greatly changed; the French are not nearly so polite as they were fifteen years ago; their manners now border on rudeness and they are detestably self-conceited.[60]

In Paris Mozart thus had an opportunity to reinforce his animosity toward nobles who thought themselves superior to him as a birthright. As Norbert Elias said of Mozart, "He was, in a word, an exceptionally gifted creative human being, born into a society which did not yet know the Romantic concept of genius, and whose social canon had no legitimate place for the highly individualized artist of genius in their midst."[61] Mozart's tragedy, in Elias's view, was based on the fact that both as a person and in his creative activities he sought by himself to break social barriers when he was in fact a member of that society and subscribed to its tradition of taste. His battle was a solitary one: a personal, not a political one. Elias observes that as far as we know, Mozart was not interested in humanitarian or relatively abstract generic political ideals.[62]

Mozart was undeniably an innovator in the musical realm, but he preferred to be a moderate in politics. He was not fond of the noble and the powerful, but he lived in their midst and he needed them. The 1777–1778 journey without Leopold, however, was making him more independent of aristocratic circles. After his unpleasant encounter with the young nobles in Augsburg who had made fun of the medal of the papal Order of the Golden Spur, Wolfgang decided no longer to wear the decoration, even if it did reflect a higher grade of knighthood than the one that Christoph Willibald Gluck continually flaunted.[63] Mozart belonged to a much younger generation than Gluck, and he certainly did not think that a knighthood served to distinguish him from the commonality: he was content to be Mozart. Secure in that knowledge, he knew himself to possess qualities far superior to those of any of the many dukes and princes who peopled the world.

Mozart was critical of French high society both for the snobbery it had shown toward him and for its poor musical taste. He wrote to his father on 5 April: "What annoys me most of all in this business is that our French gentlemen have only improved their *goût* to this extent, that they can now listen to good stuff as well. But to expect them to realize that their own music is bad or at least to notice the difference—Heaven preserve us! And their singing! Good Lord! Let me never hear a Frenchwoman singing Italian arias. I can forgive her if she screeches out her French trash, but not if she ruins good music! It's simply unbearable."[64]

On 9 July, imagining the obstacles that he might meet if he were commissioned to write an opera in Paris, he also states that the French language seemed to him absolutely unsuited for music.[65] The mutual incomprehension that had grown up between Mozart and the French was also confirmed by the tortuous dealings surrounding a *sinfonia concertante* for winds and orchestra that he had composed for the Concert Spirituel, the score of which he had delivered Monsieur Legros, but which the latter always "forgot" to have copied for the orchestra members. Behind this forgetfulness Mozart saw the hostility and the jealousy of enemies and rival composers. The work has been lost, but there is a dubious version of it cataloged as K. 297b/C14.01.

Mozart's only genuine success in Paris was his *Paris* Symphony (K. 297/300a), a work also commissioned by Legros for the Concert Spirituel. Mozart wrote it in a style somewhat different from that of his other symphonies, precisely in order to suit Parisian tastes. He was always extremely able in imitating all musical styles, and he decided to make deliberate use of this talent to have a success. Because he was a great innovator, however, he not only imitated French tastes but brought new life to them through his art. The *Paris* Symphony sweeps the listener along, particularly in the finale. Mozart had trouble with it during the rehearsals, however, because the orchestra seemed unable to play it properly. On 3 July he wrote his father:

> I was very nervous at the rehearsal, for never in my life have I heard a worse performance. You have no idea how they twice scraped and scrambled through it. I was really in a terrible way and would gladly have had it rehearsed again, but as there was so much else to rehearse, there was no time left. So I had to go to bed with an aching heart and in a discontented and angry frame of mind. I decided next morning not to go to the concert at all; but in the evening, the weather being fine, I at last made up my mind to go, determined that if my symphony went as badly as it did at the rehearsal, I would certainly make my way into the orchestra, snatch the fiddle out of the hands of Lahoussay, the first violin, and conduct myself! I prayed God that it might go well, for it is all to His greater honor and glory.[66]

This was indeed the case. There was great applause in the middle of the first movement, and even greater acclamations toward the beginning of the final allegro: "Having observed that all last as well as first allegros begin here with all the instruments playing together and generally unisono, I began mine with two violins only, piano for the first eight bars—followed instantly by a forte; the audience, as I expected, said 'hush' at the soft beginning, and when they heard the forte, began at once to clap their hands."[67] In those days no one hesitated about applauding in the middle of a work of music. The concert was held on 18 June, and to celebrate his success Wolfgang went to the Palais Royale gardens, where he treated himself to "a large ice." He then said a rosary, as he had vowed to do if the performance were a success, and returned to his mother.

A few days earlier, on 12 June, Wolfgang had been applauded at the premiere of a ballet choreographed by Jean-Georges Noverre, *Les petits riens* (K. 299b/Anh.10), for which Mozart had provided over half of the music. His name did not even appear on the publicity for the show. The ballet was performed after an opera composed by Niccolò Piccinni, *Le finte gemelle.* Mozart judged Piccinni's opera to be mediocre, and his contribution to the ballet comprised the overture and the contredanses—twelve pieces in all (of twenty)—written as a courtesy to Noverre, whom he had met in Vienna five years earlier. The music for *Les petits riens* is elegant and pleasing, but not of any great importance. It represents an obvious homage to the light taste of Parisians. The ballet was performed six times, as usual attached to other works, and it met with a constant success, in part because at one point a ballerina disguised as a shepherd, wishing to put an end to the advances of two shepherdesses, bared her breasts on the stage to demonstrate that she, too, was a woman. The spectators could be counted on to demand a repetition of this emotion-laden scene.

## The Illness and Death of Anna Maria Mozart (June–July 1778)

Wolfgang's mother led a solitary and melancholy life in Paris, even in their new lodgings on rue du Gros-Chenet. On 14 May she wrote to Leopold that Paris was much bigger and much more spread out than it had been twelve years before. Not that she had been able to see much of it: she was judging from a new map and had remarked on how different it was from the one they had used earlier. For Nannerl's benefit she reported on doings in the world of fashion:

The "mode" here is to wear no earrings, nothing round your neck, no jeweled pins in your hair, in fact, no sparkling jewels, either real or imitation. The powdered wig women wear, however, is extraordinarily high, not a heart-shaped wig, but the same height all round, more than a foot. The cap, which is even higher than the wig, is worn on top, and behind is the plait or chignon which is worn right down low into the neck with lots of curls on either side. The wig, however, consists entirely of back-combed, not of smooth, hair. They have worn this wig even higher, so that at one time the roofs of the carriages had to be raised, because no woman could sit upright in them. But they have now lowered them again. The *Polonesi* [Polish-style coats] are extremely fashionable and most beautifully made. The coats worn by unmarried girls are fitted at the waist in front and have no pleats.[68]

The monotony of Anna Maria's days was often interrupted by visits from Anton Raaff, a famous tenor then sixty-seven years old, whom Wolfgang had met in Mannheim (and who would still be sufficiently energetic, despite his advanced age, to sing the title role in the premiere of *Idomeneo* in 1781). Raaff went almost daily to call on the Mozarts, and, as Anna Maria wrote in a letter dated 12 June, "He calls me 'Mother,' is very fond of us, and often spends two or three hours with us. One day he came especially to sing to me and sang three arias, which gave me great pleasure. And now whenever he comes to see us he always sings something to me, for I am quite in love with his singing. He is a most honorable man and sincerity itself; if you knew him, you would love him with all your heart."[69]

On 29 May Anna Maria sent her husband another letter that reveals her many interests and her common sense. After a brief analysis of the War of Bavarian Secession that shows her to be rather well-informed about the intentions of the Turks, the Russians, the Swedes, and the Danes—information that she probably gleaned from an attentive reading of the newspapers—she informs Nannerl that walking sticks are the latest rage. Women use them when they go out, whether to church, to pay calls, or simply to walk. She explains why: "It is very slippery here under foot, particularly after the rain. It appears that some woman twisted her foot a while ago, and a doctor declared that it would be better if women carried walking sticks; upon which it immediately became the fashion."[70] She then informed Leopold about the price of various foodstuffs, adding that prices rose daily.

Anna Maria, who probably was already not feeling well, then gives some information about her own health. Given that Leopold had recommended bloodletting, she adds, "I will remember to be bled; only I must first look about for a good [barber-] surgeon, for people in Paris are no longer bled as commonly as they used to be."[71] Wolfgang states later in his letter of 31 July that many people had advised against having his mother undergo further bloodletting, suggesting she "take a lavement" instead. Hence it is possible that at the earlier date she was already suffering from disturbances of the digestive system.[72]

On 11 June, obedient to her husband's wishes, she submitted to the traditional spring bloodletting, which weakened her system even more. She wrote her last letter to Salzburg the following day. She said that she had gone to the Luxembourg Gardens, had returned terribly tired, and had supped alone because Wolfgang had gone with Raaff to call on Baron Grimm. The letter ends with these words: "Addio. Keep well, both of you. I kiss you several thousand times and remain your [Mozartin] faithful wife." She then adds, "I must stop, for my arm and eyes are aching."[73] In the days that followed, Anna Maria's condition began to worsen; she suffered from diarrhea and ran a fever. On 23 June she suddenly lost her hearing. On 24 June she was finally visited by an elderly German physician, because she had refused to have French doctors. She was given rhubarb powder in wine, since the famous black powder that was Leopold's standby was not to be found in Paris. The German doctor ordered that she be bled again. According to Wolfgang, his mother's diarrhea, as was the usual case with foreigners, came from drinking the pestilential water of the Seine. Before Parisians would drink water from their garbage-filled river, they left it to settle in pitchers for a day so that at least they would not consume the solids it contained. When Mozart expressed surprise at wine being prescribed for his mother, he was told that it was not wine but water that caused inflammations. The result was that poor Anna Maria, feverish and desperately thirsty, was not permitted to drink as much as one glass of fresh water.

On 30 June, Anna Maria, who had resigned herself to death, confessed, and received communion and extreme unction. After being delirious for three days, on the afternoon of 3 July she lost consciousness and went into a coma. She died about ten-thirty that evening. Wolfgang, who up to then had never seen a human being die, was at her side, holding her hand and speaking to her. The only others present were a musician friend, François Haina, and a nurse. At two in the morning Wolfgang sent off two letters to Salzburg, one to his father, in which he limited himself to saying that Anna Maria was seriously ill, and another to a family friend, Abbé Joseph Bullinger, begging him to prepare Leopold for the terrible news. Everything went according to his plan. The two letters arrived in Salzburg on 13 July, and Leopold, terribly alarmed to learn of his wife's illness, suspected the worst. He wrote to Wolfgang immediately asking for details and expressing doubts about her treatment, saying "perhaps she wasn't bled sufficiently?" Even before receiving certain news of his wife's death, he already fussed about cost of "the funeral expenses, and so forth. Great Heavens! There are innumerable expenses about which you know absolutely nothing. People deceive, overcharge, delude a stranger, lure him into unnecessary extravagance and, if he has no honest friends, squeeze him dry. You can have no conception of it."[74] Leopold was writing this letter when Bullinger, who already knew the truth, arrived, and gradually informed him of all that had occurred.

In the meantime Wolfgang had written another letter to his father on 9 July in which he no longer hid from him that Anna Maria had died and had been buried in the cemetery of Saint Eustache. Given that letters took days to travel from Paris to Salzburg, Wolfgang correctly calculated that Bullinger would have had time to accomplish his mission. In the following weeks, however, Leopold, rather than appreciating Wolfgang's tact in his handling the news, and instead of sympathizing with him for the difficult times he had gone through, treated his son as if he had been partially responsible for his mother's death. On 3 August Leopold wrote his son, admitting that Anna Maria had always neglected her health, but adding: "You had your engagements, you were away all day, and as she didn't make a fuss, you treated her condition lightly. All this time her illness became more serious, in fact mortal."[75] He also noted that his wife would have preferred to return to Salzburg, and had instead sacrificed herself by accompanying Wolfgang to Paris. She had been miraculously saved in childbirth in 1756, but Divine Providence had foreordained that she die because of him in 1778. On 27 August Leopold sent a letter to his son in which he transcribed a message that Anna Maria had sent to him in secret from Mannheim on 5 February, in which she stated her disapproval of Wolfgang's idea of going to Paris with the flutist Johann Baptist Wendling and the oboist Friedrich Ramm. To counteract the influence of these dangerous friendships, Anna Maria felt herself obliged to run the risks of the voyage. Leopold rubs it in: "If your mother had returned home from Mannheim, she would not have died." Wolfgang had decided not to travel with either of these men, but he had been wrong not to inform his father of this wise change of mind in good time. Clearly, if he had done so, Leopold reminded him, his mother would not have died. Even Anna Maria herself bore some responsibility for her death for not taking proper care of herself and other instances of disobedience, but she had paid with her life. There were no excuses and no pardon for Wolfgang's faults. "I cannot forgive you for having neglected, during your very long stay in Mannheim, to go to Mainz" rather than taking "that stupid trip of yours to Kirchheim-Bolanden" with the Webers.[76] In short, even Wolfgang's passion for the Weber family, whom Leopold already abhorred, had obliged the mother not to let the son out of her sight and became one of the reasons for Anna Maria's death.

Wolfgang might have replied point by point, perhaps even have attempted to demonstrate to Leopold how much he himself had contributed to Anna Maria's tragic demise with his anxieties and his erroneous advice, but he preferred not to do so. His intuition had led him to some insights, however. He wrote his father on 31 July:

> First of all, I must tell you that my dear departed mother *had to die.* No doctor in the world could have saved her this time—for it was clearly the will of God; her time had come—and God wanted to take her to Himself. You think she put off being bled until it was too late? That may be. She did postpone it a little. But I rather agree with the people here who tried to dissuade her from being bled—and to persuade her to take a lavement. She would not, however, have this—and I did not venture to say anything, as I do not understand these things and consequently should have been to blame if it had not suited her.[77]

In any case, Wolfgang wrote less frequently to his father. In the two months between 18 July and 17 September 1778 Leopold sent his son eight letters, while Wolfgang sent his father only four. In reality Leopold's scorn of his son's musical innovation, his disapproval of Wolfgang's relationship with the Webers in 1777, and his bad feeling about Anna Maria's death led to Wolfgang's genuine and profound detachment from both his father and his sister. Nannerl lived with their father, under his strong authority, and would have found it difficult to disagree with him. Moreover, for her own personal reasons she suffered from competition with her younger but much greater brother.

Wolfgang's biographers have varied in their interpretation of his actions on the occasion of his mother's death. Let me limit my remarks to two scholars who disagree sharply: Wolfgang Hildesheimer, whose biography was published in 1977, and Maynard Solomon, who published his work in 1995. Hildesheimer judges that "Mozart's emotion" at the death of his mother, as he expressed it in the letter to Abbé Bullinger, "is kept within the limits of baroque conventions." Hildesheimer adds that the letter, "which Mozart wrote at two in the morning," reflects "an inadequate contact with the superficial necessities of life," regarding which "he always fled into the realm of the artificial and declamatory." As if that were not enough, Hildesheimer declares being disconcerted, after examination of the autograph letter, to find it "a calligraphic jewel, so beautiful one would think it had been intended for future admiring generations as an exemplary document of its special kind." Nor did the letter that Mozart wrote to his father on 31 July please Hildesheimer, because Mozart, after excusing himself for having to be brief, then went on for twelve long pages, "going into the minutest details . . . with cruel precision" to describe his mother's complaints, symptoms, and pains and the treatments administered, but without revealing "what the illness was."[78] Hildesheimer seems not to realize that if Wolfgang went into such detail, it was because his father asked him for particulars and because he felt the need to justify himself in light of his father's accusations. Hildesheimer seems equally unaware that in 1778 not only Wolfgang but the medical profession was incapable of saying "what the illness was."

Maynard Solomon, on the other hand, defends Wolfgang and severely criticizes Leopold. To his mind Wolfgang, who, among other things, had never been present at a death, was profoundly shaken with grief at the loss of his mother. And Leopold, who was aware of his own responsibility for having obliged the fifty-eight-year-old Anna Maria to follow their son on a difficult voyage, sought—this is still according to Solomon—to "shift the responsibility—to his wife, to God, and, primarily, to Wolfgang."[79] Solomon points out that in his letters Leopold began to harp on the possibility that Wolfgang, by his bad behavior, not only hastened his mother's death but put his only remaining parent's life in danger. Referring to himself as "a distressed soul," Leopold states, "You alone can save me from death."[80] Moreover, on 19 November he returned to the theme: "I hope that you, after your mother had to die so inappropriately in Paris, that you will not also have the furtherance of your father's death on your conscience."[81] (In the original letter, "inappropriately" is *mal à propos*.) In reality, Solomon points out, Wolfgang did not at all deserve his father's tirades: he had not caused his mother's death, he had not put his father's life in danger, he was not inept but was earning his living, and he had not reduced his father or his sister to poverty.

It is true that in some of the letters he wrote to his father immediately after Anna Maria's death Wolfgang might seem a bit disconcertingly abrupt when he shifts from the topic of her death to other, more worldly topics and even to frivolous matters. We should try to understand his state of mind, however. His mother had been placed at his side because his father did not trust him. Now that his mother was no more, he had to show Leopold that he had not lost his wits, was not in despair or depressed, and knew how to conduct himself wisely in the midst of the difficulties of this world. Moreover, he did not want to communicate his torment to his father for fear of increasing his father's nervousness and prompting further persecution on his father's part. On 9 July, six days after his mother's death, Mozart sent his father these words:

I have, indeed, suffered and wept enough—but what did it avail? So I have tried to console myself: and please do so too, my dear father, my dear sister! Weep, weep your fill, but take comfort at last. Remember that Almighty God willed it thus—and how can we rebel against Him? Let us rather pray to Him, and thank Him for His goodness, for she died a very happy death. In those distressing moments, there were three things that consoled me—my entire and steadfast submission to the will of God, and the sight of her very easy and beautiful death which made me feel that in a moment she had become so happy; for how much happier is she now than we are! Indeed I wished at that moment to depart with her. From this wish and longing proceeded finally my third source of consolation—the thought that she is not lost to us for ever—that we shall see her again—that we shall live together far more happily and blissfully than ever in this world. We do not yet know when it will be—but that does not disturb me; when God wills it, I am ready. Well, His heavenly and most holy will has been fulfilled. Let us therefore say a devout Paternoster for her soul and turn our thoughts to other matters, for all things have their appropriate time.[82]

Wolfgang was more serene than his father, perhaps because he had been at his mother's side. He knew that there was nothing to do to save her, and he felt that he had fulfilled his duty to the last. Thus he had nothing with which to reproach himself. Leopold, on the other hand, was anxious, agitated, and hardly at peace with himself.

# A Difficult Homecoming

## The Last Months in Paris (Summer 1778)

Soon after the death of his mother Mozart moved to the house of Madame d'Épinay and the Baron Grimm, in Chaussée d'Antin. "I have a pretty little room with a very pleasant view and, so far as my condition permits, I am happy," he reports.[1] Leopold had told him that his hosts were far from rich and it would be appropriate to find a way to recompense them. Leopold himself wrote to Baron Grimm to thank him directly, but especially to beg him, now that Anna Maria was dead, to take her place and keep an eye on Wolfgang. The baron responded on 27 July, refusing the responsibility. Unfortunately, Grimm's letter to Leopold has been lost, but some phrases from it are quoted in Leopold's letter to Wolfgang of 13 August. Leopold tells his son that the baron had declared himself too busy to look after him, and he transcribes Grimm's rather negative judgment of Wolfgang: according to Grimm, he was "too trusting, too inactive, too easy to catch, too little intent on the means that may lead to his fortune. To make an impression here one has to be artful, enterprising, daring." In Grimm's opinion, what Wolfgang needed to be successful was "but half his talent and twice as much shrewdness."[2] In other words, Grimm thought Mozart totally incapable of finding a niche for himself in Paris. In Grimm's opinion, there were in theory—but only in theory—two paths open to him. The first would be to survive by giving harpsichord lessons, but the profession of teacher, aside from being exhausting, had the disadvantage of not suiting the young maestro, who wanted to dedicate himself wholly to composition. The second would be to become a famous composer, but in France at least, the majority of the public understood nothing of music, looked only to names it already knew, and was currently "ridiculously" divided in two camps, one supporting Piccinni and the other Gluck. Wolfgang would find it very difficult to navigate between them. Leopold adds that Piccinni and Gluck would undoubtedly prevent him from getting a commission for an opera. What Grimm reported about the hostility of musical circles in Paris was well founded, as Wolfgang was aware. It was true that the Concert Spirituel had commissioned him to write a symphony, but that was not enough. It was true that he had been offered a post as organist to the court of Versailles, but the offer had not appealed to him.

Thus, after the death of Anna Maria, everyone—Leopold, Grimm, and, above all, Wolfgang himself—was coming to the conclusion that it would be better for Wolfgang to abandon Paris. He himself was anxious to go back to Germany to embrace his beloved Aloysia. Grimm was eager to be rid of a guest who created problems for him. Leopold wanted his son to return to Salzburg, and he was already working behind the scenes, with the aid of Countess Maria Franziska Wallis, the sister of the prince-bishop, and Countess Maria Antonia Lodron, another member of Salzburg high society, to have Wolfgang readmitted into the service at the court of Colloredo.

That Mozart was still thinking of marrying Aloysia can be seen in various allusions in his letters. On 3 July 1778, the very day of his mother's death, he wrote to his father, "I have a project in my mind for the success of which I daily pray to Him. If it is His divine will, it will succeed, and if not, then I am content also—at least I shall have done my part. When all this has been set going and if all turns out as I wish, you too must do your part, or the whole work would be incomplete—I trust to your kindness to do so."[3] On 7 August, he wrote to Abbé Bullinger, in full expectation that the Abbé would show the letter to Leopold, "I placed my entire confidence in him [Leopold] and trusted completely to his fatherly care, love, and goodness. I feel sure that *some day* he will not deny me a request on which the whole happiness and peace of my life depend and which will certainly be quite fair and reasonable."[4]

But the best evidence of the love between Mozart and Aloysia and his affection for the entire Weber family is found in a letter that Mozart wrote to Fridolin Weber. From it we gather that the two corresponded frequently. Mozart had written him on 27 June, 29 June, and 3 July, and it is a real pity that all of the letters have been lost. From his letter of 29 July (which, fortunately, still exists) it is clear that at that point Wolfgang's feelings were warmer toward Fridolin than toward his father. "My friend," Mozart writes, "if I had the money which many a man, who does not earn it, squanders so disgracefully—how gladly would I then help you!"[5] He explains to Fridolin that he could undoubtedly find work with the Concert Spirituel, but there were no contracts for Aloysia. Thus he discouraged Weber from moving to Paris. He himself, he declared, hoped to leave as soon as possible to look for work in Mannheim or Mainz. On 30 July Mozart sent a letter to Aloysia expressing his eagerness to see her again. He writes to her in a somewhat pompous Italian, rather like the style of an opera libretto: "My condition and my situation will be the happiest on that day when I shall have the infinite pleasure of serving you again and embracing you with all my heart. This too is all that I can long for and desire, and my only consolation and my sole comfort lie in this hope and desire."[6]

There was little comfort left in Paris. Even Wolfgang's relationship with Grimm had gone sour, a situation to which Leopold had contributed by passing on to his son the baron's negative opinion of him. A break soon followed, among other reasons, because Grimm had joined the Piccinni camp and had sought in vain to persuade Wolfgang to do the same. "In a word," Mozart wrote to his father on 11 September, "he is of the Italian faction—he is false and is even trying to down me. This seems incredible, does it not? But it is true, and here is the proof: I opened my whole heart to him as a true friend—and good use he has made of it! He always gave me bad advice."[7]

Wolfgang went so far as to say that, before she died, his mother had told him that she found Grimm much changed. Madame d'Épinay, on the other hand, had "a better heart" than her companion. But even the room that Madame d'Épinay had so kindly made available to him and that he had found so agreeable in July now no longer pleased him: "The room I am living in belongs to her and not to him. It is the sickroom—that is, if anyone in the house is ill, he is put up there; it has nothing to recommend it, except the view; only four bare walls; no cupboard or anything." In the same letter of 11 September, Mozart adds that Grimm spoke to him "harshly, boorishly, and stupidly" and had practically thrown him out. "He makes out that I must leave Paris in a week—*he is in such a hurry*. I have told him that this is impossible—and have given him my reasons." When Grimm responded that it was Leopold's desire that he leave, Wolfgang retorted, "Excuse me, in his last letter he said that he would let me know in his next when I was to leave."[8] Mozart wanted to have the time to compose another six trios, collect some money he was owed, and correct the proofs of some of his sonatas. But the decision to leave had in any case been taken.

Mozart's biographers usually describe this Paris sojourn as one of the most unhappy times in his entire life. It is true that he had many difficulties to confront, not to speak of the terrible trial of his mother's death. These difficulties and his unhappiness, however, contributed much to Mozart's maturity: it was in Paris that he finally found himself, for the first time in his life, completely alone and his own man. Confirmation of his psychological and artistic growth can be seen in the works that he composed in the French capital. These were not many, given the scarcity of patrons and the hostility of musical circles, but they were almost all of the highest quality. The *Paris* Symphony (K. 297/300a), composed for Jean Legros and the Concert Spirituel, has already been mentioned, but it was also in Paris that Mozart composed the well-known Concerto for Flute and Harp (K. 299/297c, which Hildesheimer, somewhat astonishingly, calls "one of his insignificant works of this period").[9] There can be no doubt, however, regarding the quality of the sonatas for violin and piano (K. 304/300c, 306/300l), the variations for piano (K. 353/300f, 354/299a), and the five piano sonatas (K. 310/300d, 330/300h, 331/300i, 332/300k, 333/315c), almost all of which were composed during Anna Maria Mozart's illness or after her death. The sonata K. 332/300k in particular displays striking innovations in the first movement. The sonata K. 310/300d, which is often considered the first of Mozart's "tragic" works, was completed on 6 July 1778, three days after the death of Anna Maria. Perhaps all that he had undergone in Paris had something to do with the quality and force of nearly all of Mozart's Paris compositions.

Obviously, this music was thought "difficult" at the time. By composing in his own way, Wolfgang demonstrated that he was acting on the basis of his criteria, not on the suggestions of his father, who never lost an opportunity to tell his son that only music that was easy to follow permitted a composer to make a career. Leopold wrote to his son on 27 August:

> [Georg] Kreusser went [to Mainz] at the right time, that is, just after Jacobi, the Konzertmeister, had died. His easy symphonies, which are pleasant to listen to, were a success, so that he was immediately appointed Konzertmeister. At present he is working hard to fit himself for the post of Kapellmeister. I cannot forgive you for having neglected, during your very long stay in Mannheim, *to go to Mainz*. If you consider everything impartially, you will have to acknowledge that you have very seldom followed my advice and precepts.[10]

In other words, if Wolfgang continued to "engage [his] thoughts with mere idle dreams," he would never get ahead. "You are forever writing about the embarrassed circumstances of the Weber family. But tell me, how, if you have any common sense, can you entertain the idea that you could be the person capable of making the fortune of these people?" Leopold had already reminded his son that the debts he had incurred with his mother in Paris would lead him to poverty, and here he asks, "Are our resources sufficient to succor a family with six children? Who can do this?—I?—You? You, who have not yet been able to help your family?" Moreover Wolfgang's notion that Aloysia could earn a thousand florins a year was ridiculous: "Where, pray are the Courts, where is there a single Court, which will give a thousand gulden to a singer?" (Here Leopold was wrong, however, because Aloysia proved capable of earning large sums of money.) Leopold ends this tirade with a warning: "Unless you turn your present circumstances to profit and advantage to yourself, you will spend your life in ineffectiveness, remain unknown and poor, ruin yourself and me and thus help nobody."[11]

On 31 August Leopold announced to his son that Archbishop Colloredo had agreed to take him back into his service, permitting him to travel to other cities if he obtained commissions for operas there. The yearly stipend would be 1,000 florins—to be divided in equal parts between the father and the son.[12] Yet on 28 December 1778 Wolfgang had not returned, and as a further incentive Leopold wrote him that the 1,000 florins would be divided instead, giving 400 to the father and 600 to the son. In 1779, when Wolfgang did finally return home, Leopold (with the consent of the archbishop) increased his own stipend but reduced his son's to 450 florins, most of which he siphoned off to help repay the family's debts.

Leopold cried poverty but, as we see from a letter that he wrote to Wolfgang on 31 August 1778, he and Nannerl lived in Salzburg in an eight-room apartment with an attached stables and kept a large carriage. He was thinking of selling the carriage and replacing it with a smaller but more fashionable conveyance, perhaps a *Würstl* (literally, a sausage).[13] Maynard Solomon's opinion is that Leopold "had accumulated large sums of money," thanks to Wolfgang, but "feared to let anyone know of his wealth, lest others seek to take it from him. . . . He genuinely dreaded poverty and even believed that he was on the verge of impoverishment."[14] It is thus possible that the very debts that Leopold claimed to be laboring under were an invention of his or a strategy for deceiving people about his claimed poverty—his son first among them, in the aim of creating a guilt complex in Wolfgang and keeping him tied to him. On 19 November 1778 Leopold accused Wolfgang of having spent, in the fourteen months that he was traveling with his mother, the sizable sum of 863 florins, and he demanded payment, without taking it into account that the great expenses for the voyage had been decided in common, that half of the sum regarded Anna Maria, not Wolfgang, and that when he was a child Wolfgang had earned figures a good deal higher than 863 florins, which his father had pocketed.[15] Leopold returned to the charge in his next letter, dated 23 November, but raised the sum that Wolfgang should repay to him to 1,000 florins.[16]

Leopold reiterated his demand that Wolfgang return to Salzburg. But Wolfgang was recalcitrant. Above all, he was not fond of Salzburg and felt that if he returned he would risk ruining his career. He had already expressed a condemnation of his native city in a letter of 9 July 1778, where he explains that "one of my chief reasons for detesting Salzburg" was "those coarse, slovenly, dissolute court musicians."[17] He goes into greater detail on 11 September:

> The only thing that disgusts me about Salzburg is the impossibility of mixing freely with the people and the low estimation in which the musicians are held there—and—that the archbishop has no confidence in the experience of intelligent people, who have seen the world. For I assure you that people who do not travel (I mean those who cultivate the arts and learning) are indeed miserable creatures; and I protest that unless the archbishop allows me to travel every second year, I can't possibly accept the engagement. A fellow of mediocre talent will remain a mediocrity, whether he travels or not; but one of superior talent (which without impiety I cannot deny that I possess) will go to seed, if he always remains in the same place.[18]

Wolfgang was also less than eager to return to Salzburg because, as he explains in the same letter, his relations with Paris and the Parisians were improving. He felt that success might come to him there, after all: "I am now fairly well known, or—rather, people know me, even if I don't know *them.* I have made quite a name for myself by my two symphonies, the second of which was performed on the 8th."[19] These two symphonies were the *Paris* Symphony (K. 297/300a), which we have already seen, and another one (perhaps the spurious K. 311a/C11.05), which we cannot evaluate because it has been lost. Wolfgang's third reason for not wanting to return to Salzburg was the obvious one that he would have preferred to rejoin the Webers, in particular his beloved Aloysia. There is a fourth possible reason: we cannot exclude the notion that in spite of so many declarations of his affection for his father, Wolfgang had begun to detest him, and perhaps his sister as well. Why, then, should he go back and live with them? After the death of Anna Maria, and after the bitter epistolary exchange that we have seen, the family equilibrium had been upset forever.

Leopold sought nevertheless to persuade Wolfgang, using all the weapons he had at his disposal. He tried to instill a sense of guilt in his son, accusing him of wanting to reduce his father and his sister to poverty; worse, he accused him of intended parricide. He also tried to use blandishments, pointing out the supposed advantages of a sojourn in provincial Salzburg, seeming not to realize how insignificant these advantages would be in his son's eyes. You will not be far from Munich, he reminded Wolfgang on 3 September, where you might be able to put on an opera, and you can always send your compositions to the Paris publishers, thus earning you money and making you famous. He painted a rosy picture of life in Salzburg: "You will certainly have enough to entertain you because, if we are not obliged to pay back even the last *Kreuzer,* everything will be fine. During Carnival we can go to all the municipal balls. Actors from Munich arrive at the end of September and stay through the whole winter, until Lent, to perform in comedies and *Singspiele.* Every Sunday we amuse ourselves with target shoots, and if we then want to go out in *compagnia,* that is our choice."[20] Leopold was trying to persuade his son to be content with little, while the son, by this time, felt the magic fire of greatness within him.

### Return to Salzburg: Four Months of Travel (September 1778–January 1779)

On 26 September 1778 Wolfgang left Paris for Germany. His project had been to rent a cabriolet, a small one-horse carriage with one pair of wheels that was all the rage: a closed vehicle with glass windows, it could provide rapid transport for two people of normal weight. Baron Grimm, who must have been sick of his guest and was not a rich man, did not give him the time to make arrangements for such luxurious transportation and obliged him to travel in a very slow but less costly coach. Wolfgang was furious, and when he wrote his father from Nancy on 3 October he expressed his rage, maligning the baron's intelligence: "He sent me off by this slow conveyance simply to save money, without ever considering that, as I should have continually to be making use of inns, my expenses would be just the same. . . . It was his own money which he saved, and not mine, as he paid for my journey, but not for my keep; whereas, had I stayed eight or ten days longer in Paris, I should have been able to arrange for my journey myself and much more comfortably."[21]

The maddeningly slow coach, which took over a week to cover the approximately two hundred fifty miles between Paris and Nancy, forced Mozart to keep to a rugged schedule: "We were off every morning at four o'clock, so we had to get up at three; and twice I had the honor of getting up at one o'clock, as the carriage was to leave at two."[22] He went on to remind his father that he never could sleep in a carriage, and because he was exhausted he had determined to go on to Strasbourg in another conveyance. In reality he stopped in Nancy for a few days, without telling his father, and arrived in Strasbourg only in mid-October.

On 17 October Wolfgang gave a first concert in Strasbourg in the presence of Prince Max von Zweibrücken—without an orchestra, to cut costs. It was well received, but earned him no more than three louis d'or. On 24 October he gave a second concert, with an orchestra this time, but he ended up earning no more because the theater was half empty. "All who were present loudly and publicly abused their fellow-citizens—and I told them all, that if I could have reasonably supposed that so few people would have come, I should gladly have given the concert gratis merely for the pleasure of seeing the theater well filled."[23]

Wolfgang borrowed eight louis d'or from Johann Schertz, the Strasbourg representative of the Haffners, wholesale merchants in Salzburg (it was in honor of Haffner's daughter that he had composed the *Haffner Serenade* [K. 250/248b] in 1776). Wolfgang justified the loan, saying it was "just by way of precaution, for one can never know what may happen on a journey, and a bird in the hand is always worth two in the bush."[24] On 31 October he gave a third concert, again with an orchestra, and again, not well attended. Strasbourg was clearly not his city, but then, Wolfgang was not an expert in organizing concerts. He had given many and in many cities of Europe, but organization had always been left to the able Leopold.

Leopold lived in great anxiety for days because he was not receiving news from his son. On 19 October he wrote that he was upset to hear from some merchants in Strasbourg that Wolfgang had not even arrived there yet. He hoped that his son had lingered in Nancy (as was indeed the case), but the very idea that Wolfgang was ill or even dead threw him into a "dreadful state of anxiety." He writes his son that he had not slept for four "ghastly" nights, adding, "I have confessed and received Communion together with your sister and have prayed God most earnestly to preserve you. Our excellent Bullinger prays daily for you at Holy Mass." Travel was in fact full of perils, and Leopold reminded Wolfgang that three days before, two French merchants had been attacked by highway robbers in Bavaria. He ends this tragic letter saying, "I can hardly await the hour when I shall see you" and signing himself, "your very anxious father."[25] He takes the opportunity to stress the fact that, for a number of reasons, there were few good opportunities for work in Munich. The message was: Why on earth continue to wander about from one city to another instead of heading with all speed for Salzburg?

Mozart attempted to calm his father with a letter sent from Strasbourg a week later, on 26 October, which reached Salzburg after a few days. He reports how much admired he was in Strasbourg, adding, with a certain ingenuity, "You cannot think how much they esteem and love me here. They say that everything about me is so distinguished—that I am so composed—and polite—and have such excellent manners."[26] The Silbermanns, famous organ builders, were a Strasbourg firm, and two members of the family came to call on Mozart as soon as they learned of his presence in their city, after which they took him to a number of churches to try out organs they had manufactured. Wolfgang went so far as to tell his father that if the bishop, Cardinal Louis Constantin de Rohan (who was very ill at the time) had died, he might have gotten an appointment as an organist. Leopold, who was hoping for concrete facts and not unsubstantial hypotheses, must have been furious all over again.

On 3 November, against Leopold's wishes, Wolfgang left for Mannheim, arriving there on 6 November. He remained there for a month. Clearly, Wolfgang was doing everything possible to delay his return to Salzburg and to find work elsewhere. The Weber family, of whom he was so fond, had left Mannheim and moved to Munich, however, as had other musical families. In fact, Karl Theodor, the elector of Palatine, transferred his court to Munich soon after he inherited the Duchy of Bavaria upon the death of Maximilian III. All the musical life of the two cities was turned upside down by this transfer, and even the extraordinary orchestra of Mannheim suffered from it. The director, Johann Christian Cannabich, soon moved to Munich as well.

During his stay in Mannheim, Wolfgang began to compose music for a "duodrama" *Semiramis* (K. 315e/Anh.11), by Baron Otto von Gemmingen, an influential Freemason, a work in all probability based on the tragedy of the same name by Voltaire. Mozart explained to his father what a "duodrama" was: "You know, of course, that there is no singing in it, only recitation, to which the music is like a sort of obbligato accompaniment to a recitative. Now and then words are spoken while the music goes on, and this produces the finest effect."[27] Mozart was promised forty louis d'or to write the music for this play, but he may never have finished it, and the manuscript score, if there was one, has been lost. On 12 November he wrote to his father about *Semiramis* and the welcome he had received in Mannheim in such glowing terms that we can presume that his words aroused still further agitation and jealousy in Leopold:

> I arrived here safely on the 6th and pleasantly surprised all my good friends. God be praised that I am back again in my beloved Mannheim! I assure you, if you were here, you would say the same. I am staying with Madame Cannabich, who, with her family and all my good friends here, was almost beside herself with joy at seeing me again. . . . Since I came here I have not been able to lunch at home once, as there is a regular scramble to have me. In a word, Mannheim loves me as much as I love Mannheim.[28]

In mid-November Wolfgang began to compose a concerto for piano and violin (K. 315f/Anh.56), which he failed to complete, however, and the score remains a fragment. Wolfgang, who had always worked tenaciously, was obviously going through an inconclusive, unfocused phase. He was twenty-two years old, and for the first time in his life, was enjoying the pleasure of relaxing and being able to do what he wanted to with no one at his side to supervise or dominate him.

Leopold was in despair. "Mon très cher fils!" he writes in his letter of 19 November, "Really, I don't know what to say to you. I shall go mad or die of a decline. The very recollection of all the projects which since your departure from Salzburg you have formed and communicated to me is enough to drive me crazy. They have all amounted to proposals, empty words ending in *nothing whatever.*" He goes on to accuse Wolfgang of throwing money out of the window and draws up a list of all of his debts.[29] He returned to the charge in another letter dated 23 November:

> I am tired of your projects, thanks to which you render vain the best plans that I have so often made, a fact that you do not understand because you cannot—or you will not—reflect with a cool head and without prejudice. . . . Two things seem to be turning your head and altogether preventing you from thinking out matters sensibly. The first and chief one is your love for Mlle Weber, to which I am not at all opposed. I was not against it when her father was poor, so why should I be so now, *when she can make your happiness*—though you cannot make hers?[30]

In short, Leopold never missed a chance to wound his son by treating him as worthless.

Leopold then goes on to the second reason for Wolfgang's refusal to think straight: his obstinate determination not to live in Salzburg. Seeking to demonstrate that by returning to serve the Salzburg court, Wolfgang would have been able to travel freely to Italy and even elsewhere, Leopold writes, "This service is absolutely indispensable, unless you have the shameful and vile thought of casting your worried father into dishonor and mockery: your father, who has sacrificed to his children every hour of his life in order to gain credit and honor, given that I am not able to pay a debt that amounts, in all, to 1,000 florins, if you do not facilitate repayment with the earnings from your stipend in such a way that I can reimburse 400 florins per year, continuing to live magnificently with you two."[31] This was the same 1,000 florins that Leopold mentions in his letter of 19 November as Wolfgang's accumulated debt to him. Leopold also reproached his son with not reading his letters with proper attention, with letting himself be cheated, and with insufficient knowledge of the ways of the world.

On 9 December 1778 Mozart left Mannheim in the company of Abbot Coelestin Angelsprugger, the superior of the Abbey of Kaisheim, the oldest Cistercian abbey in the diocese of Augsburg. The party arrived at Kaisheim on 13 December, where Wolfgang stayed as a guest of the abbey for ten days or so. He left on 24 December, arriving in Munich on Christmas day, when he was finally reunited with the Weber family, Aloysia in particular. He even lodged with the Webers, all of whom welcomed him warmly—except for Aloysia, who was cool to him and rejected his approaches. It is usually said that Aloysia behaved as she did because she was disappointed that Wolfgang, after having promised her the moon—that is, a splendid musical career in Italy or in Paris—came back from France with empty hands, bringing her as a gift only a new virtuoso aria for soprano, the famous "Popoli di Tessaglia"/"Io non chiedo eterni dei" (K. 316/300b). It is probable, however, that there were other reasons behind the sentimental crisis; the situation is difficult to reconstruct because the letters between Wolfgang and Aloysia have been lost, with the exception of the one letter that Wolfgang wrote her, in Italian, from Paris on 30 July 1778, which we have already quoted and which is not much help for reconstructing their relationship. Aloysia was seventeen; she had not seen Wolfgang for months, and she may have met someone else. Three years later Wolfgang labeled her "a false, malicious person and a coquette."[32] On the other hand, just one day before he left for Munich, where he knew he would see Aloysia, Wolfgang had sent a letter full of obscenities to his famous "little cousin," Anna Thekla Mozart, with whom he had established an intimate friendship in the past. He had even invited her to come to Munich.

Some sort of break had occurred between Wolfgang and Aloysia, and Wolfgang went to lodge with Johann Baptist Becke, a friend and a flutist in the chapel orchestra of the court. He soon recovered from this sentimental setback, and on 31 December he responded energetically to his father's urging, stating his decision not to return to Salzburg immediately. He told Leopold that he wanted to remain another few days in Munich to attend the performance of *Alceste*, an opera by Anton Schweitzer, and in fact he did so. But he also hinted at his unhappiness. Given his father's past reproaches about his "gay dreams," he defended his right to give in to dreams that, if they had come true, would have turned a life that was "more sad than cheerful" into a "more endurable" one.[33] While he was in Munich, Wolfgang went with Cannabich on 7 January 1779 to call on the princess-electress, Elisabetta Maria Augusta of Bavaria, bringing her as a gift the Paris edition of his six sonatas for violin and piano (K. 301–303/293a-c, 304/300c, 305/293d, 306/300l), all of them dedicated to her.

On 8 January Wolfgang wrote his father to tell him that he was looking forward to returning to him and to his sister, but not to Salzburg. "I swear to you on my honor," he states, "that I cannot bear Salzburg or its inhabitants (I mean, the natives of Salzburg). Their language — their manners are quite intolerable to me." Later in the letter he adds:

> My little cousin is here — and why? Well, to please me, her cousin! That indeed is the ostensible reason. But — well, we shall talk about this in Salzburg — and on this account I should very much like [her to] come home with me! . . . She would like to come. So, if it would really give you pleasure to have her in your house, be so kind as to write at once to your brother, saying that it is all right. When you see her and get to know her, you will certainly like her, for she is a favorite with everyone.[34]

The body of the letter is followed by a series of postscripts, first by Anna Thekla, who humbly asks her uncle to welcome her in Salzburg, then by Wolfgang, who signs himself "votre invariable cochon" (still your same old pig). Leopold gathered from Wolfgang's allusions to his sadness, from the return of the "little cousin," and from information that the flutist Becke may have sent to Salzburg that the danger from Aloysia was now a thing of the past. But there was a new danger: the "little cousin." Leopold had many weapons he could use, and he did. At first he made the best of a bad deal, however, given that Wolfgang had to be treated with care and persuaded to return to Salzburg. On 11 January, therefore, Leopold invited his son to come back immediately, traveling with a Salzburg business-man, Joseph Franz Gschwendtner, in his carriage. He explains to his son that he had already told everyone that Wolfgang would be arriving with Gschwendtner, and he did not care to look like a liar. In his letter Leopold does not object to the idea of Anna Thekla's coming to Salzburg, but he in-dicates that she should wait for her father's approval and come on the mail coach from Munich on 20 January.

Wolfgang did indeed leave Munich on 13 January or thereabouts, ar-riving in Salzburg a few days later. We do not know his precise departure or arrival dates, nor do we know whether he traveled with his cousin after all, or whether she arrived later. A room had been prepared for her in the Salzburg house, and it seems that Anna Thekla spent some days as her un-cle's guest. It is certain, however, that she did not stay long. According to Maynard Solomon, Mozart "twice betrayed the Bäsle—first by preferring Aloysia and then by failing to stand against his father in early 1778, lead-ing to her humiliation and withdrawal."[35]

## In the Service of Archbishop Colloredo Again
## (January 1779–November 1780)

Toward the middle of January 1779 Wolfgang humbly begged Archbishop Colloredo to be taken into his service as court organist. The archbishop deigned to grant the request of his restless subject and named him organ-ist, charging him with furnishing new compositions to the court. His an-nual salary was to be 450 florins. Wolfgang pocketed a good deal less, how-ever, as his father took care to confiscate nearly the entire sum. Many biographers assert that Wolfgang, once he had returned home penniless to a father who crushed him and to a city that he disliked, became so dispirited and melancholy that he lost all taste for writing music. Wolf-gang himself stated later, in a letter dated 26 May 1781, that he could never settle down to work in Salzburg because he was never happy there.[36] In re-ality, during the almost two years that he spent in Salzburg after his trip to Paris, Mozart continued to produce music despite everything, and he probably even managed not to be too sad. He had many resources and was highly capable of adapting to circumstances. Nor had he lost hope of flee-ing at the earliest opportunity.

The list of major works that Mozart composed during this period stands as proof that he had not lost all capacity for producing music. First of all, there is the Mass in C, called the *Coronation* Mass (K. 317), a work dated 23 March 1779 composed for the cathedral of Salzburg for the feast of the Coronation of the Virgin Mary. Between January and March, Mozart wrote both the Concerto for Two Pianos (K. 365/316a) and one of his loveliest sonatas, for violin and piano (K. 378/317d). Between April and July he wrote two fine symphonies: the Symphony in G (K. 318), a short work but an innovative one, and, especially, the Symphony in B-flat (K. 319), which has an extremely attractive minuet and finale. Between spring and summer he composed a divertimento for horns and strings (K. 334/320b). On 3 August he finished the *Posthorn* Serenade (K. 320), and during the summer of 1779 he wrote a genuine masterpiece, the Sinfonia Concertante for Violin and Viola (K. 364/320d). Thereafter, it is true that his creative capacities seemed to diminish, but only relatively.

As we have seen, in his letter dated 3 September 1778 Leopold had mentioned among the attractions of Salzburg the yearly presence of ac-tors from Munich who arrived in late September and stayed through the winter, until Lent, offering plays and operettas. During Wolfgang's resi-dence in Salzburg the itinerant company of Johann Heinrich Boehm, a thirty-nine-year-old actor and impresario, did indeed arrive in Salzburg sometime in April or May 1779, returning in September to stay for several months. There were some forty artists in the company, and with the addi-tion of local musicians, they performed theatrical works with music, singspiels, comedies, and tragedies. Mozart became good friends with Boehm, and it was for his troupe that he wrote the chorus and entr'acte music of *Thamos, König in Ägypten* (K. 345/336a), a heroic drama of Ma-sonic inspiration set in Heliopolis in the age of the pharaohs, which in some ways anticipated *The Magic Flute*. He also composed either for Boehm's troupe or that of Emanuel Schikaneder (librettist of *The Magic Flute)* music for *Zaide* (K. 344), a singspiel the original title of which was *Das Serail, oder, Die unvermutete Zusammenkunft zwischen Vater, Tochter und Sohn* (The Seraglio, or, The Unexpected Encounter between a Father, a Daughter, and a Son). The action of this work, with a text by Andreas Schachtner, takes place in the harem of the sultan, Soliman, thus antici-pating *The Abduction from the Seraglio*. There is even a grumpy guardian named Osmin, a bass, who much resembles the Osmin in the later opera. Although Mozart never wrote the music for the concluding scene of *Zaide*, the portions he did complete have a playing time of about two hours. *Zaide* is an unbalanced work, but it has some splendid music, and some claim it is the most beautiful incomplete opera of the eighteenth century.

Boehm never produced *Thamos* or *Zaide*. He used the incidental music for *Thamos* for another theatrical work, while *Zaide* was forgotten until 1866, when it had its first performance in Frankfurt. In 1779 Mozart and Boehm did collaborate, however, to produce a German version of *La finta giardiniera*, an opera that Wolfgang had written, with success but little fortune, four years earlier. First performed in Augsburg on 1 May 1780, the work long remained in Boehm's repertory, where it had many performances.

In March 1780 Wolfgang wrote the Missa solemnis (K. 337), the Benedictus of which Alfred Einstein has called "the most striking and revolutionary movement in all Mozart's Masses."[37] This was the last mass that Mozart completed, given that the Mass in C Minor (K. 427/417a) does not contain a Credo, and the 1791 Requiem was completed by others. During the month of August, Mozart completed his Symphony in C (K. 338), a highly dramatic work, even in the final movement, written as a tarantella.

In short, it does not seem to me that Mozart was dozing during those twenty-two months in Salzburg. Between masses, concertos, sonatas, symphonies, and demanding works like *Thamos* and *Zaide*, he was rather active. Moreover, after Boehm's, another theatrical company arrived in Salzburg, that of Emanuel Schikaneder, who became a good friend of Wolfgang's and of the Mozart family. Meeting Schikaneder, a very generous and likable person, was an important moment in Wolfgang's life, also because he was to become the librettist of *The Magic Flute* and played the part of Papageno in the premiere production. Thanks to his friendship with Boehm and with Schikaneder, Wolfgang frequented actors, singers, and dancers, and we cannot exclude the possibility that he consoled himself for the loss of Anna Thekla and Aloysia with one or more of them. Aloysia had obtained a fabulous contract with the Vienna opera, and she and her entire family moved to that city in September 1779. Fridolin, the head of the family and at one time a good friend of Wolfgang's, died suddenly a month later.

The most important and most conclusive event during Wolfgang's time in Salzburg occurred during the summer of 1780, when Karl Theodor, the prince-elector, commissioned him to write an *opera seria* to be performed in Munich during Carnival 1781. This opera was *Idomeneo,* and Wolfgang set to work on it in October. He respectfully requested the permission of the prince-bishop, Colloredo, to go to Munich to put the finishing touches on the opera and see it through production. Colloredo could hardly refuse him, because the prince-elector of Munich outranked him. During this same period, Aloysia Weber, now twenty years old and an established singer, married the actor and painter Joseph Lange, a man ten years her senior, in Vienna. Aloysia was pregnant by Lange, and he had promised to pay seven hundred florins a year to Caecilia Weber, her mother. By marrying Aloysia, Joseph Lange was in effect taking a notable source of income away from his mother-in-law. We do not know when or how Wolfgang came to know of Aloysia's marriage with Lange, which took place on 31 October. Five days later Wolfgang was on his way to Munich for the production of *Idomeneo* and on his way to glory.

# Winning Freedom

## Idomeneo, re di Creta (K. 366)
### (November 1780–March 1781)

On 5 November 1780 Wolfgang climbed up into the post coach, waving good-bye to his father and his sister. This was the first time that he had left Salzburg alone. He could not have known it as he was leaving, but he was to return to his city of birth only once, with Constanze his wife, during the summer of 1783, and then just for two months. The fame he was to win in Munich thanks to Idomeneo would contribute to a permanent change in his life and a definitive separation from his father and from Salzburg. It is curious to note that the libretto of Idomeneo presents a family situation with which Wolfgang could easily have identified: as the opera opens we learn that a son, Prince Idamante, is supposed to be sacrificed for his father, but at the end it is the father, King Idomeneo, who must sacrifice himself and abdicate in favor of his son.

Mozart reached Munich at one o'clock in the afternoon on 6 November, after a decidedly rough trip. He describes it to Leopold in these terms: "That carriage jolted the very souls out of our bodies—and the seats were as hard as stone! After we left Wasserburg I really believed that I should never bring my behind to Munich intact. It became quite sore and no doubt was fiery red. For two whole stages I sat with my hands dug into the upholstery and my behind suspended in the air. But enough of this; it is all over now, though it will serve me as a warning rather to go on foot than to drive in a mail coach."[1] This description of his discomfort probably contains a reproach to his father, who—just like Baron Grimm in September 1778—obliged Wolfgang to use an economical but uncomfortable means of transport to save money.

Fortunately, however, as soon as he arrived in Munich, Wolfgang was immediately thrust into the vortex of the social and musical life of the city. According to his wife Constanze, speaking some years later, the period in Munich during which he completed *Idomeneo* was one of the happiest in his life.[2] He found everything inviting: "So far," he wrote his father on 15 November, "I have not lunched once at home—and consequently have had no expenses save for friseur, barber and laundress—and breakfast."[3] He went to the theater and to concerts. He dined with Countess Maria Josepha von Paumgarten, who had served as intermediary in procuring the commission for *Idomeneo* for him. Or he dined at the house of Count Joseph Anton Seeau, the superintendent of the court theater, to discuss the production of the opera. On 12 November he was presented "en passant" to the prince-elector, Karl Theodor, who expressed his pleasure at seeing Mozart again, clapped him on the shoulder, and assured Wolfgang that he had no doubt of the opera's success: "A piano piano, si va lontano" (little by little will get you far) Mozart adds, in Italian.[4]

Mozart had many friends in Munich, and a good number of them were involved in *Idomeneo*. There was Johann Christian Cannabich, who was to conduct the opera, but Mozart also knew several of the singers: the tenor Anton Raaff, who had often come to see Wolfgang and his mother in Paris, and Dorothea and Elisabeth Wendling, mother and daughter, both sopranos. Wolfgang had enjoyed their company as early as 1777, even though Leopold had severely criticized them because Elisabeth, who was twenty-five at that time, was said to be the lover of the then prince-elector, the fifty-year-old Maximilian III.

The subject of the opera had been chosen by the court, and the Abbé Giambattista Varesco, the court chaplain in Salzburg, was selected to write an Italian libretto based on a French tragedy, Antoine Danchet's *Idoménée*. Mozart discussed Varesco's libretto with Count Seeau, the superintendent, but above all, he consulted with Leopold, who had remained in Salzburg but acted as an intermediary with Varesco. Thanks to the correspondence between Wolfgang and Leopold, we possess detailed documentation regarding the genesis of the opera and all the changes made in it up to the very last minute. As the end of their work together drew closer, relations between Leopold and Varesco reflect a predictable tension. In a letter to Wolfgang dated 4 January 1781, Leopold writes that Varesco was "horribly angry" and that he "said the most foolish things, as Italians or half-Italians do."[5] (In reality, both of Varesco's parents were Italian.) At Leopold's suggestion, Varesco's text was translated into German by Andreas Schachtner, the librettist of *Zaide* and also a Salzburger. In that way, listeners who did not know Italian could follow the opera.

Not only Varesco, but some of the singers as well proved to be a hand-ful. It was not the excellent tenor, Domenico de' Panzacchi, who caused difficulty, nor the two sopranos, Dorothea and Elisabeth Wendling, who declared themselves delighted with their parts. But the celebrated Raaff, the sixty-six-year-old tenor, who expressed enthusiasm about the opera, often asked Mozart to make changes in his arias. Mozart writes in a letter dated 15 November, "The man is old and can no longer show off in such an aria as that in Act II—'Fuor del mar ho un mar nel seno.'" Almost as if he were sorry to have said so, he adds, "As for Raaff, he is my best and dear-est friend!"[6] Still, he returned to the topic in a later letter: "He is indeed a worthy and thoroughly honest fellow! But he clings to old habits—it is enough to make you sweat through seven shirts. Writing for him is thus a tough job—or, if you prefer, a very easy one, on the condition of writing him banal arias."[7] The other singer who caused problems was the castrato, Vincenzo Dal Prato, who was young but inexperienced. He ran out of breath in the middle of an aria, and Mozart complained in his letter of 15 November, "I shall have to teach [him] the whole opera. He has no no-tion how to sing a cadenza effectively, and his voice is so uneven!"[8] Dal Prato's contract was for only one year, and Mozart was aware that the singer would be replaced when it ran out, but still he continued to criticize him.

To complete the list of his problems, while Mozart was writing and re-hearsing *Idomeneo*, he was suffering from a rather bad cold that obliged him to stay in his lodgings for several days and sapped his energy. Luckily, he was in Munich, not in Salzburg, where his father would have insisted that he be bled. In a letter of 4 December the anxious Leopold, a physician manqué, offered his son a long list of therapeutic suggestions:

> That your cold should have become worse after the rehearsal is only natural, for, owing to the concentration upon *hearing* and *seeing*, all the nerves of the head become excited and strained, and eagerness and attention extends this tension *to the chest also*. Breathing becomes dif-ficult and irregular, and at times one holds his breath or breathes too rapidly and too strongly, etc. All of this fatigues and heats up the chest, the blood boils, and the cold cannot calm down, and in fact the ob-struction increases. You have done *very well* to take the violet syrup and the oil of sweet almonds: black powder and margrave powder would have done you no harm.[9]

According to Leopold, attention to diet was the chief remedy for every-thing. That meant eating little: all the soup you want, but not beef soup. A little boiled veal or mutton was acceptable, but boiled tongue was better, or well-cooked rice or barley. Then take a warm foot bath, which frees the head by forcing "flows" to the nose. No wine, and no cold foods. Boiled carrots were excellent. Leopold's advice of course did not stop there, as he worried about his son like the tenderest and most apprehensive mother. An earlier letter, of 25 November, contained other advice: "Take care of your health, and do not go to bed too late. Young people, particularly when they are engaged in mental work, must have their proper amount of sleep. Otherwise their nerves become weak, their stomach gets out of order and they fall into a decline. If people come in and settle on you in the morning, just drop it. That sort of thing is no joke, for in the end you will have to compose until you are half dead."[10] Leopold was concerned because he saw his son as the source of his own wealth, thus as something that had to be protected, but he also saw his son as his own true glory, his greatest creation, and the purpose of his entire existence.

In spite of his inferiority to his son in musical matters, Leopold continued to send Wolfgang advice from Salzburg in that area as well. Wolfgang was in fact continuing to write music for *Idomeneo* even during rehearsals, since composers of the time were considered craftsmen and were called on to create the music for an opera according to the specific talents and desires of the singers engaged for the premiere. In a letter of 18 November Leopold even seems to urge haste: "I ask you not to put off everything until doomsday. When haste is necessary, then one *no longer has a choice*, you have to write something. . . . At a given moment it must be ready: whether good, middling or bad, there's nothing that can be done about it. When the work is over, you can laugh heartily."[11] Wolfgang was attentive and scrupulous, however. He was intent on composing a masterpiece and, as always, he was exploring new paths because they were the only way to set oneself off from others. Leopold had totally different ideas: he wanted "easy" music, which he probably thought would make more money faster, devil take the quality. "I advise you," he writes Wolfgang on 11 December, "when composing to consider not only the musical, but also *the unmusical public*. You must remember that to every *ten real connoisseurs* there are a *hundred ignoramuses*. So do not neglect the so-called *popular* style, which tickles *long ears*"—that is, ass's ears.[12] Leopold had already recommended to his son, in his letter of 1 November 1777, that if he had a chance to write a German opera, "I need not urge you to imitate the natural and popular style, which everyone easily understands."[13] In another letter written 6 May 1778, he states: "If you compose something which is to be engraved, make it easy, suitable for amateurs, and *rather popular*."[14] Wolfgang did not agree with his father, however, and wrote to him from Munich on 16 December 1780, "As for what is called the popular taste, do not be uneasy, for there is music in my opera for all kinds of people, except for the long-eared."[15] In the meanwhile, the Munich musicians who had played in the orchestra for *Idomeneo* or had heard parts of the opera were enthusiastic. In the letter to his son dated 15 December, Leopold passed on to Wolfgang the contents of a letter that the flutist Becke had sent to a Salzburg colleague, where he had written that tears of joy and delight came to his eyes as he listened to the first act of *Idomeneo*. According to Becke, the performers declared it "the most beautiful music they had ever heard" and stated that "it was all new and strange and so forth."[16]

Mozart continued composing the opera even after rehearsals for *Idomeneo* had begun. On 1 December he rehearsed act 1 with part of the orchestra. On 16 December they rehearsed the first two acts. On 23 December they rehearsed the recitatives and the famous quartet in act 3, "Andrò ramingo e solo." Karl Theodor, the prince-elector, attended a rehearsal on 27 December, crying "Bravo!" at the end of act 1. He complimented Wolfgang, saying, "Who would believe that such great things could be hidden in so small a head?"[17] On 3 January 1781 Mozart was still writing the music for the third act, which he stated "has cost me more trouble than a whole opera."[18] On 18 January the recitatives were rehearsed on the stage for the first time. On 26 January Leopold and Nannerl arrived in Munich to take part in Wolfgang's triumph, coming just in time to attend the dress rehearsal the following day, which was also Wolfgang's twenty-fifth birthday.

The premiere of *Idomeneo, re di Creta, dramma per musica in 3 atti* finally took place on 29 January 1781 in the Residenz Theater in Munich, under the direction of Cannabich. The opera had only two other performances, on 3 February and 3 March, and we know nothing about how the public received the work. Maynard Solomon states, "No letter, diaries, or serious reviews describe the work's performance and reception. A Munich newspaper praised the scenery and reported that 'the text, music, and translation—all are by natives of Salzburg,' but neglected to give the composer's name. A report in a Bavarian literary annual wrote, 'The music for this season is by the younger Herr Mozzard of Salzburg.'"[19] We do not even know what the prince-elector's final judgment of the opera was, nor why he gave Mozart no more commissions. Nevertheless, the prince paid Mozart 450 florins, a sum equal to his annual stipend from Colloredo.

Probably *Idomeneo*, an excellent work in many of its parts, was considered a success, but only up to a point, given the modest number of repeat performances. It may also be that because the music was in large measure new and strange, breaking with the traditional rules of *opera seria*, many operagoers found it disconcerting, precisely as Leopold had feared. On the other hand, if *Idomeneo* is performed and appreciated today, two centuries later, it is because of the very novelties that contemporary listeners may have found disconcerting. Mozart himself loved *Idomeneo*, and in the years to come he sought to have it performed again, although with little success. On 13 March 1786 the opera was put on in Vienna, under Mozart's own direction and with some adaptations, for a private audience in the palace of Prince Johann Adam von Auersperg, a great lover of music.

Evaluations of *Idomeneo* have always varied, but my impression is that with the passage of time they have become more favorable. Norbert Elias deemed it "an opera in the old style."[20] Wolfgang Hildesheimer, to the contrary, wrote that *Idomeneo* breaks "out of the bonds of the *opera seria*."[21] Massimo Mila, while appreciating the work's better qualities, declares that it "is not a fully vital opera."[22] Ferenc Fricsay, the conductor of a memorable production of *Idomeneo*, disagreed, stating that its nobility, force, and savage emotion are not to be found together in any other Mozart opera: "Starting with the overture," Fricsay writes, "something unheard of occurs, something up to that moment unknown in musical literature. The first measures express the heroic nature of the drama and, immediately after, we hear the murmur of the sea and gigantic waves breaking. Mozart forces us to feel, right away, that the sea will play a decisive role in the opera."[23] When Fricsay turns to the quartet in act 3, "Andró ramingo e solo," he remarks that here, for the first time in the history of music, four different states of mind are being expressed at once: Elettra's anger, Ilia's renunciation, the desperation of Idomeneo, and the growing awareness of the situation on the part of his son, Idamante, the character with whom Mozart may have identified the most. "Mozart," Fricsay concludes, "will never again, not even in the masterpieces of his maturity, write such tragic pages."[24]

While Mozart was in Munich completing *Idomeneo*, he permitted himself the luxury of time off to write two *lieder* for voice and mandolin (K. 349/367a; 351/367b), one concert aria for soprano (K. 369), an oboe quartet for his friend Friedrich Ramm (K. 370/368b), and possibly the extraordinary Kyrie in D Minor (K. 341/368a). In Munich Wolfgang was full of energy, enthusiastic, happy to have created a masterpiece in *Idomeneo*, and not at all concerned about returning to Salzburg. He sensed that, thanks to what was happening, his life might be coming to a turning point, and in fact he stressed his detachment from Salzburg and from its prince-bishop in his letters to Leopold. On 16 December, when the six weeks of absence that Colloredo had conceded to him were about to run out, Wolfgang wrote to his father:

A propos, what about the archbishop? Next Monday I shall have been away from Salzburg for six weeks. You know, my dear father, that it is only to please you that I am staying on there, since, by Heaven, if I had followed my inclination, before leaving the other day I would have wiped my behind with my last contract, for I swear to you on my honor that it is not Salzburg itself but the prince and his conceited nobility who become every day more intolerable to me. Thus I should be delighted, were he to send me word in writing that he no longer required my services; for with the great patronage which I now have here, both my present and future position would be sufficiently safeguarded.[25]

In reality, Wolfgang remained in Munich until mid-March 1781; hence his absence was not the six weeks he had agreed to, but more than four months. This delay was increased by the fact that in January Colloredo was obliged to go to Vienna to be near his father, who was ill. Still, Colloredo was mightily annoyed, also because he had continued to pay Wolfgang's stipend during those months.

Between 7 and 10 March 1781, after the last performance of *Idomeneo,* the three Mozarts made a short trip to Augsburg. They returned to Munich 10 March and went their separate ways two days later, Leopold and Nannerl returning to Salzburg, taking with them Heinrich Marchand, the eleven-year-old son of Theobald Marchand, the director of the court theaters of Mannheim and Munich and a Freemason.[26] The boy was a paying guest in the Mozarts' house in Salzburg: the idea was that Leopold would make him into a great musician and composer, more or less as he had done for Wolfgang. Aware of the fact that his son was slipping out of his control, Leopold was seeking a substitute for him. He wanted, moreover, to assert his ability to forge musical geniuses, and he would have liked to demonstrate to himself, to his son, and to the world at large that, having created one Wolfgang Amadé Mozart, he was capable of producing another. Finally, and more concretely, taking on a live-in pupil swelled his earnings. In 1782 Maria Margarethe Marchand, Heinrich's sister, was also a guest and a pupil of Leopold's and Nannerl's, and in 1783 they were joined by yet another paying guest, a female Marchand cousin. All three of these pupils remained with Leopold and Nannerl until 1784—when Nannerl married—but not one of the three managed to become a new Wolfgang.

Rather than follow his father and his sister back to Salzburg, Wolfgang left for Vienna. Archbishop Colloredo, who was by now in Vienna to be with his ailing father, had ordered Wolfgang to come to the capital, where the archbishop wanted to show off all of his best musical talent. Wolfgang, who loved Vienna, was happy to comply. For one thing, Empress Maria Theresa, who had shown so much hostility toward the Mozart family, had died on 29 November, while preparations for *Idomeneo* were advancing in Munich. This imperial death might open up opportunities for work, and Wolfgang, who certainly was unaware of the contents of the letter that the empress had written on 12 December 1771, may yet have sensed the sovereign's hostility. In fact, writing to Leopold on 5 December 1780, Wolfgang indicates that the death of Maria Theresa was hardly a cause of sorrow for him:

> The death of the Empress does not affect my opera in the least, for none of the theaters have been closed and plays are being performed as usual. The entire mourning is not to last longer than six weeks and my opera will not be performed before January 20th. I beg you to have my *black suit* thoroughly brushed, shaken out, done up as well as possible and sent to me by the next mail coach—for next week everyone will be in mourning—and I, who have always to be about, *must also weep* with the others.[27]

## Vienna: The Break with Colloredo (Spring 1781)

Mozart arrived in Vienna at nine o'clock in the morning on 16 March. His patron, Colloredo, was enraged that Wolfgang had overstayed his leave in Munich, had earned a considerable sum thanks to *Idomeneo,* and in spite of this, had continued to receive his salary from Salzburg. Colloredo also understood that Mozart's Munich experience and the appreciation that had greeted *Idomeneo* might take the young composer away from him forever. A few hours after his arrival in Vienna, at four o'clock in the afternoon, Mozart was summoned by Colloredo and told to comply with his obligations, appear in concert, and demonstrate publicly that he belonged to the prince-bishop's court. Thus began Wolfgang's sojourn in Vienna—one that was to last until his death ten years later.

In the spring of 1781 the population of Vienna was some 50,000 souls; counting the suburban population, the total came to between 200,000 and 300,000. It was a big city, with theaters, musicians, a vast public of music lovers, and a major music publishing house, Artaria & Co., founded by two brothers originally from Lombardy who had moved to Vienna in 1766. The Artarias had made their reputation by publishing the music of Franz Joseph Haydn, Johann Christian Cannabich, and Jan Stamitz, and in 1781 they began to issue Mozart's compositions as well. Another leading Viennese musical publisher was Franz Anton Hoffmeister, who also printed a number of Mozart's works and eventually became his friend.

When Wolfgang arrived in Vienna, Joseph II had been emperor and sole ruler for some months. The emperor had an interest in music, since music had an important place in Vienna and could even become a state affair. It was thanks to his support that Mozart composed *Die Entführung aus dem Serail* (The Abduction from the Seraglio) in 1781–1782, *Le nozze di Figaro* (The Marriage of Figaro) in 1785–1786, and *Così fan tutte* in 1789–1790. Some historians have described Joseph II as an authoritarian and overbearing person, spoiled and egocentric, destructive and rebellious. But his character was a good deal more complex and contradictory than such adjectives might lead one to think. His first wife, Isabella of Bourbon Parma, had fallen in love with her sister-in-law, Maria Christina, Joseph II's sister. When Isabella died in 1763, some two hundred letters were discovered that the two women had secretly exchanged. Joseph, in an attempt to recover his lost wife, proposed marriage to Isabella's sister, but she was already engaged. Two years later, in 1765, Joseph agreed, for political reasons, to marry Josepha of Bavaria, whom he described as "low in stature, thickset, and without a shadow of fascination. Her face is covered with spots and pimples. Her teeth are horrible." Josepha had a good disposition, however, and Joseph accepted living with her in a friendly fashion but without love. Perhaps he was less overbearing that he is thought to have been.

Joseph II has gone down in history as an enlightened reformer. The ecclesiastical policy to which he lent his name as "Josephinism" was intended to assert the supremacy of the state over the national clergy. Joseph suppressed the contemplative religious orders and set rather severe regulations for ecclesiastical rites. In October 1781 he greatly improved the position of non-Catholics in the empire. In 1781–1782 he abolished peasant servitude, thus rendering the peasantry free to change their place of residence, to marry as they wished, and to choose their work. At the same time, he sought to reduce noble privileges, thus arousing discontent among the aristocracy. In 1783 he made marriage dependent on civil law, not religious law. In short, during the very years in which Mozart was newly arrived in Vienna, Joseph II was pursuing an intensive modernization program. The capital of the empire had the same poverty and lack of hygiene as all other big cities of the age, but in more fortunate circles it was a lively, elegant, and wealthy city.

From his first days in Vienna, Wolfgang frequented such elegant circles. The day after his arrival in the capital (that is, 17 March) he gave a highly successful concert in the house of Prince Dmitri Galitzin, the representative of the Czar of Russia. In the days that followed he called on Countess Maria Wilhelmine Thun-Hohenstein, Count Franz von Cobenzl, and the Auernhammer, Mesmer, and Fischer families; and Countess Maria Karolina Thiennes de Rumbeke became his first pupil. He very probably also moved immediately to reestablish contact with his friends the Webers. Archbishop Colloredo, who jealously defended his hold on Wolfgang and was spiteful by nature, continued to treat him as a servant and had him eat at the servants' table, as was customary at the time for court players. Mozart was enraged: how could anyone dare to treat him in such a manner, he who was now the well-established composer of *Idomeneo* and had eaten at kings' tables since childhood!

On 24 March Archbishop Colloredo was invited to a reception at Prince Galitzin's house, a highly flattering invitation that he probably received only so that he would bring Mozart with him. Ceremonial protocol of the time demanded that musicians wait in the antechamber until a valet gave them permission to enter the salon, at which point they would wait in a corner of the room until needed. In his book about Mozart, Aleksandr Ulybyshev describes Mozart making his entry into the Galitzin house without even being announced:

> The composer of *Idomeneo* thought that he had no need of a liveried major domo to enter into a music room. He thought so, and he acted accordingly. . . . He passed right by the valet, swept by the servants who came running at the latter's cry of alarm, walked right through the room, and went directly to the prince, presented his compliments, and sat down in the post of honor that his courage had won him. While he conversed familiarly with the owner of the house, he saw his colleagues Brunetti and Ceccarelli lodged in a corner of the orchestra, totally unable to move. Such great audacity provoked the clerical ire of the archbishop to the highest degree, and from that moment on he felt it his duty to punish any minimal lack of respect on the part of our hero. The most insulting epithets were copiously dealt him on a daily basis and, in the interest of keeping him far from the pride that comes from worldly successes and the temptations to which a well-filled purse exposes one, he was refused permission to give concerts.[28]

Fashionable Vienna was so displeased with this odious prohibition that in only a few days the archbishop was obliged to rescind it.[29] Thus on 3 April, Wolfgang performed, without an admission charge and to great applause, in the Kärntnertortheater (the Hotel Sacher now occupies the site) in a concert organized by the Wiener Tonkünstlersocietät, a society that benefited the widows of musicians. The next day Wolfgang gave his father a report of the concert: "I had to begin all over again, because there was no end to the applause."[30] Four days later he returned to the topic in another letter to his father: "I told you about the applause in the theater, but I must add that what delighted and surprised me most of all was the amazing silence—and also the cries of 'Bravo!' while I was playing. This is certainly honor enough in Vienna, where there are such numbers and numbers of good pianists."[31] The program on that occasion probably included the *Paris* Symphony (K. 297/300a), and Mozart himself mentions playing the twelve Variations in E-flat on "Je suis Lindor" (K. 354/299a) as well as other unspecified compositions and improvisations.

Colloredo had absolutely prohibited Mozart from organizing concerts or "academies" (performances that charged admission, with the proceeds going to the artist) on his own initiative. Wolfgang complains of this prohibition in his letter to his father of 4 April. Obviously, the prince-bishop wanted to keep the best of his musicians tied to himself by preventing him from taking advantage of the open market. On 8 April Wolfgang gave a concert in the house of the prince-bishop's father, an occasion for which he composed the allegro movement of his Sonata for Violin and Piano (K. 372),[32] as well as the Rondo in C for Violin and Orchestra (K. 373). Pleased with his own rapidity, Mozart wrote his father that he had composed them "last night between eleven and twelve," adding that to save time "I . . . retained my own part in my head."[33] Mozart continued to complain, however. That concert had prevented him from participating in one at the house of Countess Thun at which Emperor Joseph II had been present. Mozart states that if he had gone to play there, he would have earned a fine reward, whereas the archbishop had given him nothing.

It is in fact in the letter of 8 April that Wolfgang first mentions "resigning my post."[34] The previous December he had already talked about wiping his behind with his contract with Colloredo. But now the word "resigning" implies that he was considering more serious action. Within only a few days things came to a point of decision. On 12 April, Colloredo told Mozart that he was to leave Vienna on Sunday 22 April to return to Salzburg with the other court musicians. Wolfgang did not leave, however, which launched a contest of wills between the prince-bishop and his underling. It is impossible to document many particulars of this affair because, although more than a hundred letters that Mozart wrote to his father after 22 January 1781 have been preserved, his father's letters to him after that date are missing. We do not know for sure whether Leopold's letters were deliberately destroyed by someone (probably Constanze Weber), returned to the sender, or simply lost in Wolfgang's many changes of lodgings in Vienna. In any event, the correspondence between the father and the son, a precious source for the reconstruction of Mozart's biography, has serious gaps, beginning with Leopold's arrival in Munich to attend the performance of *Idomeneo,* and thus several weeks before Mozart's Viennese sojourn began. We can presume that between 1781 and 1787, the year of Leopold's death, he must have written his son over a hundred letters. We can only partially reconstruct them from Wolfgang's responses.

It is certain that in April 1781 Leopold fought like a lion to prevent his son from abandoning Salzburg. He at least managed to make him hesitate. On 18 April Wolfgang wrote his father in response to his most recent missives, "I can only say that you are both right and wrong," adding, "but the points where you are right far outweigh the points where you are wrong." He seems to have decided to return to within the paternal embrace: "I shall certainly return and with the greatest pleasure, too, as I am fully convinced that you will never prevent me from making my fortune."[35] Still, he avoids setting a date for his departure. What Wolfgang had in mind was evidently a short stay in Salzburg, given that Johann Gottlieb Stephanie the Younger was preparing the libretto of *Die Entführung aus dem Serail* (The Abduction from the Seraglio) for him, and he would have to be on hand in Vienna for the rehearsals of the new opera. On 28 April he repeated to his father that he would soon return to Salzburg, but he posed a condition that his father must solemnly promise to let him return to Vienna the following year for the end of Carnival and for Lent: "This depends on you alone and not on the archbishop. For if he does not grant me permission, I shall go all the same; and this visit will certainly not do me any harm!"[36] In short, his only reason for returning to Salzburg was his father. Wolfgang writes his thoughts in normal German, without using the code the family had devised to circumvent the censors, indicating that he has done so "so that the whole world knows and should know that the Archbishop of Salzburg has only you to thank, my most beloved father, that he did not lose me yesterday forever." Stephanie was on the point of giving him the entire libretto of *The Abduction from the Seraglio,* and Wolfgang put off his trip to Salzburg for a year, until the next Carnival, the season when the new opera might be produced.

While Leopold and Wolfgang were discussing the matter by letter, Colloredo sent a footman to Wolfgang on 1 or 2 May with an order to leave immediately for Salzburg. Wolfgang did not comply: "All the others had been informed of the day of their departure, but not I. Well, I shoved everything into my trunk in haste, and old Madame Weber has been good enough to take me into her house, where I have a pretty room. Moreover, I am living with people who are obliging and who supply me with all the things which one often requires in a hurry and which one cannot have when one is living alone."[37]

Mozart refused to leave without prior notification, and the Weber family was for him a secure port in which to take refuge to gain time, find protection, and take care of the last details of his business in Vienna. Fridolin Weber was dead by that time, and Aloysia was married, but the two younger sisters and the "old" mother, Caecilia (she was fifty-two at the time) were still at home. In Massimo Mila's opinion, Mozart rather enjoyed the simple and common human qualities of Caecilia and her two daughters.[38]

Wolfgang delayed returning to Salzburg. He had told Colloredo's functionaries that he would leave on 9 May, but later he decided to postpone his departure once more. When he presented himself at the archbishop's residence in Vienna, the valets informed him that his employer had a parcel he wanted taken to Salzburg immediately. Having already decided to put off the trip, Wolfgang did not comply with the order. In the letter he wrote to his father that same day, he describes his dramatic confrontation with Colloredo:

> *Archbishop:* "Well, young fellow, when are you going off?" *I:* "I intended to go tonight, but all the seats were already engaged." Then he rushed full steam ahead, without pausing for breath—I was the most dissolute fellow he knew—no one served him so badly as I did—I had better leave today or else he would write home and have my salary stopped. I couldn't get a word in edgeways, for he blazed away like a fire.

At this point Mozart, hoping to be dismissed, replied:

> "So Your Grace is not satisfied with me?" "What, you dare to threaten me—you scoundrel? There is the door! Look out, for I will have nothing more to do with such a miserable wretch." At last I said, "Nor I with

you!" "Well, be off!" When leaving the room, I said, "This is final. You shall have it tomorrow in writing."[39]

Wolfgang repeated to his father that he disliked Salzburg: "There is no stimulus for my talent! When I play or when any of my compositions are performed, it is just as if the audience were all tables and chairs."[40] He explained to his father that he was "seething with rage" but also that he was happy at the thought of no longer having to serve the archbishop:

> Do not be the least bit anxious about me. I am so sure of my success in Vienna that I would have resigned even without the slightest reason. . . . Now please be cheerful, for my good luck is just beginning, and I trust that my good luck will be yours also. Write to me that you are pleased—and indeed you may well be so—but in public rail at me as much as you like, so that none of the blame may fall on you. But if, in spite of this, the archbishop should be the slightest bit impertinent to you, come at once with my sister to Vienna, for I give you my word of honor that there is enough for all three of us to live on. Still, I should prefer it if you could hold out for another year.[41]

In the meantime, given that he knew his father well, Wolfgang sought to soothe him by announcing that he would send money in the days that followed "to show you that I am not starving."

On 10 May Wolfgang called on Count Karl Joseph Felix Arco, the chief chamberlain, counselor of war, and grand master of the kitchens to Colloredo, to hand in the written resignation he had promised and return the advance for travel expenses that he had just received. Count Arco refused to accept either, however, claiming that Wolfgang could not resign without his father's consent. In saying this Arco was deliberately putting Mozart in a difficult position. The law did not permit him to resign, and without an explicit letter of dismissal or a formal acceptance of his resignation, Wolfgang would end up in a murky situation from the juridical point of view, thus making it difficult, if not impossible, for him to be taken into the service of another prince. This was indeed what happened. We can imagine Wolfgang's thoughts and feelings at this point: he had returned, much against his will, to serve Colloredo as court organist in January 1779; at that time he had obtained a salary much lower than he had been promised, almost all of which had been confiscated by his father. Now, to complete the offense, the archbishop wanted to make it difficult, if not impossible, for Wolfgang to be employed by any other prince for the rest of his life, due to his unhappy service with him. In a letter written to his father on 12 May 1781 Wolfgang explained that the main reproach made to him—we do not know if this came from Colloredo or Arco—was that he had not fulfilled his duties as a valet: "I did not know that I was a valet—and that was the last straw. I ought to have idled away a couple of hours every morning in the antechamber. True, I was often told that I ought to present myself, but I could never remember that this was part of my duty, and I only turned up punctually whenever the archbishop sent for me."[42]

Mozart had been so perturbed by the injustice of which he felt himself the victim that after the unpleasant confrontation with the archbishop of 9 May he had felt ill: "In the evening I was obliged to leave the opera in the middle of the first act and go home and lie down. For I was very feverish, I was trembling in every limb, and I was staggering along the street like a drunkard. I also stayed at home the following day, yesterday, and spent the morning in bed, as I had taken tamarind water [a light laxative]."[43]

Leopold was anguished over the break with Colloredo; he reproached his son and tried to persuade him to return to the archbishop's service. He also feared the influence of the women of the Weber household. Wolfgang replied on 16 May to the paternal reprimands. By this time he was determined not to return to Salzburg. He also defended the Webers, in whose house he was living:

> What you say about the Webers, I do assure you is not true. I was a fool, I admit, about Aloysia Lange, but what does not a man do when he is in love? Indeed I loved her truly, and even now I feel that she is not a matter of indifference to me. It is, therefore, a good thing for me that her husband is a jealous fool and lets her go nowhere, so that I seldom have an opportunity of seeing her. Believe me when I say that old Madame Weber is a very obliging woman and that I cannot do enough for her in return for her kindness, as unfortunately I have no time to do so.[44]

Wolfgang's later letters indicate that Leopold did not give an inch. He insisted that his son return to Salzburg and his service with the archbishop, and he continued to rebuke him. His son was not moved: "I must confess that there is not a single touch in your letter by which I recognize my father!" he exclaimed in a letter of 19 May.[45] In a letter dated 26 May Wolfgang explained his point of view: "The more I consider the whole question, the more I realize that the best way for me to serve myself and you, my most beloved father, as well as my dear sister, is to stay in Vienna. It seems as if good fortune is about to welcome me here, and now I feel that I *must* stay. . . . Believe me when I say that I do not like to be idle but to work. I confess that in Salzburg work was a burden to me and that I could hardly ever settle down to it. But why? Because I was never happy."[46] Leopold must have accused him of not understanding the need to earn money or the value of money. Wolfgang responded "Why, where could I have learnt the value of money, when up to the present I have had so little to handle? All I know is that once when I had twenty ducats, I considered myself wealthy. Necessity alone teaches one to value money."[47]

In June the last act of the drama of Mozart's break with Colloredo ended with the famous kick delivered by Count Arco to Mozart's backside. Wolfgang had presented to the count several petitions and memoranda in the hope of eliciting from him a formal acceptance of his resignation, but as always the count refused. On 8 June, Arco lost patience and literally kicked Wolfgang out. Wolfgang described the encounter in a letter to his father dated 13 June: "Instead of taking my petition or procuring me an audience or advising me to send in the document later or persuading me to let the matter lie and to consider things more carefully—enfin, whatever he wanted—Count Arco hurls me out of the room and gives me a kick on my behind. Well, that means in our language that Salzburg is no longer the place for me, except to give me a favorable opportunity of returning the Count's kick, even if it should have to be in the public street."[48] He repeated his threat to give the count a good kick in a letter dated 16 June, adding, however, "unless I am so unlucky as to meet him first in some sacred place,"[49] where extracting his revenge would be inappropriate.

In his letters in this period Wolfgang implores his father not to grovel before the archbishop. He also defends himself against other accusations that were bombarding him from Salzburg: "It is not true," he tells Leopold, "that I boasted of eating meat on all fast-days; but I did say that I did not scruple to do so or consider it a sin. . . . I attend Mass every Sunday and every Holy day and, if I can manage it, on weekdays also, and that you know, my father." He also had to defend himself against the accusation of frequenting ladies of easy virtue: "The only association which I had with the person of ill repute was at the ball, and I talked to her long before I knew what she was, and solely because I wanted to be sure of having a partner for the contredanse. Afterwards I could not desert her all at once without giving her the reason; and who would say such a thing to a person's face?"[50]

Wolfgang also expressed distress because his father had compared him to Aloysia Weber, who, upon achieving success, had abandoned her mother and thrown herself into the arms of the actor Joseph Lange. Relations between Wolfgang and Leopold, although not interrupted, had changed irremediably for the worse, to the point that in his letter of 20 June Wolfgang told his father, "Unless I have something particularly important to tell you, I shall only write to you once a week."[51]

In front of others, however, Leopold continued to defend his son, going so far as to criticize Colloredo, who was nevertheless still his prince and his employer. In a letter to Johann Breitkopf, the Leipzig music publisher, dated 10 August 1781, for example, Leopold gives a brief summary of the controversy between Colloredo and Wolfgang. He concludes the letter saying, "As His Grace the Prince treated my son extremely badly in Vienna and as, on the other hand, all the great noble families marked him out for their special favors, he was easily persuaded to resign a service to which a miserable salary was attached, and to remain in Vienna."[52]

Wolfgang was unhappy about the crisis between his father and himself, and for some time he attempted to patch things up. Thus in a letter of 19 September 1781 he advises his sister Nannerl to marry the man she loves, Franz Armand d'Ippold, a Salzburg nobleman, and to come to Vienna with her husband and their father. "We could live very happily together again," he suggests, adding that he had always wanted his father to "enjoy his rest and not to have to worry and torment himself."[53] This hope never became a reality, and neither did the marriage between Nannerl and Franz d'Ippold, seemingly because Leopold opposed it.

## Points of View: Colloredo's, Arco's, Leopold's, and Wolfgang's

Colloredo may have preferred not to lose Wolfgang's services. According to Norbert Elias, in fact, the archbishop wanted to "impose obedience on Mozart," but he never imagined that his young musician could take the initiative and resign: "From the archbishop's standpoint the young man's reaction was quite irrational. He had scoured the country for a post and found nothing until the Salzburg court graciously received him back, and with an increased salary."[54]

Perhaps Colloredo had not fully understood Mozart's greatness, and so thought himself the stronger man. Or perhaps he had sensed that greatness, but could not tolerate having a subordinate break court discipline and set a bad example for others. The power of a prince is such a fragile thing that respect for the court rules, ceremonials, and hierarchy must always be enforced with the greatest of care precisely because they, too, are fragile. Colloredo also knew that he had an ally in Leopold (perhaps even a hostage) who could stand up to Wolfgang's obstinate refusal to compromise. Finally, by not accepting Wolfgang's resignation, Colloredo left him in such an unclear and difficult juridical position that he might perhaps be forced to return to his native city.

Count Arco seconded his employer's plans. He played the mediator and drew out the affair, hoping that the passage of days and weeks might enable the two parties to arrive at a positive solution or at least an agreement to negotiate. He told Mozart that he had not transmitted his petitions and memoranda to Colloredo, but he may perhaps have done so. He may have said he had not done so in order to gain time and permit Colloredo to reach an agreement with Wolfgang without losing face. At the end there was the famous kick in the ass. Arco may have reached the end of his patience, or he may have realized that he had failed. Perhaps there never was such a kick, as Piero Buscaroli suggests in *La morte di Mozart*. Buscaroli wonders whether the episode was not an invention or an exaggeration on Wolfgang's part, in the interest of "getting to the climax of his *indignatio* and making the pusillanimous paternal heart vibrate with indignation for the irreversible wrong he had suffered."[55] Or perhaps it was an exaggeration, a partial invention, designed to make everyone involved—not just Leopold—come to terms with a fait accompli and to turn the fracture that Arco had attempted to patch up into a definitive break.

As for Leopold, he sensed that a major era in his life risked coming to an end forever. For almost a quarter century he had lived for his son, but he had also been the prime beneficiary of his son's filial virtues. He suffered indescribably at the idea that he would have to continue to live without his magnificent creation by his side. He felt himself lost. And perhaps he understood, more or less unconsciously, that he could no longer help Wolfgang to grow as an artist. It is a pity that we do not have the letters that Leopold wrote to Wolfgang in this period, for they might have helped us to reconstruct his state of mind. We do not even know what arguments he used or what moral blackmail he applied to increase his son's sense of guilt. The indirect information that we can glean from Wolfgang's letters leads us to suppose that Leopold did not spare his blows. If he often hit his target, he also had some misses. It was a bit silly, for example, to reproach Wolfgang for eating meat on fast days or for speaking to a woman of ill repute. And certainly it was a mistake to ask him for more money. In his letter of 16 June 1781 Wolfgang felt obliged to make excuses for having sent his father only thirty ducats, even after declaring (a month earlier, on 16 May) that he never had in hand more than twenty ducats. This means that his father must have confiscated the 450 florins (the equivalent of a hundred ducats) that his son had received for *Idomeneo*. Mozart felt obliged to excuse himself again on 25 July for having sent twenty ducats to Salzburg instead of thirty.

Leopold behaved as he did either out of cupidity or because he supposed that by doing so he could tie his son to him more strongly. He wanted Wolfgang to live in Salzburg, accumulate money, pay the family debts, and help a father who had done so much for him. These were times in which parents counted on their children as insurance against their old age. In contrast, there is every indication that Mozart's decision to leave Leopold was also based on the notion that, once separated from him, he could at last make use of the money he earned. And enjoy it. As he reminded his father in his letter of 26 May, "Apart from my health I now think that there is nothing so indispensable as money."[56]

Wolfgang was a model son. He was aware of the fact that without his father it would have been difficult, if not impossible, for him to have become the great artist that he in fact was, but he felt that he had sufficiently repaid his father and teacher. He loved him, but he judged him with lucidity. He did not want to lose Leopold's paternal affection, but he realized that by then his father was no longer able to help him rise, and in fact even risked blocking his advance. Leopold had become an obstacle, not only because he wanted to isolate his son in an unstimulating Salzburg, or because by speaking constantly about debts he robbed him of an incentive to earn money, but also because from an artistic point of view he could no longer contribute anything, and with his anxious disposition, was even trying to dissuade Wolfgang from musical innovation.

Not only was Leopold a problem from a professional point of view; he had become a problem from a human standpoint as well. He wanted to continue to feel himself indispensable, so he sought to arrange matters so that his son would be incapable of administering his own affairs—in short, so that he would remain an eternal child. The image of Wolfgang as a genius, but a totally irresponsible, overgrown child that is presented in Miloš Forman's 1984 film *Amadeus,* derives in part from Leopold's (and Nannerl's) prejudices, which were rather far from reality. Wolfgang was of the opinion that he had become a man in the full sense of the word and a composer much greater and more mature than his father. We cannot exclude the idea that he might have had information about Leopold's financial status that, out of filial piety, he did not mention. All this did not prevent him from leaving his father's house with a profound sense of guilt which he never completely overcame. After their separation in 1781 he saw his father only twice: in Salzburg during the summer and autumn of 1783, and for several weeks in Vienna in 1785. When Leopold died, in May 1787, Wolfgang did not go to Salzburg to pay his last respects.

After Wolfgang moved to Vienna, Leopold did not send the clothing that his son had left in Salzburg. The son had rebelled against his father and deserved to be punished. This irritated Wolfgang, and he did not hide the fact. In a letter dated 5 September he chastised his father, accusing him of not believing in him but only in the "gossip and scribblings" of others. He reproached his father with making his hostile sentiments public, and begged him to keep them to himself:

> Do trust me always, for indeed I deserve it. I have trouble and worry enough here to support myself, and it therefore does not help me in the very least to read unpleasant letters. From the first moment I came here I have had to live entirely on my own means, that is, on what I could make by my own efforts. . . . It is certainly not my fault, my dearest father, that you have not yet had any money from me; it is due to the present bad season. . . . I wrote you for clothes, for I had nothing with me but my black suit. The mourning [for Empress Maria Theresa] was over, the weather was hot, and my clothes did not arrive. So I had to have some made, as I could not go about Vienna like a tramp, particularly in the circumstances. My linen was a pitiful sight; no house porter in Vienna wore shirts of such coarse linen as mine. . . . That meant more expense. . . . One must not make oneself cheap here—that is a cardinal point—or else one is done. Whoever is *most impertinent* has the best chance. From all your letters I gather that you believe that I do nothing but amuse myself. Well, you are most dreadfully mistaken. I can truthfully say that I have no pleasure—none whatever—save that of being away from Salzburg.[57]

Leopold hung on to his son's clothes because he hoped that he would return home. If he had sent them on, it would indicate that he approved of his son's flight and had given up any idea of having him back again.

## Free in Vienna without His Father and without Colloredo (1781)

After the break with Colloredo and separation from his father, Wolfgang seemed to be in a good mood, but perhaps somewhat less so than his letters might lead us to believe. When he wrote to Leopold, Wolfgang had to show that he was sure of himself, doing well financially, and confident of what the future would bring; otherwise his father would have been merciless. Vienna was a city full of resources, and Mozart was confident that he could draw profit from them, but at the beginning, as is understandable, the young composer encountered many difficulties. To survive he had to give piano lessons, an activity that he had never particularly enjoyed. Moreover, his pupils were few, given that most of the high society of Vienna left the city during the summer. By 16 June 1781 his only paying pupil was the twenty-six-year-old Countess Maria Karolina Thiennes de Rumbeke, who paid him six ducats (twenty-seven florins) for every twelve lessons. In July his finances were in even worse shape. "My pupil," he wrote his father on 25 July, "remained three weeks in the country, so I made nothing, while my own expenses went on." Concert subscriptions were languishing, because "all the people with money are in the country."[58]

On the other hand, Mozart was happy because Vienna had offered an opportunity to compose a new grand opera in German, *Die Entführung aus dem Serail* (The Abduction from the Seraglio). In April of that year Gottlieb Stephanie had already started adapting the libretto, which he reworked from one by Christoph Friedrich Bretzner. But, more important, in June, Count Franz Xaver Wolf Rosenberg-Orsini, a high official of the court and the general director of court entertainments, had formally given Mozart the commission to write the music. Rosenberg-Orsini had met the fourteen-year-old Mozart eleven years earlier, when Rosenberg was in Florence in the service of Grand Duke Pietro Leopoldo, the same Leopold whom we have met as a child and who later became emperor as Leopold II. In Vienna Rosenberg had received Mozart with great courtesy on several occasions and had heard him play the score of *Idomeneo* on the piano in the house of Countess Thun. Emperor Joseph II, who championed the imposition of German as the common language of the Austrian Empire, expressed great interest in having a singspiel in the German language that would contribute to the linguistic unification of the empire's various populations, and he was delighted that Mozart had formally taken on the task.

Mozart was in turn happy to live in Vienna, both for the opportunities for work that the city afforded and because he could meet musicians who enlarged his experience. In particular, there was a group of musicians and music lovers who met under the aegis of an Austrian dilettante and patron, Gottfried Bernhard van Swieten, a forty-eight-year-old Freemason who was prefect of the court library, had been a diplomatic representative of the court in Brussels, Paris, Warsaw, and Berlin, and was the son of the personal physician of Empress Maria Theresa. Evenings in van Swieten's house included music by Handel, Hasse, and Johann Sebastian Bach, the great German composer who was almost totally forgotten in those years (to the point that none of his compositions were printed between 1750 and 1800). Wolfgang might also have seen Franz Joseph Haydn in Vienna as early as 1781. Haydn usually lived in Hungary, in the castle of Prince Nikolaus (Miklós Ferdinand) Esterházy, in whose service he was, but in November 1781 he came to Vienna and remained there for two months. Mozart and Haydn had already met in Salzburg, but it was only in Vienna that they kindled the friendship and artistic understanding that was to influence both men as composers.

Mozart's residence in Vienna had important consequences for his sentimental life as well. In early May, as we have seen, when he failed to comply with Colloredo's order to return to Salzburg immediately, Wolfgang found himself without lodgings, and decided to take refuge with the Weber family, of whom he was deeply fond. He remained there for several months, at the end of which, he explained to his father in a letter dated 25 July 1781, he intended to move elsewhere "solely because people are gossiping." They were "spreading entirely groundless reports" linking Wolfgang and Constanze, and the only way to put an end to the talk was to change lodging immediately. "If there was a time when I thought less of getting married, it is most certainly now!" Wolfgang wrote his father. "God has not given me my talent that I might attach it to a wife and waste my youth in idleness. I am just beginning to live, and am I to embitter my own life?" He went on to offer some comments about Constanze: "I will not say that, living in the same house with the Mademoiselle to whom people have already married me, I am ill-bred and do not speak to her; but I am not in love with her. I fool about and have fun with her when time permits (which is only in the evening when I take supper at home, for in the morning I write in my room and in the afternoon I am rarely in the house) and—that is all. If I had to marry all those with whom I have jested, I should have two hundred wives at least."[59] Mozart left the Webers' and, after some further moves, settled into a very agreeable room on Graben 1175 (today number 17) at the end of August.

On 23 October 1781 Wolfgang sent to his "little cousin" Anna Thekla the last extant letter in their correspondence. He confided that "the gossip which people have been so kind as to circulate about me, is partly true and partly false." In short, something had happened between Wolfgang and Constanze Weber. Nonetheless, he intimated to his cousin that their relationship could continue and even grow: "If you had shown more confidence and friendship and had applied to me directly (and not to others—and what is more . . . !) But silence. If you had addressed yourself directly to me, you would certainly have heard more than everyone else—and, possibly, more than—I myself! But—" He then insists, "I hope that our correspondence, dear little cousin, will now start off again!"[60] We do not know if this was truly the last letter to Anna Thekla. If it was, it was because Mozart's sentimental relations were taking another and much more absorbing turn in Vienna.

The feast day of St. Wolfgang is 31 October, and Mozart celebrated his name day in the house of a new Viennese acquaintance, Baroness Martha Elisabeth von Waldstätten, née Schäffer, who was thirty-seven at the time and lived apart from her husband. The Waldstätten residence was in the suburb of Leopoldstadt (today, Praterstrasse 15). Wolfgang arrived at noon, and that evening at eleven o'clock, when everyone in the house was getting ready for bed, he was surprised to hear six musicians, sent by the baroness to play in his honor his very recent and delightful Serenade for Winds (K. 375). The musicians, according to Wolfgang, were "poor beggars who, however, play quite well together, particularly the first clarinet and the two horns."[61] The surprise was a very welcome one. Baroness Waldstätten was an experienced and fascinating woman, and Mozart was probably attracted to her. Norbert Elias writes that the relationship between them, "of whatever kind it might have been, was the only one [in Mozart's life] that followed the familiar pattern of a liaison between an experienced older woman and a relatively inexperienced young man."[62] In the months to come, however, the baroness approved of Wolfgang's marriage with Constanze Weber and had an exchange of letters with Leopold Mozart, who had met her in Vienna, admired her, and was himself fascinated by her.

A totally different sort of woman was Wolfgang's pupil Josepha Barbara von Auernhammer, who was twenty-three years old and to whom Wolfgang began to give piano lessons—free—in June 1781. "The young lady," Wolfgang declared in a letter to his father of 27 June, "is a fright, but plays enchantingly."[63] Her playing needed only polishing, and she secretly confided to Mozart that she wanted to study for two or three years more, then go to Paris to make her living as a pianist. She knew that she was ugly, and she had no intention of marrying a chancery clerk, the best she could hope for. She preferred to remain single and live by her artistic talent. Mozart speaks of her again in a letter dated 22 August: "If a painter wanted to portray the devil to the life, he would have to choose her face.

She is as fat as a farm wench, perspires so that you feel inclined to vomit, and goes about so scantily clad that really you can read as plain as print: '*Pray, do look here.*' True, there is enough to see, in fact, quite enough to strike one blind. . . . She tries to be attractive. But, what is worse still, she is *sérieusement* in love with me! I thought at first it was a joke, but now I know it to be a fact."[64]

Mozart made up his mind to treat her harshly when she simpered, but she pretended not to notice and fed rumors of a possible matrimony. Still, she was a good enough pianist to play with him in a concert on 23 November at the Auernhammer residence, in the presence of such eminent figures as Countess Thun, Baron Gottfried van Swieten, Baron Karl Abraham Wetzlar, Count Ernst Firmian, and the court councilor Johann B. A. Daubrawa von Daubrawaik and his son Franz Anton. The teacher and the pupil played together the Concerto in E-flat for Two Pianos (K. 365/316a), which Wolfgang had composed in Salzburg in 1779,[65] and the Sonata in D for Two Pianos (K. 448/375a), composed in Vienna for the occasion.

Appreciation for Mozart's mastery was growing in Viennese musical circles, to the point that in November and December 1781 he hoped to be chosen as the pianoforte teacher of the fourteen-year-old princess, Elisabetta of Württemberg, who was engaged to the son of the future Emperor Leopold II, at this date still grand duke of Tuscany. Mozart's hopes were in vain, because Emperor Joseph II gave the post to Antonio Salieri, who, at the age of thirty, occupied the permanent post of Kapellmeister to the court of Vienna. "The emperor has spoilt everything," Wolfgang wrote to his father on 15 December, "for he cares for no one but Salieri. The Archduke Maximilian recommended *me* to [the princess] and she replied that had it rested with her, she would never have engaged anyone else, but that on account of her singing the emperor had suggested Salieri. She added that she was extremely sorry."[66]

In the preceding days Mozart had attended a masked ball at the court in honor of Friedrich Eugen, Duke of Württemberg, the father of his would-be pupil. And on 16 November, Archduke Maximilian Franz, who openly protected Mozart, had asked him to participate in a concert in honor of the same duke. All these maneuvers failed to produce the desired result, however.

Toward the end of November, Artaria & Co. published six sonatas for keyboard and violin (K. 296, 376/374d, 377/374e, 378/317d, 379/373a, and 380/374f), works that Mozart had composed between 1778 and July 1781. Publication of these works by the prestigious Artaria firm was tantamount to major recognition.

## Constanze

In spite of his declarations to the contrary, Mozart was moving toward marriage. On 16 May 1781 he had admitted that he could not yet think of Aloysia with indifference. On 25 July he had declared to his father that he could not think of marrying any woman. Either he was not completely sincere or something in the weeks that followed made him change his mind. The reasons for this change may have been many: the vexations of the bachelor life, an aversion to solitude, need for a companion, thoughts of Constanze and the sparks that may have been struck between them, the advice of the worldly-wise Baroness Waldstätten, and, finally, a desire to assert himself as a man and a father after having played the son for so long. What we know for sure is that on 15 December 1781 Wolfgang wrote to Leopold, revealing his matrimonial intentions with a simple explanation:

> The voice of nature speaks as loud in me as in others, louder, perhaps, than in many a big strong lout of a fellow. I simply cannot live as most young men do in these days. In the first place, I have too much religion; in the second place, I have too great a love of my neighbor and too high a feeling of honor to seduce an innocent girl; and, in the third place, I have too much horror and disgust, too much dread and fear of diseases and too much care for my health to fool about with whores. So I can swear that I have never had relations of that sort with any woman.[67]

He even insists on the veracity of what he says: "I stake my life on the truth of what I have told you."

Are we to believe that Mozart was stating that at twenty-five he was still a virgin? Perhaps not. In fact, if we reread the text of his letter to his father carefully, we can see that Wolfgang was only declaring that he had not seduced innocent girls or had recourse to prostitutes. His cousin Anna Thekla, for example, was neither innocent nor a prostitute. And we might also recall the many ballerinas, singers, or women and ladies of all ages—perhaps including Baroness Waldstätten—whom Mozart had frequented. In his 15 December letter Mozart also offered another, quite practical, explanation:

> But owing to my disposition, which is more inclined to a peaceful and domesticated existence than to revelry, I who from my youth up have never been accustomed to look after my own belongings, linen, clothes, and so forth, cannot think of anything more necessary to me than a wife. I assure you that I am often obliged to spend unnecessarily,

simply because I do not pay attention to things. I am absolutely convinced that I should manage better with a wife (on the same income which I have now) than I do by myself. And how many useless expenses would be avoided![68]

In sum, Mozart declared that he was convinced that "A bachelor . . . is only half alive." Given a desire for a full and satisfying life, matrimony seemed an indispensable step. As for Constanze, Mozart attempted to reassure his father by his description of her, but he ends up sounding not very enthusiastic:

> She is not ugly, but at the same time far from beautiful. Her whole beauty consists in two little black eyes and a pretty figure. She has no wit, but she has enough common sense to enable her to fulfill her duties as a wife and mother. It is a downright lie that she is inclined to be extravagant. On the contrary, she is accustomed to be shabbily dressed. . . . She would like to be neatly and cleanly dressed, but not smartly, and most things that a woman needs she is able to make for herself; and she dresses her own hair every day.[69]

Constanze, in other words, was more enterprising and thriftier than Nannerl, who was incapable of dressing her own hair. But Wolfgang's praises of his future wife did not stop here: "She understands housekeeping and has the kindest heart in the world. I love her and she loves me with all her heart. Tell me whether I could wish myself a better wife?"[70]

We can imagine Leopold's desperation at receiving this news: if his adored son married, he would be even more out of his reach, and forever. If he really felt it necessary to marry, he should seek a better match. In all probability Leopold expressed himself frankly about Constanze and the Webers, which may explain why Constanze herself could have destroyed the letters that Leopold sent Wolfgang after January 1781. Wolfgang's letters to Salzburg also contained opinions that might have offended Constanze, but they ended up in Nannerl's hands, and she saved them. This is how we know that in his letter of 15 December Wolfgang permitted himself rather severe criticisms of the two elder Weber daughters: "The eldest [Josepha] is a lazy, gross perfidious woman, and as cunning as a fox. Mme Lange [Aloysia, once the object of his affections] is a false, malicious person and a coquette." The youngest, Sophie, was spared because she "is still too young to be anything in particular." Constanze, according to Wolfgang, was "the martyr of the family" and the best of the lot.[71]

In December 1781 Wolfgang and Constanze's matrimonial plans were clouded by the intervention of Caecilia Weber, Mozart's future mother-in-law, and Johann Franz Joseph von Thorwart, Constanze's legal guardian. An official of the court of Vienna, Thorwart was the administrator of the court theaters, a post that gave him power to affect Mozart's career. On December 1787, for example, it was Thorwart who signed the decree naming Mozart as court composer. He was a highly influential person and one who could command Mozart's respect. Herr Thorwart did not know Mozart personally, but he had heard rumors about him regarding a certain flightiness in love affairs. We know from Mozart's letter to his father of 22 December that he had requested and obtained an audience with Constanze's guardian, but had not succeeded in persuading him that his intentions were serious. Thorwart then prohibited Wolfgang from continuing to frequent the Webers' house until he had signed a prenuptial agreement. Wolfgang explains to his father, "So I drew up a document to the effect 'that I bound myself to marry Mlle Constanze Weber within the space of three years and that if it should prove impossible for me to do so owing to my changing my mind, she should be entitled to claim from me three hundred florins a year.'"[72] We can just imagine Leopold's rage—his yearly pay was four hundred florins—when he read these lines. Wolfgang took entire responsibility for this unpleasant contract, stating that Caecilia Weber had nothing to do with it, since she, too, was subjected to Thorwart's demands. As for Constanze, Wolfgang told his father that "the angelic girl" had torn the contract to pieces as soon as it was signed and her guardian had left. We will never know whether she was sincere or was playing a part. Leopold probably thought the latter. Wolfgang, on the other hand, in a clumsy attempt to find other arguments to reassure his father that he had made the right choice, ingenuously writes that Constanze "has everything but money." At the time dowries and promises of marriage subject to monetary sanctions were fairly common, as we have already seen. It was the same Thorwart who had obliged Joseph Lange, Aloysia's husband, to promise a sizable sum to Caecilia Weber. I believe, however, that our Mozart, although sincerely in love with Constanze, was being pressured by Thorwart, by Caecilia Weber, and by Constanze herself.

We can judge from the response that Wolfgang sent on 16 January 1782 that Leopold must have written him a letter full of particularly harsh remarks about his son, Caecilia Weber, and Constanze's guardian. "I quite agree with you," Wolfgang states, "in thinking that Madame Weber and Herr von Thorwart have been to blame in showing too much regard for their own interests, though the Madame is no longer her own mistress and has to leave everything, particularly all matters of this kind, to the guardian, who (as he has never made my acquaintance) is by no means bound to trust me." Thus Thorwart had been too hasty, too diffident, and for that reason had made a mistake: "Herr von Thorwart did not behave well," Mozart adds, "but not so badly that he and Madame Weber 'should be put in chains, made to sweep streets, and have boards hung round their necks with the words *seducers of youth.*' That too is an exaggeration." Leopold had obviously suggested that Caecilia Weber and Thorwart should be arrested for having deliberately promoted an affair with Constanze as a means for fanning the flames of Wolfgang's love and snagging him. Wolfgang told his father, "Even if what you say were true, that in order to catch me she opened her house, let me have the run of it, gave me every opportunity, etc., even so the punishment [going about in chains, etc.] would be rather severe."[73]

The marriage took place a few months later, on 4 August 1782, and the intervening months were filled with frantic activity. Several times Constanze was the guest of Baroness Waldstätten, who functioned as protector of the engaged couple. Leopold, writing from Salzburg, accused Constanze of harboring "evil thoughts," an accusation that Wolfgang denied in a letter to his father of 30 January: "Please do not suspect my dear Constanze of harboring such evil thoughts. Believe me, if she had such a disposition, I could not possibly love her." In short, the entire episode of the guardian and the prenuptial contract had been unpleasant. If there were any "evil thoughts," Wolfgang attributed them only to his future mother-in-law: "Both she [Constanze] and I long ago observed her mother's designs. But the latter is very much mistaken, for she wishes us (when we marry) to live with her, as she has apartments to let. That is out of the question." Constanze herself, Mozart declared, "intends to see very little of her mother and I shall do my best to stop it altogether, for we know her too well."[74]

Caecilia Weber was strong-willed, and she managed to get Constanze back under the family roof until the wedding. Wolfgang, in a letter to Nannerl dated 13 February describing his daily schedule, notes that in the evening, when he had finished working, he would go to see Constanze, "though the joy of seeing one another is nearly always spoilt by her mother's bitter remarks."[75] She was probably trying to hasten their wedding day. Wolfgang, writing to his father on 10 April, states that Frau Weber "likes wine, and more so, I admit, than a woman ought to." He adds quickly, "Still, I have never yet seen her drunk and it would be a lie if I were to say so. The children only drink water—and, although their mother almost forces wine upon them, she cannot induce them to touch it. This often leads to a lot of wrangling — can you imagine a mother quarreling with her children about such a matter?"[76] In short, Constanze was an angel, whereas the mother was stupid [*dumme*], as Wolfgang confided to Baroness Waldstätten on the eve of his wedding.

Leopold did not wish to give his consent to the marriage. He made up his mind to do so only at the last moment, indeed so late that it arrived in Vienna the day after the wedding had been celebrated. We get the impression that Leopold finally realized that he was facing a fait accompli, and that he came around to sanctioning it only to prevent an irreparable break with his son.

Toward the end of 1781, while all this was going on, Wolfgang scored a striking success, both musical and social, with a concert given at court in the presence of Emperor Joseph II, where both Mozart and Muzio Clementi played. Wolfgang treated his Roman rival with a touch of disdain, writing to his father, "Another clavier-player, an Italian called Clementi, has arrived here. He too had been invited to court. I was sent fifty ducats yesterday for my playing, and indeed I need them very badly at the moment."[77] Wolfgang returned to the subject of Clementi in two following letters (12 and 16 January 1782), indicating that his father had asked him for particulars. Wolfgang judges Clementi severely and in nearly the same terms in both letters: "Now a word about Clementi," he writes on 16 January, "He is an excellent cembalo player, but that is all. He has great facility with his right hand. His star passages are thirds. Apart from this, he has not a farthing's worth of taste or feeling; he is a mere *mechanicus*."[78] A year and a half later, in a letter dated 7 June 1783, Wolfgang commented with equal severity about some Clementi sonatas, summing up his remarks with "Clementi is a *ciarlatano*, like all Italians."[79]

The emperor had wanted Clementi to play first: he was a guest, and he came from the holy city of Rome, thus he deserved precedence. Mozart played his first piece immediately after Clementi. Both musicians were then to perform some sonatas by Paisiello, pick out a theme from them, and improvise variations on two fortepianos. Although Mozart's instrument was out of tune and had three keys that stuck, the emperor declared, "Never mind!" At the end, Joseph II seemed satisfied with the duel. According to Francis Carr, the emperor had wagered on the contest with Archduchess Maria of Russia, choosing Mozart.[80] In his letters Mozart makes no reference to winner or loser, however. "The emperor," he states, "was very gracious, said a great deal to me privately, and even mentioned my marriage. Who knows? Perhaps—what do you think? At any rate I might make the attempt. More of this in my next letter."[81]

During that same period Caecilia Weber and Thorwart, the guardian, were plotting to hasten Constanze's and Wolfgang's wedding. Mozart was by now much in view, and he had the emperor's confidence. He was gaining ground as a composer and was in the process of composing *The Abduction from the Seraglio;* hence he could be considered a good match and it wouldn't do to let him get away. In that opera the male protagonist, the noble Belmonte, makes fun of Osmin, the guardian of the harem, and plots with the woman he loves (whose name is Konstanze) to carry her off. In real life, however, during the months in which the opera was being composed, there was another plot in which a girl named Constanze succeeded, with the help of a mother and a guardian not too unlike Osmin, in carrying off Wolfgang.

## *The Abduction from the Seraglio* and Wolfgang's Marriage (July 1781–August 1782)

The libretto for *The Abduction from the Seraglio* (K. 384) was in preparation from the spring of 1781. In June, Count Rosenberg had approved the text in German by Johann Gottlieb Stephanie and commissioned Mozart to write the music. By 30 July, Wolfgang had received part of the libretto. By early August he had already set several scenes to music and had finished the chorus for the Turkish Janissaries. By 22 August the first act was ready. At that point Wolfgang had to stop because Stephanie had not sent him the text of the other two acts. The composition of the opera lasted nearly a year, reaching completion only in May 1782.

*The Abduction* is a singspiel, which means that it is a theatrical work in part sung and in part spoken. Mozart had already composed two other similar works: *Bastien und Bastienne* in 1768 and the incomplete *Zaide* in 1779–80. The latter took place in the harem of a Turkish sultan, and thus was an anticipation of *The Abduction*. *Zaide* too had an Osmin, guardian of the harem and a basso, as does *The Abduction*, but in the latter work the proprietor of the harem is not a sultan but a Turkish pasha named Selim.

We might well wonder how on earth Mozart, in Vienna, was induced to compose a singspiel, a work halfway between *serio* and *buffo*, in the Turkish vogue. One explanation lies in the broad diffusion of a mode that began after a memorable battle that took place at the gates of Vienna in 1683, a Turkish defeat that launched the decline of the Ottoman Empire.

A "Turkish problem" still remained, however, as Bernard Lewis has observed,[82] but now it centered on Turkey's weakness, not its strength. The
Austro-Turkish wars that had marked the entire eighteenth century came
to an end in 1791, the year of Mozart's death. In 1781–1782 the Turks no
longer inspired fear, as they once had, and an author or a composer could
permit himself the luxury of putting them on stage in a singspiel, even of
setting them up as objects of laughter. In *The Abduction from the Seraglio*,
however, Pasha Selim is neither ridiculous nor cruel (as is Osmin, the
overseer of the harem), but rather an adroit, noble, and generous man,
who at the end of the singspiel consents to the marriage of his slave Konstanze to Belmonte and permits her to return to freedom in Spain. Selim
is the bearer of a message of humanity and peace and, as Claudio Casini
has observed, in order for that message of peace to come through clearly
to the audience, Mozart wanted the part to be played not by a singer but
by an actor speaking prose unaccompanied by music.[83] All the other characters are singing roles. As for "Turkish" music, Mozart uses echoes of it
only in the overture, the first act chorus, and the final chorus, where he
reinforces the orchestra with a piccolo, horns, trumpets, timpani, cym-
bals, triangle, and a bass drum. Whenever he mentions these pieces in his
letters, however, he always notes the Viennese partiality for this style.[84]

Mozart created this singspiel in his own manner, that is, without respect for the traditions of the genre, but rather by innovating and blurring
the confines between serious drama and farce. The mix met with some bewilderment on the part of the spectators, first among them Joseph II, who
had commissioned the work. The emperor would have preferred something much more facile and popular, something pleasing to the broader
public that would further his project of linguistic "germanization." *The
Abduction from the Seraglio* was far from this: it was a noble and refined
work overflowing with new music. Even the overture could be considered "revolutionary" from a musical standpoint, as Stefan Kunze has remarked.[85] Mozart himself commented, in a letter dated 26 September
1781, that listening to it, "I doubt that anyone, even if his previous night
has been a sleepless one, could go to sleep over it."[86] The premiere of the
opera took place at Vienna's Burgtheater on 16 July 1782, only two weeks
before Wolfgang's wedding. According to one of Mozart's first biographers, at the end Joseph II commented, "Very many notes, my dear Mozart," to which Mozart is supposed to have responded, with his usual bold-
ness, "Exactly as many as are necessary, Your Majesty."[87] This exchange
may never have taken place, but it expresses the work's uneasy reception.
The emperor feared that the music was too sweeping, too much the pro-

tagonist, and that it might give the singing too humble a role and prove distracting to the audience. Wolfgang firmly wanted the text to be subordinate to his music. He had said as much in a letter to his father dated 13 October 1781: "I should say that in an opera the poetry must be altogether the obedient daughter of the music. Why do Italian comic operas please everywhere—in spite of their miserable libretti—even in Paris, where I myself witnessed their success? Just because there the music reigns supreme and when one listens to it all else is forgotten."[88]

In any event, the Viennese audience gave a warm welcome to *The Abduction from the Seraglio,* to the point that the Burgtheater had to give fifteen repeat performances within the year. The following year the opera was also produced in Prague, Mannheim, Berlin, and five or six other big cities in Germany, making Mozart's name known everywhere. The composer's recompense from the emperor, however, was half of what he had received in Munich for *Idomeneo.*[89]

Leopold Mozart gave an even cooler reception to *The Abduction.* He did not even think it appropriate to go to Vienna for the premiere, nor did he deign to open the packet containing the score of the singspiel, which Wolfgang had sent him immediately. On 31 July 1782 Wolfgang wrote his father, "I received today your letter of the 26th, but a cold, indifferent letter, such as I could never have expected in reply to my news of the good reception of my opera. I thought (judging by my own feelings) that you would hardly be able to open the parcel for excitement and eagerness to see your son's work, which, far from merely pleasing, is making such a sensation in Vienna that people refuse to hear anything else, so that the theater is always packed."[90] We can find many explanations for this paternal coldness. First of all, Leopold was in a contrary mood because of the imminent wedding. Second, the success of *The Abduction* proved that Wolfgang was able to make his way alone brilliantly, and that hurt his father immensely: this was the first great opera that Wolfgang had created and composed without having Leopold at his side. Third, Leopold was still suffering because his son had abandoned him, and the success in the Burgtheater wiped out all hope of his return to Salzburg.

As we have already noted, paternal consent to Wolfgang's marriage with Constanze Weber arrived in Vienna after the wedding had taken place. In the preceding months Leopold had done his utmost to oppose the marriage, while Wolfgang tried in vain to soothe his father's and his sister's nerves. Leopold and Nannerl were in anguish, suspected the worst, and feared, also because they had never had an opportunity to meet Constanze or any other member of the Weber family. They spun fantasies about the bride-to-be and her family on the basis of what Wolfgang had written, and perhaps on the basis of gossip and malicious rumors that reached Salzburg. Wolfgang himself contributed to their anxiety in letters that told about the marriage contract and gave a less than flattering description of his future mother-in-law and Constanze's sisters. They could hardly have found such details reassuring.

It is possible that in his heart of hearts even Wolfgang himself had some doubts, up to the last minute, about the wisdom of getting married. On 29 April, for example, he felt obliged to write a letter to Constanze after a spat over a parlor game that had taken place, in his absence, in the house of Baroness Waldstätten. The game involved paying a forfeit in which Constanze had permitted a young gallant to measure her calves (perhaps her thigh?). Constanze became furious at Mozart's reprimand. In order to understand why Mozart was so disturbed, we should recall that in those days self-respecting women did not show even their ankles in public. Wolfgang writes to her, "I entreat you, therefore, to ponder and reflect upon the cause of all this unpleasantness, which arose from my being annoyed that you were so impudently inconsiderate as to say to your sisters — and, be it noted, in my presence — that you had let a *chapeau* [young man] measure the calves of your legs. No woman who cares for her honor can do such a thing."[91] To Wolfgang's way of thinking, there was no excuse for such behavior, and it did not matter whether the Baroness Waldstätten had been subjected to the same penalty during the game. The baroness was a mature woman ("past her prime") and known for being "inclined to be promiscuous with her favors." Wolfgang wanted Constanze to be different from the baroness. He offered her his final warning:

> I hope, dearest friend, that, even if you do not wish to become my wife, you will never lead a life like hers. If it was quite impossible for you to resist the desire to take part in the game . . . then why in the name of Heaven did you not take the ribbon and measure your own calves *yourself* (as *all self-respecting women* have done on similar occasions in my presence) and not allow a *chapeau* to do so?—Why, I myself *in the presence of others* would never have done such a thing to you. I should have handed you the ribbon myself. Still less, then, should you have allowed it to be done to you by a stranger—a man about whom I know nothing.[92]

I have lingered over this episode because, examined closely, it offers some explanation of the attraction that Constanze exerted over her fiancé. Wolfgang was clearly very jealous, as this letter demonstrates. Still, he must have been strongly attracted by a certain atmosphere of erotic co-quetry that radiated from Constanze, and perhaps also from Baroness Waldstätten. The baroness, whom Mozart calls "past her prime," was only thirty-eight in 1782, and must have been a most attractive woman. There was a pervasive eroticism in all of Viennese high society of the time and many liberties were winked at, to the point that extraconjugal love affairs were often exhibited without creating problems.

Constanze, Baroness Waldstätten, and the frivolity of the city of Vienna may have excited and appealed to Wolfgang. But back in Salzburg, Leopold was worried to distraction. The letter that he sent to Baroness Waldstätten on 23 August gives illuminating evidence of his state of mind in those difficult days. He first thanks her for having generously organized a nuptial banquet in honor of Wolfgang and Constanze in her palace. Then he adds, referring to his son, "Since he must realize that both morally and materially I am being punished for his conduct, all I can now do is to leave him to his own resources (as he evidently wishes) and pray God to bestow on him His paternal blessing and not withdraw from him His Divine Grace."[93] These are strong words, and they hint at a decision to disinherit Wolfgang. In the same letter Leopold adds:

> On the whole, I should feel quite easy in my mind, were it not that I have detected in my son an outstanding fault, which is, that he is far too *patient* or rather *easy-going*, too *indolent*, perhaps even too *proud*, in short, that he has the sum total of all those traits which render a man *inactive*; on the other hand, he is too *impatient*, too *hasty* and will not bide his time. Two opposing elements rule his nature; I mean, there is either too *much* or too *little*, never the golden mean. If he is not actually in want, then he is immediately satisfied and becomes *indolent* and *lazy*. If he has to bestir himself, then he realizes his worth and *wants to make his fortune at once*. Nothing must stand in his way; yet it is unfortunately the most capable people and those who possess outstanding genius who have the greatest obstacles to face.[94]

Thus Leopold was depicting his son as unbalanced and slothful, at the very moment in which this disgraceful son, thanks to *The Abduction from the Seraglio*, was receiving well-deserved recognition of his mastery and his labors. Leopold preferred to continue to think that without him, Wolfgang would be unable to achieve anything.

*The Abduction from the Seraglio* was in fact a masterpiece, even if many commentators think it inferior to the great Italian operas yet to come, *Don Giovanni*, *The Marriage of Figaro*, and *Così fan tutte*. Even Hildesheimer, who judges *The Abduction* inferior to the other three operas, states, "Even *Idomeneo* and *Die Entführung* are already more than mere masterpieces of their kind; even they break out of the bounds of the *opera seria* and *Singspiel* genres."[95] Goethe was shaken after hearing *The Abduction*. He too had thought of writing a singspiel in German with a friend, but, he stated, "all our endeavor . . . was lost when Mozart appeared. *Die Entführung aus dem Serail* conquered all, and our own carefully written piece has never been so much as mentioned in theater circles."[96] Wolfgang had taken great pains with *The Abduction* and had meditated every detail. There is a famous extract from the letter he sent his father on 26 September 1781 in which he explains why Osmin, the overseer of the harem, although a boor, an impertinent lout, and a man given to violence, deserves music that, while appropriate for depicting his rage, nevertheless observes stylistic proprieties. This is, Mozart explains, "since passions, whether violent or not, must never be expressed to the point of exciting disgust, and as music, even in the most terrible situations, must never offend the ear, but must please the listener, or in other words must never cease to be *music*."[97]

In *The Abduction from the Seraglio,* Pasha Selim eventually renounces his threatened revenge and permits the marriage of Belmonte and Konstanze. In Mozart's life the opposite happened, given that Leopold refused his consent. On 3 August 1782 the marriage contract was signed by the spouses before two witnesses, the surgeon Franz Gilowsky von Urazowa and Johann Cetto von Kronstorff, a government official. The religious ceremony took place the next day in the cathedral of St. Stephen in Vienna. Wolfgang and Constanze confessed and took communion before the ceremony. Aside from the bride and bridegroom, the others present were Constanze's mother and her sister Sophie, their guardian Johann Thorwart, and the two witnesses. After the ceremony Baroness Waldstätten gave a reception for her young friends and protégés and the wedding party in her house. As we have seen, Leopold's consent arrived only the following day, but in his defense it should be said that although in his letters Wolfgang repeatedly begged his father's authorization for his marriage, he never gave him a date for the ceremony. Even after the wedding, Wolfgang "forgot" to tell Leopold until 31 August what day the wedding had been celebrated. It is quite probable that his bad memory can be attributed to a desire to hide from his father the inconvenient fact that he had married before receiving his consent. In that era to marry without parental consent was considered disgraceful. Given the circumstances, we can understand why neither Leopold nor Nannerl sent any sort of wedding gift.

## Mozart and the Marketplace

From Leopold's point of view, Mozart had rebelled against him because he had separated from him and married Constanze, but also because he had chosen to live in Vienna without finding the fixed post that would guarantee the financial security of his entire family—that is, of Leopold, his sister Nannerl, Constanze, himself, and any children yet to be born of his marriage. Wolfgang thought he had no other choice, however. In Salzburg he was the prisoner of Colloredo and of a city in which he found no stimulation. Outside Salzburg there seemed to be no other court willing to pay him a salary. Only the free music market, then at its birth, could offer salvation. And this was in fact what happened.

At the beginning of his residence in Vienna, Wolfgang was still claiming to be seeking a permanent post. On 15 December 1781 he went so far as to promise his father one half of his future earnings in such a post. On 23 January 1782 he drew up a list for his father of three possibilities for stable employment. The first was to serve Alois Joseph von Liechtenstein, who was planning to create a wind-instrument band, for which Mozart might compose music: "This would not bring in very much, it is true, but it would be at least something certain, and I should not sign the contract unless it were to be for life." The second was to be taken into the service of Emperor Joseph II; the third, to obtain a post as Kapellmeister to Archduke Maximilian Franz, Joseph II's brother.[98]

Weeks and months went by without any word of these three projects, which Wolfgang may have invented just to satisfy Leopold. Mozart understood, and he perhaps may have known for some time, that henceforth he had to manage on his own. Moreover, thanks to his father, he had already gained experience with the resources of the marketplace in his childhood years, when they had traveled all over Europe. Everywhere they went he had collected prizes, money, and gifts of notable value, which had permitted his father to realize a sizable sum, in spite of the high cost of travel. Leopold did not believe for a minute that Wolfgang—by now twenty-six—could manage to get by without his aid. He was convinced that his son's organizational skills were inferior to his own, and, as we have seen from his letter of 23 August 1782, he thought Wolfgang indolent, unenterprising, lazy, proud, impatient, and incapable of administering his own affairs.

Leopold might also have thought that, whereas a child prodigy could be offered to the caprices of the public without harm, it would be demeaning for a mature and well-appreciated composer, as Wolfgang now was, to expose himself to its whims. In the late eighteenth century, musical compositions—sacred music aside—were considered mere entertainment, and the figure of the autonomous artist, fully aware of his own worth, respected for his talent and for that reason prized by the public, did not yet exist. Concerts with paid admission, the so-called "academies," in which secular music such as symphonies, quartets, or quintets was offered, were in their early stages. And as for an opera or any theatrical production, no composer could even dream of putting one on without munificent princely backing: a theatrical spectacle was an extremely costly affair involving singers, an orchestra, scenery, a hired theater, lights, and so forth. Only a court that had its own theater and sufficient funds could permit itself the luxury. Even the prince-bishop of Salzburg found keeping up a court theater beyond his means. Moreover, a paid audience was always likely to be more capricious and unpredictable in its demands than a court. Out of long tradition, in short, all the best musicians and composers preferred to be supported by a stipend from an enlightened prince.

Mozart would have preferred that route as well. But he possessed the talent and the courage that permitted him to break with tradition. The historian Edward Crankshaw, writing about the changing role of the artist in the society of the time, points out that Gluck still needed to rely on his papal title as a Knight of the Golden Spur to give himself status, that Haydn possessed no title, but that Mozart, who held a papal title of a grade superior to Gluck's, never used it, having decided that his genius was enough to distinguish him.[99] He was judged to be foolhardy for doing so, too autonomous, and proud—just as Leopold said. In those days it was inconceivable that a musician survive on the open market for the simple reason that copyright and royalties did not yet exist. The composer of an opera or of any musical work was paid for the first performance alone, receiving no further remuneration if the work was played again. The success of an opera and its repeat performances might encourage the sale of sheet music for arias and duets, which would provide the composer with further earnings, but all too often it was the copyists who pocketed the receipts. Even the publishing of musical scores was in its infancy. In Italy, where opera dominated the musical scene, all scores were copied by hand because there were as yet no Italian music publishers. It would have seemed like folly to invest large sums to print the score of an opera when fashion changed rapidly. This situation meant that copyists played an important role. Many of them were highly capable musicians, sometimes even composers, and they were expected to be able to rework musical texts and on occasion complete them, filling in instrumental parts that a composer may barely have sketched out or even omitted, While Mozart rarely made "fair copies" of his own compositions—a job he left to professional scribes—he always worked out his music in full.

The idea of guaranteeing the authors of books, theatrical texts, and musical works a permanent monetary income from their production began to appear in England during the eighteenth century, but the first official recognition of authors' rights seems to have occurred in Paris after the French Revolution in 1791, the year of Mozart's death. In Italy authors' rights were introduced by Napoleon in 1801. In England the Dramatic Copyright Act, which also protected operas, was decreed in 1833 by William IV. Any practical application of copyright, both within each country and in international commerce, came slowly, so slowly that the first member of the Mozart family to benefit from them was one of Wolfgang's sons, Carl Thomas, who was born in 1784 and became a civil servant in Milan. In 1844, fifty-three years after his father's death, he bought a modest property in Brianza, north of the city, thanks to royalties from performances of *The Marriage of Figaro* in France.

As Marcello Sorce Keller has observed, before copyright was introduced, a composer, who was given a one-time payment for each new work, was eager to have his compositions meet with sufficient success to stimulate other commissions that would generate new income, but was not eager to have a work be such a success that it became a classic, repeated time after time without any economic profit to him.[100] The notion of a permanent repertory was long to form. The situation was somewhat similar to that of the cinema market today: films are usually consumed in one season, after which they are shown in cinema clubs, seen on television, or distributed on tape or disk, but seldom projected in first-run or even second-run houses. Thus the market requires a constant supply of new material. This is why eighteenth-century opera composers such as Niccolò Piccinni, Domenico Cimarosa, and Giovanni Paisiello found it to their advantage to churn out three or four operas a year to maintain their visibility and earn money.

Mozart behaved differently. In all of his life as a composer of theatrical works—that is, from 1767, the year in which he wrote *Apollo et Hyacinthus*, to 1791, the year of his death—he wrote only seventeen stage works, or an average of fewer than one per year. In his last ten years in Vienna he completed only seven operas, a very low average for the time. These seven, however, include *The Abduction from the Seraglio, The Marriage of Figaro, Don Giovanni, Così fan tutte,* and *The Magic Flute.* There are several explanations for this relatively low theatrical production. First, Wolfgang did not have a fixed post that obliged him to produce works frequently and with a particular production date in mind. Second, Mozart's music contained many new elements, and contemporary audiences found it somewhat difficult to accept. Consequently, commissions did not flow in, which may in fact be the principal reason for his not composing more operas. But another explanation might lie in Mozart's complicated relationship with money. He earned large sums, but he spent even larger ones and ran up debts. He gambled, and he gave sumptuous gifts to himself, to Constanze, and perhaps even to other women. He loved money, to the point of writing to his father on 4 April 1781: "My sole purpose [for remaining in Vienna] is to make as much money as possible; for after good health it is the best thing to have."[101] He did not love money to the point of sacrificing his music to it however. He would have refused to lower the quality of his operas by turning out one after another. During his Viennese years only once did he agree to write a comedy with music in haste (*Der Schauspieldirektor*, K. 486).

This is why Mozart ranks seventh in a numerical listing of composers whose operas were produced most in Vienna, after Paisiello, Vicente Martín y Soler, Cimarosa, Pietro Guglielmi, Giuseppe Sarti, and of course the highly privileged Salieri, whom Mozart disrespectfully referred to as "Bombonieri" (bonbon boxes).[102] Mozart did not have great luck as a composer during his lifetime. He was recognized as being highly talented, he was esteemed, and he obtained striking successes with audiences, but in the musical hierarchy of Vienna he ranked much lower than our current estimation of his worth would indicate. He was, however, the most-played composer of theatrical works with German librettos: all those who ranked higher in the overall category of opera were Italians, except for Martín y Soler, who was Spanish.

Mozart was great because, in spite of the extreme fragility of the market of his day, he succeeded in composing works that have stood the test of time. To be sure, many of his works were forgotten for some time after his death. But from the latter half of the twentieth century on, they have conquered a dominant position in the world repertory, precisely because their vitality and modernity have kept them fresh. Mozart composed works of lasting value because he was highly gifted, creative, had a strong sense of fantasy, and did not intend to waste his talent. Aware that we have one and only one life to live, he did not want to go through his own without leaving a profound mark. The composers who were more successful in Vienna in his day are either forgotten today or, at best, played much less often.

Piero Buscaroli tells us that Wolfgang suffered the market rather than seeking it because, like Leporello in *Don Giovanni*, he would have liked to "find a better master"—that is, an employer different from Colloredo in a city more lively than Salzburg.[103] Norbert Elias also states that Wolfgang became a "freelance artist," not because that was his true aspiration, but because he could not stand Salzburg.[104] He accepted the market as a provisory solution, as the only solution possible at the moment. If this is true, however, it is also true that, considering the results, Wolfgang adapted himself very well to the rules of commerce. We might even think that it was precisely thanks to those rules that Mozart managed to find the point of equilibrium between tradition and innovation, between the facile and the difficult, that makes his music so fascinating. If his music had been too innovative and complicated, it would have pleased no one and he would not have earned a penny.

Wolfgang disdained facile music, even though he realized that it would have brought him popular success. He sought some sort of middle road. He shared thoughts on the matter with his father in a letter of 28 December 1782, written in reference to the piano concertos (K. 413/387a and K. 414/385p) that he had just finished composing: "These concertos are a happy medium between what is too easy and too difficult; they are very brilliant, pleasing to the ear, and natural, without being vapid. There are passages here and there from which the connoisseurs alone can derive satisfaction; but these passages are written in such a way that the less learned cannot fail to be pleased, though without knowing why."[105] Nevertheless, Mozart was very uncertain of how the audience would greet his work. He comments in the same letter, "The golden mean of truth in all things is no longer either known or appreciated. In order to win applause one must write stuff which is so inane that a coachman could sing it, or so unintelligible that it pleases precisely because no sensible man can understand it." In any event, Wolfgang never forgot the demands of his listeners, whose ears must never be offended, not even by the music that accompanied the singing of the repellent Osmin.

According to Edward E. Lowinsky, much of Mozart's best music is based on irregularities and asymmetries that create a tension in the listeners and predispose them to clarifying resolutions.[106] But if we want to grasp the extreme novelty of many passages in Mozart we need to recall that even Arnold Schoenberg, the inventor of the twelve-tone method, took pains to acknowledge his debt to Mozart, stating that it was from him that he had learned how to vary the length of the musical phrase, how to form a thematic unity out of heterogeneous elements, and how to avoid constructions based on even numbers, but also how to develop secondary musical ideas.[107]

More than once, Mozart went too far, tipping beyond the delicate balancing point between what was acceptable to his contemporaries and what they judged to be too revolutionary, too free, and musically irregular—a criticism that today's listeners find difficult to grasp. In 1778 the Paris music publisher Sieber refused to print the *Jenamy* Piano Concerto (K. 271) because he found it too boldly written, and the Viennese publisher, Hoffmeister, refused to put out other compositions by Mozart after he had printed the Piano Quartet in G Minor (K. 478) in 1785.[108] We have already seen Joseph II's dismay at the overflowing of music in *The Abduction from the Seraglio*. In January 1787 the *Magazin der Musik* offered this severe evaluation of Mozart's six string quartets dedicated to Haydn (K. 387, 421/417b, 428/421b, 458, 464, and 465): "The pity is only that he aims too high in his artful and truly beautiful compositions, in order to become a new creator, whereby it must be said that feeling and heart profit little; his new Quartets for 2 violins, viola, and bass, which he has dedicated to Haydn, may well be called too highly seasoned—and whose palate can endure this for long?"[109]

Peter Gay gives a good description of the vicissitudes of the reception of Mozart's music through the ages. Throughout the nineteenth century his piano concertos were hardly ever played because they gave little scope to "virtuosos" for spectacular exhibitions of their talents. Those concertos have an intensity, a linearity, and a rigor that made them unfashionable in the romantic era. Until the early twentieth century the greater public remembered Mozart as the composer of *Eine kleine Nachtmusik* (K. 525), the Turkish March in the Piano Sonata K. 331/300i, and other "easy-listening" compositions. In the collective memory Mozart remained a child prodigy sitting erect at the keyboard. The volcanic composer that we know and admire today was much less famous. Peter Gay points out that for a century and a half Wolfgang was understood and appreciated only by such other great musicians as Mendelssohn, Beethoven, Schubert, Schumann, Chopin, Tchaikovsky, Brahms, and Richard Strauss.[110] In spite of having the stamp of approval of such authoritative musicians, Mozart's compositions still failed to enter into the repertory of opera theaters and concert halls. They were rediscovered late, to the point that a conductor of the stature of Bruno Walter confessed that at the beginning of his career, in the early years of the twentieth century, Mozart's works were somewhat alien to him.[111] *Don Giovanni* was performed at the Rome Opera House for the first time in 1886, not to be repeated until 1935. *Le nozze di Figaro* was produced in Rome for the first time in 1931, *The Magic Flute* in 1937, *The Abduction from the Seraglio* in 1941, and *Così fan tutte* in 1950. Although in Great Britain and the United States *Figaro* was staged as early as 1812 and 1824, respectively, *The Magic Flute* in 1811 and 1833, and *The Abduction in 1827* and 1860, no American opera house produced *Così fan tutte* before 1922.[112]

# Vienna: Difficulties and Successes

## Earning a Living in Vienna (1782–1783)

Given that he had to make his living in the market, Wolfgang took pains to reassure his father and sister that he was neither indolent nor lazy. He probably stretched the truth to burnish his merits: "Every morning at six o'clock my friseur arrives and wakes me, and by seven I have finished dressing. I compose until ten, when I give a lesson to Frau Trattner and at eleven to the Countess Rumbeke, each of whom pays me six ducats for twelve lessons."[1] On 13 February 1782 he gave his sister a particularly detailed account of his schedule: "Then I lunch, unless I am invited to some house where they lunch at two or even three o'clock, as, for example, today and tomorrow at Countess Zichy's and Countess Thun's. I can never work before five or six o'clock in the evening, and even then I am often prevented by a concert." He adds that immediately thereafter he went to see Constanze, who was not yet his wife, then returned home, unless there was a concert: "It is my custom (especially if I get home early) to compose a little before going to bed. I often go on writing until one — and am up again at six."[2] Thus in order to have time for composing he slept no more than five hours a night.

On 28 December 1782, after his marriage, Wolfgang continued to try to reassure his father that he was working hard: "Altogether I have so much to do that often I do not know whether I am on my head or my heels. I spend the whole forenoon giving lessons until two o'clock, when we have lunch. After the meal I must give my poor stomach an hour for digestion. The evening is therefore the only time I have for composing and of that I can never be sure, as I am often asked to perform at concerts."[3] These descriptions were an attempt on Wolfgang's part to counter the bad opinion that his father and sister had of him, but is indisputable that during the Vienna years he worked with a will, performing in academies, giving lessons, and composing concertos, operas, and music of many other sorts.

When Leopold came to Vienna, he himself was struck by the frenetic atmosphere in his son's house. On 12 March 1785 he wrote to Nannerl:

> We never get to bed before one o'clock and I never get up before nine. We lunch at two or half past. . . . Every day there are concerts; and the whole time is given up to teaching, music, composing, and so forth. I feel rather out of it all. If only the concerts were over! It is impossible for me to describe the rush and bustle. Since my arrival your brother's fortepiano has been taken at least a dozen times to the theater or to some other house. He has had a large fortepiano pedal made, which stands under the instrument and is about two feet longer and extremely heavy. It is taken to the Mehlgrube [the ballroom near the New Market where Wolfgang organized his academies] every Friday and has also been taken to Count Zichy's and to Prince Kaunitz's.[4]

From the beginning of his Viennese sojourn Mozart successfully participated in concerts and academies, but there were also difficulties. In a letter dated 17 August 1782, written after the encouragement he had received from *The Abduction from the Seraglio,* Wolfgang wrote his father that he was thinking of leaving Vienna to seek his fortune in Paris, finding work with the Concert Spirituel of Jean Joseph Legros, with the Concert des Amateurs, and giving lessons: "I should have plenty of pupils— and now that I have a wife I could superintend them more easily and attentively—and then with the help of compositions and so forth—but indeed I should rely chiefly on opera commissions."[5] He added that he had recently been studying French and had taken three English lessons and hoped that soon he would be able to read books in that language fairly easily. He was not only thinking about moving to Paris but of going to London. No one had offered him permanent employment in Vienna. As for the open market, there were too many musicians competing with one another and concert halls were scarce.

Mozart did not leave Vienna, however, and little by little his position in the capital improved. As early as 1783 he was engaged for a growing number of performances in private houses and concerts for a paying public. On 4 January 1783 he took part in an academy at the residence of councilor Anton von Spielmann. On 11 March he performed, with his sister-in-law Aloysia Lange, in an academy at the Burgtheater, with Gluck in the audience. The following day he took part in another academy in the house of Count Johann Esterházy, a major patron and a prominent Freemason. Sunday 23 March another academy was organized, for his benefit, at the Burgtheater. Emperor Joseph II, who was present, give him twenty-five ducats (112½ florins). Wolfgang's earnings, which included the entire proceeds, amounted to almost 1,600 florins, or four times his annual stipend in Salzburg. The following Sunday he performed once more at the Burgtheater with the singer Teresa Teyber, again in the presence of Joseph II, in an academy at which he played the Piano Concerto in C Major (K. 415/387b) and improvised variations on themes by Gluck and Paisiello. Unfortunately, we have no documentation regarding the improvisations, but according to Mozart's contemporaries, the Viennese found him even more impressive as an improviser than as a composer.

The academy of 23 March 1783 was a triumph for Mozart. In it he also presented a revised and corrected version of his latest symphony (no. 35), better known as the *Haffner* Symphony (K. 385). This work is certainly among Mozart's finest, thanks in particular to the last movement, in which a theme taken from one of Osmin's arias in *The Abduction from the Seraglio* is elaborated with impetuous energy. The work had originally been composed as a serenade in 1782 at the request of the Haffner family, Salzburg merchants, who wanted to celebrate the ennoblement of Sigmund Haffner the Younger. We know that earlier, in 1778, Wolfgang had turned to the Strasbourg office of the Haffner firm for a loan of eight louis d'or. The Haffners were illustrious and powerful members of the very Salzburg society on which Mozart had turned his back, and the fact that they had thought of him for this commission must have been a particular satisfaction to him. In the same period Wolfgang enjoyed another bit of revenge on his native city when the eighteen-year-old Countess Pálffy, niece of his archenemy, Prince-Bishop Colloredo, became his pupil. He wrote to his father on 4 January 1783, "I got a new pupil today . . . the daughter of the archbishop's sister. But please keep this news to yourself for the present, for I am not quite sure whether her family would like it to be known."[6]

Concertos for piano and orchestra were often featured in the academies that Mozart organized. The pianoforte was becoming a popular and highly fashionable instrument. It was attracting a new audience to music, and Mozart knew just how to dazzle this new public, since he himself conducted the orchestra, played the piano, and improvised on it as well. Between the end of 1782 and the first months of 1783 Wolfgang wrote three fine piano concertos (K. 413/387a in F, 414/385p in A, and 415/387b in C), and he hoped to earn handsome sums from them. On 28 December 1782

he announced to his father that was going to perform them in public subscription concerts, and that the subscription price was six ducats (twenty-
seven florins). Leopold was alarmed, finding the figure exaggeratedly
high. In a letter of 22 January 1783 Wolfgang sought to reassure him: the
ticket cost only four ducats (eighteen florins) and was good for any two of
the three concerts, if enough subscriptions were sold. The target number
was never achieved, and once more his father had an opportunity to treat
his son as conceited and rash. The concertos were excellent, however, and
all three were published by Artaria & Co. in 1785.

## Between Haydn and Bach: Opera Projects and the Birth of Wolfgang's First Son (December 1782–November 1783)

On 31 December 1782 Mozart completed the first of the six string quartets
dedicated to Franz Joseph Haydn (K. 387), a difficult and novel work, and
one that inspired a degree of bewilderment, as is the case with all new,
bold, and truly innovative works. Mozart had already composed a dozen
or so string quartets, but had written none for a decade. It was Haydn who
prompted him to return to the quartet by the example of his six Russian
Quartets, written in 1781 on the occasion of the visit to Vienna of Grand
Duke Paul of Russia, the future Czar Paul I. Haydn claimed to have written these quartets "in a special and completely new form."[7] Mozart found
them fascinating, and he was immediately motivated to imitate them and
go Haydn one better.

The last movement of Mozart's first *Haydn* Quartet (K. 387) shows
the clear influence of his counterpoint studies and his growing awareness of the music of Johann Sebastian Bach. The weekly musical evenings
in Gottfried van Swieten's house, which Mozart attended, often featured
works by Bach, whom the general public had forgotten but whose music
Mozart studied: although Mozart was quite aware of being a great composer, he never ceased learning, with a humility known only to superior
minds. Bach's influence on Mozart can be seen not only in the first *Haydn*
Quartet, but also in such piano pieces as the Fantasia in C Minor (K.
396/385f) and Prelude and Fugue in C Major (K. 394/383a), in his arrangements of six preludes and fugues of Bach and his son W. F. Bach for violin,
viola, and cello (K. 404a) and five fugues of J. S. Bach for string quartet
(K. 405), as well as the three concertos for piano and orchestra composed
between the end of 1782 and the beginning months of 1783, not to mention the Canon in B-flat (K. 233/382d), which has a blatantly vulgar title,
"Lech mir im Arsch," which needs no translation. Written for his friends,

the canon has not only playful, vulgar, even indecent elements, but also an appealing melody and profoundly daring polyphony. Mozart composed other canons to obscene texts, and his publishers found them worth issuing—with other words substituted for the original ones.

It should also be noted that despite his declared interest in writing operas, after *The Abduction from the Seraglio* in 1782 Mozart completed no other opera in Vienna until *The Marriage of Figaro* in 1786. On 5 February 1783 he told his father that he was eager to produce a new opera, but not in Italian: "I do not believe that the Italian opera will keep going for long, and besides, I hold with the Germans." His greatest operatic success had been a work in German, *Die Entführung aus dem Serail*, and he dearly wanted to repeat that success. His letter continues: "Every nation has its own opera and why not Germany? Is not German as singable as French and English? Is it not more so than Russian? Very well then! I am now writing a German opera for myself. I have chosen Goldoni's comedy 'Il servitore di due padroni,' and the whole of the first act has now been translated. Baron Binder is the translator. But we are keeping it a secret until it is quite finished. Well, what do you think of this scheme? Do you not think that I shall make a good thing of it?"[8] Nothing came of the project, and nothing remains of the music composed by Mozart, with the possible exception of two arias (K. 433/416c, a fragment, and 435/416b).

In December 1782 Count Rosenberg-Orsini, acting for Joseph II (the count had commissioned *The Abduction from the Seraglio* the year before), proposed to Mozart that he write a new Italian opera, but he did not offer a formal contract. Mozart, who loved writing operas, went to work immediately to find a text. He wrote to Leopold on 7 May 1783: "I have looked through at least a hundred libretti and more, but I have hardly found a single one with which I am satisfied." In the same letter Mozart speaks to his father of Lorenzo Da Ponte for the first time: "Our poet here is now a certain Abbate da Ponte. He has an enormous amount to do in revising pieces for the theater and he has to write *per obbligo* an entirely new libretto for Salieri, which will take him two months. He has promised after that to write a new libretto for me. But who knows whether he will be able to keep his word—or will want to?" Mozart had little confidence in Da Ponte or in Italians in general: "As you are aware, these Italian gentlemen are very civil to your face [*ins Gesicht*]! Enough, we know them! If he is in league with Salieri, I shall never get anything out of him."[9] He was wrong. Da Ponte furnished the libretto for Salieri's opera, *Un ricco di un giorno,* but he went on to write for Mozart. In any event, since he wanted an Italian text right away, Wolfgang turned once more to Abbé Varesco, the librettist of *Idomeneo*, and Varesco gave him the text of an *opera buffa*, *L'oca del Cairo* (The Cairo Goose), on which Mozart worked with great concentration, especially toward the end of the year 1783.

At the same time, the life of the young married couple went on, surrounded by the dazzle of Vienna. On 22 January 1783 Wolfgang wrote his father that he had organized a dance party in his house, the men contributing to the expenses by paying two florins each. The party began at six in the evening and ended at seven the next morning. Among the guests were Baron Raimund Wetzlar von Plankenstern, Baroness Waldstätten, Aloysia Weber and her husband Joseph Lange, and various other members of the aristocracy, along with professors, actors, actresses, and singers. "It would be impossible to name them all," Mozart adds. It was Carnival time, and he intended to enjoy himself: "I should like you to send me your Harlequin costume,"[10] he says in the same letter. Leopold sent the costume, and Wolfgang wore it on 3 March, the Monday before Mardi Gras, when he took part in a pantomime ballet of his devising for which he had written music on the theme of Pantalone, Colombine, and Harlequin (K. 446/416d). The music has been reconstructed from two autograph manuscripts (which vary slightly) for the first violin part. Aloysia was Columbine, her husband, Joseph Lange, was Pierrot, an old dancing master was Pantalone, and Wolfgang played Harlequin.

Wolfgang wrote to his father on 7 June 1783, inviting him to come to Vienna and asking him to stand as godfather for their first child, whose birth was imminent. He told his father that if the baby were a boy he would be christened Leopold; if a girl, Leopoldina. Leopold responded from Salzburg with a letter that has not come down to us, but in which, after explaining that he could not come, he probably said that he had no rigid demands concerning the child's name. In any event, Constanze gave birth to a boy on 17 June, who was baptized with the name Raimund, given that Baron Raimund Wetzlar von Plankenstern acted as the child's godfather. The baron was a wealthy gentleman of Jewish origin who had converted to Catholicism and had taken the young Mozart couple under his protection. Wolfgang described the events surrounding the christening to Leopold with a bit of embarrassment. When the baron was notified of the child's birth, he immediately volunteered to act as godfather:

> I could not refuse him and thought to myself, "After all, my boy can still
> be called Leopold." But while I was turning this round in my mind, the
> Baron said very cheerfully: "Ah, now you have a little Raimund"—and
> kissed the child. What was I to do? Well, I have had the child christened

Raimund Leopold. I must frankly confess that if you had not sent me in a letter your opinion on the matter, I should have been very much embarrassed, and I am not at all sure that I should not have refused his offer! But your letter has comforted me with the assurance that you will not disapprove of my action! After all, Leopold is one of his names.[11]

The fact remains that the baby was not named for his grandfather, yet another sign of the distance that had grown up between Wolfgang and Leopold.

In the same letter of 18 June Mozart gives his father news of the newborn baby and his mother that tells us much about the customs of the time. They feared that Constanze would develop milk fever because her breasts were very swollen, so Raimund was put out to a wet nurse. Mozart writes:

> I was quite determined that whether she should be able to do so or not, my wife was never to feed her child. Yet I was equally determined that my child was never to take the milk of a stranger! I wanted the child to be brought up on water, like my sister and myself. However, the midwife, my mother-in-law, and most people here have begged and implored me not to allow it, if only for the reason that most children here who are brought up on water do not survive, as the people here don't know how to do it properly. That induced me to give in, for I should not like to have anything to reproach myself with.[12]

## A Disheartening Return to Salzburg; A Stop in Linz (August–October 1783)

Leopold was still very much present in Wolfgang's life, as demonstrated by the letters that continued to go back and forth. His son was constantly on Leopold's mind, and he still hoped for a miracle that would bring him back to him. On his side, the son could not forget the twenty-five years they had spent together, nor his father's efforts to assist him in the past. Leopold's constant presence had eventually become such an encumbrance for his son that Wolfgang abandoned his father. But even that abandonment had contributed to arousing in Wolfgang a profound sense of guilt, and hence it served—perhaps to a pathological extent—to keep him bound to his father.

Leopold had not yet met Constanze Weber, and the problem of how to introduce her into the family had existed for some time. Twenty days after the wedding, in a letter dated 24 August 1782, Wolfgang spoke of coming to Salzburg with his bride. The trip was continually put off, however, first because of Mozart's many obligations in Vienna, the concerts he was organizing, the music lessons to be given, and also the success of *The Abduction from the Seraglio.* Then that autumn Constanze became pregnant. After the birth of their son on 17 June 1783, there were no more excuses. They left the tiny Raimund with his nurse and left. This was standard practice at the time: newborn babies were considered more or less like little animals who could be left wherever it was convenient. No one yet believed that to help them to grow well — or even to save their lives — they sorely needed attention, mother's milk, and maternal tenderness.

Wolfgang had always feared returning to Salzburg for at least two reasons. Above all, because the tension that existed between him and Leopold and Nannerl threatened to make a stay with them fairly unpleasant. But also because the laws covering the working relations between musicians and their employers might have led to his arrest by Colloredo's forces. Mozart had rebelled against Colloredo two years before, and the archbishop had never formally freed him from his service. Wolfgang could well have chosen to go to Salzburg in the summer precisely because Colloredo left the city during the hot months. If Mozart had come when the archbishop was in residence, his arrival might have been considered a serious provocation. In the letter that Wolfgang sent to his father on 5 July, a few days before his 12 July departure, he wrote explicitly about his fears. Using the family's secret code to circumvent the censors, he reports that many people had warned him: "Well, you will see, you will never get away again. You have no idea of what that wicked malevolent prince is capable of! And you cannot conceive what low tricks are resorted to in affairs of this kind. Take my advice and meet your father in some third place."[13] Wolfgang was looking for reassurance from Leopold, who duly sent it, and he probably added that all of Wolfgang's fears seemed like simple excuses aimed at putting off the trip. This Wolfgang denied, stating, "My friends' anxiety amounted to this: that, as I have never been discharged, the archbishop might have me arrested. But you have now set my mind completely at rest and we shall come in August, or certainly in September at the latest." As for Constanze, "She is always a little bit nervous lest you should not like her, because she is not pretty. But I console her as well as I can by telling her that my dearest father thinks more of inward than of outward beauty."[14] Nonetheless, Constanze feared her father-in-law and her sister-in-law for "inward" reasons as well, since she was well aware of their prejudices against her and that they felt themselves better educated, better mannered, and of a different nature from her and from Wolfgang.

We can understand her uneasiness if we read the short but by no means unconstrained letter that she wrote to Nannerl on 19 July 1783, a few days before their departure. Among other faults (in their eyes), like her mother Caecilia, Constanze could not even write correct German.[15]

Leopold was right, however, when he said they would not be arrested or tried. In Salzburg no one disturbed Wolfgang, and he and Constanze prolonged their stay until 27 October. On 24 August, moreover, the Mozarts were received by Franz Lactanz von Firmian, lord high chamberlain to the archbishop. On 26 October, just before Wolfgang's and Constanze's departure, the court orchestra performed Mozart's incomplete but beautiful Mass in C Minor (K. 427/417a) in the Abbey of St. Peter. Wolfgang had brought the score with him from Vienna to pay homage to his city of birth. (The score has no clarinet part, given that the clarinet was not yet common in Salzburg.)

It seems that Leopold's welcome to Constanze and Wolfgang was somewhat cold, and Nannerl's even more so. Years later Constanze stated that they had both thought this coldness unjustified.[16] We also know that little Raimund, left behind with his nurse, died on 18 August of intestinal convulsions, and we can surmise that news of his sudden death did little to make the atmosphere in the Mozart home any more cheerful. Much later, in 1829, when Constanze spoke of those days with the Vincent and Mary Novello, she told them that some time during that August the four members of the family had sung through Mozart's *Idomeneo,* and when they arrived at the third-act quartet, "Andrò ramingo e solo / morte cercando altrove / fin che la incontrerò," Wolfgang was "so overcome that he burst into tears and quitted the chamber and it was some time before she could console him."[17] We can guess that Nannerl continued to be envious of a brother who had gained success, married the partner of his choice, and was privileged to live in the alluring city of Vienna. After this time together in the summer and fall of 1783 the two siblings never saw one another again.

When they left Salzburg at the end of October, the young couple went to Linz, where they were the guests of Count Johann Thun-Hohenstein, and where Wolfgang composed, in only four days, his *Linz* Symphony (K. 425). "On Tuesday, November 4th," he wrote his father, "I am giving a concert in the theater here and, as I have not a single symphony with me, I am writing a new one at breakneck speed, which must be finished by that time. Well, I must close, because I really must set to work."[18] At the end of November the couple returned to Vienna. By the end of December Constanze was pregnant again.

# A Creative Turning-Point; The Webers; Concerts; *The Cairo Goose* (November 1783–November 1784)

The reunion with Leopold and Nannerl in Salzburg may have been difficult, but there are indications that Wolfgang emerged from the experience stronger and with a lessened sense of guilt. Immediately after his return to Vienna he worked joyfully and with great intensity. According to Wolfgang Hildesheimer, "Mozart's creativity reached a high point both qualitatively and quantitatively in the four years from the beginning of 1784 to the end of 1789."[19] The *Linz* Symphony (K. 425), a fine work even if Mozart had composed it in only four days, was the harbinger of a productive and happy new period. Much of the credit should undoubtedly go to Constanze. For the first time after the death of his mother, Wolfgang was not alone to face Leopold. There was a new woman at his side who loved him dearly and, unlike his mother, did not have a dependent relationship with Leopold. Constanze was even biased concerning her father-in-law, and for months, if not for years, she, her sisters, and her mother Caecilia had analyzed the difficult relations between Wolfgang and Leopold and Nannerl. Constanze was prepared to judge her in-laws and stand up to them, basing her actions on her intuition and on suggestions from the other Weber women. If this was indeed the case, as I think it was, Wolfgang would have been very grateful to Constanze, thus further reinforcing the ties that kept them united. They may not have been madly in love with one another, but their attachment was a lasting one that included all the ambivalence that is commonly a part of affection and love. They never lived apart, aside from occasional trips.

Mozart grew closer to all the women of the Weber family, including his mother-in-law Caecilia. He had become fond of the Webers in 1778 in Mannheim, when Fridolin was still alive and he was infatuated with Aloysia. After Fridolin's death that infatuation subsided, and in 1781–1782, when he became engaged to Constanze, Wolfgang spoke in derogatory terms of the whole family, with the exception of his fiancée. After the visit to Salzburg, Mozart understood that his wife's family had become his true family. In the Webers he found a serenity and a tolerance that Leopold and Nannerl were incapable of giving him. He grew fond of Caecilia and even began to call her "Mama."[20] He even succeeded in reestablishing a solid understanding with Aloysia. On 25 January 1784 Mozart conducted a performance of *The Abduction from the Seraglio* as a benefit for his former love.

In this new and happier climate, Wolfgang immediately began to work setting to music Abbé Varesco's libretto for *L'oca del Cairo* (The Cairo Goose). The action of this *opera buffa* takes place in an imaginary locality near the sea called Ripasecca (Dry Shore), in the house of a marquis, Don Pippo, who, erroneously thinking himself a widow, has fallen in love with his daughter's companion, Lavina, and wants to force his daughter to marry the Count Lionetto di Casavuota (Little Lion of Empty House). The plot involves complicated subplots and many surprises, including the arrival from Cairo, at the end of act 2, of a gigantic feathered goose. Like a Trojan horse, the Cairo goose is in reality a mechanical contraption manipulated from the inside, a device designed to conceal the young and noble Biondello (Blondie), who wants to marry Don Pippo's daughter. A fireworks display on the stage was planned for the finale. Writing to his father on 24 December 1783, Mozart sought to assure him that there was no danger: "I am not at all alarmed at the notion of a few fireworks, for the arrangements of the Viennese fire brigade are so excellent that there is no cause for uneasiness about having fireworks on the stage. Thus 'Medea' is often performed here, at the end of which one half of the palace collapses, while the other half goes up in flames."[21]

The text of *L'oca del Cairo* contained a number of incongruities, which may be why Mozart set only parts of it to music. Or he may have left the work incomplete because no one came forward with a formal commission. In all, some forty minutes of music make up the work identified as number 422 in the Köchel catalog. There is a recording conducted by Peter Schreier (who also sings the role of Biondello), with Dietrich Fischer-Dieskau in the role of Don Pippo. The work is amusing and very pleasant to listen to, but it is so fragmentary and incomplete that evaluation is difficult. There are fine moments in the trio "Siano pronte alle gran nozze cento e trenta e sei carrozze" (let 136 carriages be readied for the wedding) and also in the finale, written for seven voices and chorus. Here and there we can hear hints of *The Marriage of Figaro*, yet to come.

On 9 February, in another sign of new times, Mozart began to keep an orderly catalog of all of his compositions. His father had begun one (much earlier, but it remained incomplete). Wolfgang was giving one concert after another: there was one on 26 February at the residence of Prince Galitzin, the Russian ambassador; another on 1 March in the house of Count Johann Esterházy; others on 4 March, again at Prince Galitzin's palace, and on March 5 and 8, again at the Esterházy palace. On 15 March, once more at the Esterházy residence, Mozart gave the first performance of the Piano Concerto in B-flat (K. 450), a work composed specifically for the occasion and containing a number of stunning musical innovations, especially in the final movement. On 17 March he gave the first in a series of subscription concerts in the Trattner Saal, playing the Piano Concerto in E-flat (K. 449), another strikingly new work that he had composed only a few weeks earlier. From 18 March to 29 April he participated in many other concerts in the Burgtheater, the Trattner Saal, or in the houses of Galitzin, Esterházy, or Count Pálffy, the brother-in-law of Archbishop Colloredo. On 10 April Mozart was the guest of Prince Kaunitz, the state chancellor of the empire. Finally, on 29 April, in a concert in the presence of Emperor Joseph II, Mozart played the Sonata in B-flat Major for Piano and Violin (K. 454) with Regina Strinasacchi, a twenty-year-old violinist from Mantua. They performed the work without any rehearsal, Mozart playing from an incomplete piano part. All in all, in the sixty days from 26 February to 29 April 1784, Mozart played in at least twenty-five concerts. This was a feat he was never to repeat.

In a letter dated 20 March 1784 Wolfgang gave his father a detailed list of the 174 people who had paid six florins each to subscribe to his concerts (a total intake of 1,044 florins).[22] Analysis of these names by gender and social condition tells us that men represented 83 percent of the names and women 17 percent; half of the subscribers belonged to the high aristocracy, 42 percent to the lower aristocracy, and only 8 percent to the middle class. State and court officials made up 41 percent of the total; diplomats 12 percent; the military another 12 percent. Almost all the best names in Viennese high society are represented, including some of Mozart's known supporters (Galitzin and Esterházy), Count Czernin, Prince Dominik Kaunitz (the son of the state chancellor), and the great scientist and Freemason Ignaz von Born.

As if all that activity were not enough, during this time Wolfgang also completed a considerable number of compositions. Between 9 February and 21 April he wrote four piano concertos (K. 449, 450, 451, 453), the *Strinasacchi* Sonata for Piano and Violin (K. 454), and the Quintet for Piano, Oboe, Clarinet, Bassoon, and Horn (K. 452). Considering that during the second half of the year he wrote two other piano concertos (K. 456 and 459), the fourth Haydn String Quartet (K. 458), and the Variations in G Major for Piano (K. 455), we can agree with Francis Carr when he remarks that 1783 was "a year of masterpieces"—an *annus mirabilis*—for Mozart.[23]

On 18 August Wolfgang sent his sister a letter of congratulation on her upcoming marriage. Nannerl, who by then had passed her thirty-third birthday, was in fact about to become the third wife of the forty-eight-year-old Johann Baptist von Berchtold zu Sonnenburg, the father of six living children from his previous marriages (another five babies had died in infancy). Berchtold was the administrative governor of the region of St. Gilgen, the same position that Nannerl's and Wolfgang's maternal grandfather had held years before. With his daughter married, Leopold was left completely alone, and Wolfgang suggested to him that he resign from his position with the archbishop and live with Nannerl in St. Gilgen or in Vienna with him, but Leopold was not to be moved. Leopold went to Nannerl's wedding, which took place on 23 August in St. Gilgen. Wolfgang did not attend. We do not know whether he sent a wedding gift to his sister or not. In the 18 August letter, however, he sent her a short and joking poem on the topic of matrimony. It said, among other things:

> Experience soon will teach to you
> What Eve herself once had to do
> Before she could give birth to Cain.

Toward the end of the same poem he referred to the uncertainty of marital relations, perhaps thinking of his own experience with Constanze:

> Yet no state is an unmixed joy
> And marriage has its own alloy,
> Lest us its bliss perchance should cloy.

He ends the poem saying that if during the daytime her new husband might seem to her in a black humor, she would do well to turn to God and pray:

> . . . Lord, thy will be done by day,
> But mine at night you'll do.[24]

The day after the wedding Nannerl received from her husband a "Morgengabe" of five hundred florins, a premium for entering into marriage a virgin, as stipulated in the marriage contract. The marriage lasted until 1801, the year of Berchtold's death, and the couple had three children.

On 23 August 1784, the very day of Nannerl's wedding, Wolfgang went to the Burgtheater to attend the premiere of *Il re Teodoro in Venezia*, a new opera by Giovanni Paisiello for which the composer received three hundred ducats, triple the usual amount. The libretto, by Giambattista Casti, was based on the sad story of Theodore von Neuhoff, a German adventurer and soldier who was crowned king of Corsica in 1736 and died in London in 1756 after being imprisoned for debt. Some commentators believe that Casti drew the plot of his libretto from chapter 26 of Voltaire's *Candide*, where King Theodore is indeed mentioned; but he was a real person and must still have been alive in people's memories in 1784. Casti's libretto for *Il re Teodoro in Venezia* broke with many conventions, and as Mozart listened to this tale emphasizing the precariousness of power he may have realized that *opera buffa* was capable of expressing profound meanings. Roberto Parenti even goes so far as to state that without *Re Teodoro* Mozart could never have written *The Marriage of Figaro*.[25] Perhaps at the premiere of Casti and Paisiello's new work, perhaps at a later performance, Wolfgang was seized by a violent colic with drenching sweats and shivering that lasted four days, followed by digestive and intestinal disturbances for another three weeks.

On 21 September 1784 Constanze gave birth to their second son, Carl Thomas, who lived to 1858 and was the first and last in the family to receive royalties from Wolfgang's works. On 31 October the Mozarts, who had moved to a new house, celebrated Wolfgang's name day with a little concert offered by his pupils. On 17 November the Salzburg premiere of *The Abduction from the Seraglio* took place in the presence of Archbishop Colloredo, thus representing a new sign of respect, after all their difficulties, on the part of his former employer toward the great musician who had rebelled and quit his service. The opera met with continued success in later Salzburg productions.

## Mozart and Freemasonry

On 14 December 1784 Wolfgang became a Freemason in Vienna, joining the lodge Zur Wohltätigheit (Beneficence) at the level of an apprentice. Ten days later he was welcomed as a visitor into the lodge Zur wahren Eintracht (True Concord). On 7 January 1785 he became a member of the latter and obtained the rank of journeyman. A few weeks later, on 22 April, he earned the rank of master mason.

As we have seen, it is very probable that Leopold had turned to Freemasonry as early as 1762 for help and protection during the family's travels. The dating to 1772 of the aria "O heiliges Band" (K. 148/125h) indicates a clear manifestation of Wolfgang's appreciation of Freemasonry even before he became a member of a lodge. The choruses and entr'actes he composed for the play *Thamos, König in Ägypten* (K. 345/336a) in 1773 and 1779 constitute another clear sign. During his lifetime Wolfgang had ongoing relations with many Freemasons. In Mannheim in 1778 he had begun to set music to a text, *Semiramis,* by Otto von Gemmingen, a Freemason, who may have played the role of Wolfgang's sponsor when he was admitted to the Beneficence lodge, given that Gemmingen was a venerable master. Another Freemason was Legros, the director of the Concert Spirituel who had commissioned Mozart to write the *Paris* Symphony (K. 297/300a). Franz Anton Weber, the uncle of Constanze and Aloysia, was also a Freemason, as was Tobias Philipp von Gebler, the librettist for *Thamos, König in Ägypten*. Van Swieten, the patron who had introduced Bach and Handel to Wolfgang, was a Freemason, and so was Ignaz von Born, the scientist and subscriber to Wolfgang's concerts, who aided his entry into the lodge. Count Johann Esterházy, in whose residence Wolfgang put on concerts, was a Freemason as well, as was Haydn, who served the Esterházy family. Haydn joined the same lodge as Wolfgang on 11 February, a few days after Wolfgang's admission. In short, Freemasonry cast a wide net throughout society and musical circles.

Wolfgang never explained why he had decided to join a Masonic lodge, but he could easily have had many reasons. First, there would have been his need of moral support, given that by 1784 he had lost his father's protection and was ready to become a father himself. If up to that point he had benefited from Leopold's Masonic affiliation, he now had to take direct responsibility. A second reason lies in probable invitations to join a lodge on the part of many of his friends. Mozart frequented a number of intellectually inclined Masons such as van Swieten, the economist Joseph von Sonnenfels, and the scientist Born. Mozart was a prominent musician, and many Masons must have thought that Freemasonry would derive prestige and even glory from his participation. A third reason was that Masonry provided artistic opportunities. Indeed, Claudio Casini declares, "There was a precise connection between Mozart's artistic convictions and the cultural projects of Freemasonry, a connection that lay in Mozart's intent [and that of Masonic circles] to create a German national opera." German opera was scorned in conservative circles in Vienna, which preferred Italian *opera seria*, which was politically less provocative because it was an elite, artificial genre involving heroes of classical antiquity and was sung in a foreign language that the common people did not speak. Even Italian *opera buffa* was politically innocuous. German opera, or singspiel, was totally different. "Created by the intellectuals and by progressive-minded aristocrats with the intention of demanding a national identity," Casini continues, "German opera was deliberately addressed to all social classes."[26]

In his *Fire in the Minds of Men: The Origins of the Revolutionary Faith*, a vast and demanding work, James H. Billington discusses the vital political role of music, opera in particular, in the national revolutions of nineteenth-century Europe.[27] The insurrection that broke out in Brussels in 1830 as a result of a performance of Daniel Auber's *La muette de Portici* (The Mute Girl of Portici) is simply an extreme example of this, and there were many other operas—Rossini's *La gazza ladra* (The Thieving Magpie), *Mosè* (Moses), and *William Tell;* Bellini's *Norma;* not to mention Verdi's operas—that lent themselves to a revolutionary reading. *The Thieving Magpie,* for example, a work based on an actual event, contains a political message, in that the action turns around a serving woman, unjustly accused of having stolen a small silver fork, who is condemned to death but eventually pardoned. It was not for nothing that the censors' office focused on operatic works and demanded cuts and changes. Strong words, fused with orchestral music, presented in a closed theater before people of nearly all social classes who felt free to shout out their comments, risked becoming all too exciting and provocative. Billington's study focuses on nineteenth-century opera, but during the years in which Mozart was working, the problem relating to communicating a political message by theatrical means had already been posed.

Many scholars have stressed the importance of Wolfgang's participation in Freemasonry. Maynard Solomon, for example, even maintains that Masonic ideals had a powerful ideological appeal for Mozart, to the point that his joining went well beyond any banal economic and career-building aims, in particular because he had already achieved clamorous successes by December 1784.[28] I am not totally persuaded of this point of view, both because Mozart, whose numerical production ranked seventh among opera composers working in Vienna, was quite aware of the discrepancy between that standing and his merits, and because his failure to be named Kapellmeister made him insecure and discontented.

Wolfgang Hildesheimer disagrees with Solomon. He does not discern any strong presence of Masonic ideology in Mozart, maintaining instead that "the image of Mozart the Freemason has often been idealized." When he became a Mason, Wolfgang was only partially swept up by any collective fervor: "The 'meaning of life,' man's task on earth," Hildesheimer states, "were not things he wondered about consciously. On the other hand, he needed company, and he found it in the lodge." This hardly explains the seriousness and intensity of Mozart's Masonic musical compositions, but Hildesheimer minimizes the ideological content of these works as well. The texts, he avers, were stolid, "heavy, well-meaning but ineffectual" and "have the forced quality of required exercises." Hildesheimer also notes, "It was harder for Mozart than for Beethoven to set the word 'mankind' to music." Even regarding the impressive Masonic funeral march, *Mauerische Trauermusik* (K. 477/479a), a work that cannot be accused of having a "stolid" text because it has no words, Hildesheimer diminishes Mozart's involvement: "This piece . . . is one of those wonderful occasional works ordered and delivered punctually and in perfect condition by the great man, himself as little involved as a painter who paints a burial scene."[29] Hildesheimer even expresses a number of reservations regarding the Masonic elements in *The Magic Flute*.

Regarding Mozart's relationship with Freemasonry, there is in reality a much greater underlying problem, which is his relations with politics. More than one biographer has sought to present a Mozart inflamed with political passions, but their reasoning and their proofs do not hold up to critical examination. Not even the case of the "revolutionary" *Marriage of Figaro* clinches the matter. In fact, politics were marginal in Mozart's life; he considered politics an art that was, in the final analysis, much inferior to his own. This is why, among Mozart's reasons for becoming a Freemason, ideology occupied a secondary place, and the need for reassurance was primary.

As for Wolfgang's attitude toward the philosophers of the Enlightenment, we need only recall what he wrote to his father on 3 July 1778: "Now I have a piece of news for you which you may have heard already, namely that that godless arch-rascal Voltaire has kicked the bucket [*crepirt*, probably a Germanized adaptation from the Italian *crepare*] like a dog, like a beast! That is his reward!"[30] Leopold had indeed heard the news, and had written his son five days earlier, "So Voltaire is dead too! And died just as he lived; he ought to have done something better for the sake of his reputation with posterity."[31] Rumors were circulating that church authorities had refused Voltaire a regular burial (he was in fact buried in the Abbey of Sellières).

## Leopold's Visit to Vienna (February–April 1785)

On 15 January 1785, in his own house and in the presence of Haydn, Mozart performed three of the six string quartets that he dedicated to Haydn: K. 387, K. 421/417b (the most dramatic of the six, which he had finished composing on 17 June 1783, the day Constanze gave birth to their first son), and K. 428/421b (composed a few weeks after the previous one). There have been a number of explanations for the dedication to Haydn. First, Haydn was the true inventor of the quartet for two violins,

Louis Carrogis de Carmontelle, *Leopold Mozart Playing Music with Wolfgang and Nannerl* (1763). Watercolor. Musée Condé, Chantilly, France. Photograph copyright: Erich Lessing / Art Resource, New York.

Johann Nepomuk della Croce, *The Mozart Family* (1780–1781). At the piano, Nannerl and Wolfgang, and Leopold with violin, with mother Anna Maria, dead by the time the painting was made, present in her portrait. Oil on canvas, 140 × 168 cm. Mozart House, Salzburg, Austria. Photograph copyright: Erich Lessing / Art Resource, New York.

Franz Xaver Koenig, *Portrait of Prince-Archbishop Hieronymus Count Colloredo of Salzburg.* Leopold and Wolfgang were musicians at the archbishop's court. Oil on canvas, 80 × 100 cm. Austria. Photograph copyright: Erich Lessing / Art Resource, New York.

Anon., *Konstanze Mozart* (1802). Wolfgang's wife (née Constanze Weber) after her marriage to Georg Nikolaus Nissen. Oil on canvas. Mozart House, Salzburg, Austria. Photograph copyright: Erich Lessing / Art Resource, New York.

Andreas Unter-
berger(?), *Reception
at a Freemasons Lodge
in Vienna* (ca. 1784).
In the foreground is
Count Esterházy;
on the bench on the
right side is probably
Wolfgang. Mozart
became a Freemason
in 1784. Oil on can-
vas. Historisches
Museum der Stadt
Vienna, Austria.
Photograph copy-
right: Erich
Lessing / Art Re-
source, New York.

Joseph Lange, *Wolfgang Amadeus Mozart* (1789). The last (unfinished) portrait, by Mozart's brother-in-law, an actor and painter. Oil on canvas, 34.6 × 29.7 cm. Mozart House, Salzburg, Austria. Photograph copyright: Erich Lessing / Art Resource, New York.

viola, and cello. Second, Mozart considered Haydn a great friend and teacher. Third, Mozart had been so struck by Haydn's *Russian* quartets, composed in 1781, that he took them as his model, imitating them but also attempting to go Haydn one better. In the past Mozart had more than once taken other people's compositions as a stimulus for his own works, imitating them, but also improving on them and attempting to show himself to be the superior composer. On several occasions he had made an enemy by ceding to that temptation. There was no jealousy between Mozart and Haydn, however, and in fact Mozart's homage solidified their friendship. They were both great artists, they knew their own worth, and they did not fear one another. Moreover, Haydn was fourteen years older than Mozart, and he accepted the role of older brother, even of father, to his restless, worthy, and ambitious young friend.

Mozart's real father, Leopold, arrived in Vienna on 11 February 1785. After Nannerl's marriage and her move to St. Gilgen, Leopold had sent away the pupils who had been living in his house and resided alone. On 3 September 1784, writing to his son, he presented a somewhat melancholy picture of his isolation: "I'm now quite alone in eight rooms, in a really deathly silence. By day, to be sure, it doesn't bother me at all; but at night, as I write this, it's rather melancholy. If I could at least still hear the dog snoring and barking."[32] That was not to be, as Pimperl, the household's little dog, had died a few days earlier. Leopold went to Vienna to visit his son to escape that melancholy atmosphere, but also because his son remained uppermost in his thoughts.

Leopold left Salzburg on 20 January and stopped first in Munich, where he stayed with Theobald Marchand. During his stay in that city he attended Carnival opera performances, and when he left he took with him Heinrich Marchand, his former pupil, who was then sixteen years of age and whom he hoped to exhibit in Vienna. Leopold arrived in Vienna on 11 February, the day of the first of Wolfgang's Lenten subscription concerts. That same day he heard Wolfgang play his brand new Piano Concerto in D Minor (K. 466). The concerto had been completed that day, and Leopold wrote to his daughter in amazement, "We had a new and very fine concerto by Wolfgang, which the copyist was still copying when we arrived, and the rondo of which your brother did not even have time to play through, as he had to supervise the copying."[33]

Leopold was dazzled by his son's standard of living: "That your brother has very fine quarters with all the necessary furniture you may gather from the fact that his [annual] rent is 460 [florins]."[34] This was indeed a large sum in a Vienna where the average stipend of a university professor was 300 florins a year and a domestic servant had to make do with one florin a month (but was given food, lodging, and livery). A middle-class family with two children needed 500 florins a year to live decently but without luxuries. Wolfgang could permit himself this fine apartment because his income was a good deal higher than that of a university professor. In the year 1785 alone, according to data cited by Solomon, he took in a total of almost 3,000 florins: 1,500 from the subscription concerts, 559 with the academy concerts, and 900 from publications. In 1784 he had earned even more.[35] Leopold of course set to work estimating Wolfgang's net worth: "If my son has no debts to pay," he wrote to Nannerl on 19 March, "I think that he can now lodge two thousand gulden in the bank. Certainly the money is there, and so far as eating and drinking is concerned, the housekeeping is extremely economical."[36] Leopold hints that in spite of sizable earnings, the young couple's family budget might also contain debts.

The day after his arrival in Vienna, Leopold participated in another emotionally charged concert, this time in his son's house. Wolfgang, the two brothers Bartholomäus and Anton von Tinti, and Leopold performed the final three Haydn quartets (K. 458, 464, and 465) with Haydn himself present. Leopold reported to his daughter that the quartets were "somewhat easier [than the first three quartets dedicated to Haydn] but at the same time excellent compositions." He also reports that Haydn had told him, "Before God and as an honest man, I tell you that your son is the greatest composer known to me either in person or by name. He has taste and, what is more, the most profound knowledge of composition."[37]

On 13 February, the third day of his busy stay in Vienna, Leopold attended an academy concert in the Burgtheater to benefit the twenty-five-year-old soprano Luisa Laschi. Laschi, who sang only two arias on this particular occasion, was to become the first Countess Almaviva in the premiere performance of The Marriage of Figaro in 1786. In the 13 February academy Wolfgang played his recent Piano Concerto in B-flat, dedicated to the pianist Maria Theresia Paradies (K. 456), which Leopold found so moving that he wept. He reported to Nannerl that "when your brother left the platform the emperor waved his hat and called out 'Bravo, Mozart!'"[38]

There were other concerts in the days that followed. Then, on 17 February, Leopold had the honor of being invited to supper by Wolfgang's mother-in-law, Caecilia Weber, whom he had never met. The other guests included Wolfgang, Constanze, Sophie Weber, and Leopold's young pupil, Heinrich Marchand. All we know about the occasion is that the food was delicious. "I must tell you," Leopold writes his daughter on 21 February, "that the meal, which was neither too lavish nor too stingy, was cooked to perfection. The roast was a fine plump pheasant; and everything was excellently well prepared."[39] That is all that Leopold says about the evening, but we can imagine a certain tension around the table: three years earlier, when Wolfgang and Constanze became engaged, Leopold had stated that Caecilia should be put in irons and made to sweep the streets, and even Wolfgang had severely criticized Caecilia and her two elder daughters. Leopold had always expressed his detestation of the entire Weber family, but on 21 February, when he was suffering from rheumatism and got out of bed only in time for lunch, he found Sophie Weber, who was twenty-two at the time, there to keep him company. Because Wolfgang and Constanze were dining out, she remained with him until after eight o'clock that evening. We do not know whether Sophie's affectionate presence served to change Leopold's mind regarding the Webers.

A few of the many academies, concerts, and receptions that enlivened Leopold's stay in Vienna between 11 February and 25 April 1785 merit special mention. The first of these, in chronological order, is the academy given by Heinrich Marchand, Leopold's pupil, on 2 March at the Burgtheater. Leopold wrote to his daughter: "Heinrich's academy was both *bad* and *good*: bad because there were so few people there that, after having deducted 115 florins for expenses, he had only 18 ducats [81 florins] left; but it was *good* because he played so well that we can hope to earn more in a second academy the day after tomorrow, on the 14th."[40]

Leopold had taken on Marchand as a pupil in the hope of turning him into a new Wolfgang, and he had brought the youngster to Vienna to score a triumph. He would have liked to show the world that he knew how to forge musical geniuses, one after another. This was unlikely and in fact did not happen. Marchand probably became a competent musician, but little more than that. In 1786 he was taken on as a violinist and pianist by the court orchestra of Salzburg, and later he worked as a musician in Regensburg and Paris. His place in musical history is thus minuscule in comparison to Wolfgang's.

The second event that deserves to be recorded is the meeting between Leopold and Aloysia. On 25 March Leopold was the guest of Aloysia Weber and her husband, Joseph Lange, and thus the guest of the woman whose fascination had first attracted Wolfgang to the Weber family in 1777. In 1778 Leopold had attempted to quash any idea that Aloysia could become a great singer, but he was wrong. When he finally met her and heard her in Vienna he did his best to analyze her defects. As he wrote to his daughter in a letter of 25–26 March 1785:

That she sings with the greatest expression cannot be denied. I had often questioned people about her and I now understand why some said that she had a very weak voice and others that she had a very powerful one. Both statements are true. Her held notes and those she emphasizes are astonishingly loud, her tender phrases, passages, and grace notes and high notes are very delicate, so that in my opinion there is too much discrepancy between the two renderings. In a room her loud notes offend the ear and in a theater her delicate passages demand great silence and attention on the part of the audience.[41]

The last event in this period that deserves mention concerns Leopold's participation in Masonic activities in Vienna. On 4 April he was welcomed as a guest in the Beneficence lodge. Two days later he was granted the status of journeyman in his son's lodge, the True Concord. On 16 and 22 April he received two further promotions, and on 24 April, in yet another lodge, he attended ceremonies to confer the title of Knight of the Realm on Ignaz von Born, an occasion for which Wolfgang composed and directed the cantata *Die Maurerfreude* (Masonic Joy; K. 471).

Many of Mozart's biographers claim that it was at this point that Leopold became a Freemason, but Claudio Casini states that it is likely that he already belonged to a Salzburg lodge. There are no documents to enable us to give an unqualified response to the question, but Casini notes that in 1785 Leopold "had extremely easy access to Freemasonry in Vienna, as if he were a foreign brother rather than a 'postulant' outsider."[42] Whether Leopold entered into a Masonic lodge at that point or had already done so, the fact remains that all four of the musicians who played the three final *Haydn* string quartets in Wolfgang's house on 12 February—as well as Haydn himself—were already Freemasons or were about to join a lodge. We have already traced Wolfgang's and Leopold's affiliation: Haydn had become a Freemason on 11 February, the day before this musicale, and Anton and Bartholomäus von Tinti, both barons, were already Freemasons. Heinrich Marchand was probably also in attendance, but since he was only sixteen he could not have been a Mason. His father, who had been Leopold's host in Munich several days before, was certainly a Freemason.

On 25 April, after attending the ceremonies in honor of Ignaz von Born, Leopold left Vienna. Thus ended the whirl of activities, some of which Leopold describes in his letter of 12 March 1785. His son's frenetic activity left him bewildered, which may have been just what Wolfgang had in mind: he wanted to impress his father by showing him that he was capable of growing, maturing, winning successes, and earning large amounts of money without paternal assistance. His father was well aware of his son's motivation. Leopold and Wolfgang did not ever see one another again.

## Mozart's Character

Thanks to Peter Shaffer's play, *Amadeus*, and the film that Miloš Forman made from it in 1984, millions of people imagine Mozart as a half-mad, overgrown boy fond of practical jokes, yet capable of turning out marvelous pieces of music without any of the study, hard work, and serious effort that other great artists required. Both Shaffer's play and Forman's film are well constructed and appealing, but they transmit a false image of Mozart. It is true that Mozart was capable of writing excellent compositions in a short time, but this is because, aside from possessing a rare talent, he was totally serious about his work and made good use of the experience he had accumulated since childhood. I even suspect that the image that Shaffer and Forman transmitted to us was as widely accepted as it was because it corresponds to a model with broad popular appeal: it suggests that anyone can achieve success by mysterious means rather than through hard work, self-discipline, and determination—plus a bit of luck. It should be said, however, that the fallacious image purveyed in *Amadeus* has illustrious predecessors, since it derives from evaluations of Mozart repeatedly expressed by Leopold, Nannerl, and, to some extent, by Constanze, all of whom were less intelligent and less gifted than he was. It could not have been easy for them to live side by side with a genius without feeling crushed and torn between feelings of admiration and lack of respect. It is also true that a great genius can have moments of weakness, behave in small-minded ways, or be guilty of vulgarity. It is an easy game for someone who feels crushed by another to emphasize his faults. Leopold, Nannerl, and Constanze must have been prey to many frustrations, for which they blamed their son, brother, or husband.

Nannerl in particular was not only jealous of her brother but angry at him. She was the one who informed Wolfgang's first biographer, Friedrich von Schlichtegroll, that her brother had always remained a child. And Schlichtegroll, who never knew Mozart personally, repeated what she had told him:

If this exceptional being as an artist soon became a *man*, impartiality obliges me to say that in all other aspects, or nearly so, he always remained a child. He never learned to manage his own affairs. . . . He always needed a guide. . . . His father was perfectly aware of this lack of self-control, which was why he put Wolfgang's mother at his side to accompany him to Paris. . . . In Vienna [Wolfgang] married Constanza Weber and found in her a good mother of the two children of their union, and a worthy wife who, moreover, sought to restrain him from many foolishnesses and excesses. Despite a considerable income, he yet, in consequence of his exceptional sensuality and domestic disorder, left his family nothing beyond the glory of his name, and the attention of a large public fixed upon them.[43]

Schlichtegroll's description appeared in his *Nekrolog der Teutschen für das neunzehnte Jahrhundert*, published in 1793, not long after Mozart's death. From that time on, the image—superficially kindly but malevolent in substance—of Mozart as immature and detached from reality has continued to circulate. It seems a perfect fit for an artist who entered into history as a child, even as an extraordinary child prodigy.

A number of Leopold's letters contain severe judgments of what he perceived as his son's immaturity. In his letter to his wife and son of 16 February 1778, he complains to Wolfgang that, whereas "as a child and a boy you were serious rather than childish," now that he was an adult he was "hot-tempered and impulsive."[44] A few days later, on 23 February, he accuses his son of bad judgment: "First of all, you have a little too much *pride* and *self-love;* and secondly, you immediately make yourself too *cheap* and open your heart to everyone."[45] In the letter that Leopold wrote to the Baroness Waldstätten on 23 August 1782 he describes Wolfgang as unbalanced ("never the golden mean"), indolent, lazy, proud, impetuous, and hasty.[46] Among Mozart's biographers, Maynard Solomon is one of the warmest in defending Mozart against Leopold's allegations. He writes of Leopold, "He loved Mozart so profoundly that he needed to swallow him, to keep him within himself, to prevent him from getting out. He tried to keep Mozart from establishing a separate existence because, he was convinced, he himself had no separate existence without Mozart." Leopold wanted his son to play the father to him, remaining by him and procuring money for him as well as fame. In short, Solomon maintains, "If Leopold acted the willful tyrant, it was the raging willfulness that comes from feelings of downright helplessness. In a sense, then, it was he rather than his son who had really been the eternal child of the Mozart family."[47]

Leopold's wife Anna Maria had always protected and cared for him, but fate decreed that she would die in Paris in July 1778, just when Wolfgang was in love with Aloysia, was feeling himself more mature artistically, and had begun to take on more autonomy. At that time Leopold was back in Salzburg with Nannerl, who took her mother's place in caring for Leopold. According to Solomon, "Mozart, too, tried to take the mother's role, but his father's demands on him went beyond his capacity for self-subordination. . . . Eventually Mozart had to give up his struggle to aid his father, because to continue would have meant surrendering his individuality, smothering his sexual needs, and setting severe limits on his creativity. He needed to leave his father in order to survive as a person and as an artist."[48]

Leopold wanted to deny his son even the pleasurable opportunity of abandoning himself to dreams of success, as can be seen from two letters that the father and the son exchanged on 28 and 31 December 1778. In an attempt to hasten his son's return to Salzburg, Leopold summoned Wolfgang to "set all your gay dreams [*alle lustigen Träume*] aside," to which Wolfgang replied, "A propos, what do you mean by 'gay dreams'! Peaceful dreams, refreshing sweet dreams! That is what they are—dreams which, if realized would make my life, which is more sad than cheerful, more endurable."[49]

In 1778, when he wrote those words, Wolfgang was twenty-two years old, and it is absolutely normal that he should be thinking of his future and imagining attaining pleasurable goals in places far from a native city that he disliked. He was young and fully aware of qualities that authorized him to dream of a radiant future. At times his sense of superiority led him to excesses. In October 1781, for example, Carl Umlauff, who was nearly sixty and had replaced Salieri as director of the court theater in Vienna, wrote a mediocre opera. Mozart sat down at a piano and read the score at sight as if it were nothing. Umlauff had labored over his opera for more than a year, and he probably felt rather humiliated. Mozart had also treated Muzio Clementi with disdain, as we have seen. In short, Mozart felt no reverential awe before anyone, not a famous composer like Muzio Clementi, not the poet Wieland, and not the many kings, queens, princes, and princesses he had met as a child. Even Archbishop Colloredo charged Wolfgang with being "profoundly proud." Mozart admitted to this, stating in a letter written between 26 May and 2 June 1781, "It is true that I become proud when I see that someone is trying to treat me with contempt and *en bagatelle*."[50] He repeated the thought in a letter of 2 June:

"When I see that someone despises me and treats me with contempt, I can be as proud as a peacock."[51] As Alfred Einstein has observed, "There was not a trace of servility in Mozart; in that respect he was a modern, democratic man."[52]

One thing is certain: Mozart's character evolved through time. The child prodigy who amazed everyone with his skill at the keyboard differed from the young composer, who differed from the mature composer. It is also clear that 1778 was a turning point for his character: this was the year in which he lost his mother, fell in love with Aloysia and lost her, lived alone for the first time, and began to feel what it meant to be separated from his father. In the course of his adult life there was no other single year in which so many major changes took place. His state of mind and his feelings often oscillated between phases of excitement and depression. As a whole, he was fairly high-strung in temperament, as the fact that in Vienna he moved his lodgings twelve times between 1781 and 1791 seems to indicate (he remained at each address for an average of less than one year). All these continual peregrinations were a legacy of his vagabond childhood years.

As for his buffoonery, it is certainly true that Mozart liked to joke and play the fool, but this was a needed distraction from overly focused and strenuous labors. Amusing himself was indispensable to intensive composition. Karoline Pichler, an Austrian writer, tells her readers, "One day when I was sitting at the pianoforte playing the 'Non più andrai' from *Figaro*, Mozart, who was paying a visit to us, came up behind me . . . sat down, told me to carry on playing the bass, and began to improvise such wonderfully beautiful variations that everyone listened. . . . But then he suddenly tired of it, jumped up, and, in the mad mood which so often came over him, he began to leap over tables and chairs, miaow like a cat, and turn somersaults like an unruly boy." But Pichler also tells us that Haydn loved foolery as much as Mozart and indulged in crude practical jokes. She adds, "Mozart and Haydn, whom I knew well, were men in whose personal intercourse there was absolutely no other sign of unusual power of intellect and almost no trace of intellectual culture, nor of any scholarly or other higher interest."[53]

In reality, Mozart and Haydn were conscious of living in a world of their own, one that others, even Frau Pichler, were unable to share. Someone who came closer to intuiting the underlying reasons for Mozart's hilarity was the actor and painter Joseph Lange. It is interesting that it should be Lange, the husband of Aloysia, who painted one of the best-known oil portraits of Wolfgang. He states:

Never was Mozart less recognizably a great man in his conversation and actions, than when he was busied with an important work. At such times he not only spoke confusedly and disconnectedly, but occasionally made jests of a nature which one did not expect of him; indeed he even deliberately forgot himself in his behavior. But he did not appear to be brooding and thinking about anything. Either he intentionally concealed his inner tension behind superficial frivolity, for reasons which could not be fathomed, or he took delight in throwing into sharp contrast the divine ideas of his music and these sudden outbursts of vulgar platitudes, and in giving himself pleasure by seeming to make fun of himself. I can understand that so exalted an artist can, out of a deep veneration for his Art, belittle and as it were expose to ridicule his own personality.[54]

These observations on the contradictions in Mozart's personality lead us to the ambivalence present in his music. The beauty of his more important works and his major operas lies precisely in their capacity for expressing the duplicity of sentiments and situations. An allegro contains sadness, and sadness is not always what it seems. Good can also be bad, and bad, good. The Queen of the Night in *The Magic Flute* is an incarnation of evil, but she is also the mother of the excellent Pamina. Sarastro, in the same opera, is the incarnation of good, but he is the employer of the evil Monostatos. In *The Marriage of Figaro* it is unclear who is more truly noble, Count Almaviva or his servant Figaro. Don Giovanni is a libertine and a murderer, but he is a fascinating man. The last movement of the Symphony in C (K. 338) is dramatic, yet it is set to a dance rhythm, a tarantella. Mozart gave expression to his great secret precisely in his ability to miaow and turn somersaults. He seems to say: I am a great composer, but also a child, and all of you out there in the world are just like me. You are adults, but also infants; good, but also bad; intelligent, and at the same time a bit stupid; women, but with a masculine side; men, but with female aspects. Mozart had arrived at these conclusions by living and suffering. As a child he had been obliged to behave like a man. As a man he was determined to preserve those childlike aspects that then permitted him to become the great artist we know.

## Mozart's Physical Aspect, Elegance, Dwellings

Around 1768 the composer Johann Adolph Hasse called the boy Mozart "handsome, vivacious, graceful, and full of good manners."[55] The German writer Ludwig Tieck, who met Mozart in 1789, wrote that he was "small, rapid of movement, restless, and with a stupid expression on his face: an unprepossessing figure in a gray overcoat."[56] Wolfgang himself realized that, great as his stature as an artist may have been, his physical stature was modest. He signed a letter to Baroness Waldstätten of 2 October 1782 "Mozart magnus, corpore parvus."[57] We also read in Nannerl's memoirs that Mozart was "small, thin, pale in color, and entirely lacking in any pretensions as to physiognomy and bodily appearance."[58] Johann Nepomuk Hummel, Mozart's leading pupil, said of him that "he was small of stature and of a rather pale complexion; his physiognomy had much that was pleasant, and friendly, combined with a rather melancholy graveness; his large blue eyes shone brightly."[59] The tenor Michael Kelly, who sang the role of Don Basilio in the first production of The Marriage of Figaro, remembered Mozart as a "remarkable small man, very thin and pale, with a profusion of fine fair hair, of which he was rather vain."[60] In 1785 the Englishman John Pettinger went to visit Mozart as the composer was working on some quartets. Pettinger reports, "I was surprised, when he rose to find him of not more than about five feet and four inches in height and of very slight build. . . . His face was not particular striking, rather melancholy until he spoke, when his expression became animated and amused and his eyes . . . were full of kind concern in our doings about which he inquired with obvious interest."[61]

Photography had not yet been invented, so that, aside from the written testimony, we have only the contemporary paintings, engravings, and drawings to help us reconstruct a physical image of Mozart. The works of painters and other artists are often not very persuasive, however, because they tend to prettify their subjects. Mozart's death mask can be of no help to us because it has disappeared, perhaps destroyed by Constanze. That does not prevent biographers from describing Mozart's physical appearance, and many of them stress the fact that he had a deformed left ear but usually kept the anomaly hidden under his hair or a wig. Some medical texts relate this malformation to the kidney problems that made Mozart's life miserable and, according to some, led to his death. As we have already seen, Mozart contracted smallpox at the age of ten and was left with his face pockmarked. As if that were not enough, his fingers were deformed, either because of continual keyboard exercises from childhood on or from arthritis. Whatever the cause, this condition made it diffcult for him to cut meat or anything resistant. Hildesheimer suggests that Mozart deteriorated physically as the years went by, and he provides us with a description of Mozart that is the most pitiless of them all: "In the last years of his life he became physically unattractive. His face was pockmarked, the skin grew yellowish and puffy; toward the end he developed a double chin. His head was too big for his body. His nose was outsized: a newspaper once called him the 'great-nosed Mozart.' His eyes protruded more and more; he grew stout."[62]

Although this description may be somewhat exaggerated, it is true that Wolfgang always sought to compensate for his physical limitations by an elegance in dress. The care he took with his clothing and his hair must have helped him to deal with the powerful on an equal basis. Moreover, as a man of the theater in its more spectacular mode, he wanted to be a spectacle himself and to be noticed. Lorenzo Da Ponte, his famous librettist, was also something of a dandy in dress. The story goes that Muzio Clementi, on seeing Mozart for the first time in December 1781, on the occasion of the piano contest organized by Joseph II, took him "for one of the emperor's chamberlains" because he was so sumptuously dressed.[63] A few weeks earlier Mozart told his father in a letter dated 5 September 1781 that he had been obliged to have some new clothes made because his father had failed to send him the clothing he had left in Salzburg. He protests, "I could not go about Vienna like a tramp," and he justifies his actions: "One must not make oneself cheap here—that is a cardinal point—or else one is done."[64] On 28 September 1782 Mozart wrote to Baroness Waldstätten about a red coat that he fancied. The letter clearly displays his love of fine clothing:

> As for the beautiful red coat, which attracts me enormously, please, please let me know *where it is to be had and how much it costs*—for that I have completely forgotten, as I was so captivated by its splendor that I did not take note of its price. I must have a coat like that, for it is one that will really do justice to certain buttons which I have long been hankering after. I saw them once, when I was choosing some for a suit. They were in Brandau's button factory in the Kohlmarkt, opposite the Milano [café]. They are mother-of-pearl with a few white stones round the edge and a fine yellow stone in the center. I should like all my things to be of good quality, genuine, and beautiful.[65]

Not only suits and coats, but shirts, underwear, and handkerchiefs were then costly items, to the point that after being used, even for years, they were listed in detail as death goods. The inventory drawn up after Mozart's death lists a wardrobe not to be scorned, considering the averages for the age. Among other items, it includes six complete suits of different colors, two fur coats, four vests, and nine pairs of breeches. It also includes

"1 green cloth billiard table with 5 balls, 12 cues, one lantern," as Mozart was very fond of gambling at billiards, ninepins, and cards.[66]

As we have already seen from the letter that Leopold wrote immediately after his arrival in Vienna in February 1785, Wolfgang and Constanze lived in a costly apartment, the rent for which amounted to 460 florins a year. This ostentatious apartment, Mozart's taste for fine clothing, and the young couple's high standard of living seem to have been part of a strategy aimed at reassuring themselves of their success.

## After Leopold's Departure (1785–1786)

The seventy-some days that Leopold had spend in Vienna with Wolfgang were filled with frenetic activity: concerts, receptions, and get-togethers, all organized by Wolfgang in order to impress his father and show him that he had obtained satisfactions in Vienna that Salzburg never could have offered. After 25 April 1785, however, once his father had left, Wolfgang must have made a lucid, detached evaluation of his relations with Vienna, the city in which he had now lived for four years. It was true that he had achieved things in Vienna that would have been unthinkable in Salzburg, but there was still a real disproportion between his worth as a composer and the position he had reached. He felt he was worth more than Sarti and Salieri, but they and other musicians had been more successful at reaching Viennese audiences than he had. His concertos for piano and orchestra were new and marvelous, and yet the Viennese preferred the superficial concertos of the Bohemian composer Leopold Kozeluch. Wolfgang loved composing operas and had moved to Vienna precisely because the capital city of the empire had a great opera house. And yet for four years—from the day *The Abduction from the Seraglio* was commissioned—he had received no new commissions. Joseph II had liked that opera—up to a point. The emperor esteemed Mozart, enjoyed his concerts, and even cried "Bravo!" from his box, but he paid a fixed salary to Salieri, not to Mozart. Wolfgang earned money from academies, subscription concerts, performances in people's private music rooms, lessons, and publications, but in the final analysis he worked very hard to earn lesser sums than those earned by composers who were less talented than he but more privileged. In one scholar's opinion, in 1785 Mozart was a loser.[67] We have no idea whether he himself considered this to be the case, but it is clear that he was not a winner. After the whirl of events organized to impress Leopold, he probably fell into a phase of exhaustion and depression.

Some time during the latter half of 1785—probably in September— Mozart received the commission to write *The Marriage of Figaro*, the premiere of which was to take place at the Burgtheater on 1 May 1786. This was the big chance that he had been waiting for. The new commission raised his morale, to the point that while he was writing *Figaro* he found the time to compose three more piano concertos: in E-flat (K. 482) in December 1785, in A (K. 488) in February and March 1786, and the Concerto in C Minor (K. 491), which he completed soon after. He played all three of these in the Burgtheater. As if that were not enough, while he was writing *Figaro*, he also managed to compose (in only two weeks) a singspiel in German, *Der Schauspieldirektor* (The Impresario) (K. 486). Thus once again he moved into a period of intensive creation and consistent earnings.

On 1 September 1785 Artaria & Co. published the six *Haydn* String Quartets, paying Mozart a hundred ducats (450 florins) for them. In his dedication to Haydn, written in Italian, Mozart defined the quartets as "these six children of mine . . . the fruit of long and laborious endeavor," sending them off to his friend Haydn, and asking him to "be their Father, Guide, and Friend."[68] In the course of the year 1785 Wolfgang submitted many other compositions to publishers: Leopold states in a letter to his daughter dated 3 November that he had recently met Lorenz Hübner, a professor and a journalist, who had told him, "It is really astonishing to see what a number of compositions your son is publishing. In all the announcements of musical works I see nothing but Mozart." Hübner reported that the publicity announcements for the *Haydn* Quartets were accompanied by the words "It is quite unnecessary to recommend these quartets to the public. Suffice it to say that they are the work of Herr Mozart."[69]

Nannerl's first child was born during that same period, on 27 July 1785. She was delivered in Salzburg, in her father's house, and she named the child Leopold and asked her father to be godfather. Not only that, but when Nannerl returned to St. Gilgen from Salzburg on 1 September of that year, she left little Leopold as a boarder in his grandfather's house. Leopold was delighted, both because he felt less alone and because he hoped to create a new great composer. When the child was not yet four months old, Leopold dreamed out loud about the child's musical gifts in a letter to Nannerl of 11 November 1785:

I can never look at the child's right hand without being moved. The most skilled pianist cannot place his hand so beautifully on the keyboard as he customarily holds his hand; often he doesn't move the fingers; often the fingers are placed with curved hand in the playing position, and when he sleeps his hands lie in such a way as though the fingers were really touching the clavier, as well as with the most proportional relaxation and curvature of the fingers. In brief! One could not see anything more beautiful—I am often truly saddened when I see this, for I wish he were already just three years old . . . so that he would already be able to play.[70]

Leopold died in 1787, when little Leopold was two years old, so we will never know what the result of his grandfather's upbringing might have been had he lived longer. We do know, however, that Leopold von Berchtold lived until 1840, and that he became a government official (like his father), not a musician or a composer. Leopold wanted to keep secret the presence of his infant grandson in Salzburg, and in a letter to Nannerl of 17 November 1786 he complained that the painter Johann Michael Müller had praised the child to Wolfgang, thus inadvertently informing him that the baby had been living with his grandfather for over a year. Leopold had kept his presence a secret, perhaps because he was attempting, once more, to create a rival to Wolfgang, perhaps because he did not want Wolfgang and Constanze to leave their offspring with him as well. In any event, the entire episode offers a new proof of the competition and lack of openness between Leopold and Nannerl and Wolfgang.

Between 1785 and 1786 Wolfgang continued to attend the Masonic lodges and to compose Masonic music. On 11 December 1785 Joseph II ordered that the two Viennese lodges be combined into one, and on 14 January 1786 the new lodge, the New Crowned Hope, was inaugurated. Mozart composed two pieces for the occasion, "Zerfliesset heut', geliebte Brüder" (K. 483) and "Ihr unsre neuen Leiter" (K. 484), both for male chorus. Mozart was not present because he was ill.

It took Mozart only two weeks (between 18 January and 3 February) to compose Der Schauspieldirektor (K. 486), a singspiel for seven actors and three singers. It narrates the story of a theatrical impresario trying desperately to find actors and singers for a production to be given in Salzburg. In order to write it, Wolfgang was obliged to suspend work on The Marriage of Figaro. The libretto of the Schauspieldirektor was written by Johann Gottlieb Stephanie the Younger, who had written the libretto for The Abduction from the Seraglio. The spoken parts take up most of the performance time, the sung parts accounting for only some twenty minutes in all. The music is good, but not exceptional, and the entire singspiel is something of a musical joke. The entry in Karl Johann Zinzendorf's diary states, "The whole was very mediocre."[71] The actors for the premiere included the librettist, Johann Stephanie, and Joseph Lange, the husband of Aloysia Weber. Aloysia herself was among the singers. The imperial court had commissioned Mozart to write this singspiel to be performed on 7 February in the Orangerie of the Schönbrunn Castle. On the same day a short opera by Salieri was performed as well, *Prima la musica, poi le parole*, a work to a text by Giambattista Casti that was also set in the world of the theater. Mozart's compensation was fifty ducats; Salieri's was a hundred ducats, because his opera was longer.

On 19 February 1786, Wolfgang attended a ball in the Hofburg, the imperial palace, disguised "in the robes of an Oriental philosopher." During the course of the festivities he distributed a sheet of paper containing riddles and proverbs written by himself or his friends, but supposedly penned by the Iranian prophet Zoroaster or Zarathustra. The riddles were ironic, at times pungent, and at times ingenuous or somewhat inane, but very much in the taste of the times. One was, "One can possess me without seeing me. One can carry me without feeling me. One can give me without having me." The answer was a cuckold's horns. Another was, "We are many sisters; it is painful for us to unite as well as to separate. We live in a palace, yet we could rather call it a prison, for we live securely locked up and must work for the sustenance of men. The most remarkable thing is that the doors are opened for us quite often, both day and night, and still we do not come out, except when one pulls us out by force."[72] The answer was, of course, teeth.

In this period of his life Mozart forced himself to expend enormous amounts of energy because he was so eager to win over Vienna with *The Marriage of Figaro*. Given his nature, this meant that he also sought to let off steam and amuse himself even with such frivolities as writing silly riddles and disguising himself as a Persian philosopher.

# The Great Italian Operas

## Le nozze di Figaro (May 1786)

Mozart began composing *Le nozze di Figaro* (The Marriage of Figaro) (K. 492), on a libretto written by Lorenzo Da Ponte, in 1785. The libretto was in turn based on a famous comedy by Pierre Augustin de Beaumarchais that had first been performed in Paris the year before. In his play Beaumarchais makes fun of the nobility and invokes freedom of thought and speech: *La folle journée, ou, Le mariage de Figaro* elicited such passions and scandal that almost all history books maintain that it helped to undermine the foundations of the ancien régime and bring on the French Revolution. As a result, many of Mozart's biographers state that when he and Da Ponte moved quickly to adapt Beaumarchais' play and set it to music, their opera was also a politically bold and revolutionary act. This is true, but in a very difference sense, and if anyone was responsible for a political operation, it was neither Mozart nor Da Ponte, but the highest representative of imperial power, Joseph II.

*The Marriage of Figaro* was commissioned by Joseph II, and he followed Mozart's and Da Ponte's progress attentively, working through the supreme director of the court theater, Count Franz Rosenberg-Orsini. On 11 November, Leopold wrote to his daughter that Wolfgang had to get down to serious work, "for Count Rosenberg is prodding him [*getrieben wird*]."[1] Two years later, as we learn from a letter of Wolfgang's of 15 October 1787, Joseph II insisted, over the protests of the local aristocracy, that the Prague opera house put on *The Marriage of Figaro*.[2]

Joseph II was a sovereign interested in reform, imbued with Enlightenment ideas, and inclined to reduce the privileges of the nobility. Already from the time of Maria Theresa, however, policies had been initiated in an attempt to subordinate the interests of the nobility to those of the imperial crown. Thus *Figaro* fitted right in with the imperial house's program for modernization. It may be useful to offer a brief review of the opera's plot. Count Almaviva has given his consent to the imminent marriage of Susanna and Figaro, both of whom are in his employ, but he has taken a fancy to Susanna and intends to claim the *jus primae noctis*—the lord's right to a "first night"—with her. This leads to a series of suspicions, clandestine meetings, and disguises, in the course of which Figaro, the count's manservant, behaves more intelligently and with more nobility than his master, and Susanna, the countess's maidservant, acts with a wisdom and a dignity equal to those of the countess herself. At the end of the opera the count is placed in a position where he must beg the countess's pardon and bless the marriage of his servants. The plot of *Figaro* paralleled the sovereign's objectives: to revolutionize the institution of marriage by making it subject to a simple civil contract; to facilitate marital separations; and to reduce the privileges of the noble lords. Hence the emperor's policies were in direct contradiction to the *jus primae noctis* to which Almaviva claims a right.

In 1786 and 1787 the French Revolution had not yet broken out, and no one at the time imagined that a play or opera could help to bring about revolutionary uprisings. Beaumarchais himself, much like Joseph II and like Mozart, wanted to see a constitutional monarchy put into place, not to set off a revolution, and when revolution did break out in France, he bitterly disapproved of it. He was persecuted, had to flee, was imprisoned, and his goods were confiscated. Joseph II acted prudently. He ordered the theatrical censor to prohibit Beaumarchais' comedy if changes were not made in it, and he made sure that Da Ponte's libretto did not contain Figaro's famous tirade against the nobility. Where Beaumarchais had Figaro inveighing against nobles, Mozart's and Da Ponte's Figaro sighs about women: "Son streghe che incantano / per farci penar. / Sirene che cantano / per farci affogar" (They are witches who enchant us to make us suffer; sirens who sing to us to drown us).

Piero Buscaroli has done a particularly good job of clarifying these politically significant aspects of *The Marriage of Figaro*. In *La morte di Mozart* Buscaroli states that while Mozart was composing *Figaro* he made a "secret alliance" with Joseph II. In Lorenzo Da Ponte's memoirs, which are often not to be trusted, the librettist claims that Mozart suggested Beaumarchais' *Figaro* to him as a possible departure point for an opera libretto. Buscaroli does not believe that the initiative came from Mozart, and I tend to agree with him.[3] What is important, however, is not that Mozart,

Da Ponte, or someone else was the first to think of Beaumarchais' *Mariage de Figaro*, given that in those days everyone was talking about it. What is important is that Joseph II decided to commission an opera based on that scandalous and supposedly indecent comedy. This is why I have suggested that he was the person truly responsible for the political project of *The Marriage of Figaro*. Without the emperor's *placet* the opera would never have been written.

By composing *Figaro* Mozart put himself in a bad light with the nobility whom Joseph II was combating. He may not have understood immediately that the new opera could bring him harm from a public largely composed of aristocrats. Even if he did understand, however, he had little choice, and once the decision had been taken to write the opera there was no turning back: the emperor was a man too powerful to oppose, since he could block access to the theaters of Vienna and access to the fixed salary that Mozart had dreamed of for years. What is more, the political message contained in *Figaro* did not disturb Mozart, who for some time had disdained those who thought themselves superior by right of some privilege of birth, and thus he was all too happy to make them dance to his *chitarrino*. Be that as it may, as Wolfgang Hildesheimer points out, *Figaro* "was to be the beginning of his ruin," because the high society of Vienna, who were used to seeing themselves mirrored in the magnanimous and noble personages of *opera seria*, "did not feel offended exactly, but they didn't much like it." Their reaction at first "began with sneers," and if they took offense, it came later.[4]

It is not easy to establish how much of a success *The Marriage of Figaro* was when it was first performed in the Burgtheater of Vienna on 1 May 1786. Some of Mozart's biographers declare that it was a great success and point to the nine repeat performances. Others state the contrary. Still others note that the success of the work was intense but short—nothing to compare with the triumph of *Una cosa rara*, the new opera of Vicente Martín y Soler, which was produced in Vienna not long after. The music critic of the *Wiener Realzeitung* recognized that Mozart's opera was a masterpiece, but in his opinion the first performance, "owing to the difficulty of the composition," was "none of the best." The same source reports that the public did not know what to make of the work; that some "unbiased connoisseurs" shouted "Bravo!" but also that "obstreperous louts in the uppermost story exerted their hired lungs with all their might to deafen singers and audience alike with their *St!* And *Pst!*"[5] Count Zinzendorf, who was present at the premiere, was bewildered: he found "Mozart's music singular, hands without head."[6] It is probable that much of the original audience was put off by both the difficulty of the music and the political and social message in the text. The letters that Wolfgang wrote in those particular days have unfortunately been lost, but we know that Leopold, writing to his daughter on 28 April, was concerned about what the "very powerful cabals" and "Salieri and all his supporters" would do to mar the premiere of *Figaro*.[7] In a later letter, dated 18 May, Leopold reported that at the second performance five arias and other pieces were repeated, by popular demand, and seven had to be repeated at the third performance.

Nearly all the singers who performed in the first production of *Figaro* were excellent, in particular the forty-year-old bass-baritone, Francesco Benucci, who gave a stellar performance as Figaro. The tenor Michael Kelly, who played Don Basilio, has left us a lively description of a rehearsal: "I remember at the first rehearsal of the full band, Mozart was on the stage with his crimson pelisse and gold-laced cocked hat, giving the time of the music to the orchestra." When Benucci began to sing Figaro's aria, "Non più andrai, farfallone amoroso" with great vivacity and power, Mozart's excitement grew. Kelly writes: "I was standing close to Mozart, who, *sotto voce,* was repeating, Bravo! Bravo! Bennuci [Kelly's spelling]; and when Bennuci came to the fine passage, 'Cherubino, alla vittoria, alla gloria militar,' which he gave out with stentorian lungs, the effect was electricity itself, for the whole of the performers on the stage, and those in the orchestra, as if actuated by one feeling of delight, vociferated Bravo! Bravo! Maestro."[8]

The twenty-one-year-old Nancy Storace was the first Susanna, but—perhaps because of her youth—she seems to have made less of an impression than Benucci. Luisa Laschi, who was twenty-seven at the time, sang the role of Countess Almaviva, and the thirty-six-year-old Stefano Mandini was Count Almaviva. All the singers, as was the custom of the times, discussed their arias with Mozart during the rehearsals, and he often made modifications on the basis of their preferences, but also to respect their jealousies and caprices. It appears that the Countess's aria, "Dove sono i bei momenti" cost Mozart much effort and a good deal of trouble, as we can see from the evidence in his drafts. As a reward for his labors Mozart received 450 florins from the Burgtheater, and Da Ponte 200 florins.

Lorenzo Da Ponte, who in the years to come also wrote the librettos for *Don Giovanni* and *Così fan tutte* for Mozart, was born in Ceneda (now Vittorio Veneto) in 1749, into a Jewish family who had converted to Catholicism. As a child he was called Emmanuel Conegliano, but at the age of fourteen, after his family had converted, he took the name of the bishop who had baptized him, Lorenzo Da Ponte. He was educated in a seminary and became a priest and a pedagogue. He fled the Venetian Republic when he became involved in a trial for adultery and went to Gorizia, Dresden, and then Vienna. Da Ponte had lived an adventurous life before he met Mozart, and he ended his days in New York City as the first professor of Italian literature at Columbia University. He died in 1838.

We have already seen that Da Ponte furnished Salieri with the libretto for his opera, *Un ricco di un giorno,* performed for the first time on 6 December 1784. The opera was a fiasco. Salieri, enraged, swore never again to put to music so much as one line of Da Ponte's verse, which meant that the latter found himself in a somewhat precarious situation in 1785. Aleramo Lanapoppi, Da Ponte's biographer, tells us, "In the autumn of 1785, when Mozart and Da Ponte began to work on *Le nozze di Figaro,* no one would have wagered much on the results of their collaboration: from more than one point of view, their meeting might even seem that of two losers relegated to the margins of Viennese musical life."[9] Instead, they were about to bring to life one of the most extraordinary operas in the entire history of music. And soon after, they produced two others.

## Vienna's Betrayal (June 1786–March 1787)

Nothing gives a better idea of the isolation into which Mozart was plunged after *The Marriage of Figaro* than the fact that when he attempted to organize a new series of subscription concerts in March 1787 he found only one subscriber—his friend van Swieten—whereas in 1784 there had been 174. The aristocrats, the military, the upper middle class, and even Baroness Waldstätten, all of whom had paid eighteen florins for the concerts three years before, kept their purses closed this time. There are at least three probable reasons for this. The first was the opera itself: *Figaro* had disturbed and offended the better part of the nobility, who, because they made and unmade fashions, induced the military and the middle class to follow their lead in finding Mozart less attractive. After all, why spend so many florins if the event was not fashionable? A second reason is that all fashions are ephemeral by nature, and the Viennese elite, totally apart from the political and social messages contained in *Figaro,* already lived in an elitist consumer society within which everything moved fast and soon became passé. Even the fascination with Mozart was a consumer product. The third and last reason is that Mozart's music is not easy. According to the criteria of the era, concerts functioned mainly as light entertainment. Mozart's music, on the other hand, forced the listener to think, and thinking is always tiring. It was much more comfortable to let oneself be caressed by the "easy listening" music of Kozeluch and his ilk.

Embittered, Mozart contemplated leaving Vienna and moving, at least for a time, to England. On 18 October 1786 he became the father of a third son, which meant that he and Constanze had two children at home (the first, Raimund Leopold, had died two months after his birth). The newborn was named Johann Thomas Leopold: Johann Thomas from his godfather, Baron Johann Thomas von Trattner; and Leopold—once more tacked on at the end—for his grandfather. We can imagine that once again, second billing did not exactly delight the aging Leopold. Whether Leopold was pleased or not, around mid-November Wolfgang proposed to his father that he take charge of the two children for the entire time that he and Constanze would be in England. There is every indication that Leopold rejected the proposal. Johann Thomas Leopold passed on to a better life on 15 November, less than a month after his birth. Even so, a trip to London with the remaining two-year-old would not have been easy, considering the difficulty of travel at the time.

Wolfgang probably did not immediately give up the idea of going to England. We know, in fact, that in February 1787 Nancy Storace, the Susanna of *The Marriage of Figaro,* whose father was Italian and mother English, left for England along with her mother Elisabeth, the tenor Michael Kelly (the first Don Basilio), and Thomas Attwood, a pupil of Mozart's. Among the departing group was also Stephen Storace, Nancy's brother, a young composer who would enjoy extraordinary success in London two years later. These friends left Vienna with the idea in mind of finding contracts in London for Wolfgang as well as themselves. They stopped on their way in Salzburg, where they met Leopold, and we have a report of this encounter thanks to a letter that Leopold sent Nannerl on 1 March 1787. He told her that Attwood wanted to secure "a definite engagement for [Wolfgang] in London, I mean, a contract to compose an opera or a subscription concert." He adds that Nancy Storace must have "filled him with stories to the same effect," and we gather that the entire English traveling party did not please Leopold a bit. In his letter Leopold declares his intention to write to Wolfgang immediately, tell him to get his feet back on the ground, and persuade him that if he did not have "at least two thousand gulden in his pocket before undertaking such an expedition" it would not be worth the trouble.[10]

In the meantime, Mozart watched his earnings drop, and on 24 April 1787 he moved to a less luxurious apartment. His father referred to the fact in a letter to Nannerl of 10 May, the last he wrote before his death:

"Your brother is now living in the Landstrasse no. 224. He does not say why he has moved. Not a word. But unfortunately I can guess the reason."[11] The final word of this letter—*leider* (unfortunately)—was the last word that Leopold wrote about his extraordinary son. If we reread Wolfgang's accounts for the year 1787, we realize that, given the high standard of living in the Mozart household, only partially altered by moving to less luxurious lodgings, the thousand florins that he inherited at the death of his father were highly useful for continuing to live with a certain ease.

In the period from 1768 to 1788 Wolfgang, like his father before him, had a young pupil in his house. From all we can tell, Mozart was giving him free lessons. There is a difference, however: Leopold's pupils never went far, while Wolfgang's student, Johann Nepomuk Hummel, like Mozart, became a child prodigy and gave concerts in many cities of Europe. In 1788 and 1789, when he was ten and eleven years old, Hummel traveled with his father and performed in Prague, Berlin, Dresden, and Copenhagen, then in England and Scotland. In his adult years Hummel became a much-appreciated composer as well as a skilled pianist and conductor. He was only thirteen when Wolfgang died, which meant that Hummel had to turn to other teachers, including Salieri. Thanks to Hummel, Wolfgang had another source of satisfaction in his rocky relationship with his father: not only had he been a child prodigy himself, he was capable of developing another prodigy.

While he was worrying over the premiere of *The Marriage of Figaro*, wondering whether he should go to England, and teaching Hummel, Mozart produced such stunning compositions as the Piano Quartet in E-flat (K. 493), the Piano Trio in G (K. 496), and the Trio in E-flat for Piano, Clarinet, and Viola (K. 498), known as the *Kegelstatt* Trio (Skittles trio) because Mozart is supposed to have gotten the idea for it while playing that game, one of his favorites. That he wrote so many compositions for small chamber groups can be explained by his urgent need for earnings and by the publishers' requests for "house" music to be played by three or four relatives or friends, which was easier to market than scores for large orchestras. In the same vein, Wolfgang composed a Sonata in F for Piano Four Hands (K. 497), the *Hoffmeister* String Quartet (K. 499), the Variations in B-flat on an Original Theme for Piano (K. 500), and Variations in G on an Original Theme for Piano Four Hands (K. 501). Although there were some problems regarding the E-flat Piano Quartet (K. 493), all of these compositions were published by Artaria & Co. or Hoffmeister that year or during the two following years.

The Piano Concerto in C (K. 503) that Mozart composed in December

1786, intending to play it at one of the subscription concerts to which only van Swieten had subscribed, was published posthumously in 1798. In that same December of 1786 Mozart completed a symphony to be performed not long after in Prague, the famous *Prague* Symphony (K. 504).

## The First Triumph: Prague (January 1787)

On 8 January 1787, just after five o'clock in the morning, while it was still dark, Wolfgang and Constanze left for Prague with their dog Gauckerl, their future brother-in-law Franz de Paula Hofer (a violinist who married Josepha Weber the following year), and a few other friends, among them the clarinetist Anton Stadler and the thirteen-year-old-violinist Marianne Crux. Wolfgang and Constanze were also accompanied by their servant Joseph Deiner, nicknamed Primus, to distinguish him from Josephus Secundus, the emperor. They were all gay and excited because *The Marriage of Figaro* had been produced in Prague at the Nostitz theater and had been a triumphant success. Mozart had been invited to the capital of Bohemia by the theater's orchestra, together with a group of music lovers, so that he could enjoy his triumph. Just before he left Vienna, Wolfgang signed the album of his cousin by marriage, Franz Edmund Weber, with the words "Be industrious—shun idleness—and never forget your cousin, who loves you with all his heart." He added a postscript: "5 o'clock in the morning, before departure" and signed himself "Wolfgang Amadé Mozart" followed by a Masonic triangle.[12]

Today it takes five hours by train to go from Vienna to Prague. Mozart, Constanze, and their friends spent three days to make the trip in a carriage. During those three days of good-humored companionship they amused themselves by giving one another the oddest possible nicknames, which Wolfgang lists in a letter dated 15 January. "*I* am Punktititi. *My wife* is Schabla Pumfa. *Hofer* is Rozka-Pumpa. *Stadler* is Natschibinitschibi. *My servant Joseph* is Sagadaratà. *My dog Gauckerl* is Schmanuzky," and so on for the rest of the group.[13]

Prague was the third-largest city in the empire, after Vienna and Budapest. It had a population of about 70,000 inhabitants and a sizable Jewish community. Until only a few years before, it had been divided into four separate and independent administrative sectors, but the city had been unified by Joseph II in 1782. This quite recent unification and other provisions that the emperor had adopted to modernize the city had given it a notable boost, and in the years that followed Prague became the nerve center of Bohemian industrialization. Thus Mozart found a very lively, dynamic atmosphere there. Even the Nostitz theater, where *Figaro* was to be performed, was new. The theater, inaugurated in 1783, had been constructed with the support of Count Franz Anton von Nostitz, whose name had figured among the subscribers to Mozart's concerts. The new theater's managers, Pasquale Bondini and Domenico Guardasoni, were both Italians and former singers.

Mozart arrived in Prague around noon on 11 January. He lodged at the Three Golden Lions inn, and as soon as he arrived he was immediately escorted to the theater. Franz Niemetschek, one of Mozart's first biographers, was in Prague at the time, and he states, "At once the word spread about that he was present in the stalls, and when the symphony was over, the whole public applauded and welcomed him with their clapping."[14] The day after their arrival, Wolfgang and Constanze moved to the house of Count Johann Thun-Hohenstein, whose wife had been among the subscribers to Mozart's academy concerts in Vienna. Wolfgang met many figures in the better society of Prague at parties, balls, and concerts, but his greatest pleasure was to discover that melodies from *Figaro* had become popular among the people as well. He writes in his letter of 15 January, "I looked on . . . with the greatest pleasure while all these people flew about in sheer delight to the music of my 'Figaro,' arranged for contredanses and German dances. For here they talk about nothing but 'Figaro.' Nothing is played, sung, or whistled but 'Figaro.' Certainly a great honor for me!"[15] Franz Niemetschek confirms that arias from *Figaro* could be heard on the streets of the city, and that café orchestras had to play the music for "Non più andrai, farfallone amoroso" first if they wanted anyone to listen to anything else.

On 19 January, Mozart gave a concert at the Nostitz theater, conducting the symphony he had composed for the purpose before he left Vienna (K. 504) and playing other compositions on the piano. It must have been a truly memorable concert. The *Prague* Symphony is one of his most beautiful, and the public gave it a warm welcome. Enthusiasm reached its peak when Mozart improvised on the pianoforte for more than a half hour. Niemetschek, who was also present on this occasion, writes,

Never had the theater been so full of people as it was on this occasion: never had there been greater or more unanimous delight than his playing aroused. Indeed, we did not know what to admire the more — the extraordinary composition, or the extraordinary playing. . . . But at the end of the concert, when Mozart extemporized alone for more than half an hour at the pianoforte, raising our delight to the highest degree, our enchantment dissolved into loud, overwhelming applause. And indeed, this extemporization exceeded anything normally understood by pianoforte playing, as the highest excellence in the art of composition was combined with the most perfect accomplishment in execution. For sure, just as this concert had no parallel for the citizens of Prague, so Mozart counted this day as one of the finest of his life.[16]

An anonymous contemporary confirmed this impression, saying, "At the end of the concert, Mozart improvised for a good half hour. . . . When he appeared for the third time . . . in the absolute silence of the hall a voice cried out, *Figaro!* And so Mozart attacked the theme of the aria, 'Non più andrai' and improvised a dozen extraordinary variations, which finished in a hurricane of applause."[17] For that concert Mozart was paid one thousand florins.

During his sojourn in Prague, Mozart also won a contract for a new opera (which would become *Don Giovanni),* to be written as soon as possible for performance before the end of the year. It was Domenico Guardasoni, one of the two managers of the Nostitz theater, who suggested the story of Don Juan to Mozart. This is according to Lorenzo Da Ponte, writing in a brief and rare work, *An Extract from the Life of Lorenzo Da Ponte . . . ,* published in New York in 1819. In his much more famous *Memoirs* of 1823, however, Da Ponte claimed the merit of having proposed the subject to Mozart. "For Mozart I chose the *Don Giovanni,* a subject that pleased him mightily."[18] This was a fabrication, however: the earlier version was more accurate. In it, Da Ponte asks rhetorically, "Why did Mozart refuse to set to music the *Don Giovanni* (of evil memory) written by [Giovanni] Bertati and offered consigned to him by one Guardasoni . . . manager of the Italian theater of Prague? . . . Why did he [Mozart] insist upon having a book written by Da Ponte on the same subject *and not by any other dramatist?* Shall I tell you why? [Da Ponte's emphasis]"[19] Da Ponte implies that the response to these rhetorical questions was that Mozart trusted Da Ponte more, which was true. But in his *Memoirs* Da Ponte modifies his earlier version, not so much to take credit himself for proposing the subject, but to sweep aside Giovanni Bertati's libretto, which was set to music by Giuseppe Gazzaniga and produced in Venice in February 1787 with the title *Don Giovanni, o sia Il convitato di pietra.* In point of fact, Da Ponte lifted from Bertati's work, although he also added variations and improvements.

In an exultant mood after his triumphs in Prague and the commission to write *Don Giovanni,* Mozart returned to Vienna early in February. On

15 January he had written his friend Gottfried von Jacquin, "I must frankly admit that, although I meet with all possible courtesies and honors here and although Prague is indeed a very beautiful and pleasant place, I long most ardently to be back in Vienna."[20] He added that he yearned to see von Jacquin and other dear friends. It may seem odd, but it is a fact that Mozart longed to return to the city that now treated him with a certain coldness, preferring to abandon a public and a city that had treated him very well indeed. Perhaps the fascination of a worldly Vienna seemed without equal; perhaps leaving Vienna now seemed to him an admission of defeat; perhaps he had friendships and loves in Vienna that he did not care to give up; perhaps Constanze vetoed any move for similar reasons of her own. What is sure is both that in February 1787, after the Prague triumph of *The Marriage of Figaro,* and then again in November of that year, after the triumph of the *Don Giovanni* premiere, Wolfgang headed back to Vienna.

## The Death of Leopold (May 1787)

When he returned to Vienna, Mozart could not set to work immediately composing *Don Giovanni* because he had to wait for Da Ponte to write the libretto. We can imagine, however, that from the beginning he followed his librettist's work intently, intervening with suggestions and corrections. At the same time, however, he was composing other music and giving concerts. In March 1787 he completed the famous Rondo for Piano in A Minor (K. 511), which Hoffmeister published immediately, as well as a very dramatic concert aria for bass, "Alcandro, lo confesso"/"Non so d'onde viene" (K. 512) on a text by Metastasio, which was performed at the Kärntnertortheater, together with other of Mozart's compositions. There were other concerts as well, although to a diminished audience. Between April and May, Mozart wrote two splendid string quartets (K. 515, 516), which were offered for sale "at the price of 4 ducats, or "18 florins, Viennese currency," as was stated in a publicity announcement in the *Wiener Zeitung* of 2 April 1788 .[21]

Between 7 and 20 April 1787, Ludwig van Beethoven, who was sixteen at the time, stayed in Vienna and may have been taken to play and improvise for Mozart. Several comments supposedly made by Mozart at this encounter are probably apocryphal. According to the story, Mozart's first remark about his playing was decidedly cool: "Really very graceful, but too mechanical." This troubled the young Beethoven, who asked for a theme on which to make other improvisations. According to the legend, when Mozart heard him play again, he declared, "Keep an eye on this young man; he will have something to say."[22] In any case, Beethoven, who may have been hoping to take lessons from Mozart, had to leave Vienna because his mother was ill.

Leopold fell ill and died on 28 May. He was not yet sixty-eight years old, but in those times people aged early and were usually considered old before that. He probably had some sort of cardiac insufficiency, but his physician attributed his death to a "congestion of the spleen," while the *Salzburger Intelligenzblatt* of 2 June 1787 stated that he had died "of consumption."[23] Leopold had been in good health in February, so much so that he had gone to Munich for the Carnival opera season. In mid-March he fell ill, and his daughter Nannerl went to Salzburg to take care of him. Nannerl remained with her father for two months before returning to St. Gilgen. On 10 May Leopold wrote his last letter to her.

Wolfgang was duly informed of his father's illness, and although he understood that Leopold might die, he did not go to see him. He wrote his father a letter from Vienna on 4 April, seeking to console him and to prepare him to accept death with serenity. Many of Mozart's biographers have been struck by the profundity of the sentiments expressed in this letter without realizing that these conceits were copied from Moses Mendelssohn's *Phädon, oder über die Unsterblichkeit der Seele,* a work on the immortality of the soul published in 1767. Moses Mendelssohn was a Masonic philosopher of Jewish origin and the grandfather of the composer Felix Mendelssohn-Bartholdy. Wolfgang owned a copy of the *Phädon,* as we know from the inventory of his possessions after his death and from other evidence.[24] As he was writing his father to tell him of the latest developments in Vienna, he received word that Leopold's illness had taken a turn for the worse. "This very moment I have received a piece of news which greatly distresses me, the more so as I gathered from your last letter that, thank God, you were very well indeed." He wishes his father a speedy recovery, but immediately goes on to speak about death, indicating that he knew there was nothing to be done. Taking inspiration from Mendelssohn, he writes, "As death, when we come to consider it closely, is the true goal of our existence, I have formed during the last few years such close relations with this best and truest friend of mankind, that his image is not only no longer terrifying to me, but is indeed very soothing and consoling! And I thank my God for graciously granting me the opportunity (you know what I mean) of learning that death is the *key* which unlocks the door to our true happiness."[25] The parenthetical "you know what I mean" was an allusion to their joint allegiance to Freemasonry, which, incidentally, Moses Mendelssohn shared. Wolfgang continues:

> I never lie down at night without reflecting that—young as I am—I may not live to see another day. . . . I hope and trust that while I am writing this, you are feeling better. But if, contrary to all expectation, you are not recovering, I implore you by . . . [the ellipses are another reference to Freemasonry] not to hide it from me, but to tell me the whole truth or get someone to write it to me, so that as quickly as is humanly possible I may come to your arms. I entreat you by all that is sacred—to both of us. Nevertheless I trust that I shall soon have a reassuring letter from you; and cherishing this pleasant hope, I and my wife and our little Carl kiss your hands a thousand times and I am ever your most obedient son, W: A: Mozart.[26]

Leopold lived another fifty-four days, and even Nannerl left his side two or three weeks before he died, returning to St. Gilgen. She may have thought that her father's illness could last a long time, and we do not know whether she returned to Salzburg in time to see the dying Leopold one more time. We do know that Wolfgang did not go to embrace him for the last time, even though his letter of 4 April shows him well aware of the gravity of his father's illness. Unfortunately all of the other letters that Wolfgang wrote to Leopold during the summer of 1784 are lost, and without them it is very difficult to reconstruct the evolution of his filial sentiments. Whatever they may have been, we can imagine that Leopold's death was a hard blow for him, in spite of the resentment he had expressed in recent years, or perhaps because of it. The death of a father who had to some extent disappointed him could have struck him just as hard, and perhaps harder, than the death of a father with whom relations had remained serene to the end. Wolfgang certainly must have been flooded with a sense of guilt for having abandoned a parent who had brought him up, had given him his musical training, and had done so much, up to 1777, to facilitate his success.

If we want to understand fully the trauma that his father's death caused for Wolfgang, we should recall the bad relations between Wolfgang and Nannerl at the time, and also the problems that arose with Nannerl regarding Leopold's estate, which had to be resolved immediately. Brother and sister had not met since 1783. In 1784 Wolfgang did not attend Nannerl's wedding (for that matter, neither did she attend his). In her conversations with Leopold over the years, Nannerl must have accumulated increasingly hostile feelings toward a brother who was judged to be superficial, squandering his money right and left, a prisoner of the Webers, and incapable of baptizing a son with Leopold's name. To cap it off, this miserable brother had not come to the bedside of his ailing and dying father for as much as one day.

With her father's death Nannerl could give free rein to her desire for revenge, and we suspect that she managed to garner almost all of Leopold's estate. If this was the case, it was made possible by the fact that her brother did not go to Salzburg even after his father's death to make a personal count of the inheritance goods. Wolfgang was represented by a proxy. Leopold's will has never been found, and his assets can be reconstructed only partially from the few short letters that Wolfgang sent to his sister and his brother-in-law. The letters that Nannerl wrote to Wolfgang in that period have been lost.

By what remains we know that on 2 June, five days after his father's death, Wolfgang explained to Nannerl that he could not leave Vienna, and that he agreed with her in the decision to sell Leopold's household goods at auction. He refers to a will, however, adding, "But if, as Herr F. d'Yppold has written to tell me, there is a dispositio paterna inter liberos, then, of course, I must be informed of this dispositio beforehand, so as to be able to make further arrangements."[27] In the same letter he presents his friend Franz d'Ippold as his proxy. This *dispositio paterna inter liberos* was nothing other than a will, but unfortunately no such document has come down to us and Mozart does not mention it again in his letters. Thus many of Mozart's biographers speak of his inheritance from his father as if Leopold had made no will, but this cannot be true. In the first place, Wolfgang himself speaks about a will in his 2 June letter. The fact that in later letters he fails to mention it again might be because his father's provisions had left him chastised and saddened. In the second place, it seems to me impossible that a man as astute as Leopold would die without stipulating his last wishes, in particular regarding a daughter who had always been devoted to him, had sacrificed herself to him for years, and deserved to be rewarded for it. It seems to me impossible that he should want to treat her as he had Wolfgang, who, in his mind, had betrayed him, who earned enormous sums of money, and whom he considered a spendthrift.

On 16 June Wolfgang wrote to his sister again, in response to a letter that has not come down to us. In that letter Nannerl must have told Wolfgang that he was expected to agree that she have everything, or almost everything, including the household objects. "My dearest, most beloved sister!" Mozart writes, and we sense his resentment: "If you were still unprovided for, all this would be quite unnecessary, for as I have already said and thought a thousand times, I should leave everything to you with the greatest delight. But as the property would really be of no use to you, while, on the contrary, it would be a considerable help to me, I think it my duty to consider my wife and child."[28]

An inventory of Leopold's goods and chattels was made in Salzburg, but this document is also lost. We know, however, that it listed nearly 600 items, among them a large pianoforte and some optical instruments, for a total worth of 999 florins, a figure that must represent the base price for an auction sale. Nannerl proposed an agreement: given that the auction sale price usually represented half of the actual value, Wolfgang could declare himself satisfied to receive 1,000 florins, which was to be paid at the end of September, after the auction. Wolfgang accepted, but in a letter dated 1 August he asked that the 1,000 florins be sent to him in Viennese currency, a sum equivalent to 1,200 Salzburg florins. Nannerl accepted his proposal. The auction took place in Salzburg between 25 and 28 September. Three hundred twenty-four items were sold for a total of 1,507 florins, and Nannerl took the 265 items that failed to sell.[29] On 29 September Mozart wrote to his brother-in-law Berchtold, directing him to send his thousand Viennese florins addressed to Johann Michael Puchberg at the palace of Count Walsegg in Vienna. Wolfgang took for himself none of the things that had belonged to his father.

According to Maynard Solomon, Leopold's will left all of his estate to his daughter, with the exception of his personal effects, which were to be sold at auction with the proceeds going to Nannerl and Wolfgang in equal parts.[30] Also according to Solomon, Leopold never revealed to Wolfgang the full extent of the profits earned during their European travels by way of all the gifts they received. One observer who was lucky enough to view them stated that it was "like inspecting a church treasury."[31] In his relations with his son, Leopold had always cried poverty, but in Salzburg he had always lived a life of ease in a fine house with a carriage and servants. It seems quite unlikely that his entire patrimony amounted to less than two thousand florins. Nannerl knew Leopold's secrets; she was the adored daughter, devoted and ever present, and it is quite possible that as the years went by she used all her advantages to triumph over her brother at her father's death. Her need for revenge was great, and at Leopold's death it found fulfillment. Thereafter Wolfgang responded to two letters from Nannerl, and no more. In the second one, written 2 August 1788, he hints that it may be the last from him. As indeed it was.

After his father's death Wolfgang threw himself into his work with a passion, in part out of sheer necessity, as *Don Giovanni* was scheduled for the month of October. On 14 June, however, he found the time and the will to complete a "musical joke"—*Ein musikalischer Spass* (K. 522)—a work in four movements for two horns and strings that made fun of village musicians, third-rate artists who hit wrong notes, played out of key, and produced tonal absurdities. On 24 June he composed an evening song for soprano voice, "Abendempfindung an Laura" (K. 523), a work full of melancholy more in tune with a period of mourning. On 10 August he returned to a happier frame of mind, however, with the famous *Eine kleine Nachtmusik* (K. 525). On 24 August he turned to serious meditations with the Sonata for Piano and Violin in A Major (K. 526), which Hoffmeister immediately published. These oscillations between recollection and amusement must have corresponded to his shifting moods in those difficult weeks.

A number of scholars have sought to understand why, only a few days after he learned of the death of his father, Wolfgang should feel the urge to compose *A Musical Joke*. According to Roberto Parenti, the work was written "as a pure emotional outlet for the composer," and even as a "compensation and substitute for a keen sorrow, a sense of guilt that could not be given too free a rein and that had to be done away with as soon as possible."[32] Hildesheimer, too, thinks that the *Musikalischer Spass* represented something like an unconscious reaction to Leopold's death, hence self-administered therapy.[33] There is no direct testimony, no documents to guide us, however, and we will never get to the bottom of how Mozart reacted to his father's death. Nor will we understand why, on 4 June—two days after receiving word—he wrote a poem of twenty-two rhymed lines, not on the occasion of his father's death, but on that of his pet starling, who had also died suddenly: "A little fool lies here / Whom I held dear— / A starling in the prime / of his brief time / He was not naughty, quite / But gay and bright," and so on in the same tone.[34]

## Don Giovanni (October 1787)

Between March and October 1787 Mozart composed *Don Giovanni* (K. 527) or, to give the original title more precisely, *Il dissoluto punito, ossia Il Don Giovanni*, as printed in the announcement put out by the theater in Prague on the day of the opera's premiere, 29 October 1787. Wolfgang and Constanze left for Prague on 1 October, with the opera still to be completed, arriving there on 4 October. They lodged first at the Three Golden Lions inn, then in Villa Betramka, with their friends Franz and

Josepha Duschek. Franz Duschek was an elderly and famous musician; his much younger, wealthy wife was a well-known singer. Their villa is now a Mozart museum.

On 15 October, Mozart conducted a performance of *The Marriage of Figaro* in honor of Archduchess Maria Theresia, the daughter of the future emperor, Leopold II, who was passing through Prague. On 25 October, Giacomo Casanova, by then near the end of his career as a libertine and adventurer, arrived in Prague, and we can presume that he attended the premiere of *Don Giovanni* and met its composer. Mozart put the finishing touches on the score on 28 October, only a few hours before the opera went on the stage.

It was Mozart and Da Ponte who determined that the opera was a "dramma giocoso in due atti." In fact, drama explodes on the stage immediately, when Don Giovanni kills the Commendatore, and the opera ends even more dramatically with Don Giovanni being swallowed up by the flames of hell. Between these two violent deaths the audience is invited to be amused, even to laugh. The action takes place in Spain, in sixteenth-century Seville. Don Giovanni, a licentious "young nobleman," begins a series of amorous adventures by "forcing" Donna Anna, a lady of Seville, and killing her aged father, the Commendatore. During the rest of the opera Don Giovanni takes an interest in a number of other women, the peasant girl Zerlina, Donna Elvira, a lady from Burgos, and another woman who is only mentioned and may even be the wife of Leporello, the Don's servant. Among all of the characters in this profoundly immoral "merry drama," there is only one person who permits himself to laugh all the way to the end: Don Giovanni. He even laughs in the cemetery, before the tomb of the Commendatore, the man he has killed, when the dead man's statue announces his imminent death: "Di rider finirai pria dell'aurora" (You will stop laughing before dawn). On hearing this, Don Giovanni, in a paroxysm of audacity, invites the statue to supper. Nor is he afraid when this "stone guest" actually does present himself at the supper table and, refusing to be seated, sends his host down to eternal fire. At the very end, but only at the end, when he is swallowed up by the flames, Don Giovanni takes fright and cries out, "Che terror!"

Obviously, the plot of the opera is much richer and more complicated than this brief summary indicates. In fact, hundreds of thousands of pages have been written about the interpretation of Mozart's *Don Giovanni*, based on elements selected out of the enormous quantity of more or less mysterious allusions in the libretto and the music. I am inclined to share the authoritative opinion of Stefan Kunze, who notes first that *Don Gio-*

*vanni* is an opera that "fits into no preexistent category, least of all in that of tragedy." Kunze cuts short a number of complicated theories, noting, "Mozart and Da Ponte wanted a success. They had not the least intention of ennobling their subject matter with literary or aesthetic pretensions."[35] Both the composer and the librettist were in fact very down-to-earth artists who were interested in acquiring fame and money by seeking to stupefy, move, amuse, and disturb the spectators, even with an immoral story. They had had to ready *Don Giovanni* in great haste, with no time for splitting hairs, whereas the critics and scholars of Mozart's life and works have had plenty of time to do just that.

Mozart was of course aware that, like all works offered to the public, *Don Giovanni* would take on a meaning through time that its authors had not foreseen. Wolfgang had poured all of his talent as an artist into composing the opera, and that was enough to make him confident. He also knew that he had remained faithful to one of his basic principles: to represent the ambiguities and the follies of life and the strength and weaknesses of human relations. The drama that he brought to life on the stage fully expressed the ambivalences of everyone's realities, precisely because it was merry—*giocoso*. Only by uniting pain with irony, mixing the serious and the ridiculous, and breaking out of preordained schemes could he conquer the public and leave his mark.

All of the characters in the opera are guilty of duplicity. To mention a few: Don Giovanni boasts of being a "nobil cavaliere," but he behaves like a lout. When he meets Donna Anna, who is in mourning for the death of her father, killed by Don Giovanni himself, he has the effrontery to ask, "Perché così piangete? Il crudele chi fu che osò la calma turbar del viver vostro?" (Why are you crying? Who is the cruel man who has dared to perturb your calm?). At the very moment when he is lying to Zerlina in order to seduce her, he has the nerve to say, "la nobiltà ha dipinta negli occhi l'onestà" (nobility has honesty imprinted in its eyes). He speaks of love to all women, but in reality he is incapable of loving a woman and is only interested in "putting them on his list," the old and the ugly included. He is cruel, yet he manages to arouse sympathy and have his offenses forgotten. In the final scene he even displays flashes of heroism.

In Molière's *Don Juan,* the opera's antecedent, the servant Sganarelle calls his master an "esprit fort," a term applied to the libertine philosophers of his time. Mozart's and Da Ponte's Don Giovanni is also an *esprit fort,* one who does not hesitate to raise a toast to "Liberty" but who understands the term to mean erotic license. His cry of "Viva la Libertà" is repeated by all the participants in the party at the end of act 1, where it takes on broader meaning, but that same liberty has negative overtones: it accompanies the chaos and confusion of the ball, where three orchestras play at once.

Leporello, Don Giovanni's manservant, is pusillanimous: he judges his master severely, but he would dearly love to "play the gentleman" himself. In fact he disguises himself as Don Giovanni, switching cloaks with his master, who takes on his own servant's guise. In doing so, Leporello risks having his own wife betray him in the dark, thinking that Don Giovanni is her husband. This may even be what happened. "Then I realized that it was your beauty," his master tells him, at which Leporello responds, "And if she had been my wife?" The answer comes: "Better still." At this Don Giovanni laughs heartily (the libretto reads, *ride molto forte*). This is what prompts the Statue's pronouncement: "Di rider finirai pria dell'aurora."

Donna Anna loses both her father and her honor thanks to Don Giovanni. She is so disturbed by these events that she is unable to return the love of Don Ottavio, the only true gentleman in the whole opera (apart from the Commendatore, who is soon eliminated, although he returns in the form of a statue). Don Ottavio declares on several occasions that he is Donna Anna's husband and friend, or her husband and father; he sings dulcet arias in which he nobly asserts his intention to avenge the ill done to the woman he loves, yet, in comparison with Don Giovanni—or even with Donna Anna—he seems to us spineless, vapid, and in the final analysis untrustworthy. When Don Ottavio finally presses his suit, demanding Donna Anna's love ("Non mi far languire ancor"; Do not make me languish still longer), she persuades him to respect her mourning for another year ("Lascia, o caro, un anno ancora allo sfogo del mio cor"; Let my heart, dear one, grieve for another year). The thought might be overly malicious, but she may even fear that she is pregnant by Don Giovanni.

At first Donna Elvira, the noblewoman from Burgos, is furious at Don Giovanni for having abandoned her on some previous occasion. She goes so far as to menace him: "Vo' farne orrendo scempio, gli vo' cavare il cor" (I want to slaughter him horridly; I want to tear out his heart). She remains true to her desire for revenge for the whole of act 1. In the second act, however, she forgets all this and becomes compliant, even to the point of calling Leporello, masked as Don Giovanni, "adorato mio sposo." Even toward the end Donna Elvira comes to Don Giovanni's house to offer him "the ultimate proof of her love" ("l'ultima prova dell'amor suo") in a final attempt to redeem him. Desperate, she declares her intention to become a nun or worse: "Io men vado in un ritiro / a finir la vita mia!" (I will go off to a retreat to end my life), but, given her temperament, it is to be doubted that she will actually do so.

The peasant girl Zerlina is also full of quite comprehensible contradictions. Courted by Don Giovanni, who is much higher than she is on the social scale, she hesitates ("vorrei e non vorrei"; I would like to, but then I wouldn't), and she ignores her peasant lover Masetto, whom she is supposed to marry that very day. She and Don Giovanni sing together, "Andiam, andiam mio bene, a ristorar le pene" (Let us go, let us go, my dear, to refresh ourselves from troubles), and she seems perfectly willing to sneak off to a "little house" in the garden with her aristocratic seducer before they are prevented from doing so—for the moment—by the arrival of Donna Anna, Donna Elvira, and Don Ottavio. Very soon, at the end of the first act, Don Giovanni gives a great ball, during which, the stage directions indicate, "while dancing he leads Zerlina to a doorway and makes her enter almost by force." Something serious apparently takes place behind those closed doors, because loud noises and voices are heard and Zerlina eventually cries out for help.

Masetto is just as weak as Don Ottavio, but for different reasons. He is well aware of his social inferiority and he is less clever than Don Giovanni. At first he gives in to him immediately: "Ho capito, signorsì! Chino il capo e me ne vò. Giacché piace a voi così, altre repliche non fo" (I understand, yes my lord. I bow my head and go. Since it so pleases you, I make no other response). Later, although he attempts to organize the assembled peasants to revolt against the lord who has insulted his wife-to-be, he is stupid enough to hand over to Don Giovanni the musket and pistol he intended to use. In short, among all the male characters in this *dramma giocoso*, the only ones with any virility are Don Giovanni and the Commendatore.

## A Fixed Salary, at Last, but No End to Debts
### (December 1787–April 1789)

On 4 November, Mozart wrote to his friend Gottfried von Jacquin that in Prague *Don Giovanni* had been "received with the greatest applause" and expressed his hope that the opera would be performed in Vienna. He then adds, "People here are doing their best to persuade me to remain on for a couple of months and write another one. But I cannot accept this proposal, however flattering it may be."[36] In mid-November Mozart returned to Vienna. We have already noted his reasons for preferring that city. In autumn 1787 he added another: dissatisfaction with the technical level of the Prague musicians. On 15 October, in fact, he had written his friend Jacquin that the production of *Don Giovanni* had been delayed because "the stage personnel here are not as smart as those in Vienna, when it comes to mastering an opera of this kind in a very short time."[37]

Still, Mozart's success in Prague and the fact that people there had proposed to him that he remain in that city produced an important result: on seeing Mozart's fame as a composer grow and fearing that he might accept offers in Prague or some other city, in December, Emperor Joseph II decided to give him a fixed stipend of eight hundred florins a year to keep him by his side and block other offers. Many biographers write that the emperor offered him the post that had previously been held by Gluck, who died on 15 November. The situation was somewhat different, however. Gluck's position was "court composer," which commanded a high salary, whereas Mozart was given a more generic post of "chamber musician" (*Kammermusicus*), a designation that in the strict sense was a sinecure, without expressing any specific obligation. In the four remaining years of his life Wolfgang limited his duties for the imperial court to writing thirty-six minuets and thirty-one dances. This is why he noted on a receipt for his salary, "Too much and too little."[38] Too much for the nothing he was obliged to do; too little in respect of his great artistic merits, which should have guaranteed him a more prestigious and better paid charge. In any event, the eight hundred florins were enough to persuade him not to leave the imperial capital, at least for the moment. It goes without saying that the first contredanse that he wrote after receiving the appointment was a lively one: it was entitled "Das Donnerwetter" (*Donner*, thunder; *Wetter*, storm; K. 534). The term can also be used to describe a fit of rage, uproar, and confusion, or as an mild oath. Hence by likening his first court dance to a *Donnerwetter*, Mozart was trying once again to make a noise like thunder, to entertain, and to amuse himself.

He was instead beginning a rather difficult period in his life, one full of financial setbacks and musical disappointments. On 27 December 1787 a fourth child was born to the couple, a girl, Theresia Constanze, who died seven months later. On 7 May 1788 *Don Giovanni* was produced on the stage of the Burgtheater of Vienna, exactly as Mozart had hoped. He had modified the libretto and the score to adapt the work to Viennese tastes, but in spite of these attempts to please the public, the opera was less a success than was expected. Perhaps Viennese aristocratic circles were still smarting from the attack they had received in *Figaro*. Perhaps they thought the music too difficult, aimed at a few connoisseurs, and too unlike the style they were accustomed to. Many of the singers were excellent, however. Francesco Benucci, an impeccable Figaro in 1786, sang the part of Leporello, and the celebrated Caterina Cavalieri was Donna Elvira. Wolfgang's sister-in-law, Aloysia, sang Donna Anna, and Francesco Albertarelli sang Don Giovanni. Luisa Laschi was seven months pregnant, and we do not know how she managed to reconcile the girlish grace of Zerlina, after whom Don Giovanni lusts, with her expanding belly.

In spite of a decidedly cool reception, *Don Giovanni* had fifteen repeat performances in Vienna in 1788, and Lorenzo Da Ponte wrote in his *Memoirs* that Joseph II, after attending one of them, commented, "That opera is divine; I should even venture that it is more beautiful than *Figaro*. But such music is not meat for the teeth of my Viennese!" Da Ponte relates that when he reported this to Mozart, his response was, "Give them time to chew on it."[39] Most biographers, basing their opinion on the authority of Da Ponte, believe the anecdote to be true, but Piero Buscaroli denies that this exchange ever took place, for the simple reason that Joseph II never attended any performance of *Don Giovanni*. In February of that year the emperor had declared war on Turkey and was out of Vienna. He returned from army headquarters on 5 December and he might have been able to attend the performance on 15 December, but Buscaroli notes that Joseph II, "exhausted and ill, did not go again to the theater,"[40] as the emperor himself wrote to his sister Maria Christina.

The fruitless and costly war with the Turks that had taken the emperor out of Vienna launched an inflation that called for a climate of austerity and savings that did little to help Mozart out of his financial difficulties. The years 1788 and 1789 were in fact the worst ones of Mozart's time in Vienna, in spite of the 800 florins he now received from the court. Whereas from 1781 to 1787 his earnings had always oscillated between 2,000 and 4,000 florins a year, for the years 1788 and 1789 this estimate has to be reduced to 1,400 florins, or at most 2,100 florins. It was not until 1790 and 1791 that his earnings improved sharply.[41] Hence, beginning in June 1788 Mozart sent Johann Michael Puchberg at least twenty letters requesting money. Puchberg, a friend, fellow Freemason, and the owner of a company that sold Mozart's music to the public, had advanced him money on a number of occasions. In four years Wolfgang asked Puchberg for 4,000 florins, and received from him loans for 1, 415 florins.

The letters to Puchberg and other creditors have led to the notion that in the last years of his life Mozart lived in poverty. That is not true. Mozart earned a good deal and, even in the critical two-year period of 1788–1789, he earned enough money to live in ease. The fact is that he spent more than he earned, and it was the gap between what came in and what went out that unbalanced his accounts. That leaves us with the question of why Mozart had a need to spend so much. Perhaps his high expenditures can be attributed to his character and to an inability to resist his desires; perhaps to the couple's luxurious standard of living; perhaps even to Mozart's gambling and his frequenting of women, actresses and singers in particular; perhaps to Constanze's demands and her habit of squandering money. These are all suppositions. What is certain is that Mozart entered into a downward spiral in which he very probably was borrowing from one person to pay interest to another, even to lend out to others himself. In July 1788 he pawned some objects. On 2 April 1789 he signed a draft for a hundred florins for the benefit of Franz Hofdemel. In a letter dated 17 May 1790 he told Puchberg he was obliged to borrow money from the usurers. On 1 October 1790 he took out a loan of a thousand florins, offering all of his furniture as a guarantee, from the merchant Heinrich Lackenbacher in a contract endorsed by the publisher Hoffmeister.

All this time Mozart was composing dances and contredanses for the court balls. On 4 February 1788 he produced *The Abduction from the Seraglio* at the Kärntnertortheater. On 24 February he completed a new, difficult, and by no means traditional Piano Concerto in D Major (K. 537), which, due to the economic crisis that had struck Vienna, he played for the first time over a year later, on 14 April 1789 in Dresden.[42] On 26 February and 4 March, in the house of Count Johann Baptist Esterházy, Mozart conducted compositions by Carl Philipp Emanuel Bach, which he had reorchestrated. On 22 June he composed the Piano Trio in E Major (K. 542). Finally, between June and August 1788 he completed his last three great symphonies, the *Swan Song* Symphony (K. 543), the famous G-Minor Symphony (K. 550), and the Symphony in C, only later dubbed *Jupiter* for its Olympian power and solemnity (K. 551). Thus Mozart composed the three most important symphonic works of his entire life (and perhaps of the entire eighteenth century) in only a few weeks. The symphony K. 543 is highly dramatic; K. 550 has won such popularity that today its opening measures provide the incoming call alert for millions of cell phones. The *Jupiter* Symphony contains a surprising minuet and an equally surprising final movement. It would be interesting to know, given Mozart's declining public appeal in those years, whether these three extraordinary symphonies were played in public or not. Scholars are divided on this point, and only a few conclude that they were.

From the middle of 1788 through the spring of 1789 Mozart worked at a slower pace. He composed the admirable Divertimento in E-flat for String Trio (K. 563) for the musicales of his friend and creditor, Michael

Puchberg, and he wrote the Piano Trio in G (K. 564). At the behest of Gottfried von Swieten he also arranged and reorchestrated two works by Handel, *Messiah* (K. 572) and the pastorale *Acis and Galatea* (K. 566.) This was too little activity for a volcanic mind like Mozart's. Hence he decided to leave Vienna.

## A Strange Trip to Germany and Jealousy in the Family

On 8 April 1789 Mozart left Vienna without Constanze, but in the company of Prince Karl Lichnowsky. The prince was twenty-eight years old, a Freemason, a pupil of Mozart's, and still a bachelor. In November he was to marry the daughter of Countess Thun-Hohenstein, who had protected Mozart from his earliest years in Vienna. In years to come the prince and his wife were to become major patrons of Beethoven. It seems to have been the young Lichnowsky who had inspired the trip and had invited Mozart to join him to shake off the melancholy of Vienna. Mozart, for his part, wanted to go to Berlin in the hope of winning favor with Frederick William II, the king of Prussia, and turn around the bad luck that seemed to have pursued him for some time. On the eve of their departure Wolfgang wrote a short poem for Constanze that began, "To Berlin I must travel, / Hoping there to gain much honor and fame."[43]

In the early afternoon of 10 April, Mozart and Lichnowsky arrived in Prague, but they left that same evening at nine o'clock. In the few hours that he spent in Prague Mozart went to the Duschek's house, where he was told that Josepha Duschek was in Dresden. Wolfgang and Lichnowsky then decided to depart immediately for that city, but before they left, Wolfgang took the time to meet Guardasoni, the impresario of the Nostitz theater, and draw up an agreement with him to provide him with a new opera that autumn, for which he was to be paid two hundred ducats, plus reimbursement for his travel expenses. This projected new opera for Prague was never produced, because that summer Mozart was charged by the emperor to write the opera that became *Così fan tutte* for the Burgtheater of Vienna.

On 12 April, at six o'clock in the evening, Mozart arrived in Dresden, lodging at the Hotel Polonia, where he remained for nearly a week. The evening of his arrival he paid a visit to the Duscheks, and the following day he gave a concert with Josepha Duschek at the Hotel Polonia. In the days that followed he gave concerts in the residence of the czar's ambassador, Prince Alexander Beloselsky, and in the palace of the highest authority in Dresden, the elector of Saxony, Frederick Augustus III. Mozart played the

Piano Concerto in D Major (K. 537), and the next day the prince-elector sent as a gift a magnificent box containing a hundred ducats. Thus the trip seemed to begin auspiciously.

On 18 April, Mozart and Lichnowsky left Dresden; after stopping at Leipzig they reached Potsdam on 25 April. The palace of Sans-Souci at Potsdam, only a few kilometers from Berlin, was one of the residences of Frederick William II of Prussia. Mozart was received there by Jean Pierre Duport, a court composer. In Potsdam Mozart composed the Piano Variations in D on a Minuet by J. P. Duport (K. 573), presumably with the aim of obtaining Duport's favor and, through him, of being received by the king. The king did not receive Mozart, however, and at an unspecified date (perhaps 6 May) Wolfgang left Potsdam. We are sure that he gave a concert at the Gewandhaus in Leipzig with the participation of Josepha Duschek, and that he remained in Leipzig for at least six days.

We also know from the Mozart papers that there is a gap in communications between Wolfgang and Constanze of almost one month, from 16 April to 16 May 1789. We also know that Constanze complained of not receiving any news of her husband during that month, and that finally, in a letter from Berlin dated 23 May, Wolfgang did his utmost to explain to his wife why four letters that he had sent from Leipzig and Potsdam on various dates had all mysteriously disappeared. In his letter of 16 April, written on the eve of that "disappearance," Wolfgang tells his wife, with more concern for appearances and for honor than for the substance of their relations, "I beg you in your conduct not only to be careful of *your honor* and *mine*, but also to consider *appearances*. Do not be angry with me for asking this. You ought to love me even more for thus valuing our honor."[44] These are words that make us suspect the existence of some slight disagreement and of a relationship that had become somewhat elastic, perhaps because Constanze was constantly pregnant. In a letter of 23 May, the first after a month of silence, Mozart announces his imminent return (in fact he arrived only on 4 June) and seeks to cheer up his wife by evoking the nights they would spend together after this long abstinence: "Arrange your dear sweet nest very daintily, for my little fellow deserves it indeed, he has really behaved himself very well and is only longing to possess your sweetest . . . [word blotted out in the autograph]. Just picture to yourself that rascal; as I write he crawls on to the table and looks at me questioningly. I, however, box his ears properly—but the rogue is simply . . . , and now the knave burns only more fiercely and can hardly be restrained. Surely you will drive out to the first post-stage to meet me?"[45]

Mozart is being daringly provocative here, but we might suspect that he was being so deliberately, to create a curtain of smoke around a recent betrayal of the marriage bed. One even suspects that he might have neglected his regular correspondence with Constanze because he was distracted by a dalliance with some lady, or even with Josepha Duschek herself, a woman of thirty-six who was married to a man much older than she and was used to traveling alone to pursue her career as a singer. Mozart's contradictory statements about how long he would stay in Potsdam, not to mention his prolonged stays in Dresden and Leipzig, where he certainly might have met with Josepha Duschek, only increase our suspicions.

On 17 May Mozart left Leipzig. Two days later he arrived in Berlin, and that evening he attended a performance of *The Abduction from the Seraglio* in the Royal Theater, where he met the poet Ludwig Tieck. On 23 May he probably went to a concert given by his pupil Hummel, who was then ten years old. Many of Mozart's biographers write that on 26 May he gave a concert before the court, and that on that occasion Frederick William II "very probably" commissioned him to write six string quartets and six easy piano sonatas.[46] That "very probably" derives from the fact that in his letters to Puchberg, Mozart states that he was busy composing "for" the king of Prussia. This may well be true. But he never indicates that he had received either a formal invitation to do so or any money for having carried it out. On the contrary, he states in his letter to Puchberg of 12 July that he is planning to have the sonatas and the quartets printed "at my expense," probably in the hope that the king of Prussia will reimburse him and reward him at a later date.[47] In short, there may be reason to believe that the concert at the court of Prussia on 26 May never took place, and that there was no commission to compose any music whatsoever.[48] According to Maynard Solomon, Mozart may have set up this entire fable to justify a useless and expensive trip, to placate Constanze, and to reassure Puchberg, his creditor.[49] Finally, in order to demonstrate that his trip had been a success and to reinforce his image as a respected artist, he probably felt constrained to borrow a large sum of money, letting it be known that the money represented his earnings. He may have obtained this money from his traveling companion, Prince Lichnowsky, who, in fact, requested restitution of 1,435 florins in 1791.

On 28 May Mozart left Berlin, and by 4 June he was back in Vienna. He set to work immediately composing "for" the king of Prussia a string quartet (K. 575) and a piano sonata (K. 576). On 12 July Constanze fell ill (she suffered from varicose veins) and Wolfgang, arguing that his wife's illness brought additional expenses, asked Puchberg for more money. He told Puchberg that whereas in Vienna he had had little luck, outside Vienna his operas were very successful. *The Abduction from the Seraglio* in particular was in fact performed in many German cities, and even in Vienna the Burgtheater was about to revive *The Marriage of Figaro.* In early August Constanze moved to Baden for a cure and Wolfgang, who may easily have been unfaithful to her during his trip through Germany, sent her a letter in early August extolling fidelity and damning betrayals and jealousies. He wrote this admonishing letter even though he was leaving the next day at five o'clock in the morning to join her in Baden.

We can surmise that matrimonial relations were undergoing a crisis, but that Mozart intended to do his best to save their marriage. "You have no reason whatever to be unhappy. You have a husband who loves you and does all he possibly can for you," he writes. After this, Wolfgang speaks as if Constanze were the one who was unfaithful: "In my opinion you are too free and easy with N.N. . . . and it was the same with N.N., when he was still at Baden." The published letters give "N.N." here because an unknown hand had rendered the original names illegible. Mozart follows this by giving Constanze instructions on correct behavior: "A woman must always make herself respected, or else people will begin to talk about her. My love! Forgive me for being so frank, but my peace of mind demands it as well as our mutual happiness." He then delivers a low blow: "Remember that you yourself once admitted to me that you were inclined to *comply too easily.* You know the consequences of that." In short, Mozart admits that he is aware of "compliances" on Constanze's part. Toward the end of the letter he gives her further advice on how to save their marriage: "Be merry and happy and charming [*gefällig*] to me," after which he adds a phrase that can be read as an implicit admission of guilt on his part: "Do not torment yourself and me with unnecessary jealousy." Hence Constanze might have had legitimate reasons for being jealous. The letter ends with these words: "Believe in my love, for surely you have proofs of it, and you will see how happy we shall be. Rest assured that it is only by her prudent behavior that a wife can enchain her husband. Adieu. Tomorrow I shall kiss you most tenderly."[50]

Analysis of this letter raises the question of the evolution of the institution of marriage in the society of which Wolfgang and Constanze were a part. Legend has it that Emperor Joseph II stated one day that if the city of Vienna were covered with a great tent it might be taken for the biggest house of pleasure in the entire world. Betrayals, adventures, and more or less fleeting love affairs must have been the order of the day. Faced with a choice between an impossible eternal passion and resigned conjugal boredom, Viennese of the upper classes would probably have sought a third way out in ephemeral amusements. At that point jealousy becomes "unnecessary," as Mozart preached to his wife. We do not have sufficient evidence to understand the matrimonial relations of the author of *Don Giovanni* in depth, but it is worth remarking that on 4 November 1787, precisely when he was in Prague supervising the staging of that opera, Wolfgang wrote a letter to his friend Gottfried von Jacquin in which he attempts to persuade him to abandon his "restless way of living," arguing, "Surely the pleasure of a transient, capricious infatuation is as far removed as heaven from earth from the blessed happiness of a deep and true affection?"[51] Another translation of the last phrase, "vernünftige Liebe," might be "reasonable love," which may be what Mozart himself preferred over unreasoning passion. This means that in Wolfgang's letter to Constanze of August 1789, written to try to save their marriage, his true appeal to her may lie in his statement "Forgive me for being so frank, but my peace of mind demands it." It is true that Mozart adds, "as well as our mutual happiness," but we need to recall that he had a fairly relative concept of happiness. In a letter written to Leopold from Mannheim on 29 November 1777, he had in fact claimed that "happiness consists— simply in imagination."[52] Tranquility may have seemed to him a more stable and certain value.

On 29 August 1789, a month and a half after the outbreak of the French Revolution, *The Marriage of Figaro* was put on for the second time at the Burgtheater. The emperor clearly did not fear that this opera would affect Vienna. Mozart revised the opera for the occasion and composed two new arias for Susanna. It is true that Vienna was less fond of Mozart, and that among the composers of the operas most often performed in the city he ranked below Salieri and others, but it is also true that Mozart ranked first among the composers of German operas and that his 1789 *Figaro* was well received and had twelve repeat performances.

On 29 September Wolfgang completed the splendid Clarinet Quintet in A Major (K. 581), sometimes known as the *Stadler* Quintet because it was dedicated to his friend Anton Stadler, a famous clarinetist and a Freemason. On 16 November Constanze gave birth to her fifth child, a girl, Anna Maria, who died an hour after her birth and was buried the next day. In October Wolfgang had begun composing his last masterpiece to a text of Da Ponte, *Così fan tutte,* an opera exploring the matrimonial and extramatrimonial customs of the Viennese that had been so much on his mind during the previous summer.

## *Così fan tutte* (January 1790)

We know very little about the genesis of *Così fan tutte, ossia La scuola degli amanti* (K. 588). Mozart's letters furnish scant information, and Lorenzo Da Ponte only briefly mentions the opera in his *Memoirs*, referring to it by its subtitle, the "School for Lovers."[53] It seems, however, that Joseph II commissioned the work after the success of the second production of *The Marriage of Figaro* at the Burgtheater. Some commentators believe that the emperor himself suggested the subject matter and that the plot is based on events that actually took place in Vienna or another city some time before. In reality, however, the somewhat risqué theme of couples exchanging partners had already been used in various ways in operatic theater, and in Vienna of the time there must have been plenty of tales of couples involved in libertine behavior. All we can glean from the Mozart correspondence regarding the genesis of *Così fan tutte* is that two hundred ducats (nine hundred florins) were to be paid him in January 1790 and the dress rehearsal was to take place on 21 January. The premiere was on 26 January, at the Burgtheater, and there were four repeat performances before Joseph II died on 20 February and the theater was closed for the mourning period. Thus the opera's beginnings were not fortunate, but another five performances were given from June to August of the same year, when the period of mourning for the emperor had ended.

Naples provides the setting for *Così fan tutte*. Two young officers, Guglielmo and Ferrando, are engaged to two sisters from Ferrara, Fiordiligi and Dorabella. Sure of their two loves, the two men bet a hundred zecchini that their girls would never be unfaithful to them, wagering with the elderly and philosophical Don Alfonso, who holds the opposite view. The young men agree to do whatever Don Alfonso demands. He tells them that they must first pretend to go off to war, but return soon after, presenting themselves to the sisters disguised as Albanians visiting Naples. Don Alfonso has an ally in Despina, the girls' clever serving maid, and he orders each young "Albanian" to pay court to the other one's fiancée. The two sisters hesitate for a while, but of course they end up accepting their new lovers, going so far as to sign marriage contracts provided by Despina, crudely disguised as a notary. Don Alfonso has won his bet. At the end of the opera the two officers come back unexpectedly, stating that a counterorder arrived and they do not have to go off to war after all. When the whole story is explained, the two girls are obliged to confess their infidelity.

Summaries of the opera's plot often state, out of some sort of respect for what is "proper," that the original couples are reconciled, and singers usually follow that rule. But if we read the libretto carefully, there is no explicit mention of such a reconciliation: it indicates only that the four lovers are present and Don Alfonso "unites them and makes them embrace each other," without stating who embraces whom. The exchange may be definitive, in other words. When the opera is performed, the director is free to choose. Perhaps the better interpretation would be to end the opera with the new couples embracing: at least they can try to live in harmony, since the love of the original couples would have lost its innocence. In any event, in the theatrical ambiguity of the final scene Mozart remained faithful to his firm principle of representing on stage the dualities and unconventional sides of life. After all, he himself fell madly in love with one of the Weber sisters and married another.

*Così fan tutte* is an opera about the fragility of human relations and, in a broader sense, the ways in which we can all lose our moorings in life. Some commentators believe that the opera is limited to describing a bet, a more or less indecent joke. All we need do is listen to the intense and often pain-laden music to understand that this is not so. Once more Mozart has given us a *dramma giocoso* in which either the drama or the merry qualities can be accentuated, and perhaps there is more drama in it than playfulness. The opera contains moments in which we laugh or smile, and Mozart is always ironic: when he offers the opposite to *opera seria*, as he does here, he is also laughing at himself, the great composer of *Idomeneo*. Here, however, the irony and the smiles are always accompanied by a certain bitterness. Hildesheimer writes that *Così fan tutte* "does, in fact, pose greater riddles than all Mozart's other operas." He also remarks that the opera's title could just as well be *Così fan tutti*, because the women's infidelity is outmatched by the men's lack of morality.[54] Giovanni Carli Ballola and Roberto Parenti call *Così fan tutte* Mozart's most mysterious opera.[55]

The two men, Guglielmo and Ferrando, who are aware of the false identities from the start since they made the bet, set to work with a will, each attempting to rob the other man of his fiancée, even though they know that if they are successful each will lose fifty zecchini as well as a future spouse. Their male vanity proves stronger, however, and each one wants to tell the other man, "I am as good as you and perhaps even better than you" because he has been able to win over the other's beloved. They are also urged on by the pleasure of novelty and a desire to change partners to see what secret arts another man's woman might possess. At this point the fifty zecchini represent the price to be paid for that knowledge. A passion for gambling as an end in itself may also be part of the picture. Guglielmo and Ferrando are young, superficial, and thoughtless; they are perfectly willing to disguise themselves as Albanians with fake moustaches and play with human emotions, heedless of the consequences.

It is possible that the two women, Dorabella and Fiordiligi, are genuinely unaware of the masquerade until the dénouement. This is doubtful, however, not so much because theatrical tradition dictates that the two lovers remain recognizable under their turbans, their false moustaches, and their vaguely Turkish robes, but rather because their voices, their looks, and their gestures ought to betray their identities to even the most ingenuous girls. The Ferrarese sisters are not all that inexperienced, as we can surmise both by what takes place in the opera and by what may have occurred earlier, given that at one point Fiordiligi states that there are "many uniforms of Guglielmo's and Ferrando's" in the girls' house. Even if we accept the notion that Dorabella and Fiordiligi understand nothing, the fact remains that the action of the opera takes place in one day, within a few hours, as Ferrando exclaims ("In un giorno! . . . In poche ore!"). Thus the two sisters are capable of betraying their fiancés immediately, with no hesitation, and with two absurd "Albanians." The women, too, haven't a thought in their heads, are superficial, and are willing to play with the emotions of others. Or perhaps they are creatures not too unlike all others when constrained to try to live up to the mad demands of one true love. This is clear in Fiordiligi's exclamation: "Inorridisci! Io amo! E l'amor mio non è solo per Guglielmo" (Horrors! I love, and my love is not only for Guglielmo). In short, Fiordiligi loves two people at once, Guglielmo, who has departed for the wars, and the false Albanian (Ferrando) who has just arrived on the scene. We can guess that the box seats of the Burgtheater contained plenty of married persons capable of feeling strong ties to both a spouse and a lover. It is probable that Mozart himself, who wanted to salvage his marriage with Constanze, found himself in a similar situation.

Despina, the maid, is a very clever young woman who lends aid (in exchange for money) to Don Alfonso and the Albanians. She must have smelled a ruse from the beginning, even if at the end of the opera she displays great surprise when the two officers confess that they had disguised themselves. She does the same, and twice, once as a doctor and then as a notary. Disguised as a doctor, she enters on stage holding an enormous magnet in her hand, an obvious reference—as all Vienna would recognize immediately—to the "magnetism" that Mesmer was using at the time as a therapeutic procedure. Don Alfonso is a café philosopher, a skeptic given to mockery. He quite obviously does not believe that love is eternal, and he finds some inspiration in Enlightenment thought. Everything points to the notion that Mozart identified with him. Some passages in the opera seem to raise an echo of Wolfgang and Constanze's discussions about fidelity and betrayals during that same period. The final chorus ends the opera with a moral not unlike Mozart's definition of the fortunate man as one who "lets reason guide him" and who can keep calm in the midst of the whirl of life—that is, who find the "tranquility" that Wolfgang preached to Constanze.

We do not know how the Viennese public reacted to *Così fan tutte*, but it appears that the work's reception was somewhat tepid. This opera, too, contained elements that the aristocracy of the capital might find distasteful. The maid Despina is much shrewder than her mistresses, whom she defines as two *buffone*. She also turns out to be better educated because, disguised as a doctor, she manages at least to improvise some macaronic Latin—"Salvete amabiles bonae puellae"—that leaves the two ladies from Ferrara open-mouthed and forces them to confess that "he is speaking a language that we do not know." At the beginning of the opera Despina, after having prepared chocolate for the two ladies, complains that she herself cannot taste a drink reserved for her betters, then has to watch Dorabella thoughtlessly throw the tray, the cups, and the chocolate to the floor. And as if that were not enough to annoy the gentlefolk of Vienna, the two women and their lovers, all of whom belong to the upper classes, seem marionettes manipulated by Despina, the servant, and by Don Alfonso.

But *Così fan tutte* might also have particularly disturbed the Viennese public with its immorality. The libretto is full of racy double meanings, and even the institution of marriage is derided in the scene of the nuptials between the Albanian men and the Ferrarese ladies, as the chorus compares brides to prolific hens. During the same ceremony, what is more, three of the four sing a libertine toast, set to splendid and religious-sounding music ("E nel tuo, nel mio bicchiero si sommerga ogni pensiero"; Let every thought be drowned in my cup and in yours). Only Guglielmo is disturbed, and says to himself, about the others, "Ah, bevessero del tossico, queste volpi senza onor!" (Ah, if those vixens without honor were only drinking poison). Today we attend a performance of *Così fan tutte* knowing that two centuries of history separate us from the society we see represented, but the Viennese public of the time saw itself. An emergent romantic sentimentality was wounded by the pitiless message contained in the opera, and in fact *Così fan tutte* was not performed anywhere during the entire nineteenth century.

## Leopold II (February 1789–December 1790)

On 20 February 1790 Joseph II died and the performances of *Così fan tutte* were suspended for the period of imperial mourning. Joseph's successor on the throne was his brother Leopold, who was forty-two at the time and had been grand duke of Tuscany. In 1762, when Leopold was only fifteen, he had listened to Mozart the child prodigy play in Vienna. In April 1770 he had received him in Florence in the grand-ducal villa of Poggio Imperiale and heard him play again. In January 1773 Leopold Mozart stated that he had petitioned the young grand duke to give seventeen-year-old Wolfgang a permanent position, but Leopold had not been persuaded to do so. Now, the situation was completely different. Leopold Mozart was dead, and Wolfgang had lived in Vienna for some years, was a famous composer, had written operas for the Burgtheater, and had obtained a sinecure of eight hundred florins a year from Joseph II. With the arrival of Leopold II on the imperial throne, Mozart mistakenly thought that he might be able to obtain other high and more important responsibilities at court.

When the new emperor arrived in Vienna, he found a situation of great confusion, even in economic terms, and that needed to be brought under control. The war with the Turks was costly and fruitless, which meant that the Austrian Empire found itself in a weaker position than the other great powers. Within the empire, what is more, the reforms of Joseph II had aroused hostility, not only among the aristocracy, but also among the various ethnic groups. Thus Leopold II was dealing with problems a good deal more urgent than those of the musical arts. Leopold put an end to the effort to eliminate the privileges of the nobility; he sought to conclude the war with the Turks as early as possible; and he showed himself to be rather indifferent to the promotion of cultural and artistic life that had been so close to his brother's heart.

In the general commotion prompted by the new emperor's arrival on the scene, Salieri retired from his responsibilities as director of the court theater, but he maintained his position as Kapellmeister. Da Ponte left Vienna. During the first part of May 1790 Mozart requested a post as second Kapellmeister, and he wrote to Puchberg about this modest ambition, "I now have great hopes of an appointment at court, for I have reliable information that the emperor has not sent back my petition with a favorable or damning remark, as he has the others, but has retained it. That is a good sign."[56] In reality, Mozart was without any new commissions, scraping by on his salary of eight hundred florins, and in a very marginal position. He continued to ask for money from his friend Puchberg and was obliged to give lessons in order to pay expenses. On 12 June he claimed to have been obliged to "give away" to Artaria & Co. "for a mere song" the first *Prussian* String Quartet (K. 575) and two other recent quartets, the second and third *Prussian* (K. 589, 590)—that is, all three of the quartets ostensibly written for the king of Prussia.[57] Mozart gave a concert in April, and in June he conducted a performance of *Così fan tutte*, which returned to the stage of the Burgtheater after the period of mourning for Joseph II was over. Still, he lived in the midst of great difficulties. The entire empire was in crisis, and that crisis coincided with a decline in interest in Mozart's music, which was judged to be too original, too full of ideas, and thus apt to leave the listener breathless. The fact remains that in the latter part of the year 1790, after completing *Così fan tutte*, Mozart produced relatively little, in comparison with his usual high level of production.

On 9 October Leopold of Hapsburg was to be crowned Holy Roman Emperor in the cathedral of Frankfurt am Main, and all the Viennese who had some weight in the court, including Salieri, were invited there to do honor to the sovereign. Mozart was not considered worthy of an invitation. In order to defend his image and be present at the event, Wolfgang left Vienna on 23 September, traveling in a private carriage with his brother-in-law Franz de Paula Hofer and his servant Joseph Deiner. To pay the travel expenses he had pawned the household's silverware and Constanze's jewels. During the days of great celebrations for the coronation he intended to make some money by giving concerts and mounting a performance of either *Don Giovanni* or *The Abduction from the Seraglio*. He arrived in Frankfurt on 28 September and lodged in an inn. Two days later he moved to the house of an old acquaintance, the actor and theater director Johann Heinrich Boehm. On 4 October Leopold II made his solemn entry into Frankfurt with an impressive cortege of horsemen and carriages, one of which transported Salieri and the other court musicians who, unlike Mozart, had received formal invitations.

The following day Mozart suffered a serious disappointment, because the troupe of the court theater in Mainz changed its program, not giving a benefit performance of *Don Giovanni* for the composer, as Mozart had announced in a letter to Constanze, but instead putting on an opera of Karl Ditters von Dittersdorf, *L'amore in manicomio*. Wolfgang wrote again to Constanze on 8 October, complaining about what was happening to him. He told her he was thinking of giving a concert and leaving immediately afterward: "Forthwith—tschiri-tschitschi—seek safety in flight!" He added, "I shall certainly not make enough money here to be able to pay back 800 or 1,000 gulden immediately on my return," and gave Constanze suggestions for how to obtain the money some other way.[58] Luckily, his friend Boehm did not betray Mozart, and he staged *The Abduction from the Seraglio*. On 15 October, at eleven o'clock in the morning, Mozart finally managed to organize a concert, but it was not a great financial success. Count Ludwig von Bentheim-Steinfurt, who was present, noted that Mozart had played a concerto "of an extraordinary prettiness and charm" and played beautifully, especially in a "Fantasy without the music," which he improvised at the fortepiano. Bentheim-Steinfurt adds that "the last Symphony was not given, for it was almost two o'clock and everybody was sighing for dinner." The concert had in fact lasted over three hours, with long intervals between one piece and the next. "The orchestra was no more than rather weak with 5 or six violins, but apart from that very accurate: there was only one accursed thing that displeased me very much," he adds, which was that "there were not many people."[59] A second concert, scheduled for some time in the next few days, was canceled. The trip to Frankfurt, which was to have signaled Mozart's triumph over Salieri and the other musicians invited by Leopold II, was a failure.

On 16 October Wolfgang left for Mainz by Rhine boat. On 20 October he gave a concert in that city in the presence of the prince-elector, Joseph von Erthal, and the imperial vice-chancellor, Franz de Paula Gundacker Colloredo, for which he received a fee of 165 florins. From Mainz he went to Mannheim, where his *Figaro* was performed in German translation. He passed through Augsburg, where we do not know whether he saw his "little cousin" Anna Thekla, by that time thirty-two years old and the mother of an illegitimate child. On 29 October he reached Munich, where he saw his many friends, the Cannabich family among them, which helped to improve his morale: "You can well imagine that I have had a good time with [them]," he told Constanze in a letter of 4 November 1790.[60] On 4 or perhaps 5 November Mozart participated in a concert organized in Munich by the elector of Bavaria, Karl Theodor, to honor Ferdinand IV, king of Naples, and his wife Maria Carolina, the sister of Joseph II and Leopold II. Wolfgang wrote to Constanze the day before the concert that he was happy to be able to play before the king of Naples, Leopold's brother-in-law, though, he declares ironically, he thought it "greatly to the credit of the Viennese Court that the king has to hear me in a foreign country."[61] The king of Naples had in fact been in Vienna around the middle of September, thinking to hear Mozart on that occasion, but Leopold II had invited other court musicians to play.

On 10 November 1790 Wolfgang returned to Vienna after a trip that had lasted some fifty days. There he completed the Adagio and Allegro in F Minor for Mechanical Organ (K. 594) that he had begun in Frankfurt. The piece had been commissioned by Count Joseph Deym, a bizarre personage who had something resembling a wax museum in Vienna containing automatons, busts, musical clocks, and, indeed, a mechanical organ. Mozart was happy to have a paid commission that permitted him to "slip a few ducats into the hands of my dear little wife," but he was bored with the composition task and nearly gave it up.[62] Soon after, however, he wrote another and very fine Fantasia for Mechanical Organ (K. 608), completing it on 3 March 1791. Haydn, Salieri, Beethoven, and Cherubini had also composed music for Count Deym's museum.

Realizing that Vienna had little to offer him, Mozart again thought of moving to London, where he had lived for a while as a child. As we have seen, in 1787 Nancy Storace, Michael Kelly, and Thomas Attwood returned to England with the idea of finding contracts for Wolfgang. In November 1789 the London music publisher John Bland, who was visiting Vienna, had met Haydn and perhaps Mozart as well. On 26 October 1790, when Mozart was traveling between Mannheim and Augsburg, Robert May O'Reilly, the administrator of the Italian theater in London, sent Mozart an invitation to come to the city from December 1790 to June 1791, where he would be paid three hundred pounds to compose at least two operas and be permitted to write other compositions for the concert hall. Mozart let the offer drop. In the same period the concert impresario Johann Peter Salomon also arrived in Vienna from London. He persuaded Haydn to leave for England and probably attempted, in vain, to induce Mozart to do the same. Some scholars think that rather than giving up the idea of going to London, Mozart simply put it off for a year.

On 14 December Mozart was part of the company at a farewell dinner that Haydn's close friends gave the day before he left for England with Salomon. Some think that Mozart did not follow his example because he did not have enough money to undertake the long and arduous trip or to pay his debts, as he would have had to do before leaving. Others have observed that, ultimately, Wolfgang did not suffer financially by not going to England, given than in Vienna, in 1791, he managed to resolve his financial problems and to earn sums equal to Haydn's earnings in England.

# Mozart's Last Year

## A Period of Great Activity

Mozart was exceptionally active during the final year of his life. During the course of the year 1791 he composed two operas, *La clemenza di Tito* (The Clemency of Titus) and *The Magic Flute*, but he also wrote the Piano Concerto in B-flat (K. 595), his last; the splendid motet, "Ave verum corpus" (K. 618); the String Quintet in E-flat (K. 614); the Clarinet Concerto in A (K. 622); two notable Masonic cantatas (K. 619, 623); portions of the Requiem (K. 626); and a number of arias, minuets, dances, and contredanses. The year was positive from the financial point of view as well, with earnings estimated at between 3,600 and 5,600 florins. The cost of living in Vienna had risen, but this was the most that Mozart had earned since he moved there.

The Piano Concerto in B-flat (K. 595) was completed on 5 January, but it was not performed until 4 March, when it was part of a concert given in a hall made available by Ignaz Jahn, a man whom some of Mozart's biographers call a restaurant owner, but who was in reality the purveyor for the grand dinners and banquets of the Viennese court. The concert featured the Bohemian clarinetist Joseph Bähr, court composer to the czar of Russia; Aloysia Weber Lange also sang several arias. The printed publicity announcement for the event stated that "Herr Kapellmeister Mozart" was to play "a Concerto on the *forte piano*."[1] No one could have imagined that this would be Mozart's last public appearance as a concert pianist.

Although the handbill calls Mozart "Kapellmeister," this term is not strictly accurate. Mozart's appointment was as composer for the court balls, but at the time he was pulling strings to become "deputy Kapellmeister" of the Cathedral of St. Stephen, an unsalaried post. He presented a formal request to that effect in April 1791, which was promptly rejected, perhaps because his private life was judged not totally irreproachable. On 9 May, however, he was granted this secondary, nonpaying post, but with some conditions attached.[2] Mozart was happy to accept the offer because it was a way of "reserving" the title—and the stipend—of Kapellmeister when it became available. It appears (although this is not certain) that the decree naming him to the higher post arrived only three days before he died. The salaried Kapellmeisters were by far inferior to him as musicians, but throughout his life he was unsuccessful in being recognized as their equal.

Between January and May 1791 Mozart composed a number of dances, the String Quintet in E-flat (K. 614), and two works featuring glass harmonica (K. 356/617a; 617), an instrument for which Benjamin Franklin had devised improvements in 1761. The sounds produced by the "armonica" resemble those of some modern electronic synthesizers, and the famous Doctor Mesmer used it as a therapeutic device. Mozart composed these pieces for Marianne Kirchgässner, a twenty-two-year-old musician blind from the age of three.

In May of the same year Mozart set to work composing *Die Zauberflöte* (The Magic Flute) (K. 620) on a libretto by Johann Emanuel Schikaneder. By June he had completed the orchestration for act 1. In July the impresario Domenico Guardasoni (who had commissioned *Don Giovanni* in 1787) approached Mozart with the idea of writing a new opera, *La clemenza di Tito*, for the Prague theater, to be performed in September as part of the festivities celebrating Leopold II's coronation as king of Bohemia.[3] Thus Mozart must have been working simultaneously on *The Magic Flute* and *La clemenza di Tito*. In August, however, he necessarily concentrated on the latter. As if that were not enough, in July he accepted a commission to write a requiem mass, which means that from then until December—that is until his death—he was a very busy man.

Wolfgang remained active and lighthearted until November, when he fell desperately ill. On 4 June, Constanze, who was pregnant for the sixth time, went to Baden, a spa some fourteen miles south of Vienna, for the waters, taking with her their son Carl, then seven years old. Wolfgang joined her there often, but he also sent her a number of letters. His letter of 6 June was filled with sweet nothings and jokes, some of them fairly scurrilous. In it he affectionately calls her "Stanzi-Marini," which sounds like the double surname of an imaginary Italian singer. He worries about her health, telling her that he was delighted that her appetite was good but warning her that "whoever gorges a lot, must also shit a lot—walk a lot, I mean." He sends her 2,999½ little flying kisses and alludes to more: "Listen, I want to whisper something in your ear—and you in mine—and now we open and close our mouths—again—again and again—at last we say: 'It is all about Plumpi—Strumpi—'" words that had meaning only for them.[4]

On 18 June, Mozart completed the "Ave verum corpus" (K. 618) in Baden. It was performed for the first time on 23 June, also in Baden, on Corpus Domini, a feast day that had been eliminated by Joseph II but was reinstated by Leopold II. Bernhard Paumgartner called this motet, a brief work of only forty-six bars, "perhaps the most elevated work of art that Mozart ever wrote."[5] In a letter to Constanze dated 25 June, Wolfgang states that he intended to go the next day, candle in hand, to join the Corpus Domini procession to Josefstadt, a suburb of Vienna (Corpus Domini was celebrated a week late in the suburbs).[6] This display of devotion may be explained by the fact that the ceremony was organized by the Piarist Fathers, and Mozart was trying to persuade them to accept his son Carl at their school.

While his wife was in Baden, Mozart was living alone in Vienna, but he was a man who feared solitude. On 6 June he wrote Constanze that he had gone to sleep at the house of an old acquaintance, the horn player Joseph Leutgeb, because there was no one at home, not even the servant woman. On 12 June he complains about having to eat alone in a restaurant. The malicious might say that Mozart may have been eating and sleeping in excellent company and was complaining of being alone only because he was hiding an embarrassing dalliance. This may be so. But in any event the fact that he speaks to his wife about disliking being alone indicates that she was well aware of his fears. In the same letter of 25 June, probably in response to a question from Constanze, he declares, "And where did I sleep? At home of course. And I slept very well, save that the mice kept me most excellent company. Why, I had a first-rate argument with them. I was up before five o'clock."[7]

Constanze was not suffering from loneliness in Baden: she had the company of twenty-five-year-old Franz Xaver Süssmayr, formerly Mozart's student and for about a year his collaborator. Süssmayr was working on the orchestration of The Magic Flute in Baden, and it has been suggested that Mozart sent him there to keep an eye on his wife.[8] Others have speculated that Süssmayr had become Constanze's lover. Whatever their relationship may have been, the baby born on 26 July 1791 was named Franz Xaver Wolfgang, a combination of both men's names, and in 1829, to counter suspicions that were still in circulation, Constanze felt the need to publish two drawings showing that her husband's left ear and that of her son Franz displayed the same defect. As for Mozart, the letters that he sent to Constanze in Baden often take delight in poking fun at Süss-mayr and denigrating him, even with a touch of acrimony, as if he too had his suspicions or knew something. On 25 August the three of them traveled together to Prague to attend performances of *La clemenza di Tito* and *Don Giovanni,* returning together to Vienna on 11 September.

Mozart considered the trip to Prague a step forward in his artistic career. *La clemenza di Tito* had been written to honor Leopold II, and the emperor himself had asked that *Don Giovanni* also be performed in Prague, which gave Mozart the impression that Leopold might now regard him more favorably. His fame now extended far beyond the Hapsburg Empire: as we have seen, proposals had come to him from London, and on 15 September in Vienna, Count Andrei Razumovsky, a diplomatic representative on a mission to the court of Leopold II, suggested to Prince Grigori Potemkin that he invite Mozart to Russia. Razumovsky was the brother-in-law of Prince Lichnowsky and a great music lover, while Potemkin was the chief favorite of Empress Catherine II, hence one of the most influential men in Russia. Thus in the final days of his life, Wolfgang was given definite signs that his compositions were becoming known throughout Europe.

Mozart completed *The Magic Flute* on 28 September. Two days later he conducted the opera in Schikaneder's theater, the Freihaus-Theater auf der Wieden. The critics were at first dubious, but the theater attracted a general public with whom the work was a roaring success. The following day, 1 October, Mozart conducted the opera again. He describes what happened in a letter to Constanze of 7–8 October:

> I have this moment returned from the opera, which was as full as ever. As usual the duet "Mann und Weib" and Papageno's glockenspiel in Act I had to be repeated and also the trio of the boys in Act II. But what always gives me the most pleasure is the *silent approval!* You can see how this opera is becoming more and more esteemed. . . . And the strangest thing of all is that on the very evening when my new opera was performed for the first time with such success, "Tito" was given in Prague for the last time with tremendous applause.[9]

Mozart was a happy man. On 7 October he completed the sublime Clarinet Concerto in A (K. 622).

Mozart speaks of *The Magic Flute* again in a letter dated 8–9 October. He reports that once more the opera played to a full house, declares his intention to take his mother-in-law to the theater the next day, and then criticizes an acquaintance who had attended the opera the previous night and had laughed at everything, even the "solemn scene" at the beginning of act 2, thus showing himself to be totally unaware of the opera's deeper meanings. Mozart relates that he went backstage during the second act, and that he himself played the glockenspiel that Schikaneder, as Papageno, was supposedly playing on the stage. By coming in at all the wrong moments Mozart made the audience realize that Schikaneder was faking it, and the entire hall burst out laughing. In short, Wolfgang was in a good humor and in excellent health: he tells Constanze that he slept very well and for breakfast had "thoroughly enjoyed" a half capon.[10]

On 14 October he sent Constanze the last letter of his life. In it he relates that he had taken little Carl and his grandmother, Caecilia Weber, and Antonio Salieri and the soprano Caterina Cavalieri to hear *The Magic Flute*. He reports that Salieri and Cavalieri were "charming" to him and had liked it all, "not only my music, but the libretto and everything." He adds, "They both said that it was an *operone,* worthy to be performed for the grandest festival and before the greatest monarch, and that they would often go to see it, as they had never seen a more beautiful or delightful show. Salieri listened and watched most attentively and from the overture to the last chorus there was not a single number that did not call forth from him a bravo! or bello! It seemed as if they could not thank me enough for my kindness." Little Carl had been "absolutely delighted" to be taken to the theater with his father. "He is looking splendid," his father reports, adding, in typically fatherly fashion, "He still has his old bad manners; he never stops chattering just as he used to do in the past; and he is, if anything, *less inclined to learn than before,* for out there [at the school in Perchtoldsdorf] all he does is to wander about in the garden for five hours in the morning and five hours in the afternoon, as he himself confessed."[11]

He ends his letter with a complaint that Constanze had not written him from Baden for two days, but concludes, "I hope that I shall certainly have a letter from you today, and that tomorrow I shall talk to you and embrace you with all my heart. Farewell, Ever your Mozart." There could hardly be a more tender conclusion. Still, he added a postscript, and thus Wolfgang's last written words to Constanze were "Do what you like with N.N. Adieu."[12] Many scholars believe that "N.N." probably refers to Süssmayr.

A few days later the family was all together at Baden. On 9 November Prince Lichnowsky obtained a court judgment garnishing Mozart's salary to repay a debt of 1,435 florins and 32 kreuzer, plus 24 florins for court costs. After Mozart's death Lichnowsky acted in a truly princely manner and let the matter drop. On 15 November Wolfgang finished his last complete composition, the Masonic cantata *Laut verkünde unsre Freude* (K. 623), a work for three male voices and orchestra that he himself conducted on 17 November for the inauguration of the new site of the lodge of New Crowned Hope. Three days later, on 20 November, he took to his bed.

## *La clemenza di Tito* (September 1791)

*La clemenza di Tito* (K. 621), commissioned by the impresario Guardasoni in July, was performed less than two months later, on 6 September. Legend has it that the opera was written in only eighteen days, from 19 August to 5 September, but it seems highly unlikely that Mozart could have completed it in so short a time. He probably began working on it in the month of July, perhaps using music that he had put aside for later use. It is also likely that he entrusted Süssmayr with the task of providing music for the recitatives. Even taking all of that into account, however, Mozart furnished a new and dazzling proof of his ability to write fast. Everything seems to indicate that it was precisely because Guardasoni knew how rapidly Mozart could produce music that he entrusted him with the task, luring him on with a grandiose promise of two hundred ducats (nine hundred florins). The Bohemian Estates, the governing body of Bohemia, had contacted Guardasoni early in June, signing a contract with him on 8 July. In it Guardasoni agreed to have the libretto "set to music by a celebrated master" or, because time was short, to "procure an opera newly composed on the subject of *Tito* by Metastasio."[13] As it indeed happened. Guardasoni evidently approached Salieri before Mozart and was turned down (perhaps precisely because not enough time had been allowed).[14] Mozart was capable of writing fast, liked to earn money, and was eager to ingratiate himself with Leopold II. He accepted the challenge.

Mozart wrote in his catalog of his works that Metastasio's play, *La clemenza di Tito,* had been reworked and reduced to "a true opera" by Caterino Mazzolà, a librettist born in the Veneto who had formerly been active at the court of Dresden. The Metastasio-Mazzolà libretto tells the story of a conspiracy against Titus Vespasianus, the first-century AD Roman emperor, in which a band of conspirators burn the Campidoglio and attempt to assassinate Titus. The emperor escapes, pardons the conspirators, and even takes Vitellia, who had been the brains of the operation, as his wife. The emperor's purity and mercifulness is such that he sings lines (in act 2, scene 12) that would have driven Machiavelli wild (and not only Machiavelli): "Se all'impero, amici Dei, necessario è un cor severo / o togliete a me l'impero, o a me date un altro cor" (If, O friends of the gods, a severe heart is mandatory for power, either take away my power or give me another heart).

Adopting this text in celebration of Leopold II's coronation signified that immeasurable magnanimity was expected of the new emperor. Mozart was capable of charging the opera with a further and more personal message, however: he was letting Leopold know that he expected the emperor, in his goodness, to recognize the composer as at least equal to other, less gifted musicians. Finally, it is possible that the Prague audience found in La clemenza di Tito an echo of the great events that had recently taken place in France. The conspirators setting fire to the Campidoglio could be likened to the Paris revolutionaries who stormed the Bastille in 1789. By the same token, the good-hearted Titus, who pardoned the conspirators and promised to live in harmony with them, might call to mind Louis XVI or any monarch disposed to agree to a constitution. In France the constitution of 1791 was ratified in Paris on 3 September, just three days before La clemenza di Tito was first performed at the Nostitz theater in Prague.

The emperor and the empress were present at the theater on 6 September, but the opera was less than a triumphal success. Leopold II's consort, Maria Luisa of Bourbon, is reported to have called La clemenza di Tito "una porcheria tedesca" (German hogwash). One reason for the opera's less than enthusiastic reception was that tickets for the premiere were not sold or distributed in the usual ways, but rather assigned by government officials to members of the court, dignitaries, and state functionaries. This excluded many music lovers, which meant that the audience inside the theater lacked the connoisseurs who usually guided public reaction with their musical judgment, their applause, and their cries of "bravo!" As is clear from Wolfgang's letter to Constanze of 7–8 October, when the normal public returned to the Nostitz for the final performance of the opera, the work was greeted "with tremendous applause."[15]

Mozart's critics and biographers oscillate between extremes in their judgment of La clemenza di Tito. Some consider the opera sublime, a living, pulsing masterpiece perfect in its genre; others hold that it fails to hit the mark and is conventional, cold, and boring. Aleksandr Ulybyshev, Georges de Saint-Foix, and Giorgio Vigolo considered Tito as an anticipation of Fidelio and Beethoven's Eroica Symphony.[16] In 1947 Edward J. Dent

felt that the opera could only be considered "a museum piece," and although he had good things to say about many portions of the work, he
found it a curious mix of formality, magnificence, and a certain modernity.[17] As early as 1843, the Russian critic Aleksandr Ulybyshev stated that
on the whole *La clemenza di Tito* was "incontestably the least perfect" of
Mozart's classical operas. He faulted Mozart's music for weakening the
tragedy of certain scenes, at the same time praising some portions of the
opera.[18] My own opinion is that *Tito* does indeed display a number of limitations, due in part to its hasty composition, but that it is also true that
portions of the work are very beautiful and fully repay repeated listening.
Still, anyone who hopes to find in *La clemenza di Tito* the freshness, vivacity, and modernity of *Figaro, Don Giovanni, Così fan tutte,* or *The Magic Flute*
would be disappointed.

## *The Magic Flute* (September 1791)

The Köchel catalog number for *The Magic Flute*, K. 620, precedes that of
*La clemenza di Tito* (K. 621), but it seems to me proper to discuss it after
*Tito* because it was completed at a later date, premiering on 30 September
1791, presumably with Mozart working to complete the score up to the
last minute. Since it is a German opera, it really ought to be referred to as
*Die Zauberflöte.* Just as Italians think of the opera as *Il flauto magico,* re-
membering that until a few decades ago in Italy it was sung in Italian, not
German, the English-speaking world thinks of it as *The Magic Flute.* Papageno is an *uccellatore,* or a bird catcher, rather than a *Vogelfänger.* As we
have seen, Mozart attended a performance of his *Figaro* sung in German
at Mannheim in October 1790. Even today the texts of operas are sometimes sung in translation. In February 1950, the Rome Opera production
of Wagner's *Tristan und Isolde* presented a Tristan (August Seider) who
sang in German and an Isolde (Maria Callas) who sang in Italian. If philo-
logical concerns dominate today, they did not exist in Mozart's day. Thus
Italians will continue to speak of *Il flauto magico* and the English-speaking
world will refer to *The Magic Flute* rather than *Die Zauberflöte.*
   The idea for *The Magic Flute* seems to have come from Emanuel Schikaneder. Mozart had known Schikaneder, a multitalented actor, singer,
and head comic, since they had met in Salzburg in 1780. They became re-
acquainted in Vienna in 1785–1786, when Schikaneder produced a number of works at the Burgtheater, and in 1789, when he took over the direction of the Freihaus-Theater auf der Wieden, a theater inaugurated on
12 July 1789, two days before the taking of the Bastille. The Freihaus was

a large and imposing six-story structure containing not only a theater with an audience capacity of one thousand seats, but also an inn, a church (dedicated to St. Rosalia), a number of shops, an oil works, a pharmacy, a flour mill, and over two hundred apartments. Attached to it was a small wooden pavilion not much bigger than a newspaper stand, now in the garden of the Mozarteum in Salzburg. Inside that pavilion Mozart composed the better part of *The Magic Flute*.

The opera tells the story of a young prince, Tamino, in search of love and wisdom. He finds love with the princess Pamina, and he will find wisdom in the temple of the High Priest Sarastro, who is keeping Pamina prisoner. The action takes place in Thebes, in ancient Egypt, in an atmosphere that swings back and forth between the dramatic and the comic. The plot is both magical and fantastic, and it includes specific references to Masonic rituals. Toward the end of the opera Tamino and Pamina must undergo a trial by fire, and as they make their way through the flames, Tamino plays a magical golden flute that wards off danger. The other characters in the opera include the Queen of the Night, Sarastro's sworn enemy and Pamina's mother; Papageno, a simple and timorous bird catcher who becomes Tamino's companion; and Papagena, who first appears as an ugly crone but later becomes a splendid young woman who promises Papageno that together they will produce many pretty little Papagenos and Papagenas. There is also Monostatos, a Moor and Sarastro's evil servant. In the final scene the Queen of the Night and Monostatos, the two characters who are intent on doing harm, plunge into the eternal abyss. There are also three ladies-in-waiting to the Queen, three small boys, two men in armor, an orator, a good many priests, and some slaves, all of whom help create the climate of high emotion and uncertainty around the lovers, Tamino and Pamina, that is so much a part of all human life. The dual moral of the tale is that stressful adventures prepare us for pleasures, and virtuous behavior is rewarded.

*The Magic Flute* expresses the world's ambiguities perhaps better than any other Mozart opera. Sarastro, who represents good, light, and rationality, nonetheless keeps the innocent Pamina prisoner and has in his employ Monostatos, an unctuous, perfidious person. It appears that Mozart and Schikaneder took as their model for the Sarastro character Ignaz von Born, the scientist who had introduced Mozart to Freemasonry. Born was proud and intolerant. Sarastro, like Born and like all men, is imperfect.

The Queen of the Night, who represents evil, darkness, and irrationality, is nonetheless the mother of the splendid Pamina, and it is the queen who urges Tamino to seek out Pamina, thus pointing him toward happiness, goodness, and love. Love arises from the nocturnal irrational. It is also the Queen of the Night, seated on a throne adorned with transparent stars, who sees to it that Tamino and Papageno are protected by two musical instruments, a golden flute and silver bells, thus indicating that music, which is useful and supportive to us in this life, comes from an irrational, nocturnal, and indecipherable sphere. The text of the opera tells us that the Queen of the Night had been married to the King of the Circle of the Sun in a union that created a great universal harmony, a sort of terrestrial paradise that disappeared with the death of the king. Before dying, he entrusted the Circle of the Sun to Sarastro and his initiates, but universal harmony had nonetheless been forever broken. The queen had ordered Pamina to kill Sarastro in the vain hope of getting back the Circle of the Sun and restoring that earlier harmony. *The Magic Flute* thus describes the impossibility of a return to a lost paradise. It seems hardly coincidental that in the opening scene of the opera Tamino is threatened by a serpent—just like Adam in the Garden of Eden.

The three ladies who appear on stage at that point are attendants of the Queen of the Night, and by that token they ought to be working for evil, whereas the three boys are Sarastro's servants, hence they should be working for good. Yet the ladies are the first to help Tamino by freeing him from the serpent; they are also the ones who give him the magic flute, after which they turn him over to the three boys so they can lead him to Sarastro—further proof of the close connections between the kingdoms of evil and good. The three ladies seem to be warmhearted, even emotional, and they take an immediate liking to Tamino. The three boys, like Sarastro's priests, seem cold, detached, and overly rational beings, almost as if to demonstrate that reason without passion becomes sterile.

Papageno is a mirror image of Tamino. Where Tamino is noble and courageous, Papageno is a spontaneous liar and timorous. He is more animal than man, and in fact when Schikaneder inaugurated the role in September 1791, he was costumed as a bird, complete with feathers and a tail. Tamino's immediate reaction to him is, "I can't believe you are a man." Papageno's ignorance is crushing: he is aware of nothing beyond the valley in which he lives. He asks Tamino, "Are there other lands and other men beyond those mountains?" He has no ambition, and says so cheerfully: "Basically, I claim no wisdom. I am such a simple person that I am happy to sleep, eat, and drink. And if it were possible, I would like to have a beautiful little wife." In reality Mozart's bird catcher is a caricature of many of the peasants of his day, men reduced to living almost like animals yet capable of clever dealings. The citizens of Vienna knew the type well, and they may easily have seen bird catchers very much like Papageno in the marketplace, dressed in rags rather than bird's feathers. Although he is Tamino's social inferior, Papageno manages to find Pamina before he does, to protect her, and to find the right words to reassure her and touch her heart. At the end of the opera, however, Papageno does not fully become a man; he does not go through the purifying fire, but remains the same simple individual that he was. Mozart and Schikaneder had more than one reason for giving their princely couple a common double in Papageno and Papagena: there are many more Papagenos than Taminos in the real world; Papageno provides comic relief and entertainment; and, perhaps, we all find that a certain dose of the animal is indispensable.

It is often said that *The Magic Flute* is a work that denigrates women. I disagree. Admittedly, Sarastro states that any woman will abandon her assigned sphere if she lacks male guidance. Also admittedly, the priests intone a general invitation to be wary of women's wiles. Even Tamino tells Papageno not to trust the Queen of the Night because "she is a woman and has the mind of a woman." Still, we begin to doubt Mozart's misogyny on hearing Pamina's sublime duet with the simple Papageno, who likes women very much: "Man with woman and woman with man," they state, "rise up together to divinity." Pamina is permitted to undergo the trial by fire just like a man. Tamino and the two men in armor sing, "A woman who fears neither the night nor death is worthy, and will be initiated." Tamino and Pamina enter the Temple of Wisdom together, hand in hand. *The Magic Flute* seems to me to contain an invitation to Freemasonry to permit the initiation of women if and when they show themselves worthy of it. Both Tamino and Pamina wear priestly garments after their ordeal. One might argue endlessly about the Masonic (and non-Masonic) enigmas contained in *The Magic Flute*, but probably no one holds the key to solving them all. If there is such a key, Mozart and Schikaneder took it with them to their graves.

When the opera was produced in 1791 it was a spectacle using flying machines, trapdoors, fireworks, special effects, and scenery designed to dazzle the eye and touch the emotions. Schikaneder was famous for just such productions, and as Massimo Mila reminded us some years ago, the era loved the *Zauberstück*—"magic plays."[19] Scenic effects reached a peak that we find it difficult to imagine today, and audiences lapped them up. As he put on his opera, Mozart was once again seeking success, income, and entertainment, but given that in Mozart everything is ambivalent, entertainment came with a profound and dramatic message. Toward the end of *The Magic Flute*, for example, as Tamino and Pamina are preparing to enter into the fire, they are welcomed by two men in black armor, and the four of them—Tamino, Pamina, and the two armored men—sing "Thanks to the power of music we go happily through the dusky night of death." This is the profound message of *The Magic Flute:* we will all live better and die better with music to support us than we can without music.

## Mozart and Women

Mozart was strongly attracted to women. We can debate whether his sentiments were superficial or profound and whether he did or did not experience success with various women, but there is no doubt that they exerted a strong fascination for him. Some of his biographers note that there is no existing proof that Mozart had actual sexual experience with women other than Constanze, and they point out that after he lost Aloysia, he always played the role of the unhappy lover. I do not agree with them. Even if they are right, the long list of women he is said to have pined for stands as proof of the importance of the "eternal feminine" in his life. Even the message that he leaves us in *The Magic Flute*—that Pamina and, through her, all deserving women, can be initiated into the mysteries of wisdom—confirms the respect and admiration that Mozart felt for the fair sex.

The list of the women of whom he is conjectured to have been enamored may not be as long as Leporello's list of Don Giovanni's conquests, but it is sizable. At the age of fourteen he developed a crush on a friend of his sister's, as we learn from a letter to his sister Nannerl dated 20 October 1770. The following year in Venice he became close friends with the Wider girls, playing the rough-and-tumble games with them typical of young people's first approaches to one another that serve to camouflage sexual desire. In Salzburg, after his return from Italy, there were infatuations with other young girls mentioned in letters to his sister of 24 and 31 August 1771. These may have included Teresa Barisani, perhaps Anna Barbara von Mölk, and possibly others. In any event, these were nothing important. On 28 December 1774, again writing to Nannerl, Wolfgang alludes to a love. In 1776 in Salzburg he was probably attracted to one of the daughters of Countess Lodron. In September 1777, to reverse the situation, the daughter of a Salzburg baker seems to have become enamored of him after meeting him at a ball, and Leopold teases him about her.

On 23 September 1777 the twenty-one-year-old Wolfgang went to Germany, and Leopold made sure that he was accompanied by his mother, who was charged with keeping track of him and preventing him from doing anything foolish, especially with women. In Augsburg, however, on one of the early stages of that trip, Mozart was won over by the charms of his sprightly eighteen-year-old cousin Anna Thekla, thanks to whom he probably managed to have a complete or nearly complete sexual experience. As we know, Zweig and Freud both showed interest in the erotic letters that Wolfgang wrote to Anna Thekla. At the end of October, Mozart went to Mannheim, where he may have felt some form of attraction, not for his very young pupil, Rose Cannabich, to whom he dedicated the Piano Sonata in C (K. 309/284b), but for her mother, Lisel Cannabich. It was also in Mannheim that Aloysia Weber inspired Mozart's first genuine, deep, and overwhelming love, a passion that lasted about a year and drove Leopold nearly to distraction. In a letter of 17 September 1778 that Leopold wrote to his son in the hope of extracting him from the clutches of the Weber family and bringing him back to Salzburg once and for all, he mentions to Wolfgang that an old flame, Louise Robinig von Rottenfeld, who was twenty-one at the time, sent him her love. She may be another addition to the list. The young women of the Weber household were destined to prevail, however. They must have cast some sort of spell on Wolfgang, who went on from Aloysia to Constanze.

It is also true that in Vienna, as Mozart was planning for his marriage to Constanze, the thirty-seven-year-old Baroness Waldstätten, a lovely, uninhibited, and seductive woman experienced in the world's ways, felt an intense sympathy for Wolfgang, which he returned by paying ardent court to her. In a letter dated 2 October 1782 he tells the baroness that he is sending her a gift of some books and the Rondo in D for Piano and Orchestra (K. 382). He thanks her for her promise to give him a fine red coat and jokingly describes his unhappiness, sighing and moaning as he watched her in all her beauty at a ball. Something may have occurred after the ball, as Mozart tells his friend the baroness that he had slept like a dormouse and hoped that she had done the same: "You smile! you blush! Ah, yes—I am indeed happy. My fortune is made! But alas! Who taps me on the shoulder? Who peeps into my letter? Alas, alas, alas! My wife! Well, well, in the name of Heaven, I have taken her and must keep her! What is to be done? I must praise her—and imagine that what I say is true!" He then adds, "Apart from this, I should have had occasion to write to your Ladyship, though indeed I do not dare to mention it. Yet why not? Well then, courage! I should like to ask your Ladyship to—Faugh, the devil— that would be too gross! A propos, Does not your Ladyship know the little Rhyme? A woman and a jug of beer, / How can they rhyme together?" The letter concludes, " My wife, who is an angel of a woman, and I, who am a model husband, both kiss your Ladyship's hands a thousand times and are ever your faithful vassals."[20]

It goes without saying that Wolfgang refers to the baroness with great circumspection in two letters to his father written in January 1783. On 4 January he declares her "*changeable* as the wind," and on 8 January, since the baroness had asked Leopold's advice about taking on a new piano teacher, Wolfgang writes that he knows her all too well and that at times one should be on guard with her, as she has a habit of taking men into her service, as he puts it, "for herself and not for her children," and then dismissing them. He adds, "You may put whatever construction you like on this. Suffice it to say that the result of these scenes is that people speak very lightly about her. She is weak; but I shall say no more — and the little I have said is only for yourself; for I have received a great many kindnesses from her and so it is my duty to defend her so far as possible, or at least to say nothing."[21] Leopold, too, found the charming young Baroness Waldstätten attractive. She and Leopold exchanged letters, and in Vienna in 1785 he had occasion to meet her.

After his marriage with Constanze, Wolfgang continued to pay court to beautiful women. One of these is thought to have been the soprano Nancy Storace, the first Susanna in *The Marriage of Figaro,* a woman some ten years his junior to whom he dedicated the soprano scene with rondo, "Ch'io mi scordi di te?"/"Non temer, amato bene," a work for orchestra and solo piano (K. 505) that is a genuine declaration of love: "Do not fear, my well-beloved, my heart will always be yours." In his dedication, dated 26 December 1786, Mozart wrote: "For Mlle Storace and for me." Storace was about to return to London and had suggested that Mozart move to England. According to Alfred Einstein, Mozart remained in correspondence with the young soprano, but no one knows what became of their letters. Storace may have destroyed them before she died to prevent them from being read by "profane" eyes.[22]

Another love that has been attributed to Mozart is Josepha Duschek, a famous singer married to a composer much older than she whom Mozart pursued during the strange trip that he made to Germany without Constanze in 1789. One of Mozart's pupils in Vienna was the young and beautiful Theresia von Trattner, the wife of Baron Johann Thomas von Trattner, a man forty-one years older than she, and in whom Mozart seems to have taken a lively interest. Between 1784 and 1787 Trattner and his young wife became godparents to several of Wolfgang and Constanze's children, and Mozart dedicated two piano works to Theresia von Trattner, the Sonata in C Minor (K. 457) and the Fantasy in C Minor (K. 475). Another woman in whom Mozart probably took an interest in the last months of his life was Maria Magdalena Pokorny Hofdemel. She and the scandal attached to her are treated below.

Other adventures may have enlivened Mozart's life while he was hard at work, hidden from prying eyes in the little wooden pavilion near Schikaneder's theater. A high degree of liberty, a pursuit of entertainment, and the absence of moralism ruled in Schikaneder's theatrical realm, to the point that Schikaneder himself was expelled from Freemasonry for his dissolute life. Even the prudent Hermann Abert felt that during the process of readying *The Magic Flute* for its first performance, the twenty-one-year-old Barbara Gerl, née Reisinger, the first Papagena and the wife of Franz Gerl, the first Sarastro, may have managed to snare Mozart, or vice-versa.[23] The list does not stop there, however. There are also suggestions that Anna Gottlieb, who sang the first Barbarina in *The Marriage of Figaro* in 1786 at the age of twelve and, in 1791, when she was eighteen, was the first Pamina of *The Magic Flute*, also succeeded in seducing—or being seduced by—Mozart. His letters from that period exude a joyous exultation. He would be dead only two months later, but he was just thirty-five at the time.

## A Very Incomplete Requiem

Between August and December 1791 Mozart composed a portion of the Requiem in D Minor, the last composition that Köchel listed in his catalog (K. 626) in spite of the fact that the work is incomplete. In July 1791 an intermediary—not definitely identified but almost certainly Johann Michael Puchberg, an old friend of Mozart's, a merchant, and a Freemason who has been mentioned frequently in these pages—asked Mozart to compose a Requiem Mass for the young Count Franz Xaver Walsegg-Stuppach. The count had lost his wife on 14 February, and he wanted the world to believe that he himself had written the mass. In exchange he offered to pay the real composer of the work the sum of four hundred florins. Count Walsegg was an extremely wealthy man and an amateur musician and composer known for just this sort of secret transaction. Puchberg's role as intermediary is nearly certain. He lived and had his shop in the Walsegg palace. Since Mozart had borrowed sums much greater than four hundred florins from Puchberg, he would have found it difficult to refuse the offer. With some other intermediary Mozart might have sought to protect his dignity by refusing to cooperate in this shameful commercial exchange, but with Puchberg he could not. We can imagine Puchberg's arguments: don't worry, no one will know the truth; you can just write a simple mass in a hurry, without putting in much effort, because it won't be known as your work but as Walsegg's, and he is a dilettante. Besides, you will be doing a favor to my landlord and to me, and I lend you so much money. Mozart cannot have been very displeased at the idea of the four hundred florins, almost as much as he had received for *The Marriage of Figaro*. He may have thought of pulling out at some point, but he probably had received something on account, if not the entire sum, and the contract may have stipulated penalties should he fail to produce the work.

In later years the commission of the Requiem became the subject of legends, and the first person to spread them was Constanze, in her conversations with one of Mozart's earliest biographers, Franz Niemetschek. Constanze did not mention Walsegg's name. She spoke instead of an unknown messenger who had handed to Mozart an unsigned letter and later brought him not only the honorarium that Mozart had requested "but also the promise, as Mozart had been modest in his price, that he would receive another payment on receipt of the composition." The mysterious messenger gave Mozart free rein to compose "according to his own ideas and mood," but prohibited him from making any attempt to know his patron's identity.[24]

All this air of mystery and the fact that Mozart died while he was composing the Requiem encouraged other legends about the genesis of the work, and latter-day viewers of the Miloš Forman film *Amadeus* might be led to think that the work was commissioned by Antonio Salieri, the messenger of death. A counterfeit letter from Mozart to Lorenzo Da Ponte, dated September 1791, has even been published. In it Wolfgang declares himself to be at death's door and obsessed by the unknown commissioner of the Requiem. It bears repeating that this letter is a fake, perpetrated by persons unknown for purposes unknown.[25]

Mozart was working on the Requiem as he was composing *The Magic Flute* and *La clemenza di Tito*, a fact that helps us to understand why he had not completed it when he fell ill in November. That Mozart may have felt uneasy because of the strangeness of the task offers a second explanation for why the work was left incomplete. Indeed, it was far from dignified for a great composer like Mozart to cooperate—for four hundred florins—in the fiction that Count Walsegg demanded of him. Moreover, because the composer of the Requiem was supposed to be a dilettante, it would have to be written amateurishly lest any listener with a finely tuned ear sense the deception. In other words, Mozart was obliged to hold back, to avoid any strokes of genius, hence to work against his instincts. Never in his whole life had he been in a messy situation like this one. When he died in December he left the work unfinished.

The only part of the Requiem entirely written by Mozart is the Introit. A performance of the Requiem lasts fifty minutes or so, but the Introit represents only the first five minutes. All of the rest—that is, 90 percent of the Requiem—was written or completed by other hands, in part on the basis of Mozart's sketches. They included Mozart's pupils and assistants: Franz Xaver Süssmayr, whom we have already met, Franz Jacob Freystädt-ler, and Joseph Eybler, who were brought in by Constanze, on her husband's advice, in the interest of working more swiftly. The Requiem had to be offered as a work entirely by Mozart, written before his death. It needed to be given to Walsegg immediately, both in order to receive the promised supplementary fee and to avoid trouble. In 1793, when Schlich-tegroll published his *Nekrolog* of Mozart, Constanze hastened to buy up all available copies of it and destroy them, because Schlichtegroll had dared to state that Mozart had not completed the Requiem.

The score for the Kyrie, which contains some instrumental parts in Mozart's hand, was filled in by his pupils. Both the Sequence (which includes the Dies Irae, Confutatis, and Lacrimosa) and the Offertory, for which Mozart had composed only a few passages, were completed with much more massive additions. For example, Wolfgang had composed only eight bars of the Lacrimosa, and it was finished by his pupils in a somewhat approximate and repetitive manner. The Requiem was supposed to seem the work of a dilettante, and to fulfill that task, Mozart's pupils were more suited than their master. The Sanctus, the Benedictus, and the Agnus Dei were entirely composed by Süssmayr and the others, although they may have made use of some sketches that Mozart left. For the final portion, the Communion, the pupils used a good deal of material from the Introit and the Kyrie. In short, Constanze and Mozart's disciples ended up confecting a substantially false product. This was precisely the aim of Walsegg's commission, however. Beethoven did not much like the Requiem, and many scholars have criticized various of its parts. The general public is still insufficiently informed, and believes that the work is entirely Mozart's. People find it moving that the great musician wrote it on the eve of his death.

In his biography of Mozart, Bernhard Paumgartner, the prominent scholar who served as director of the Salzburg Mozarteum for forty years, approaches the Requiem in terms that at first sight seem to coincide with the judgment of the cultivated public: "Mozart," he writes, "left us his Requiem (K. 626) incomplete, like a powerful torso. Soon after his death other hands completed it, almost under the cover of anonymity, but they were taught by him and had developed in the spirit of his school." Paumgartner adds that controversy arose immediately after Mozart's death, "But it will not be possible in the foreseeable future to claim to have said the final word." After this cautious preamble, Paumgartner offers a sharp criticism of Süssmayr's contribution, in particular of the awkward instrumentation of the Dies Irae: "The strings almost always double the vocal parts set down by Mozart, or else depart from them with impersonal accompanimental figures and tremolos. Even the trombones stay glued to the chorus in a patriarchal churchly style, which results in sonic effects irreconcilable with Mozart's mature technique." That same defect struck Paumgartner as "particularly disturbing" in the Confutatis. The repetition of the Kyrie in the Agnus Dei seemed to him a conventional move, whereas "Mozart, with the fine artistic intuition that he achieved in his last years, would certainly have found another solution, making the conclusion of the entire work much more powerful."[26]

We must keep reminding ourselves that Wolfgang, Puchberg, Constanze, Walsegg, and later Süssmayr, Freystädtler, and Eybler all schemed to produce a rough-cast Requiem with a fair share of banality to it that would only in part seem the work of a great composer. Mozart's illness and death were in a sense providential for achieving that goal, to the point that it might be appropriate to cancel the Requiem from the Köchel catalog. The Requiem is less a work written by Mozart than it is a work written by others for him.

## Illness and Death

Until 20 November, the day he had to take to his bed with a fever, Mozart does not seem to have been sick. In the current state of the documentation, all the information that Constanze later provided regarding a gradual worsening of his health beginning in September and a slow poisoning due to "Tofana water" (an arsenic-based poison) administered by some mysterious individual seems totally unfounded. It was in Constanze's interest to divulge erroneous particulars in order create a halo of legend around the Requiem and make people believe that Mozart composed the work in full awareness of his imminent death. Constanze herself denied the story some years later when she told Vincent and Mary Novello that her husband had been killed by a sudden fever. The death register of the cathedral of St. Stephen declares that Mozart died on 5 December of a "severe military fever" (*hitziges Frieselfieber*), a term that means little to us now but that probably refers to an acute rheumatic fever. Not only did the physicians of the time not know how to treat patients, but they were also unable to diagnose their illnesses. Two doctors, Thomas Closset and Matthias von Sallaba, bled Mozart profusely, taking from two to three liters of blood, according to some witnesses. If this was indeed the case, it would be reasonable to conclude that without knowing what they were doing, the doctors killed him or at least hastened his death.

Vienna was in the grip of a fever epidemic at the time. The letter that Mozart wrote Constanze on 8–9 October 1791, while she was in Baden, mentions it in passing: "Primus told me last night," he writes, "that a great many people in Baden are ill. Is this true? Do take care and don't trust the weather."[27] Giuseppe Carpani, Haydn's biographer, wrote in 1824 to defend Salieri from the accusation of having poisoned Mozart, stating that Mozart had contracted an infectious fever that was attacking many inhabitants of Vienna.[28] In his *Mozart's Last Year,* H. C. Robbins Landon reproduces a letter of the court councilor Eduard Guldener von Lobes, a friend of Dr. Closset (one of the physicians who attended Mozart), that he wrote to Carpani, denying the thesis of poisoning and confirming the presence of an epidemic. Guldener writes, "In the autumn of 1791 he fell ill of an inflammatory fever, which at that season was so prevalent that few persons entirely escaped its influence. . . . I saw the body after death, and it exhibited no appearances beyond those usual in such cases."[29] Constanze is reported to have thrown herself in despair onto the bed next to her dead husband precisely in order to be infected herself and die.

It is probable that Mozart continued to work on the Requiem as he lay ill in the apartment on the Rauhensteingasse. He may have been worried about the contract he had signed with Count Walsegg and about penalties to be incurred if he failed to do his part. He does not seem to have worked on it very intensively, however. He may have given orders and advice to Constanze and his assistants, becoming increasingly anguished as he became aware that death was near. Constanze and her sister Sophie remained at his side. Toward the end a priest was sent for to give Mozart extreme unction, an errand that seems to have proved somewhat difficult, perhaps because Mozart was a Freemason, perhaps for some other reason. On November 28, when his condition worsened, Closset and Sallaba, both prominent physicians, were called in for consultation. Sophie Haibel indicated many years later that on the evening of 4 December, the last day of Mozart's life, she and Constanze sent again for Dr. Closset, who was at the theater and sent back word that he could not leave before the end of the performance.[30] Many commentators have wondered about this delay, but it is quite possible that Closset had a professional obligation to remain until the performance was over. Or perhaps he knew that nothing could be done to save Wolfgang. He arrived after the performance. When Mozart died, at five minutes before one in the morning of 5 December 1791, Closset, Constanze, and Sophie were at his bedside.

Count Deym, the wax museum owner who had commissioned the Adagio and Allegro in F Minor for Mechanical Organ (K. 594) in 1790, took a wax death mask, which unfortunately has been lost. Mozart was placed in his coffin wrapped in a black cloak with his head hooded, as Masonic ritual required. At three o'clock in the afternoon on 6 December, thirty-eight hours after his death, the funeral service took place in the Chapel of the Crucifix of the cathedral of St. Stephen. Such relative haste may have been due to regulations regarding the epidemic in course. In any event, Constanze was not present at the funeral service because, as it was explained, she was beside herself with grief. She was now alone in the world with two children, Carl, who was seven, and the four-month-old Franz Xaver Wolfgang. Constanze may have lost control, fleeing from the house with the children, because she believed that in losing Mozart she had lost everything and, worse, would find herself in serious difficulty because of her husband's debts and contractual obligations, including the obligation to furnish Walsegg with the Requiem.

On the day after Mozart's funeral service, 7 December, Franz Hofdemel, an official in the Ministry of Justice and a dilettante musician, seriously wounded his beautiful twenty-five-year-old wife Maria Magdalena Pokorny in a fit of jealousy, then killed himself with a razor. Maria Magdalena had been a pupil of Mozart's before his illness, and according to some commentators she was so distraught by her teacher's death that she revealed to her husband that they had been lovers and that she was five months pregnant with his child. Hofdemel's attempt to kill his wife was unsuccessful, and she was found lying in a pool of blood. She survived, but her face was disfigured by scars. Hofdemel knew Wolfgang and had even lent him a hundred florins: on 2 April 1789 Mozart had signed a draft in his favor. We can easily imagine the emotions aroused in Vienna by this tragic incident and the scandal that ensued.[31] We do not know the precise hour at which Hofdemel killed himself after wounding his wife, nor do we know when Constanze learned about it. Certainly all Viennese society was shaken by the affair. Some years later Count Karl Czerny asked Beethoven if he would like to meet Frau Hofdemel, and Beethoven responded, "Hofdemel? Isn't that the woman who had the affair with Mozart?" Francis Carr, in his *Mozart & Constanze*, raises the suggestion that Hofdemel poisoned Mozart, but his theory does not seem to me persuasive.[32] Piero Buscaroli notes in *La morte di Mozart* that up to a few decades ago some Viennese insisted that Mozart died of a cerebral hemorrhage caused by being beaten by Hofdemel, a hypothesis that has been repeated in a recent book by Giorgio Taboga.[33] What is clear is that the mysteries surrounding Mozart's death have fascinated scholars and will continue to do so for some time to come.

According to the most widely accepted version of events, immediately after the funeral mass on 6 December, Mozart's coffin was placed in a mortuary chapel surrounded by candles and flowers, as was the custom. A third-class burial was contracted for, as was the norm for someone of the middle class, at the cost of eight florins, fifty-six kreuzer. With the approach of night, a hearse drawn by two horses, hired for a supplementary cost of three florins, bore the coffin to the cemetery of St. Marx, where Mozart's body was buried that same night or the next day in a simple community tomb (not in a common grave), as required by the very strict rules in effect at the time. His friends and family would not have accompanied the coffin: the cemetery lay some two miles outside the city gates, and the laws required that bodies be transported during the nighttime hours. Emperor Joseph II had demanded that religious ceremonies return to an earlier simplicity and austerity. Gravestones were permitted, but Mozart did not have one. Nor does it seem that Constanze ever went to the cemetery to visit the spot where the coffin was buried. When the idea occurred to someone it was too late, and the resting place of Mozart's mortal remains is unknown.

On 10 December a requiem mass in Mozart's honor was sung in the church of St. Michael in Vienna, the seat of the Congregation of St. Cecilia, the court musicians' guild. The Freemasons of Vienna also honored their illustrious brother with an imposing funeral celebration, the oration for which was printed. Mozart's fellow Masons also published the recently composed Masonic cantata, *Laut verkünde unsre Freude* (K. 623), with the proceeds going to Constanze. In Prague religious ceremonies were organized in Mozart's memory that were even more solemn than those in Vienna.

# Mozart Lives On

Mozart's body died, but his music and his myth are still alive, even more so today than in the past. A veritable cult has developed around Mozart, and anyone who enters his name in an Internet search engine will soon be lost among all the entries that pop up on the computer monitor. There is no composer of classical music whose works are played more than his. All stores that sell compact discs carry his works. His music has a prominent place in concert halls, opera houses, and radio programs. Orchestras, quartets, festivals, schools of music, associations, clubs, and reviews brandish his name, and Mozart's name can also be found on signs for hotels, pensions, bed-and-breakfasts, cafés, and restaurants the world over. His face and his name serve to sell desserts, bottles of liqueur, chocolates, perfumes, soap, and T-shirts. His life and his works provide subject matter for books, plays, novels, pictures, films, musical comedies, and operettas. Clinics and health centers make therapeutic use of Mozart's music to help heal patients afflicted with dyslexia, autism, or epilepsy, or as a positive influence on the psyches of newborn babies and their mothers. Many cities have streets bearing his name, and in Salzburg even the airport is named "Wolfgang Amadeus Mozart." An Internet search reveals that there is a small town in Saskatchewan, with a post office, named "Mozart." Everywhere in the world there are Masonic lodges that proudly bear the name of their brother who died in 1791. An Austrian popular singer, Hans Hölzel, called "Falco" (the Falcon), became famous thanks to a song titled "Rock Me, Amadeus." Soon after Hölzel's death in 1998 a musical comedy, *Falco Meets Amadeus*, featured imaginary encounters between the two musicians. To complete the list, thousands of cell phones announce incoming calls with the opening measures of the G-Minor Symphony (K. 550). Mozart would probably be delighted. When he went to Prague in 1787 he was enchanted to note that people on the street were whistling airs from his *Figaro* and bands of musicians were playing his tunes in cafés and restaurants. The omnipresence of Mozart in our society of mass consumption may appear to be a perfectly normal phenomenon: what is abnormal is its extraordinary extent. Mozart's current popularity seems to me clearly greater than that of all the other great composers beloved by the public—Puccini, Verdi, Beethoven, Chopin, or Tchaikovsky, to mention a few.

The explanation must lie, above all, in the nature of Mozart's music and in the extraordinary equilibrium he managed to create between tradition and innovation. Only artists capable of innovation can give a long life to their works. Innovation prompts tension, curiosity, and awe. It lights up their compositions. The works of conformist or academic composers are lifeless, precisely because they do not innovate. Their substance is bland and faded. Because they conform to fashion they may enjoy an ephemeral success but never a lasting affirmation. Mozart's compositions comply with the first rule for long survival: they surprise listeners and touch their emotions. If the composer wants to create that fecund emotion, he or she must be aware of innovating at the very moment of creation, avoiding exaggeration, however, since an exaggerated surprise is too facile and just as sterile as copying others. Thus one reason for the current triumph of Mozart's music is exactly what disturbed many listeners during his lifetime and what made more than one publisher hesitate to issue his works.

A second reason for Mozart's posthumous success lies in his profound respect for his audience. His music is intelligent, new, carefully constructed, but never harsh, strident, or violent. The third reason for his popularity today lies in the ambivalence so frequently mentioned in these pages. Osmin's rage and the delectable music that accompanies it are but one expression of ambiguities present everywhere in Mozart's music. He did not hesitate to use waltz rhythms in his *Dominicus* Mass (K. 66) or a tarantella to conclude the Missa solemnis (K. 337) or, working in the opposite direction, to accompany the libertine toast toward the end of *Così fan tutte* with solemn, religious-sounding music. Everything in Mozart can be dual and multiple: his ambivalence is extremely modern because it corresponds to the profound insecurities of the modern world. Today, in a world in radical transformation, dependable rules of conduct are fewer, and a growing number of people find it difficult to draw a clear distinction between good and evil, the good person and the bad one. The tendency today is to believe that on this earth it is no longer given to us to make clear choices between what is good and what is not, but only—and in the best of cases—between two mixtures of good and bad.

To my mind, no one has given a better account of the modernity of Mozart than Carmelo Samonà, a Sicilian author who died in 1990. He writes,

It is not too hazardous to maintain that the success of Mozart in the modern world should be seen in relation to the current crisis in ideologies, to the wearing down of accepted "morals." Never so much in our own times has the sense of the moralists' bad conscience been clearer, or of the linguistic poverty of those who debate the fate of man while enunciating general principles and forging models of behavior. This explains why many of Mozart's listeners intuit with relief that the author of *Don Giovanni* offers a totally different message: he is the repository of an art that *never strives to be* but simply *is*; of a discourse that seems alien to any reference, even a minimal hint, of ideological persuasion. Naturally, even Mozart had his own conception of the world, and he presents it in his works. But he does so without jollying us along; he limits himself to feeling it and representing it. It is the fruit of an unflinching gaze at things, not the expression of a moral project.[1]

It is quite imaginable that a composer who disseminates doubt and is endowed with a libertine spirit should encounter difficulties where certitude and moralism are the rule. Karl Dietrich Bracher tells us in a book about Hitler and the National Socialist Third Reich, the territory of which included Salzburg, Mozart's city of birth, that Joseph Goebbels, the minister for propaganda and national enlightenment, felt impelled to intervene to calm the enthusiasm of Alfred Rosenberg, who wanted to ban Mozart's works under the pretext that their author was a Freemason.[2] We do not know whether or not Rosenberg was aware that *The Marriage of Figaro, Don Giovanni,* and *Così fan tutte* might also have been candidates for prohibition because their librettist was not only a Freemason but of Jewish extraction. As for the moralism that often accompanies supreme certitudes, Luca Fontana tells us in "La casta eredità sovietica" (*Diario,* 15 March 2002) about an experience that he had as he was about to deliver a lecture at the Italian Consulate in St. Petersburg in 2002. The occasion was the premiere of the first production ever of *Così fan tutte* in Russia. Fontana had a disagreement with the Russian interpreters, who had refused to communicate to the audience that the opera's libretto is a tissue of double entendres and obscenities. "It isn't proper to say that there are obscenities in Mozart," they insisted. The same opera was first produced in the United States only in 1921, a delay determined by moralistic preoccupations.

Mozart is modern because he uses his music to liberate us from many irrelevant restraints. From that point of view *The Magic Flute* seems to be the work that best expresses the desire to liberate humanity. The golden flute that a lady-in-waiting of the Queen of the Night gives Tamino in act 1, scene 7, is highly symbolic. That flute and the sounds that it makes express the essence of music—sounds that come from the world of the irrational but are nevertheless capable of accompanying Tamino, his bride Pamina, Mozart, and all of us into life and beyond life, toward the world of the unknown and toward a greater awareness.

# Cited Works of Mozart, by Köchel Number

K. 1/1e. Minuet in G for Keyboard

K. 1a. Andante in C Major for Keyboard

K. 1b. Allegro in C Major for Keyboard

K. 1c. Allegro in F Major for Keyboard

K. 1d. Minuet in F Major for Keyboard

K. 6. Sonata in C Major for Keyboard and Violin

K. 7. Sonata in D Major for Keyboard and Violin

K. 8. Sonata in B-flat Major for Keyboard and Violin

K. 9. Sonata in G Major for Keyboard and Violin

K. 10. Sonata in B-flat Major for Keyboard (Harpsichord) and Violin

K. 11. Sonata in G Major for Keyboard (Harpsichord) and Violin

K. 12. Sonata in A Major for Keyboard (Harpsichord) and Violin

K. 13. Sonata in F Major for Keyboard (Harpsichord) and Violin

K. 14. Sonata in C Major for Keyboard (Harpsichord) and Violin

K. 15. Sonata in B-flat Major for Keyboard (Harpsichord) and Violin

K. 16. Symphony in E-flat Major (no. 1)

K. 21/19c. "Va dal furor portata," Concert Aria for Tenor and Orchestra

K. 22. Symphony in B-flat Major (no. 5)

K. 35. *Die Schuldigkeit des erstern Gebots* (The Obligation of the First Commandment), part 1 of a sacred oratorio; part 2 by Michael Haydn; part 3 by A. C. Adlgasser

K. 37. Concerto in F Major for Keyboard and Orchestra (no. 1)

K. 38. *Apollo et Hyacinthus,* Latin intermedio

K. 39. Concerto in B-flat Major for Keyboard and Orchestra (no. 2)

K. 40. Concerto in D Major for Keyboard and Orchestra (no. 3)

K. 41. Concerto in G Major for Keyboard and Orchestra (no. 4)

K. 43. Symphony in F Major (no. 6)

K. 49/47d. Missa brevis in G Major

K. 50/46b. *Bastien und Bastienne,* singspiel

K. 51/46a. *La finta semplice* (The Pretended Simpleton), *opera buffa*

K. 65/61a. Missa brevis in D Minor

K. 66. Missa in C Major (*Dominicus*)

K. 70/61c. "A Berenice"/"Sol nascente," recitative and concert aria for soprano and orchestra

K. 73/75a. Symphony in C Major (no. 9)

K. 80/73f. String Quartet in F Major (no. 1)

K. 85/73s. Miserere in A Minor

K. 86/73v. Antiphon *Quaerite primum* in D Minor

K. 87/74a. *Mitridate, Re di Ponto, dramma per musica*

K. 96/111b. Symphony in C Major

K. 108/74d. Regina coeli in C Major

K. 109/74e. Litaniae Lauretanae BVM

K. 110/75b. Symphony in G Major (no. 12)

K. 111. *Ascanio in Alba, festa teatrale*

K. 112. Symphony in F Major (no. 13)

K. 113. Divertimento in E-flat Major for Orchestra

K. 114. Symphony in A Major (no. 14)

K. 118/74c. *La Betulia liberata* (Bethulia Liberated), oratorio

K. 120/111a. Symphony. Finale only, to form a symphony with overture to K. 111, *Ascanio in Alba*

K. 124. Symphony in G Major (no. 15)

K. 125. Litaniae de venerabilis altaris sacramento

K. 126. *Il sogno di Scipione* (Scipio's Dream), *azione teatrale*

K. 127. Regina coeli in B-flat Major

K. 128. Symphony in C Major (no. 16)

K. 129. Symphony in G Major (no. 17)

K. 130. Symphony in F Major (no. 18)

K. 131. Divertimento in D Major for Orchestra

K. 132. Symphony in E-flat Major (no. 19)

K. 133. Symphony in D Major (no. 20)

K. 134. Symphony in A Major (no. 21)

K. 135. *Lucio Silla, dramma per musica*

K. 136/125a. Divertimento in D Major for String Quartet

K. 137/125b. Divertimento in B-flat Major for String Quartet

K. 138/125c. Divertimento in F Major for String Quartet

K. 139/47a. Missa solemnis in C Minor (*Waisenhaus*)

K. 148/125h. Lobgesang auf die feierliche Johannisloge ("O heiliges Band")

K. 155/134a. String Quartet in D Major (no. 2)

K. 156/134b. String Quartet in G Major (no. 3)

K. 157. String Quartet in C Major (no. 4)

K. 158. String Quartet in F Major (no. 5)

K. 159. String Quartet in B-flat Major (no. 6)

K. 160/159a. String Quartet in E-flat Major (no. 7)

K. 161/141a. Symphony in D Major (movements from the overture to *Il sogno di Scipione*)

K. 165/158a. "Exsultate, jubilate," motet in F Major

K. 168. String Quartet in F Major (no. 8)

K. 169. String Quartet in A Major (no. 9)

K. 170. String Quartet in C Major (no. 10)

K. 171. String Quartet in E-flat Major (no. 11)

K. 172. String Quartet in B-flat Major (no. 12)

K. 173. String Quartet in D Minor (no. 13)

K. 175. Concerto in D Major for Piano and Orchestra (no. 5); see also K. 382

K. 181/162b. Symphony in D Major (no. 23)

K. 183/173dB. Symphony in G Minor (no. 25)

K. 184/161a. Symphony in E-flat Major (no. 26)

K. 196. *La finta giardiniera* (The Make-Believe Garden-Girl), *opera buffa*

K. 201/186a. Symphony in A Major (no. 29)

K. 202/186b. Symphony in D Major (no. 30)

K. 208. *Il re pastore* (The Shepherd King), serenata

K. 216. Concerto in G Major for Violin and Orchestra (no. 3) (*Strasbourg*)

K. 219. Concerto in A Major for Violin and Orchestra (no. 5) (*Turkish*)

K. 222/205a. "Misericordias Domini" in D Minor

K. 233/382d. Canon in B-flat Major, *Lech mir im Arsch*

K. 242. Concerto in F Major for Three Pianos and Orchestra (no. 7) (*Lodron*)

K. 246. Concerto in C Major for Piano and Orchestra (no. 8) (*Lützow*)

K. 250/248b. Serenade in D Major for Orchestra (*Haffner*)

K. 254. Divertimento (Trio) in B-flat Major for Piano, Violin, and Cello (no. 1)

K. 271. Concerto in E-flat Major for Piano and Orchestra (no. 9) (*Jenamy*)

K. 273. "Sancta Maria, mater Dei," gradual in F Major

K. 275/272b. Missa brevis in B-flat Major

K. 279/189d. Sonata for Keyboard in C Major

K. 280/189e. Sonata for Keyboard in F Major

K. 281/189f. Sonata for Keyboard in B-flat Major

K. 282/189g. Sonata for Keyboard in E-flat Major

K. 283/189h. Sonata for Keyboard in G Major

K. 284/205b. Sonata for Keyboard in D Major (*Dürnitz*)

K. 285. Quartet in D Major for Flute, Violin, Viola, and Cello (no. 1)

K. 285a. Quartet in G Major for Flute, Violin, Viola, and Cello (no. 2)

K. 285b/Anh.171. Quartet in C Major for Flute, Violin, Viola, and Cello (no. 3); doubtful work

K. 287/271h. Divertimento in B-flat Major for Horns and Solo Strings

K. 294. "Alcandro lo confesso"/"Non so d'onde viene," recitative and concert aria for soprano and orchestra

K. 296. Sonata in C Major for Keyboard and Violin

K. 297/300a. Symphony in D Major (no. 31) (*Paris*)

K. 297a/Anh.1. Eight Movements for a Miserere by Ignaz Holzbauer

K. 297B/C14.01. Sinfonia Concertante in E-flat Major for Oboe, Bassoon, and Orchestra

K. 299/297c. Concerto in C Major for Flute and Harp

K. 299b/Anh.10. Ballet music, *Les petits riens*

K. 301/293a. Sonata in G Major for Keyboard and Violin

K. 302/293b. Sonata in E-flat Major for Keyboard and Violin

K. 303/293c. Sonata in C for Keyboard and Violin

K. 304/300c. Sonata in E Minor for Keyboard and Violin

K. 305/293d. Sonata in A Major for Keyboard and Violin

K. 306/300l. Sonata in D Major for Keyboard and Violin

K. 309/284b. Sonata in C Major for Piano

K. 310/300d. Sonata in A Major for Piano

K. 311/284c. Sonata in D Major for Piano

K. 311a/C11.05. *Second Paris* Symphony; spurious work

K. 313/285c. Concerto in G Major for Flute and Orchestra

K. 314/285d. Concerto in D Major for Flute and Orchestra

K. 315e/Anh.11. *Semiramis*, duodrama

K. 315f/Anh.56. Concerto in D Major for Violin and Piano, unfinished

K. 316/300b. "Popoli di Tessaglia"/"Io non chiedo eterni dei," recitative and concert aria for soprano and orchestra

K. 317. Mass in C Major (*Coronation*)

K. 318. Symphony in G Major (no. 32)

K. 319. Symphony in B-flat Major (no. 33)

K. 320. Serenade in D Major for Orchestra (*Posthorn*)

K. 330/300h. Sonata in C Major for Piano

K. 331/300i. Sonata in A Major for Piano

K. 332/300k. Sonata in F Major for Piano

K. 333/315c. Sonata in B-flat Major for Piano (*Linz*)

K. 334/320b. Divertimento in D Major for Horns and Solo Strings (*Robinig von Rottenfeld*)

K. 337. Missa solemnis in C Major (*Aulica*)

K. 338. Symphony in C Major (no. 34)

K. 341/368a. Kyrie in D Minor

K. 344. *Zaide*, singspiel

K. 345/336a. *Thamos, König in Ägypten, dramma per musica*

K. 349/367a. "Die Zufriedenheit" ("Was frag ich viel"), song (*lied*)

K. 351/367b. "Comm, liebe Zither," song (*lied*)

K. 353/300f. Variations in E-flat Major on "La belle françoise" for Piano

K. 354/299a. Variations in E-flat Major on "Je suis Lindor" for Piano

K. 356/617a. Adagio in C Major for Glass Harmonica

K. 364/320d. Sinfonia Concertante in E-flat Major for Violin, Viola, and Orchestra

K. 365/316a. Concerto in E-flat Major for Two Pianos and Orchestra (no. 10)

K. 366. *Idomeneo, re di Creta, dramma per musica*

K. 368. "Ma che vi fece"/"Sperai vicino," recitative and concert aria for soprano and orchestra

K. 369. "Misera, dove son!"/"Ah! Non son'io che parlo," recitative and concert aria for soprano and orchestra

K. 370/368b. Quartet in F Major for Oboe, Violin, Viola, and Cello

K. 372. Sonata in B-flat Major for Keyboard and Violin, first movement only

K. 373. Rondo in C Major for Violin and Orchestra

K. 375. Serenade in E-flat Major for Winds

K. 376/374d. Sonata in F Major for Keyboard and Violin

K. 377/374e. Sonata in F Major for Keyboard and Violin

K. 378/317d. Sonata in B-flat Major for Keyboard and Violin

K. 379/373a. Sonata in G Major for Keyboard and Violin

K. 380/374f. Sonata in E-flat Major for Keyboard and Violin

K. 382. Rondo in D Major for Piano and Orchestra; a new finale for K. 175

K. 384. *Die Entführung aus dem Serail* (The Abduction from the Seraglio), singspiel

K. 385. Symphony in D Major (no. 35) (*Haffner*)

K. 387. String Quartet in G Major (no. 14) (first *Haydn*)

K. 394/383a. Prelude and Fugue in C Major for Piano

K. 396/385f. Fantasia in C Minor for Piano

K. 404a, nos. 1–6. Preludes and Fugues in D Minor, G Minor, F Major, F Major, E-flat Major, and F Minor for Violin, Viola, and Cello (arrangements of J. S. Bach and W. F. Bach)

K. 405. Five Fugues for String Quartet (arrangements of J. S. Bach)

K. 413/387a. Concerto in F Major for Piano and Orchestra (no. 11)

K. 414/385p. Concerto in A Major for Piano and Orchestra (no. 12)

K. 415/387b. Concerto in C Major for Piano and Orchestra (no. 13)

K. 421/417b. String Quartet in D Minor (no. 15) (second *Haydn*)

K. 422. *L'oca del Cairo* (The Cairo Goose), *opera buffa*

K. 425. Symphony in C Major (no. 36) (*Linz*)

K. 427/417a. Mass in C Minor

K. 428/421b. String Quartet in E-flat Major (no. 16) (third *Haydn*)

K. 433/416c. "Männer suchen stets zu maschen," aria

K. 435/416b. "Müsst ich auch durch tausend Drachen," concert aria for tenor and orchestra

K. 446/416d. *Pantalone e Colombina*, music for a pantomime

K. 448/375a. Sonata in D Major for Two Pianos

K. 449. Concerto in E-flat Major for Piano and Orchestra (no. 14) (first for Barbara Ployer)

K. 450. Concerto in B-flat Major for Piano and Orchestra (no. 15)

K. 451. Concerto in D Major for Piano and Orchestra (no. 16)

K. 452. Quintet in E-flat Major for Piano, Oboe, Clarinet, Bassoon, and Horn

K. 453. Concerto in G Major for Piano and Orchestra (no. 17) (second for Barbara Ployer)

K. 454. Sonata in B-flat Major for Piano and Violin (*Strinasacchi*)

K. 455. Variations in G Major on "Unser dummer Pöbel meint" for Piano

K. 456. Concerto in B-flat Major for Piano and Orchestra (no. 18) (*Paradies*)

K. 457. Sonata in C Minor for Piano

K. 458. String Quartet in B-flat Major (no. 17) (fourth *Haydn; Hunt*)

K. 459. Concerto in F Major for Piano and Orchestra (no. 19) (second *Coronation*)

K. 464. String Quartet in A Major (no. 18) (fifth *Haydn*)

K. 465. String Quartet in C Major (no. 19) (sixth *Haydn; Dissonance*)

K. 466. Concerto in D Minor for Piano and Orchestra (no. 20)

K. 471. *Die Maurerfreude* (Masonic Joy), cantata

K. 475. Fantasia in C Minor for Piano

K. 477/479a. *Mauerische Trauermusik* in C Minor for Orchestra

K. 478. Quartet in G Minor for Piano, Violin, Viola, and Cello

K. 482. Concerto in E-flat Major for Piano and Orchestra (no. 22)

K. 483. "Zerfliesset heut', geliebte Brüder," Masonic song for male chorus

K. 484. "Ihr unsre neuen Leiter," Masonic song for male chorus

K. 486. *Der Schauspieldirektor* (The Impresario), singspiel

K. 488. Concerto in A Major for Piano and Orchestra (no. 23)

K. 491. Concerto in C Minor for Piano and Orchestra (no. 24)

K. 492. *Le nozze di Figaro* (The Marriage of Figaro), *opera buffa*

K. 493. Quartet in E-flat Major for Piano, Violin, Viola, and Cello (*Dite almeno*)

K. 496. Trio in G Major for Piano, Violin, and Viola (no. 2)

K. 497. Sonata in F Major for Piano Four Hands

K. 498. Trio in E-flat Major for Piano, Clarinet and Viola (*Kegelstatt*)

K. 499. String Quartet in D Major (no. 20) (*Hoffmeister*)

K. 500. Variations in B-flat Major on an Original Theme for Piano

K. 501. Variations in G Major on an Original Theme for Piano Four Hands

K. 503. Concerto in C Major for Piano and Orchestra (no. 25)

K. 504. Symphony in D Major (no. 38) (*Prague*)

K. 505. "Ch'io mi scordi di te?"/"Non temer, amato bene," scena and rondo for soprano and orchestra

K. 511. Rondo in A Minor for Piano

K. 512. "Alcandro, lo confesso"/"Non so d'onde viene," recitative and concert aria for bass and orchestra

K. 515. String Quintet in C Major

K. 516. String Quintet in G Minor

K. 522. *Ein musikalischer Spass* in F Major for Horns and Solo Strings

K. 523. "Abendempfindung an Laura" ("Abend ist's"), song (*lied*)

K. 525. *Eine kleine Nachtmusik* in G Major for Strings

K. 526. Sonata in A Major for Violin and Piano

K. 527. *Don Giovanni, opera buffa*

K. 534. Contredanse in D Major ("Das Donnerwetter") for Orchestra

K. 537. Concerto in D Major for Piano and Orchestra (no. 26) (*Coronation*)

K. 542. Trio in E Major for Piano, Violin, and Cello (no. 4)

K. 543. Symphony in E-flat Major (no. 39) (*Swan Song*)

K. 550. Symphony in G Minor (no. 40)

K. 551. Symphony in C Major (no. 41) (*Jupiter*)

K. 563. Trio (Divertimento) in E-flat Major for Violin, Viola, and Cello

K. 564. Trio in G Major for Piano, Violin, and Cello (no. 6)

K. 566. *Acis and Galatea* (arrangement of Handel)

K. 572. *Messiah* (arrangement of Handel)

K. 573. Piano variations in D Major on a Minuet by J. P. Duport

K. 575. String Quartet in D Major (no. 21) (first *Prussian*)

K. 576. Sonata in D Major for Piano

K. 581. Quintet in A Major for Clarinet, Two Violins, Viola, and Cello (*Stadler*)

K. 588. *Così fan tutte, opera buffa*

K. 589. String Quartet in B-flat Major (no. 22) (second *Prussian*)

K. 590. String Quartet in F Major (no. 23) (third *Prussian*)

K. 594. Adagio and Allegro in F Minor for Mechanical Organ

K. 595. Concerto in B-flat Major for Piano and Orchestra (no. 27)

K. 608. Fantasia in F Minor for Mechanical Organ

K. 614. String Quintet in E-flat Major

K. 617. Adagio and Rondo in C Minor for Glass Harmonica, Flute, Oboe, Viola, and Cello

K. 618. "Ave verum corpus," motet in D Major

K. 619. *Die ihr des unermesslichen Weltalls Schöpfer ehrt*, cantata

K. 620. *Die Zauberflöte* (The Magic Flute), singspiel

K. 621. *La clemenza di Tito, opera seria*

K. 622. Concerto in A Major for Clarinet and Orchestra

K. 623. *Laut verkünde unsre Freude*, cantata

K. 626. Requiem in D Minor, completed by F. Süssmayr and others

# Note on the English Translation

This translation of Piero Melograni's *WAM: La vita e il tempo di Wolfgang Amadeus Mozart* owes two tremendous debts of gratitude. The first debt is to the author, who generously responded to a number of queries, supplying information for an English edition that includes many notes, unlike his sprightly original. The second debt is to Kathleen K. Hansell, for her musicological advice and her tireless contribution of emendations to the text, for providing German bibliography, and for thoroughly checking the list of Mozart's works and their Köchel numbers.

# Notes

## Abbreviations

*Briefe*      *Mozart: Briefe und Aufzeichnungen*
Deutsch     Otto Erich Deutsch, *Mozart: A Documentary Biography*
*Letters*     Emily Anderson, ed., *The Letters of Mozart and His Family*
NMA         Mozart, Neue Ausgabe sämtlicher Werke

### PREFACE

1. Wolfgang Amadeus Mozart, *Correspondance*, trans. Geneviève Geffray, 2nd ed. rev., 6 vols. (Paris: Flammarion, 1986–1994), 3:201.

### PROLOGUE

1. "From the 'Public Advertiser,' 31 May 1764," in Otto Erich Deutsch, *Mozart: A Documentary Biography*, trans. Eric Brom, Peter Branscombe, and Jeremy Noble (Stanford, CA: Stanford University Press, 1965), 34, henceforth abbreviated as Deutsch.

2. Leopold's violin treatise is *Versuch einer gründlichen Violinschule* (Augsburg, 1756); available in English as *A Treatise on the Fundamental Principles of Violin Playing*, translated by Edith Knocker (London: Oxford University Press, 1948; reprint 1985).

3. "Zinzendorf's Diary, 17 October 1762," Deutsch, 17.

4. "From J. P. Eckermann's Conversations with Goethe, 3 February 1830," Deutsch, 550.

5. Leopold Mozart, letter to Lorenz Hagenauer, 8 June 1764, in Emily Anderson, ed., *The Letters of Mozart and His Family*, 2nd ed. (1966) rev. by Alec Hyatt King and Monica Carolan; 3rd ed. rev. by Stanley Sadie and Fiona Smart (London: Macmillan, 1985), 48–49, henceforth abbreviated as *Letters*.

---

*Substantive annotations are by Kathleen Kuzmick Hansell, who with Lydia Cochrane prepared the endnotes for this edition.*

6. "Maria Theresa to the Archduke Ferdinand at Milan: Vienna, 12 December 1771," Deutsch, 138. For the French, see Maynard Solomon, *Mozart: A Life* (New York: Harper-Collins, 1995), 93.

CHAPTER I

1. Leopold Mozart, letter to his son, 3 August 1778, *Letters*, 590–91.

2. Norbert Elias, *Mozart: Portrait of a Genius* (Berkeley: University of California Press, 1993), 80.

3. Mozart, letter to his mother, 31 January 1778, *Letters*, 456–57.

4. Schlichtegroll's account was based on Johann Andreas Schachtner's letter of 24 April 1792 to Mozart's sister; see Deutsch, 454.

5. "From the Memoirs of Placidus Scharl" (Andechs, 1808), in Deutsch, 512.

6. See Schachtner's letter, cited in n. 4; Deutsch, 453.

7. Leopold Mozart, letter to his wife and son, 16 February 1778, *Letters*, 483.

8. Mozart, letter to his father, 7 March 1778, *Letters*, 506.

9. Leopold Mozart, letter to his wife and son, 25 February 1778; letters to his son, 3 August 1778 and 13 September 1778, *Letters*, 493, 590, 609, 610.

10. Leopold Mozart, letter to Lorenz Hagenauer, 16 October 1762, *Letters*, 4–6.

11. The portrait is reproduced in Solomon, *Mozart: A Life*, facing p. 3.

12. Leopold Mozart, letter to Lorenz Hagenauer, 20 August 1763, *Letters*, 28.

13. On Mozart's "scarlet fever," see Peter J. Davies, *Mozart in Person: His Character and Health* (New York: Greenwood Press, 1989).

14. Leopold Mozart, letter to Lorenz Hagenauer, 11 July 1763, *Letters*, 22.

15. Ibid., 24.

16. Leopold Mozart, letter to Lorenz Hagenauer, 20 August 1763, *Letters*, 28.

17. Leopold Mozart, letter to Lorenz Hagenauer, 17 October 1763, *Letters*, 30.

18. Leopold Mozart, letter to Lorenz Hagenauer, 4 November 1763, *Letters*, 34.

19. Leopold Mozart, letter to Lorenz Hagenauer, 20 August 1763; this and other letters of the period are excerpted in Emily Anderson's English translation. For the complete correspondence of Mozart and his family, therefore, readers should turn to the original versions, in *Mozart: Briefe und Aufzeichnungen*, edited by Wilhelm A. Bauer and Otto Erich Deutsch, 7 vols. (Kassel: Bärenreiter, 1962–1975), hereafter abbreviated as *Briefe*. For the reference to the letter of 20 August 1763, see vol. 1, p. 88.

20. Leopold Mozart, letter to Lorenz Hagenauer, 18 December 1763, *Briefe*, 1:115.

21. Leopold Mozart, letter to Frau Maria Theresa Hagenauer, 1 February 1764, *Letters*, 33–36.

22. Leopold Mozart, postscript of 9 March 1764 to a letter to Lorenz Hagenauer of 4 March 1764, *Briefe*, 1:137.

23. Leopold Mozart, letter to Lorenz Hagenauer, 1 April 1764, *Briefe*, 1:137–38.

24. Leopold Mozart, letter to Lorenz Hagenauer, 22 February 1764, *Briefe*, 1:131.

25. Leopold Mozart, letter to Lorenz Hagenauer, 4 March 1764, *Briefe*, 1:136.

26. Leopold Mozart, letter to Lorenz Hagenauer, 22 February 1764, *Letters*, 40.

27. Leopold Mozart, letters to Lorenz Hagenauer of 22 February and 1 April 1764, *Briefe*, 1:131, 141.

28. Leopold Mozart, letter to Frau Maria Theresa Hagenauer, 1 February 1764, *Letters*, 33–39.

29. Leopold Mozart, letter to Lorenz Hagenauer, 1 April 1764, *Letters*, 41–42.

30. Leopold Mozart, letter to Lorenz Hagenauer, 13 September 1764, *Letters*, 51.

31. Leopold's highly detailed descriptions of London appear especially in his lengthy letter to Lorenz Hagenauer of 27 November 1764, *Briefe*, 1:170–75.

32. Leopold Mozart, letter to Lorenz Hagenauer, 19 March 1765, *Letters*, 56.

33. Leopold Mozart, letter to Lorenz Hagenauer, 28 May 1764, *Letters*, 46.

34. From Grimm's *Correspondance littéraire* of 15 July 1756, Deutsch, 57.

35. Leopold Mozart, letter to Lorenz Hagenauer, 28 May 1764, *Letters*, 47.

36. "Daines Barrington's Report on Mozart: Received November 28, 1769; Account of a Very Remarkable Young Musician," Deutsch, 95–100, esp. pp. 95, 97.

37. Leopold Mozart, letter to Lorenz Hagenauer, 8 June 1764, *Letters* 48–49.

38. Leopold Mozart, letter to Lorenz Hagenauer, 12 December 1765, *Letters* 63.

39. See the report in Beda Hübner's *Diarium* of 8 December 1766, Deutsch, 70.

40. Leopold Mozart, letter to Lorenz Hagenauer, 10 November 1766, *Letters*, 68–69.

41. *Die Schuldigkeit des ersten Gebots* was a joint effort: Wolfgang composed the first act, while Michael Haydn and Anton Adlgasser wrote acts 2 and 3.

42. See Daines Barrington's report of 28 November 1969, in Deutsch, 99.

43. Leopold Mozart, letter to Lorenz Hagenauer, 10 December 1762, *Letters* 14.

CHAPTER 2

1. Leopold Mozart, letter to Lorenz Hagenauer, 6 August 1768, *Briefe*, 1:275.

2. Leopold Mozart, letter to Lorenz Hagenauer, 30 January 1768, *Briefe*, 1:256; *Letters*, 82.

3. Leopold Mozart, letter to Lorenz Hagenauer, 30 July 1768, *Letters*, 88.

4. See Leopold's petition to Emperor Joseph II, 21 September 1768, Deutsch, 80–84.

5. "Maria Theresa to the Archduke Ferdinand at Milan: Vienna, 12 December 1771," in Deutsch, 138.

6. Mozart, letter to his father, 5 December 1780, *Letters*, 681–83.

7. Parts of *Bastien und Bastienne* were, however, performed at Mesmer's house in Vienna, in September or October 1768: see Deutsch, 84.

8. "Johann Adolph Hasse to Giovanni Maria Ortes at Venice, Vienna, 30 September 1769," Deutsch, 92–93.

9. Leopold Mozart, letter to Lorenz Hagenauer, 30 January–3 February 1768, *Letters*, 81.

10. In 1768, Leopold made a three-page index ("Verzeichniss") of the works his son had composed up to that time, beginning with the published compositions. For the complete list, see *Briefe*, 1:287–89, with a facsimile of the first page; see also Deutsch, 84. For the smaller works Leopold did not provide an itemized listing, but indicated "many minuets," "various marches," etc.

11. Iwo and Pamela Zaluski, *Mozart in Italy* (London: P. Owen, 1999).

12. "Programme of Mozart's Concert at the Teatro Scientifico, Mantua, 16 January 1770," Deutsch, 106.

13. Leopold Mozart, letter to his wife, 11 January 1770, *Letters*, 107.

14. Leopold Mozart, letter to his wife, 17 February 1770, *Letters*, 114.

15. See Wolfgang's postscript to his father's letter to his wife of 10 February 1770, *Briefe*, 1:314.

16. Mozart, letter to his sister, 24 March 1770, *Letters*, 120–22.

17. Leopoldo Mozart, letter to his wife, 3 April 1770, *Letters*, 125.

18. Leopold Mozart, letter to his wife, 14 April 1770, *Letters*, 126.

19. Ibid.

20. Mozart, letter to his sister, 5 June 1770, *Letters*, 142.

21. The story was included in the notes Nannerl Mozart prepared in April 1792 for her brother's first biographer, Friedrich Schlichtegroll; see "Marianne von Berchtold's reminiscences, spring 1792" in Deutsch, 459.

22. "Abbé Ferdinando Galiani to Madame d'Épinay, Naples, 7 July 1770," Deutsch, 124.

23. Mozart, letter to his sister, 5 June 1770, *Letters*, 143.

24. Ibid., 142.

25. Mozart, letter to his sister, 19 May 1770, *Letters*, 137.

26. Mozart, letters to his sister, 5 June; 4 August 1770, *Letters*, 143, 154.

27. Leopold Mozart, letter to his wife, 26 May 1770, *Letters*, 139.

28. Leopold Mozart, letter to his wife, 9 June 1770, *Letters*, 143–44.

29. Leopold Mozart, letter to his wife, 27 June 1770, *Letters*, 145–46.

30. Leopold Mozart, letter to his wife, 21 July 1770, *Briefe*, 1:370–71.

31. Leopold Mozart, letter to his wife, 11 August 1770, *Letters*, 155.

32. Leopold Mozart, letter to his wife, 20 October 1770, *Letters*, 166.

33. Mozart's postscript of 30 September 1779 to Anna Maria Mozart's (his mother's) letter to Leopold of 29 September 1779, *Briefe*, 2:30.

34. Alfred Einstein, *Mozart: His Character, His Work*, trans. Arthur Mendel and Nathan Broder (New York: Oxford University Press, 1945), 147.

35. Minutes of Mozart's examination for admittance to the Accademia Filarmonica of Bologna, Deutsch, 126.

36. Einstein, *Mozart: His Character*, 147.

37. Vernon Lee (pseud. of Violet Paget), *Studies of the Eighteenth Century in Italy* (1907; New York: Da Capo Press, 1978), 110.

38. Leopold Mozart, letter to his wife, 25 August 1770, *Letters*, 158.

39. Leopold Mozart, letter to his wife, 12 January 1771, *Letters*, 179.

40. Leopold Mozart, letter to his wife, 20 February 1771, *Briefe*, 1:420.

41. Mozart's addendum to Leopold Mozart's letter to his wife of 21 July 1770, *Briefe*, 1:372.

42. Leopold Mozart, letter to his wife, 11 August 1770, *Letters*, 155.

43. Leopold Mozart, letter to his wife, 21 August 1770, *Briefe*, 1:381–82.

44. Leopold Mozart, letter to his wife, 18 September 1770, *Letters*, 161.

45. Leopold Mozart, letter to his wife, 10 November 1770, *Letters*, 170.

46. Zaluski and Zaluski, *Mozart in Italy*.

47. See the entry "Bach, Johann Sebastian" in *The New Grove Dictionary of Music and Musicians*, ed. Stanley Sadie (London: Macmillan, 1980), 1:791–92.

48. Mozart, letter to his mother, 20 October 1770, *Letters*, 166.

49. Leopold Mozart, letter to his wife, 17 November 1770, *Letters,* 171.

50. Leopold Mozart, letter to his wife, 15 December 1770, *Letters,* 174.

51. Leopold Mozart, letter to his wife, 1 March 1771, *Briefe,* 1:421. Since Mozart's autograph score of *Mitridate* was lost and has never been recovered, these copies were crucial in reconstructing the music. See the critical edition of *Mitridate* by Luigi Ferdinando Tagliavini in Wolfgang Amadeus Mozart, *Neue Ausgabe sämtlicher Werke,* hereafter abbreviated as *NMA,* ser. 2, Werkgruppe 5, vol. 4 (Kassel: Bärenreiter, 1966); score, 1978; critical commentary, 1978.

52. In Italy conductors in the modern sense did not appear until the late 1850s.

53. Leopold Mozart, letter to his wife, 2 February 1771, *Letters,* 180.

54. Leopold Mozart, letter to his wife, 20 February 1771, *Letters,* 183.

55. Mozart to Johann Nepomuk Hagenauer, 13 February 1771, *Letters,* 182.

56. Mozart, letter to his sister, 20 February 1771, *Letters,* 183.

57. Paolo Cattelan, *Mozart: Un mese a Venezia* (Venice: Marsilio, 2000), 42.

58. Leopold Mozart, letter to his wife, 14 March 1771, *Letters,* 186.

59. For the final two quotations, see "Ortes to Hasse, Venice, 2 March 1771," Deutsch, 132. See also *Johann Adolf Hasse e Giammaria Ortes: Lettere 1760–1783,* edited and with commentary by Livia Pancino (Turnhout: Brepols, 1998).

60. "Hasse to Ortes, Vienna, 23 March 1771," Deutsch, 134.

61. Leopold Mozart, letter to his wife, 6 March 1771, *Letters,* 184.

62. Mozart, letter to his father, 11 October 1777, *Briefe,* 1:445–46.

63. Mozart, letter to his mother, 20 October 1770, *Letters,* 166.

64. Mozart, letter to his sister, 24 August 1771, *Letters,* 193–94.

65. Mozart, letter to his sister, 31 August 1771, *Letters,* 195.

66. Leopold Mozart, letters to his wife, 5 October 1771; 12 October 1771, *Letters,* 200, 201.

67. Leopold Mozart to his wife, letter of 26 October 1771, *Briefe,* 1:445. They were then invited into the archduke's own box.

68. Einstein, *Mozart,* 399.

69. Zaluski and Zaluski, *Mozart in Italy,* 170–71.

70. Mozart, letter to his sister, 24 November 1771, *Letters,* 207.

71. Leopold Mozart, letter to his wife, 19 October 1771, *Letters,* 202.

72. See Deutsch, 137.

73. "Maria Theresa, letter to the Archduke Ferdinand at Milan, Vienna, 12 December 1771," Deutsch, 138.

74. Nannerl Mozart so described her brother in a letter of 2 July 1819 accompanying three portraits of Wolfgang she sent to Joseph Sonnleithner for copying: "The one that was painted when he came back from the Italian journey is the oldest, he was then just 16 years old, but as he had just got up from a serious illness, the picture looks sickly and very yellow"; cited in Deutsch, 520. Wolfgang turned sixteen on 27 January 1772, shortly after returning from his second trip to Milan.

75. Leopold Mozart entered the name "Girolamo" over the original, which he scraped away; see the critical edition of *Il sogno di Scipione,* edited by Joseph-Horst Lederer, in *NMA,* ser. 2, Werkgruppe 5, vol. 6 (Kassel: Bärenreiter, 1974), vii and critical commentary, d/16.

76. Massimo Mila, *Wolfgang Amadeus Mozart* (Pordenone: Studio Tesi, 1980), 33.

77. Letter of 14 November 1772 in Mozart, *Correspondance*, 1:494; *Briefe*, 5:318, 320.

78. Mozart to Archbishop Hieronymus Colloredo, 1 August 1777, *Letters*, 267. For the decree, see Deutsch, 142.

79. Amedeo Poggi, *Mozart: Signori il catalogo è questo*, ed. Edgar Vallora (Turin: Einaudi, 2000), 145.

80. Quoted from Solomon, *Mozart: A Life*, 328.

81. De Gamerra sent a draft of his text to Metastasio in Vienna, who revised a few verses. For details, see Rosy Candiani, *Libretti e librettisti italiani per Mozart* (Rome: Archivio Guido Izzi, 1994). Leopold mentions the delay this caused in a letter to his wife, 14 November 1772, *Letters*, 216.

82. Mozart, letter to his sister, 28 October 1772, *Letters*, 213–14; *Briefe*, 1:458.

83. Mozart, *Correspondance*, 493 n. 9.

84. Leopold Mozart, letter to his wife, 7 November 1772, *Letters*, 215.

85. Leopold Mozart, letter to his wife, 8 November 1772, *Letters*, 217.

86. Mozart, letter to his sister, 5 December 1772, *Letters*, 219.

87. The origin of these characterizations can be traced back to Nannerl Mozart, whose attitude was probably ultimately taken over from their father. As early as spring 1792, a few months after Wolfgang's death, she wrote in the reminiscences that served as the basis for early biographies, "Apart from his music he was almost always a child, and thus he remained: and this is the main feature of his character on the dark side; he always needed a father's, a mother's, or some other guardian's care; he could not manage his financial affairs"; see Deutsch, 462. By contrast, the 1808 memoirs of Wolfgang's brother-in-law, Joseph Lange, offer a far more plausible and sympathetic explanation for his joking: "Either he intentionally concealed his inner tension behind superficial frivolity, for reasons which could not be fathomed, or he took delight in throwing into sharp contrast the divine ideas of his music and these sudden outbursts of vulgar platitudes, and in giving himself pleasure by seeming to make fun of himself"; quoted in ibid., 503.

88. Leopold Mozart noted the number of performances in his letter to his wife of 30 January 1773, *Briefe*, 1:478.

89. Leopold Mozart, letter to his wife, 9 January 1773, *Letters*, 224. Along with the letter Leopold ordered a complete copy of the score of *Lucio Silla* prepared and sent to Archduke Leopold.

90. Leopold Mozart, letter to his wife, 12 August 1773, *Letters*, 236.

91. Mozart, letter to Archbishop Hieronymus Colloredo, 1 August 1777, *Letters*, 267–68.

92. Mozart to his father, 26 May 1781, *Letters*, 737.

93. As Julian Rushton has noted, "No published libretto of *La finta giardiniera* acknowledges its authorship." Previously attributed in error to Rainieri de' Calzabigi and more recently to Petrosellini, the ascription to the latter is now questioned on stylistic grounds by Italian scholars as well. See Rushton, "Finta giardiniera, La" in *The New Grove Dictionary of Opera*, ed. Stanley Sadie (London: Macmillan, 1992), 2:211.

94. Leopold Mozart, letter to his wife, 21 December 1774, *Briefe*, 1:508.

95. Mozart, letter to his sister, 28 December 1774, *Letters*, 254.

96. Mozart, letter to his mother, 14 January 1775, *Letters*, 259.

97. Leopold Mozart, letter to his wife, 18 January 1775, *Letters*, 260.

98. The work was revived as a singspiel (with spoken dialogue) as *Die vorstellte Gärt-nerin*, an adaptation in which Mozart probably collaborated, and was first performed in 1780. See Rushton, "Finta giardiniera, La."

99. Christian Friedrich Daniel Schubart, "Deutsche Chronik, Augsburg, 27 April 1775," Deutsch, 153.

100. Since 1912, K. 271 has been known as the "Jeunehomme" concerto, although scholars were aware that Mozart wrote it for a young woman. In March 2004, however, musicologist Michael Lorenz solved the mystery and disclosed that the pianist, whom Mozart referred as "Mad.$^{me}$ Jenomy" (letter of 5 April 1778) was in fact Victoire Jenamy, daughter of Noverre, whom the Mozarts knew well. Lorenz discovered in the Vienna City Archive that Victoire Jenamy commissioned the concerto in Vienna in 1776. The discovery was announced both in the *New York Times* of 15 March 2004 and by the *Neue Mozart-Ausgabe*, Salzburg.

101. Leopold Mozart, letter to his son, 24 September 1778, *Letters*, 619; adjusted per *Briefe*, 2:485.

102. Reported in July 1785 in the commentary to Mozart's entry of K. 478 in his own list of his works, *Briefe*, 6:237.

103. Stefan Kunze, *Il teatro di Mozart: Dalla Finta Semplice al Flauto Magico*, trans. Leonardo Cavari (Venice: Marsilio, 1990), 116. Despite Kunze's use of the designation *opera seria*, *Il re pastore* does not belong to that genre.

CHAPTER 3

1. Mozart, letter to Padre Martini, Bologna 4 September 1776, *Letters*, 266.

2. Leopold Mozart, letter to his son, 30 September 1777, *Briefe*, 2:27.

3. "Mozart's Petition to Archbishop Hieronymus, Count Colloredo [August 1777]," Deutsch, 162–63. For Archbishop Colloredo's response on the verso of this document, see ibid., 163.

4. Leopold, letter to his wife and son, 25 September 1777, *Letters*, 272–73.

5. Mozart, letter to his father, 29–30 September 1777, *Letters*, 283.

6. Ibid., 285–86.

7. Ibid., 283.

8. Mozart, letter to his father, 29–30 September 1771, *Letters*, 284. Gulden and florins were equivalent, and both were abbreviated "f" (as in Wolfgang's letter).

9. Leopold Mozart, letter to his son, 4 October 1777, *Letters*, 294–95. A ducat was worth fifteen gulden (or florins).

10. Mozart, letter to his father, 11 October 1777, *Letters*, 308.

11. As reported by Anna Maria Mozart in her letter to Leopold of 14 October 1779, *Letters*, 315.

12. Mozart, letter to his father, 16 October 1777, *Letters*, 323–24.

13. Anna Maria Mozart to her husband, 14 October 1777, Mozart's postscript, *Letters*, 315.

14. Mozart, letter to his father, 17 October 1777, *Letters*, 326.

15. Mozart, letter to his father, 16 October 1777, *Letters*, 326.

16. Solomon, *Mozart: A Life,* 355.

17. Mozart, letter to his father, 17 November 1781, *Letters,* 779.

18. Mozart, letter to his father, 20 June 1781, *Briefe,* 3:133.

19. Mozart, letter to his father, 16 October 1777, *Letters,* 326.

20. Mozart, letter to Maria Anna Thekla Mozart, 5 November 1777, *Briefe,* 2:104.

21. Leopold Mozart, letter to his wife, 23 October 1777, *Briefe,* 2:77. The girl soon decided to leave the cloister for good, however, as Leopold notes in the same letter.

22. Leopold Mozart, letter to his son, 12 February 1778, *Letters,* 476.

23. Stefan Zweig, letter to Sigmund Freud, quoted from Wolfgang Hildesheimer, *Mozart,* trans. Marion Faber (New York: Farrar Straus Giroux, 1982), 109.

24. Leopold Mozart, letter to his son, 18 October 1777, *Letters,* 335.

25. Anna Maria Mozart, letter to Leopold Mozart, 20 December 1777, *Briefe,* 2:198.

26. Mozart, letter to his father, 9 July 1778, *Letters,* 562.

27. Mozart, letter to his father, 4 November 1777, *Letters,* 356.

28. Leopold Mozart, letter to his son, 27 November 1777, *Letters,* 393.

29. Leopold Mozart, letter to his son, 24 November 1777, *Letters,* 388.

30. Mozart, letter to his father, 13 November 1777, *Letters,* 369.

31. Leopold Mozart, letter to his son, 20 November 1777, *Letters,* 379–80.

32. Mozart, letter to his father, 14 November 1777, *Letters,* 373.

33. Leopold Mozart, letter to his son, 13 November 1777, *Letters,* 367.

34. Mozart, letter to his father, 29 November 1777, *Letters,* 395, 396.

35. Anna Maria Mozart, letter to her husband, 7 December 1777, *Letters,* 409.

36. Anna Maria Mozart, letter to her husband, 18 December 1777, *Letters,* 426.

37. Mozart, letter to his father, 27 December 1777, *Letters,* 435. Leopold Mozart was not a tall man either.

38. Leopold Mozart to his son, 5 January 1778, *Letters,* 442.

39. Mozart, letter to his father, 7 February 1778, *Letters,* 468.

40. Leopold Mozart, letter to his wife and son, 4 December 1777, *Letters,* 406.

41. Leopold Mozart, letter to his son, 18 December 1777, *Letters,* 424.

42. Leopold Mozart, letter to his son, 29 January 1778, *Letters,* 455.

43. Mozart, letter to his father, 7 February 1778, *Letters,* 467.

44. Mozart, letter to his father, 4 February 1778, *Letters,* 461.

45. Ibid.

46. Leopold Mozart, letter to his son, 12 February 1778, *Letters,* 475.

47. Leopold Mozart, letter to his son, 23 February 1778, *Letters,* 493.

48. Ibid., 492.

49. Mozart, letter to his father, 7 March 1778, *Letters,* 506.

50. Alexis de Tocqueville, *The Old Régime and the French Revolution,* trans. Stuart Gilbert (New York: Anchor Press [Doubleday], 1955), vi.

51. Anna Maria Mozart, letter to her husband, 24 March 1778, *Letters,* 519.

52. Anna Maria Mozart, letter to her husband, 5 April 1778, *Letters,* 520.

53. Ibid.

54. See Grimm's letter to Leopold Mozart of 21 February 1778, Deutsch, 173.

55. Mozart's postscript to his mother's letter to her husband of 5 April 1778, *Briefe,* 2:331.

56. Mozart, letter to his father, 3 May 1778, *Letters*, 532.

57. Anna Maria Mozart, letter to her husband, 14 May 1778, *Letters*, 536–38.

58. Mozart, letter to his father, 31 July 1778, *Letters*, 587.

59. Mozart, letter to his father, 1 May 1778, *Letters*, 531–32.

60. Ibid., 532.

61. Elias, *Mozart: Portrait of a Genius*, 19.

62. Ibid.

63. Mozart admitted, in a letter to his father of 16 December 1780, that when an acquaintance asked him, "Why don't I wear the golden spur, I said I had enough difficulty carrying things around in my head." A few sentences later he mentions the "spur that his friend mislaid; I mean the external one, the visible one." *Briefe*, 3:59.

64. Mozart, letter to his father, 5 April 1778, *Letters*, 522.

65. Mozart, letter to his father, 9 July 1778, *Letters*, 564.

66. Mozart, letter to his father, 3 July 1778, *Letters*, 557–58.

67. Ibid., 558.

68. Anna Maria Mozart, letter to her husband, 14 May 1778, *Letters*, 537–38. Translation corrected following the original, in *Briefe*, 2:356.

69. Anna Maria Mozart, letter to her husband, 12 June 1778, *Letters*, 550.

70. Anna Maria Mozart, letter to her husband, 29 May 1778, *Letters*, 543.

71. Ibid.

72. Mozart, letter to his father, 31 July 1778, *Letters*, 584.

73. Anna Maria Mozart, letter to her husband, 12 June 1778, *Letters*, 551. "Mozartin" is the feminine form of the surname, which Anna Maria habitually used.

74. Leopold Mozart, letter to his wife and son, 13 July 1778, *Letters*, 569, 567.

75. Leopold Mozart, letter to his son, 3 August 1778, *Letters*, 590.

76. Leopold Mozart, letter to his son, 27 August 1778, *Letters*, 604.

77. Mozart, letter to his father, 31 July 1778, *Letters*, 584.

78. Hildesheimer, *Mozart*, 79–81.

79. Solomon, *Mozart: A Life*, 85.

80. Leopold Mozart, letter to his son, 3 September 1778, *Letters*, 610.

81. Leopold Mozart, letter to Wolfgang, 19 November 1778, quoted from Solomon, *Mozart: A Life*, 186. See also the original in *Briefe*, 2:510.

82. Mozart, letter to his father, 9 July 1778, *Letters*, 561.

CHAPTER 4

1. Mozart, letter to his father, 9 July 1778, *Letters*, 561.

2. Leopold Mozart, letter to his son, 13 August 1778, *Letters*, 597. An English translation of Grimm's letter appears in Deutsch, 177.

3. Mozart, letter to his father, 3 July 1778, *Letters*, 558.

4. Mozart, letter to the Abbé Bullinger, Salzburg, 7 August 1778, *Letters*, 593.

5. Mozart, letter to Fridolin Weber, 29 July 1778, *Letters*, 576.

6. Mozart, letter to Aloysia Weber, 30 July 1778, *Letters*, 582.

7. Mozart, letter to his father, 11 September 1778, *Letters*, 614.

8. Ibid., 614, 615.

9. Hildesheimer, *Mozart*, 92.

10. Leopold Mozart, letter to his son, 27 August 1778, *Letters*, 604, 605.

11. Ibid., 604, 605.

12. Leopold Mozart, letter to his son, 31 August 1778, *Letters*, 608–9.

13. Leopold Mozart, letter to his son, 31 August 1778, *Briefe*, 2:461.

14. Solomon, *Mozart: A Life*, 156.

15. Leopold Mozart, letter to his son, 19 November 1778, *Letters*, 634.

16. Leopold Mozart, letter to his son, 23 November 1778, *Briefe*, 2:512.

17. Mozart, letter to his father, 9 July 1778, *Letters*, 562.

18. Mozart, letter to his father, 11 September 1778, *Letters*, 612.

19. Ibid., 613.

20. Leopold Mozart, letter to his son, 3 September 1778, *Briefe*, 2:465.

21. Mozart, letter to his father, 3 October 1778, *Letters*, 621.

22. Mozart, letter to his father, 26 October 1778, *Letters*, 627.

23. Ibid., 622.

24. Ibid.

25. Leopold Mozart, letter to his son, 19 October 1778, *Letters*, 626.

26. Mozart, letter to his father, 26 October 1778, addition of 2 November 1778, *Letters*, 629.

27. Mozart, letter to his father, 12 November 1778, *Letters*, 631.

28. Ibid., 630.

29. Leopold Mozart, letter to his son, 19 November 1778, *Letters*, 633.

30. Leopold Mozart, letter to his son, 23 November 1778, *Letters*, 635; *Briefe*, 2:511–12.

31. Ibid., *Briefe*, 2:512.

32. Mozart, letter to his father, 15 December 1781, *Letters*, 784.

33. Mozart, letter to his father, 31 December 1778, *Letters*, 648.

34. Mozart, letter to his father, 8 January 1779, *Letters*, 648–50.

35. Solomon, *Mozart: A Life*, 176.

36. Mozart, letter to his father, 26 May 1781, *Letters*, 736.

37. Einstein, *Mozart: His Character, His Work*, 345.

CHAPTER 5

1. Mozart, letter to his father, 8 November 1780, *Letters*, 659.

2. As reported in Vincent and Mary Novello's diaries recording their visit to Mozart's widow in July 1829, Deutsch, 539.

3. Mozart, letter to his father, 15 November 1780, *Letters*, 664.

4. Ibid., 665.

5. Leopold Mozart, letter to his son, 4 January 1781, *Letters*, 704.

6. Mozart, letter to his father, 15 November 1780, *Letters*, 664.

7. Mozart, letter to his father, 22 November 1780, *Letters*, 668.

8. Mozart, letter to his father, 15 November 1780, *Letters*, 664.

9. Leopold Mozart, letter to his son, 4 December 1780, partially quoted in *Letters*, 681. For the complete citation, see *Briefe*, 3:45.

10. Leopold Mozart, letter to his son, 25 November 1780, *Letters*, 673.

11. Leopold Mozart, letter to his son, 18 November 1780, *Briefe*, 3:24.

12. Leopold Mozart, letter to his son, 11 December 1780, *Letters*, 685.

13. Leopold Mozart, letter to his son, 1 November 1777, *Letters*, 354.

14. Leopold Mozart, letter to his wife and son, 6 May 1778, *Letters*, 536.

15. Mozart, letter to his father, 16 December 1780, *Letters*, 690, edited.

16. Leopold Mozart, letter to his son, 15 December 1780, *Letters*, 687–88.

17. Mozart, letter to his father, 27 December 1780, *Letters*, 698.

18. Mozart, letter to his father, 3 January 1781, *Letters*, 703.

19. Solomon, *Mozart: A Life*, 236.

20. Elias, *Mozart: Portrait of a Genius*, 139.

21. Hildesheimer, *Mozart*, 138.

22. Mila, *Wolfgang Amadeus Mozart*, 50.

23. Ferenc Fricsay, liner notes for *Idomeneo* CD, Deutsche Grammophon Gesellschaft, with Wiener Philarmoniker, conducted by Ferenc Fricsay.

24. Ibid.

25. Mozart, letter to his father, 16 December 1780, *Letters*, 690.

26. See Deutsch, 236. See also the commentary to Mozart's letter to his father of 24 March 1781 in *Briefe*, 6:56.

27. Mozart, letter to his father, 5 December 1780, *Letters*, 681–82.

28. Aleksandr Ulybyshev, *Nouvelle biographie de Mozart*, 3 vols. (Moscow, 1842–1858); *Mozart* (Paris: Séguier, 1991), 123–24. This account follows closely that of Mozart himself in his letter to his father of 24 March 1781, *Letters*, 716–20, esp. 717.

29. See Mozart's postscript of 28 March 1781 to his letter to his father of 24 March, *Briefe*, 3:100.

30. Mozart, letter to his father, 4 April 1781, *Letters*, 720.

31. Mozart, letter to his father, 8 April 1781, *Letters*, 722.

32. Mozart wrote only the first movement of K. 372. The sonata was later completed by M. Stadler.

33. Mozart, letter to his father, 8 April 1781, *Letters*, 722.

34. Mozart, letter to his father, 8 April 1781, *Briefe*, 3:104: "meine dienste *quittirte*"; the last two words were written in the family's code.

35. Mozart, letter to his father, 18 April 1781, *Letters*, 725.

36. Mozart, letter to his father, 28 April 1781, *Letters*, 726.

37. Mozart, letter to his father, 9 May 1781, *Letters*, 727–28.

38. Mila, *Wolfgang Amadeus Mozart*, 53.

39. Mozart, letter to his father, 9 May 1781, *Letters*, 728.

40. Mozart, letter to his father, 26 May 1781, *Letters*, 736.

41. Mozart, letter to his father, 9 May 1781, *Letters*, 727, 729.

42. Mozart, letter to his father, 12 May 1781, *Letters*, 730.

43. Ibid.

44. Mozart, letter to his father, 16 May 1781, *Letters*, 733.

45. Mozart, letter to his father, 19 May 1781, *Letters*, 733.

46. Mozart, letter to his father, 26 May 1781, *Letters*, 736.

47. Ibid., 737.

48. Mozart, letter to his father, 13 June 1781, *Letters*, 743.

49. Mozart, letter to his father, 16 June 1781, *Letters*, 746.

50. Mozart, letter to his father, 13 June 1781, *Letters*, 743.

51. Mozart, letter to his father, 20 June 1781, *Letters*, 747.

52. Leopold Mozart, letter to Breitkopf and Son, Leipzig, 10 August 1781, *Letters*, 758.

53. Mozart, letter to his sister, 19 September 1781, *Letters*, 766, 767.

54. Elias, *Mozart*, 116–17.

55. Piero Buscaroli, *La morte di Mozart* (Milan: Rizzoli, 1996), 53.

56. Mozart, letter to his father, 26 May 1781, *Letters*, 736.

57. Mozart, letter to his father, 5 September 1781, *Letters*, 764.

58. Mozart, letter to his father, 25 July 1781, *Letters*, 753.

59. Ibid, 752, 753.

60. Mozart, letter to his cousin, Maria Anna Thekla Mozart, 23 October 1781, *Letters*, 774.

61. Mozart, letter to his father, 3 November 1781, *Letters*, 776.

62. Elias, *Mozart*, 134.

63. Mozart, letter to his father, 27 June 1781, *Letters*, 748.

64. Mozart, letter to his father, 22 August 1781, *Letters*, 760.

65. For the concert at the Auernhammers' Mozart amplified the orchestration of K. 365, adding two clarinets, two trumpets, and drums to the outer movements: see Deutsch, 197.

66. Mozart, letter to his father, 15 December 1781, *Letters*, 782.

67. Ibid., 783.

68. Ibid.

69. Ibid., 784.

70. Ibid.

71. Ibid.

72. Mozart, letter to his father, 22 December 1781, *Letters*, 788.

73. Mozart, letter to his father, 16 January 1782, *Letters*, 792–93.

74. Mozart, letter to his father, 30 January 1782, *Letters*, 796.

75. Mozart, letter to his sister, 13 February 1782, *Letters*, 797.

76. Mozart, letter to his father 10 April, 1782, *Letters*, 799.

77. Mozart, letter to his father, 22 December 1781, *Letters*, 789–90.

78. Mozart, letter to his father, 16 January 1782, *Letters*, 793.

79. Mozart, letter to his father, 7 June 1783, *Letters*, 850.

80. Francis Carr, *Mozart and Constanze* (London: John Murray, 1983), 41.

81. Mozart, letter to his father, 16 January 1782, *Letters*, 793.

82. Bernard Lewis, *Islam and the West* (New York: Oxford University Press, 1993), 19; *L'Europa e l'Islam*, trans. Marina Astrologo (Rome: Laterza, 2001), 43.

83. Claudio Casini, *Amadeus: Vita di Mozart* (Milan: Rusconi, 1990).

84. See Thomas Bauman, "Coming of Age in Vienna: *Die Entführung aus dem Serail*" in Daniel Heartz, *Mozart's Operas*, edited and with contributing essays by Thomas Bauman (Berkeley: University of California Press, 1990), 69. For example, Mozart notes that

the Janissary Chorus was "written entirely for the Viennese"; letter to his father, 26 September 1781, *Briefe*, 3:163.

85. Kunze, *Il teatro di Mozart*, 400, 409.

86. Mozart, letter to his father, 26 September 1781, *Letters*, 770.

87. As reported by Franz Xaver Niemetschek in his Mozart biography (Prague, 1808); see excerpt in Deutsch, 504–5.

88. Mozart, letter to his father, 13 October 1781, *Letters*, 773.

89. For an opera seria like *Idomeneo*, however, composers of the time were generally paid much higher fees than for a comic opera or singspiel.

90. Mozart, letter to his father, 31 July 1782, *Letters*, 811.

91. Mozart, letter to Constanze Weber, 29 April 1782, *Letters*, 802–3.

92. Ibid., 803.

93. Leopold Mozart, letter to the Baroness von Waldstätten, 23 August 1782, *Letters*, 816.

94. Ibid.

95. Hildesheimer, *Mozart*, 138.

96. "From Goethe's 'Italienische Reise,' Rome November 1787," in Deutsch, 305.

97. Mozart, letter to his father, 26 September 1781, *Letters*, 769.

98. Mozart, letter to his father, 23 January 1782, *Letters*, 794.

99. Edward Crankshaw, *Maria Theresa* (New York: Viking, 1970).

100. Marcello Sorce Keller, *Musica e sociologia: Una breve storia* (Milan: Ricordi, 1996), 93.

101. Mozart, letter to his father, 4 April 1781, *Letters*, 721.

102. Casini, *Amadeus*, 204.

103. Buscaroli, *La morte di Mozart*.

104. Elias, *Mozart*, 21.

105. Mozart, letter to his father, 28 December 1782, *Letters*, 833.

106. Edward E. Lowinsky, "On Mozart's Rhythm," in *The Creative World of Mozart*, ed. Paul Henry Lang (New York: W. W. Norton, 1963), 32–33.

107. See David Macculi, "La scuola di Vienna da Mozart a Schönberg," *Lettera Internazionale* 3 (2001): 33–36.

108. K. 478 was the first of three piano quartets that Hoffmeister was to issue, but the publisher found so little interest in it that he let Mozart keep his advance payment for the other two on the condition "that he not compose the other two quartets agreed upon and that Hoffmeister was freed of his contractual obligation." As reported by Georg Nikolaus Nissen, Constanze's second husband, in his *Biographie W. A. Mozarts* (Leipzig: Breitkopf und Härtel, 1828; reprint ed. 1972), 630; noted in *Briefe*, 6:237 (commentary).

109. "From Cramer's 'Magazin der Musik,' Hamburg, 23 April 1787" (but with the dateline "Vienna, 29 January 1787"), Deutsch, 290.

110. Peter Gay, *Mozart* (New York: Lipper/Viking, 1999), 161–62.

111. Bruno Walter, *Theme and Variations: An Autobiography*, trans. James A. Galston (New York: Alfred A. Knopf, 1966), 54, quoted in Gay, *Mozart*, 163.

112. These statistics are drawn from H. C. Robbins Landon, ed., *The Mozart Compendium: A Guide to Mozart's Life and Music* (New York: Schirmer Books, 1990).

CHAPTER 6

1. Mozart, letter to his father 22 December 1781, *Letters,* 789.

2. Mozart, letter to his sister, 13 February 1782, *Letters,* 797.

3. Mozart, letter to his father, 28 December 1782, *Letters,* 833.

4. Leopold Mozart, letter to his daughter, 12 March 1785, *Letters,* 888–89.

5. Mozart, letter to his father 17 August 1782, *Letters,* 815.

6. Mozart, letter to his father, 4 January 1783, *Letters,* 834–35.

7. See Jens Peter Larsen, "Haydn, Joseph," in *The New Grove Dictionary of Music and Musicians* (1980), 8:339.

8. Mozart, letter to his father, 5 February 1783, *Letters,* 839.

9. Mozart, letter to his father, 7 May 1783, *Letters,* 848.

10. Mozart, letter to his father, 22 January 1783, *Letters,* 838, 837.

11. Mozart, letter to his father, 18 June 1783, *Letters,* 852.

12. Ibid. The "water diet" was a thin gruel of oatmeal and barley.

13. Mozart, letter to his father, 5 July 1783, *Letters,* 855.

14. Mozart, letter to his father, 12 July 1783, *Letters,* 856, 857.

15. See Constanze's original letter in *Briefe,* 3:280–81.

16. Casini, *Amadeus,* 143.

17. Constanze Mozart to Vincent and Mary Novello, quoted from Salomon, *Mozart: A Life,* 115.

18. Mozart, letter to his father, 31 October 1783, *Letters,* 859.

19. Hildesheimer, *Mozart,* 175.

20. See Wolfgang's letter to Constanze, 8–9 October 1791, *Briefe,* 4:160.

21. Mozart, letter to his father, 24 December 1783, *Letters,* 865.

22. The entire list is reproduced in Deutsch, 573–82, appendix 1: The Subscribers to Mozart's Concerts on 17, 24, and 31 March 1784.

23. Carr, *Mozart and Constanze,* 79.

24. Mozart, letter to his sister, 18 August 1784, *Letters,* 882.

25. Roberto Parenti, in Giovanni Carli Ballola and Roberto Parenti, *Mozart* (Milan: Rusconi, 1990), 109–11.

26. Casini, *Amadeus,* 116, 123.

27. James H. Billington, *Fire in the Minds of Men: The Origins of the Revolutionary Faith* (New York: Basic Books, 1980), "The Operatic Stimulus," 152–58.

28. Solomon, *Mozart: A Life,* 330.

29. Hildesheimer, *Mozart,* 314, 315.

30. Mozart, letter to his father, 3 July 1778, *Letters,* 558.

31. Leopold Mozart, letter to his wife and son, 29 June 1778, *Letters,* 556.

32. Leopold Mozart, letter of 3 September 1784, quoted from Ruth Halliwell, *The Mozart Family: Four Lives in a Social Context* (Oxford: Clarendon Press, 1998), 461.

33. Leopold Mozart, letter to his daughter, 16 February 1785, *Letters,* 886.

34. Ibid., 885.

35. Solomon, *Mozart: A Life,* 522.

36. Leopold Mozart, letter to his daughter, 19 March 1785, *Letters,* 889 n.1.

37. Leopold Mozart, letter to his daughter, 16 February 1785, *Letters,* 886.

38. Ibid.

39. Leopold Mozart, letter to his daughter, 21 February 1785, *Letters*, 887.

40. Leopold Mozart, letter to his daughter, 12 March 1785, *Briefe*, 3:378.

41. Leopold Mozart, letter to his daughter, 25–26 March 1785, *Letters*, 889.

42. Casini, *Amadeus*, 116, 118–19.

43. For the latter half of this quotation, see "From Friedrich Schlichtegroll's Nekrolog auf das Jahr 1791," in Deutsch, 469.

44. Leopold Mozart, letter to his wife and son, 16 February 1778, *Letters*, 483.

45. Leopold Mozart, letter to his son, 23 February 1778, *Letters*, 492–93.

46. Leopold Mozart, letter to the Baroness von Waldstätten, 23 August 1782, *Letters*, 815–16.

47. Solomon, *Mozart*, 218.

48. Ibid., 216.

49. Leopold Mozart, letter to his son, 28 December 1778; Mozart, letter to his father, 31 December 1778, *Letters*, 644, 648.

50. Mozart, letter to his father, between 26 May and 2 June 1781, *Letters*, 738.

51. Mozart, letter to his father, 2 June 1781, *Letters*, 739.

52. Einstein, *Mozart: His Character, His Work*, 87.

53. "From Karoline Pichler's Memoirs, Vienna, 1843–44," Deutsch, 556–57.

54. "From Joseph Lange's Reminiscences, Vienna, 1808," Deutsch, 503.

55. "Johann Adolph Hasse to Giovanni Maria Ortes at Venice, Vienna, 30 September 1769" Deutsch, 92.

56. "From Ludwig Tieck's Memoirs, Leipzig, 1855," Deutsch, 562.

57. Mozart, letter to the Baroness Waldstätten, 2 October 1782, *Letters*, 825.

58. "Marianne von Berchtold's Reminiscences, Spring 1792: 'Data for a biography of the late composer Wolfgang Mozart,'" Deutsch, 462.

59. "From Johann Nepomuk Hummel's Sketch for a Biography of Mozart, ca. 1825," Deutsch, 527.

60. "From Michael Kelly's *Reminiscences*, London, 1826," Deutsch, 530.

61. "From the papers of John Pettinger, Vienna, summer 1785," *New Mozart Documents: A Supplement to O. E. Deutsch's Documentary Biography*, ed. Cliff Eisen (Stanford: Stanford University Press, 1991), 37.

62. Hildesheimer, *Mozart*, 280–81.

63. "From Ludwig Berger's Essay on Muzio Clementi, 1829," Deutsch, 542.

64. Mozart, letter to his father, 5 September 1781, *Letters*, 764.

65. Mozart, letter to the Baroness von Waldstätten, 28 September 1782, *Letters*, 823.

66. Appendix 2, "Documents Pertaining to Mozart's Estate," Deutsch, 586.

67. Aleramo Lanapoppi, *Lorenzo Da Ponte: Realtà e leggenda nella vita del librettista di Mozart* (Venice: Marsilio, 1992), 140.

68. "Title-Page and Dedication of the String Quartets Dedicated to Haydn," Deutsch, 250.

69. Leopold Mozart, letter to his daughter, 3 November 1785, *Letters*, 893.

70. Leopold Mozart, quoted in Solomon, *Mozart*, 391.

71. "From Zinzendorf's Diary, 7 February 1786," Deutsch, 262.

72. Solomon, *Mozart*, 338, 339, in his translation.

## CHAPTER 7

1. Leopold Mozart, letter to his daughter, 11 November 1785, *Letters*, 893.

2. Mozart, letter to Baron Gottfried von Jacquin, 15 October 1787, *Letters*, 911.

3. Buscaroli, *La morte di Mozart*, 98, 99.

4. Hildesheimer, *Mozart*, 182.

5. "From the 'Wiener Realzeitung,' 11 July 1786," Deutsch, 278.

6. "From Zinzendorf's Diary, 4 July 1786," Deutsch 278.

7. Leopold Mozart, letter to his daughter, 28 April 1786, *Letters*, 897.

8. "From Michael Kelly's *Reminiscences*, London, 1826," Deutsch, 533.

9. Lanapoppi, *Lorenzo Da Ponte*, 140.

10. Leopold Mozart, letter to his daughter, 1 March 1787, *Letters*, 906.

11. Leopold Mozart, letter to his daughter, 10–11 May 1787, *Letters*, 908, n. 5.

12. "Mozart's entry in Edmund Weber's Album," Deutsch, 283.

13. Mozart, letter to Baron Gottfried von Jacquin, 15 January 1787, *Letters*, 904.

14. "From Franz Xaver Niemetschek's Mozart Biography, Prague, 1808," Deutsch, 506–7.

15. Mozart, letter to Baron Gottfried von Jacquin, 15 January 1787, *Letters*, 903.

16. "From Franz Xaver Niemetschek's Mozart Biography, Prague, 1808," Deutsch, 507.

17. Poggi and Vallora, *Mozart*, 552.

18. Lorenzo Da Ponte, *Memoirs of Lorenzo Da Ponte*, trans. Elisabeth Abbott, ed. and annotated by Arthur Livingston, new preface by Stanley Sadie (New York: Da Capo: 1988), 174.

19. Lorenzo Da Ponte, *An Extract from The life of Lorenzo Da Ponte with the History of Several Dramas by Him . . . Set to Music by Mozart* (New York, 1819), quoted in Heartz, *Mozart's Operas*, 158–59.

20. Mozart, letter to Baron Gottfried von Jacquin, 15 January 1787, *Letters*, 904.

21. "From the 'Wiener Zeitung,' 2 April 1788," Deutsch, 312.

22. As Hildesheimer, among others, remarks, this meeting probably never took place. Beethoven, though an admirer of Mozart, never mentions it. Hildesheimer, *Mozart*, 201, in the German edition. See also Solomon, *Mozart: A Life*, 366–67; H. C. Robbins Landon, comp. and ed., *Beethoven: A Documentary Study* (New York: Macmillan, 1970), 46.

23. *Salzburger Intelligenzblatt* 2 June 1787, quoted in a note to "From Dominikus Hagenauer's Diary, 28 May 1878," Deutsch, 293.

24. The inventory is cited in Deutsch, 583–602. Mozart owned the 4th edition of *Phädon* (Berlin, 1767), as noted in Deutsch, 602.

25. Mozart, letter to his father, 4 April 1787, *Letters*, 907.

26. Ibid., 908.

27. Mozart, letter to his sister, 2 June 1787, *Letters*, 909.

28. Mozart, letter to his sister, 16 June 1787, *Letters*, 909.

29. Mozart, letter to his brother-in-law, Baron von Berchtold zu Sonnenburg, 29 September 1787, *Letters*, 910.

30. Solomon, *Mozart: A Life*, 411.

31. See the entry from Beda Hübner's "Diarium" of 8 December 1766, Deutsch, 70.

32. Parenti, in Carli Ballola and Parenti, *Mozart*, 131.

33. Hildesheimer, *Mozart*, 208–9.

34. Ibid., 206.

35. Kunze, *Il teatro di Mozart*, 400, 409.

36. Mozart, letter to Baron Gottfried von Jacquin, 4 November 1787, *Letters*, 913.

37. Mozart, letter to Baron Gottfried von Jacquin, 15 October 1787, *Letters*, 911.

38. Casini, *Amadeus*, 204.

39. Da Ponte, *Memoirs*, 180.

40. Buscaroli, *La morte di Mozart*, 98.

41. Solomon, *Mozart: A Life*, "Appendix: Mozart's Vienna Earnings," 521–28.

42. See the report on the Dresden concert, at which Mozart performed before the elector of Saxony, in Deutsch, 339.

43. Mozart's poem quoted from Solomon, *Mozart: A Life*, 437.

44. Mozart, letter to his wife, 16 April 1789, *Letters*, 924.

45. Mozart, letter to his wife, 23 May 1789, *Letters*, 929.

46. According to Deutsch, 346, Mozart definitely gave a concert before the king and queen in Berlin (Potsdam), and "It may have been on this occasion that Mozart received the commission from Frederick William II to write six easy pianoforte sonatas for Princess Frederike and six string quartets for the king himself."

47. Mozart, letter to Michael Puchberg, 12 July 1789, *Letters*, 930.

48. In Mozart's own list of his works, however, in entering the string quartet (K. 570) in June 1789, he indicates it as "für Seine Mayestät dem könig in Preussen" (for His Majesty the King of Prussia), *Briefe*, 4:91.

49. Solomon, *Mozart: A Life*, 442–43.

50. Mozart, letter to his wife at Baden, first half of August 1789, *Letters*, 933.

51. Mozart, letter to Baron Gottfried von Jacquin, 4 November 1787, *Letters*, 913.

52. Mozart, letter to his father, 29 November 1777, *Letters*, 396.

53. Da Ponte, *Memoirs*, 185.

54. Hildesheimer, *Mozart*, 285.

55. Carli Ballola and Parenti, *Mozart*, 719.

56. Mozart, letter to Michael Puchberg, on or before 17 May 1790, *Letters*, 939.

57. Mozart, letter to Michael Puchberg, 12 June 1790, *Letters*, 940.

58. Mozart, letter to his wife, 8 October 1790, *Letters*, 945.

59. "From the Travel Diary of Count Ludwig von Bentheim-Steinfurt, Frankfurt, 15 October 1790," Deutsch, 375.

60. Mozart, letter to his wife, before 4 November 1790, *Letters*, 948.

61. Ibid, 947–48.

62. Mozart, letter to his wife, 3 October 1790, *Letters*, 943.

CHAPTER 8

1. "Handbill Announcing the Vienna Concert of the Clarinet Virtuoso Joseph Bähr on 4 March 1791," Deutsch, 386.

2. See "Decree of the City Council," Deutsch, 395.

3. The precise date of the commission is not known, but it was after 8 July, when Guardasoni left Prague with an agreement from the Bohemian Estates to provide an

opera for the coronation. See John A. Rice, "Emperor and Impresario: Leopold II and the Transformation of Viennese Musical Theater, 1790–1792" (Ph.D. diss., University of California Berkeley, 1987), 321.

4. Mozart, letter to his wife at Baden, 6 June 1791, *Letters*, 951–52.

5. Bernhard Paumgartner, *Mozart*, trans. Carlo Pinelli (Turin: Einaudi, 1994), 469; German orig., 1940.

6. Mozart, letter to his wife at Baden, 25 June 1791, *Letters*, 957.

7. Ibid., 956.

8. Hildesheimer, *Mozart*, 335–38, esp. 336; Casini, *Amadeus*, 13; Buscaroli, *La morte di* ˙ *Mozart*, 194, 204, 250–51.

9. Mozart, letter to his wife at Baden, 7–8 October 1791, *Letters*, 966–67.

10. Mozart, letter to his wife at Baden, 8–9 October 1791, *Letters*, 968–69.

11. Mozart, letter to his wife at Baden, 14 October 1791, *Letters*, 970.

12. Ibid., 971.

13. "Domenico Guardasoni's Contract with the Bohemian Estates, 8 July 1791," in Eisen, ed., *New Mozart Documents*, 67.

14. In a letter of August 1791, Salieri explained to Prince Anton Esterházy why he had to turn down Guardasoni's offer, even though the impresario "visited me five times to beg me to accept the commission." See John A. Rice, *Antonio Salieri and Viennese Opera* (Chicago: University of Chicago Press, 1998), 7–8.

15. Mozart, letter to his wife at Baden, 7–8 October 1791, *Letters*, 967.

16. Buscaroli, *La morte di Mozart*, 313–14.

17. Edward J. Dent, *Mozart's Operas: A Critical Study* (Oxford: Clarendon Press; 1991), 212. The work was first published in 1947.

18. Ulybyshev, *Mozart*, 696–707.

19. Massimo Mila, *Lettura del Flauto Magico* (Turin: Einaudi, 1989), 8.

20. Mozart, letter to the Baroness von Waldstätten, 2 October 1782, *Letters*, 824.

21. Mozart, letter to his father, 8 January 1783, *Letters*, 836.

22. Einstein, *Mozart: His Character, His Work*, 74.

23. Hermann Abert, *W. A. Mozart*, 2 vols., 7th ed. (Leipzig, 1956; orig. 1919–1921), 2:581.

24. Franz Xaver Niemetschek, *Life of Mozart*, trans. Helen Mautner (London: Leonard Hyman, 1956; orig. 1808), 42.

25. Published in Wolfgang Amadeus Mozart, *Lettere* (Parma: Guanda, 1991), 284. On this forgery, see Hildesheimer, *Mozart*, 193–94; and Buscaroli, *La morte di Mozart*, 267–68.

26. Paumgartner, *Mozart*, 505–13.

27. Mozart, letter to his wife at Baden, 8–9 October 1791, *Letters*, 969.

28. H. C. Robbins Landon, *Mozart's Last Year, 1791* (New York: Schirmer Books, 1988), 174.

29. Ibid., 174–75. A similar letter that Guldener sent to Carpani on 10 June 1824 is cited complete in Deutsch, 522–23.

30. Sophie Haibel's contribution to the Mozart biography by Constanze's second husband, Georg Nikolaus Nissen, dated 7 April 1825, in Deutsch, 525.

31. An article of 21 December 1791 in the newspaper *Pressburger Zeitung,* reported that "the suicide . . . as is now known, took his life from faint-heartedness rather than jealousy" and that the empress herself promised his widow assistance, since her "conduct is known to be unexceptionable," Deutsch, 426.

32. Carr, *Mozart and Constanze,* 152 (for Beethoven), 145–56 (for the poison theory).

33. Buscaroli, *La morte di Mozart,* 205 n. 10; Giorgio Taboga, *L'assassinio di Mozart* (Lucca: Akademos, 1997), 114.

EPILOGUE

1. Carmelo Samonà, "Sulla attuale fortuna di Mozart," *La cultura* 2 (July-December 1985): 360.

2. Karl Dietrich Bracher, *La dittatura tedesca: Origini, strutture, conseguenze del nazionalsocialismo in Germania* (Bologna: Il Mulino, 1969), 352.

# Bibliographical Notes

The bibliography of writings on Mozart is enormous and ever growing, surpassed perhaps only by that on Wagner. The following listing is a very selective one, aimed at the general reader more than the specialist. The principal documentary sources are the letters of Mozart and his family and his musical compositions.

The letters and notes of the Mozart family have been published in seven volumes (four volumes of documents, two of commentary, and one of indexes) by the International Mozarteum Foundation of Salzburg: *Mozart: Briefe und Aufzeichnungen, Gesamtausgabe,* edited by the Internationale Stiftung Mozarteum Salzburg, collected and with commentary by Wilhelm A. Bauer and Otto Erich Deutsch, 7 vols. (Kassel: Bärenreiter, 1962–1975). This collection appears in French translation as: Wolfgang Amadeus Mozart, *Correspondance,* translated by Geneviève Geffray, 2nd ed. rev., 6 vols. (Paris: Flammarion, 1986–1994). The French edition can be considered complete, although it does not include the letters of Leopold Mozart earlier than 9 February 1756 or some voyage notes and other peripherals. English-speaking readers will have to rely on the less complete collections originally put together and translated by Emily Anderson in 1938 as *The Letters of Mozart and His Family,* 2nd ed. (1966) revised by Alec Hyatt King and Monica Carolan; 3rd ed. revised by Stanley Sadie and Fiona Smart (London: Macmillan, 1985). For letters lacking, incomplete, or incorrectly translated in Anderson's edition, the present book has had recourse to the originals in the Bauer-Deutsch edition. See also *Mozart Speaks: Views on Music, Musicians, and the World,* selected, with commentary, by Robert L. Marshall (New York: Schirmer; Toronto: Maxwell Macmillan, 1991).

The impressive collection of Mozart letters nonetheless requires critical examination for a number of reasons. It should be noted at the start that whole parts of this correspondence are missing: for example, all the letters that Leopold wrote to his son after 22 January 1781 have disappeared. There may have been more than a hundred of them, and they were probably destroyed by Constanze Mozart after the death of her husband. Other letters—for example, those written by Mozart to his wife between mid-August 1789 and 14 October 1791—quite obviously contain deletions and additions after the fact made by Constanze or others. The well-founded suspicion exists that Constanze, who for many years had access to the Mozart papers, might have found it convenient to destroy, correct, cut up, and modify whatever might have seemed to her capable of diminishing her own reputation and that of her husband. It seems that Constanze even took care to correct and change the biography of Mozart written by her second husband, Georg Nikolaus Nissen, published posthumously in 1828, *Biographie W. A. Mozarts* (Leipzig: Breitkopf und Härtel, 1828).

A significant collection of nonepistolary documents is also indispensable: Otto Erich Deutsch, *Mozart: A Documentary Biography*, translated by Eric Blom, Peter Branscombe, and Jeremy Noble (Stanford, CA: Stanford University Press, 1965). More recently discovered documents appear in *New Mozart Documents: A Supplement to O. E. Deutsch's Documentary Biography*, ed. Cliff Eisen (Stanford: Stanford University Press, 1991).

For those interested in listening to Mozart's music, there is a complete collection of his works put out by Philips comprising 178 compact discs divided into seventeen volumes (symphonies, divertimenti and serenades, piano concertos, operas in Italian and in German, quintets, quartets, and trios, etc.). The performers are too numerous to mention. Philips has put out two editions of this complete collection; one of them (the more costly) is accompanied by ample notes and the librettos of the operas, with each CD offered in its own case; a more economical and manageable edition provides each CD in a simple paper sleeve, more limited critical notes, and no librettos. Mozart symphonies, sonatas, operas, and concertos have of course been recorded by many interpreters and put out by a number of record companies.

All of Mozart's compositions are listed in the catalog originally drawn up in 1862 by Ludwig von Köchel, a nineteenth-century Viennese botanist and mineralogist and sometime musicologist. The most recent edition is the sixth, of 1964, reprinted for the second time (unchanged) as the "eighth": *Chronologisch-thematisches Verzeichnis sämtlicher Tonwerke Wolfgang Amadé Mozarts*, edited by Franz Giegling, Alexander Weinmann, and Gerd Sieversis (Wiesbaden: Breitkopf & Härtel; New York: C. F. Peter, 1983). A useful complement to this large catalog, particularly for English-speaking readers, is Neal Zaslaw and Fiona Morgan Fein, eds., *The Mozart Repertory: A Guide for Musicians, Programmers, and Researchers* (Ithaca: Cornell University Press, 1991). Zaslaw is the head of an international team now putting together the new edition of the complete Köchel catalog. This daunting task is all the more necessary in that over half of Mozart's autograph manuscript scores, until 1939 housed in Berlin at the Prussian State Library, were evacuated by the Germans at that time for safekeeping to Lower Silesia, but their whereabouts were subsequently a mystery. Thus the sixth edition of Köchel (1964) described all of these scores as "verschollen" (missing). Not until 1980 did it become general knowledge that these music manuscripts (including *The Magic Flute*, half of *The Marriage of Figaro*, the *Jupiter* symphony, and over a hundred others) were at the Jagiellonian University Library in Krakow, Poland. The new Köchel catalog will take full account not only of these rediscovered scores, but also of many advances in Mozart scholarship since the 1960s, including the profound impact on the dating of his works furnished by studies of Mozart's paper, his handwriting, and added information from rediscovered manuscript copies of scores and parts.

There are many biographies and monographs that are indispensable to anyone who wants to understand the intense life of Mozart, dig a bit deeper, and connect facts and ideas. In alphabetical order by author they are: Hermann Abert, *W. A. Mozart*, 7th ed., 2 vols. (Leipzig, 1956; orig. 1919–1921); Saul Bellow, *Mozart* (Milan: Mondadori, 1993); see also Saul Bellow, "Mozart: An Overture," in Bellow, *It All Adds Up: From the Dim Past to the Uncertain Future* (New York: Viking Penguin, 1994), 1–14; James H. Billington, *Fire in the Minds of Men: Origins of the Revolutionary Faith* (New York: Basic Books, 1980); Marcel Brion, *La vie quotidienne à Vienne à l'époque de Mozart et de Schubert* (Paris: Hachette, 1959), in English translation by Jean Stewart as *Daily Life in Vienna in the Time of Mozart and Schubert* (New York: Macmillan, 1962); Piero Buscaroli, *La morte di Mozart* (Milan: Rizzoli, 1996); Giovanni Carli Ballola and Roberto Parenti, *Mozart* (Milan: Rusconi, 1990); Francis Carr, *Mozart & Constanze* (London: John Murray, 1983); Claudio Casini, *Amadeus: Vita di Mozart* (Milan: Rusconi, 1990); Paolo Cattelan, *Mozart: Un mese a Venezia* (Venice: Marsilio, 2000); Lorenzo Da Ponte, *Memoirs of Lorenzo Da Ponte*, trans. Elisabeth

Abbott, ed. and annotated by Arthur Livingston, new preface by Stanley Sadie (New York: Da Capo, 1988); Peter J. Davies, *Mozart in Person: His Character and Health* (New York: Greenwood Press, 1989); Edward. J. Dent, *Mozart's Operas: A Critical Study* (Oxford: Clarendon Press, 1991; orig. 1947); Sergio Durante, ed., *Mozart* (Bologna: Il Mulino, 1991); Alfred Einstein, *Mozart: His Character, His Work*, trans. from the German by Arthur Mendel and Nathan Broder (New York: Oxford University Press, 1945); Norbert Elias, *Mozart: Portrait of a Genius*, trans. Edmund Jephcott, ed. Michael Schröter (Berkeley: University of California Press, 1993); Louis Fürnberg, *Mozart Novelle* (Berlin: Dietz, 1954); Peter Gay, *Mozart* (New York: Lipper/Viking, 1999); Aloys Greither, ed., *Wolfgang Amadé Mozart in Selbstzeugnissen und Bilddokumenten* (Reinbek bei Hamburg: Rowohlt, 1962); Gernot Gruber, *Mozart und die Nachwelt* (Salzburg, 1985), in English translation as *Mozart and Posterity* (Boston: Northeast University Press, 1994); Ruth Halliwell, *The Mozart Family: Four Lives in a Social Context* (Oxford: Clarendon Press, 1998); Daniel Heartz, *Mozart's Operas*, ed. and with contributing essays by Thomas Bauman (Berkeley: University of California Press, 1990); Ernst W. Heine, *Chi ha ucciso Mozart? Delitti per amici della musica*, trans. Vittorio Tamao and Antonella Fantoni (Rome: Theoria, 1988), originally published as *Wer ermordete Mozart? Wer enthauptete Haydn? Morfgeschichten für Musikfreunde* (Zurich: Diogenes Verlag, 1984); Wolfgang Hildesheimer, *Mozart*, in English translation by Marion Faber (New York: Farrar Straus Giroux, 1982); Mary Hunter, *The Culture of Opera Buffa in Mozart's Vienna: A Poetics of Entertainment* (Princeton: Princeton University Press, 1999); Mary Hunter and James Webster, eds., *Opera Buffa in Mozart's Vienna* (Cambridge: Cambridge University Press, 1997); Pierre Jean Jouve, *Le "Don Juan" de Mozart* (Paris: Plon, 1968; orig. 1942); Søren Kierkegaard, *Mozarts Don Juan*, trans. and ed. Hermann Ky (Zurich: Atlantis, 1956); Georg Knepler, *Wolfgang Amadé Mozart: Annäherungen* (Berlin: Henschel, 1991), in English translation as *Wolfgang Amadé Mozart* (Cambridge: Cambridge University Press, 1994); Stefan Kunze, *Mozarts Opern*, 2nd ed. (Stuttgart: Reclam, 1996); Idem, *Il teatro di Mozart: Dalla Finta Semplice al Flauto Magico*, trans. Leonardo Cavari (Venice: Marsilio, 1990); Aleramo Lanapoppi, *Lorenzo Da Ponte: Realtà e leggenda nella vita del librettista di Mozart* (Venice: Marsilio, 1992); H. C. Robbins Landon, *Mozart's Last Year, 1791* (New York: Schirmer Books, 1988); Idem, *The Mozart Compendium: A Guide to Mozart's Life and Music* (New York: Schirmer, 1990); Vernon Lee (Violet Paget), *Studies of the Eighteenth Century in Italy* (New York: Da Capo Press, 1978; orig. 1907); Massimo Mila, *Wolfgang Amadeus Mozart*

(Pordenone: Studio Tesi, 1980); Idem, *Lettura del Flauto Magico* (Turin: Einaudi, 1989); Piero Mioli, ed., *Tutti i libretti d'opera* (Rome: Newton Compton, 1986); Eduard Mörike, *Mozart auf der Reise nach Prag* (Augsburg: J. G. Cotta, 1855); Franz Xaver Niemetschek, *Life of Mozart*, trans. Helen Mautner (London: Hyman, 1956; orig. 1808); Bernard Paumgartner, *Mozart* (Zurich: Atlantis, 1993; orig. 1940); Pierluigi Petrobelli, *Music in the Theater: Essays on Verdi and Other Composers* (Princeton: Princeton University Press, 1994); John A. Rice, "Emperor and Impresario: Leopold II and the Transformation of Viennese Musical Theater, 1790–1792" (Ph.D. diss., University of California Berkeley, 1987); Idem, *Antonio Salieri and Viennese Opera* (Chicago: University of Chicago Press, 1998); Stanley Sadie, *Mozart* (New York: Grossman, 1970; orig. 1965); Carmelo Samonà, "Sulla attuale fortuna di Mozart," *La cultura* 2 (July–December 1985): 357–62; Friedrich Schlichtegroll, *Johannes Chrysostomus Wolfgang Gottlieb Mozart* (Leipzig: Poeschel und Trepte, 1942; orig. 1793); Idem, *Nekrolog der Teutschen für das neunzehnte Jahrhundert (1790–1800)*, 5 vols. (Gotha: Perthes, 1802–1806); Anke Schmitt, *Der Exotismus in der deutschen Oper zwischen Mozart und Spohr* (Hamburg: Verlag den Musikalienhandlung K. D. Wagner, 1988); Emanuele Senici, *La clemenza di Tito di Mozart: I primi trent'anni (1791–1821)* (Turnhout: Brepols, 1997); Maynard Solomon, *Mozart: A Life* (New York: HarperCollins, 1995); Stendhal, *The Lives of Haydn and Mozart . . .* (London: John Murray, 1818); Giorgio Taboga, *L'assassinio di Mozart* (Lucca: Akademos, 1997); Alexis de Tocqueville, *The Old Régime and the French Revolution*, trans. Stuart Gilbert (New York: Anchor Press, 1955); Christoph Wolff, *Mozart's Requiem: Historical Studies, Documents, Score*, trans. Mary Whittall (Berkeley: University of California Press, 1994); Iwo and Pamela Zaluski, *Mozart in Italy* (London: P. Owen, 1999).

# Index